PRAISE FOR *SA MARKETING CHANNELS*

'This book is a true tour de force on all things marketing, distribution, franchising and more. Dent and White have given us a highly compelling and practical blueprint for success in times of great change and disruption. Their updated treatise gives us practical 21st-century strategic insights into sales and marketing channel and distribution management. Heed these authors' advice or risk irrelevance and peril for your business and brand.' **Joe Tripodi, CMO, Subway, and former CMO, Coca-Cola, Allstate, MasterCard, Bank of New York and Seagram's**

'With sales and marketing channels becoming ever more complex and challenging, the need for help constantly increases. This book hits the mark – I seriously suggest anyone involved in channels has this to hand. Dent and White stand head and shoulders above many others in demystifying the channel into understandable and executable components. Whether you are a channel novice or channel expert, this new edition is paramount for executives to account managers alike.' **Jeremy Butt, SVP International, Mitel**

'This is the best book available for providing a deep understanding of channel business models and has helped us build more effective relationships with our channel partners.' **Louis Gries, CEO, James Hardie Industries plc**

'This book is essential reading for any vendor working with indirect channels of distribution. The deep insights into channel business models it provides enable vendors to secure maximum value from both distributor and final-tier engagement.' **Michael Urban, Corporate Vice President, Strategy, Transformation, Global Vendor Management, Tech Data Corporation**

Third Edition

Sales and Marketing Channels

How to build and manage
distribution strategy

Julian Dent
Michael White

KoganPage

First published in Great Britain and the United States as *Distribution Channels* in 2008 by Kogan Page Limited
Second edition published as *Distribution Channels* in 2011
Third edition published in 2018

2nd Floor, 45 Gee Street	c/o Martin P Hill Consulting	4737/23 Ansari Road
London EC1V 3RS	122 W 27th St, 10th Floor	Daryaganj
United Kingdom	New York NY 10001	New Delhi 110002
	USA	India

www.koganpage.com

ISBN   978 0 7494 8214 5
E-ISBN   978 0 7494 8215 2

British Library Cataloguing-in-Publication Data

A CIP record for this book is available from the British Library.

Library of Congress Cataloging-in-Publication Data

CIP data is available.

Library of Congress Control Number: 2018003916

Typeset by Integra Software Services Pvt. Ltd., Pondicherry
Print production managed by Jellyfish
Printed and bound by CPI Group (UK) Ltd, Croydon, CR0 4YY

CONTENTS

About the authors xi
Preface xii
Acknowledgements xiv

PART ONE Introduction 1

01 How to get the best out of this book 3

About this book 3
How this book is set out 5

02 The business of getting products and services to market 9

Marketing and sales channels, and distribution strategy 9
Distribution strategy matters 13
Challenging business dynamics 15
Business models are key to value propositions 20
A structured approach to positioning your channel value proposition 21

03 Major trends and developments in market access 24

Introduction 24
The myth of disintermediation 24
From products to services 26
Emergence of the cloud, apps and microtransactions 29
Multi-channel (omni-channel) challenges 30
Consumer channels: more than just retail and e-tailer 32
Commercial channels and ecosystems 35
The 'gig economy' channels 36

PART TWO Distributors, wholesalers and intermediaries 39

04   The role of the distributor for sales and marketing channels 41

Distributors, wholesalers and intermediaries 41
Customer role – core functions 41
Supplier role 45
Supplier role – core functions 47
How distribution improves the supplier's business model 50

05   How the distributor business model works 52

What do we mean by business model? 52
Role defines business model 54
Profit is a very small number between two very big numbers 55
Managing working capital is a balancing act 55
The measures that matter and how to manage with them 58

06   Managing distributors – margins and profitability 59

Multiple margins 59
Gross margin and value-add 59
Margin mix or blended margin 62
Contribution margin 66
Net margin and operating margin 70

07   Managing distributors – working capital 73

Working capital management 73
Supplier credit 74
Inventory 75
Customer credit 78
Working capital cycle 80

08   Managing distributors – productivity 84

Earn and turn 84
Contribution margin return on inventory investment 86
Returns on working capital 89

09   Managing distributors – sustainability 94

Sustainability – longer-term business health 94
Return on net assets and return on capital employed 94
Return on invested capital 97
Value creation 98
Managing value creation on an operational basis 104

10   Managing distributors – managing growth 107

Growth dynamics 107
Internally financed growth rate formula 108
Economies of scale – profitability 109
Economies of scale – working capital management 112
Risks of growth – diseconomies of scale 114

11   Understanding the distribution landscape 115

Introduction 115
Typical landscape evolution 116

12   How to get the best from distribution strategy 119

Building and leveraging distribution partnerships 119
The engagement process 120
Managing the account relationship 125
Making compelling business cases 126
Summary of Part Two 129

PART THREE   Managing final-tier sales and marketing channels 131

13   The roles of the final-tier channel players 133

The final-tier channel players 133
The possible roles of final-tier channel players 135
Matching channel roles to channel players 139
Different roles command different compensation
   models 141
Applying this framework to your industry sector
   or channel 148

14   How the business model works for final-tier channel players 149

Role defines business model 149
Service-provision business models – people and platforms 150
Special features of the people-based service business model 151
Special features of the platform-based service business model 156

15   Managing final-tier channel players – sales and utilization 157

People-based service business model 157
Platform-based service business model 169

16   Managing final-tier channel players – gross margin and recoverability 172

People-based service business model 172
Platform-based service business model 178

17   Managing final-tier channel players – working capital management 183

The cash-to-cash cycle 183
People-based service business model 183
Platform-based service business model 188

18   Managing final-tier channel players – value creation and growth 190

Value creation and improving the numbers 190
Managing growth – the integrated business model 196

19   How to get the best from final-tier channel players 198

Introduction 198
Segmenting the final-tier trade channel 199
What the final tier looks for in a vendor 200
What the final tier looks for in a distributor 207
Managing the account relationship 211
Some rules of thumb for making compelling business cases 213
Selling 'with' the final tier in an advocacy role 216
Summary of Part Three 217

PART FOUR Managing distribution in individual industry sectors 219

20 Introduction to managing distribution in individual industry sectors 221

21 Insights from managing capital goods distribution 225

Introduction 225
Specialist challenges and how the sector tackles them 226
Exposure to the business cycle 227
Extremely high cost 228
Shifting ownership and consumption models 228
Difficult locations and extended supply chains 229
Political complexities 230
Critical competencies 231
Key metrics 239

22 Insights from managing consumer goods distribution and retailers 241

Retailers and retailing 241
Multichannel and omni-channel 246
Specialist challenges and how the sector tackles them 254
Critical attributes and competencies 259
Key metrics 265

23 Insights from managing services distribution 273

Introduction 273
Specialist challenges and how the sector tackles them 274
Critical competencies 279
Key metrics 289

24 Insights from managing hotels, restaurants, catering and travel distribution 291

Introduction 291
Specialist challenges and how the sector tackles them 292

Critical competencies 295
Key metrics 296

25 Insights from managing intellectual property distribution 297

Introduction 297
Specialist challenges and how the sector tackles them 299
Critical competencies 307

26 Insights from managing franchised distribution 315

What is a franchise? 316
The franchise system model 318
Specialist challenges and how the sector tackles them 321
Critical attributes and competencies 326
Key metrics 330

Key ratios 335
Glossary of technical terms 340
Index 353

Three online bonus chapters accompany this book:

1 Managing the people-based business model

2 How to engage with retailers

3 How to engage with franchised systems

These and other resources can be downloaded at the following URL: **www.koganpage.com/SMC3** (please scroll to the bottom of the web page and complete the form to access them).

ABOUT THE AUTHORS

Julian Dent

Julian Dent is Chairman of VIA International, a specialist routes-to-market consultancy. He has more than 35 years of global experience in distribution, specializing in channel strategy and implementation at global corporate and regional levels. His blue-chip clients cover industry sectors from finance and FMCG to hospitality, construction, healthcare and technology, including Barclays Bank, BP, Caterpillar, Cisco, Citibank, Esso, Hewlett-Packard, Hyatt, IBM, Microsoft, Pfizer, Philips, Subway and Xerox. He has also worked with many smaller businesses on their distribution strategy for growth, usually following venture or development capital injections. He also works closely with the Global Technology Distribution Council to define its industry-recognized accreditations.

Julian is a Chartered Accountant and a Freeman of the City of London.

Michael White

Michael White is General Manager for EMEA of Quadmark, a global routes-to-market and sales enablement consultancy. He has been consulting on distribution, sales and marketing channels optimization across industries and geographies for close to 30 years, covering commercial and consumer markets and taking channel strategy from formulation through to execution. He has run projects in all major world markets, but has a particular focus on Europe, where as a fluent French, Italian and German speaker he has extensive experience of working in cross-national teams, both within and across clients and their channel partners. Michael's clients include Apple, Caterpillar, Cisco, Electrolux, Google, Hewlett-Packard, Logitech, Microsoft, Orange, PayPal, Procter & Gamble and Tefal/Groupe SEB. He also works on education and research programmes with the Global Technology Distribution Council.

Michael is a graduate of the University of Cambridge and a Member of the Chartered Institute of Marketing.

PREFACE

This book represents the best part of our 35 years' personal and shared experience of sales and marketing channels in businesses of all types as management consultants with VIA International or Quadmark. In that time, we have had the opportunity to work with some of the world's leading businesses and their distribution channels, across a wide variety of sectors. Indeed, it is that variety of sectors that has delivered the best insights – each sector has some facets that are world-class practices and many that are less so. We have learnt from all of them and have done our best to distil that experience into this edition of the book, with a special focus on insights from specific sectors in the all-new Part Four.

As consultants, we are lucky enough to spend most of our time working inside some of the world's most successful brands and companies (yes, they still ask for help), which means we have seen an enormous amount of best practice. Often though, these companies are challenged by sheer scale, complexity and channel overlap or conflict, which prevents them from seeing the business issues quite as clearly as they might. They are usually relieved to find we can bring some clarity and objectivity to the situation and can recommend strategies that are rooted in commercial logic to deliver the outcomes they need. Many of these situations have found their way into this book, albeit usually with a cloak of anonymity. You will find many real companies and situations named and described in the book too, but these insights are based on facts already in the public domain or well known in the trade.

Even more usefully, much of our work requires us to go inside the distribution models of our clients' routes to market and investigate the actual measures and business model dynamics operating in the distributors and final-tier channel players. This provides the basis for much of the insight into each type of channel business model laid out in the different sections of the book.

We have also had the opportunity to work with many smaller companies and businesses, typically following the introduction of an injection of venture finance, which means that all concerned are expecting a sharp up-tick in sales. This growth often needs to come from a combination of new customer segments, new markets or new products, which usually means new channels too. There have been some hard lessons learnt along the way about establishing a value proposition that will attract the players in the channels needed to deliver the required growth; these are laid out for you here too.

The world changes fast and one of the reasons for this new edition is the speed at which the domains of sales and marketing channels and distribution channels are evolving. In this edition, we have aimed to balance the new with the proven, examining some of the most significant new trends and developments through the lens of rational, commercial analysis and proven frameworks. You will find we have aimed to give you the tools to think through your own specific challenges or situations, as well as share our own analysis and conclusions on some of the higher profile developments.

As in the first two editions, published under the title, *Distribution Channels: Understanding and managing channels to market*, all the examples, explanations and concepts come from first-hand consulting engagements conducted by VIA International and Quadmark. We have also had feedback from many clients (and non-clients) as readers of the book and they have shared many instances of how they have applied the principles from the book and the outcomes achieved. We are indebted to our clients for their continued opportunities and insights and hope that you, the reader, will find them valuable in your quest to reach the customer through the most effective sales, marketing and distribution channels.

Julian Dent and Michael White
jdent@viaint.com, michael.white@quadmark.com

ACKNOWLEDGEMENTS

The original inspiration for this book came from our clients, who would often ask for a book that went deeper into issues than we were able during the engagements and workshops of our consulting work. The fact that we sat down to respond to these book requests is largely due to the late Professor Erin Andersen at INSEAD, who was a wonderful source of encouragement. She is still much missed in the academic faculties of sales and marketing channels.

We owe thanks to our colleagues and partners at VIA International and Quadmark, for their support in allowing us time out to write this book. They have let us borrow freely from their expertise and experiences as have our many current and former colleagues and associates over the years.

Of course, none of this would have been possible without the continuing patronage of our clients, who share with us some of their more demanding challenges and issues. We can never say enough how much we appreciate their trust and candour.

Many people have helped with the deeper channel insights of their industry, and special thanks are due to Rob Abshire, Reza Honarmand of Tech Data, Wolfgang Pregel and Jorge De Jesus. They have given us invaluable feedback, but any mistakes that remain are down to us.

In the production of this book, we have had the most wonderful support from Sharon Davis, Sean Daly, who helped with the formatting of many of the original pictures and tables, and Charlotte Owen of Kogan Page, who helped to shape this latest edition.

Finally, we'd like to acknowledge the support of our families, who have left us in peace for long periods interrupted only by teas and coffees, and with just the occasional enquiry as to whether it was the butler or the gamekeeper who would be revealed as the villain in the final chapter. Well, now they will have to believe us that it just isn't that sort of book!

PART ONE
Introduction

How to get the best out of this book

About this book

This book will help you be where your customers want to buy, whether that place is real or virtual. It will help you gain market access for your products and services, whether your customers are consumers, small businesses, global enterprises or the public sector. It will help you penetrate the market, whether you touch your customers directly or rely on the most complex ecosystem of intermediaries, distributors, partners and service providers.

This book is for chief executives, chief marketing officers, chief sales officers, directors of distribution, channels or go-to-market strategy, and everyone who works in their teams. In fact, it is for anyone whose role touches the marketing, sales, distribution and service channels of their industry. It is for anyone whose responsibilities include generating demand and fulfilling customer needs through the provision of products and services. It is for those responsible for gaining market access, reaching customers, servicing customers, and working with every intermediary that they need to count on to achieve their objectives.

This book is for the managers of the businesses that market, distribute, sell and service the products and services of *other* suppliers and it is for anyone who is involved in the frontline of these relationships. It is for anyone who manages the relationship between two or more players in the distribution system, be they partner account managers, partner business managers, channel managers, sales managers, buyers, programme managers, etc. And, of course, it is for the managers and ultimate directors of these critical roles. Everyone involved in these roles needs to know how to demonstrate the commercial value of their relationship with another player to win and retain business. They also need to understand the way their own business works to build relationships that work for both parties, be they the 'buyer' or 'seller' in the relationship. This book sets out how to do this in great detail.

This book is for business students too, and aims to fill a gap in the typical reading material available for MBA, Marketing or Business courses at universities or colleges because it deals with the 'Place P' in the marketing mix (the others being Product, Price, Promotion and People to make the Five Ps). Place is the most dynamic 'P', with dramatic shifts in power occurring between producers and intermediaries. It is the most complex 'P', requiring compelling commercial value propositions up and down the value chain. Place is the 'P' that sets the most difficult management challenges, requiring the ability to influence independent partners. If you are not convinced that you should be looking at 'Place' with new eyes, consider the following recent shifts in the balance of power:

- Online Travel Agents (OTAs) now grab an 18–25 per cent commission on those (lowest-priced) hotel rooms they find for customers. Hotels are fighting back by reinventing their loyalty schemes to cut out the OTAs and engage their customers through direct channels.

- The 18 largest information technology distributors now account for over 75 per cent of the sales in the global market (for companies like Hewlett-Packard, Dell, Microsoft, Cisco and the thousands of other vendors). They now control market access only 15 years after they had to beg vendors to fill their warehouses – a total reversal of power.

- Airbnb now sells more rooms than any other hotel operator, all without owning a single room, because it created a marketplace that didn't exist five years ago.

- Almost anything that used to be sold as a product can now be sold as a service. Corporates no longer buy computers, printers or storage devices: they buy computing, printing and cloud back-up; many city dwellers no longer buy cars, they rent them by the hour using an app (when not hailing a taxi on Uber). In both examples, this completely changes what customers buy, how they buy and who they buy from. With services, place becomes a virtual battle ground for 'eyes', consideration and consumption. The consumption model will figure large in the new 'gig' and sharing economies.

We will expand on this list in the following chapters, but the combination of advancing technology, changing consumer behaviours (not just millennials), growth of social media and virtualization of location means that every business needs to work much harder to find and connect with its customers. More of tomorrow's CEOs will be drawn from today's directors of distribution and heads of channels than their colleagues in the ranks of CMOs, CFOs or CIOs.

To understand sales and marketing channels, you need to be a student of business models and be comfortable dealing with financial terms. We know that this doesn't sound much like the traditional view of marketing, but it's better for us to be straightforward with you now about this and be kind in helping you achieve the required level of mastery in the rest of the book. In fact, this book is written for people who don't consider themselves to be masters of the economics of business. It aims to provide you with confidence, as well as the competence, to talk *commercially* about your sales and marketing relationships, and to provide pragmatic insights into the challenges faced by each of the parties involved in marketing and distribution of products and services. There must be an economic incentive for every element in your sales and marketing channels. No incentive means no, or limited, market access. You will be amazed at the opportunities this insight unlocks, and so you will find that all the financial content of this book is always in the context of making you better at managing your sales and marketing channels.

There are many books and courses about finance. Some are for financial people; many are for the 'non-financial' manager. Most of these books talk about product companies; some even include a chapter or two about service companies. There are also books about distribution channels and systems, often from a sales or marketing perspective, dealing for example with how to minimize channel conflict or increase your power in the relationship with the channel. However, we have yet to find a book that deals with the business models of companies whose role is primarily to distribute products and services, written for people whose job specification does not require a qualification in accountancy... so here it is!

How this book is set out

This is the third edition of this book, and in this one we have reframed the title, updated a large proportion of the content and added a new section with multi-industry sectors to reflect the full diversity of sales and marketing channels, many of which are undergoing substantial change.

This edition is a book of two halves. The first half (Parts One to Three) lays the groundwork to enable you to analyse, understand and work with any type of distribution system across every industry sector. The second half takes you on a tour of sales and marketing channels in many different sectors, highlighting their special characteristics, unique challenges and how they solve them. It shows how sales and marketing strategies have evolved and shares some best practices that should prove thought-provoking and relevant to any sector. These sectors range from capital goods, such as cranes, factory machinery or industrial equipment, through to intellectual property such as music, films, books, software licences and brands via sectors as diverse as consumer products, travel and hotels, and services of all types. We have chosen the sectors to give you as broad an exposure to sales and marketing channels as possible so that, even if you don't work in one of these sectors, you will learn much that you can apply to yours. In addition, there will be further sectors available in the online chapters, so keep checking back as we will add to these over time.

In the first half of the book, Part One provides an overview of the business of getting products and services to market and the major trends and developments in market access and distribution strategy. This is where you will see just how fast-changing this space is, and gain an understanding of the forces that are propelling these changes.

Part Two sets out the business models of all the major types of intermediary ('players') in a distribution system, in the following structure:

- *The role of the player* – although there are some special cases and exceptions, in most industries the roles of the key players are very consistent. However, the labels that are applied in each industry can vary confusingly and, in some cases, are used interchangeably and in others can carry quite specific meanings. To make sure the labels applied in your industry do not mislead you, we define the key roles, so you can recognize which players you are dealing with.

- *How their business model works* – the principal characteristics of each player's role in the distribution system determine the fundamental shape of their business model. They will be subject to some well-understood economic dynamics and each will have one or more 'big issues' that define their management's priorities. We orientate you to the key features of the business model and show how these are driven by each player's role and the structure of the industry or distribution system. We explain the business model in plain English and provide a consistent framework for mapping the key numbers. We provide numerous examples of each type of business model so that you can see how the forces in its market have shaped its business profile and affected its business performance.

- *The measures that matter and how to manage the business using them* – we define and explain all the key measures and how and why they are used. We provide some basic benchmarks to give you a sense of the norms for each measure and help you understand what can be done to improve each one. We show you how the measures interact so that you understand the pressures that managers of each player are under and the trade-offs they are constantly juggling. We provide some case studies and examples of how failing businesses have been turned around and how successful players have executed their strategies in detail.

- *How to get the best from that player* – or how to articulate your value proposition. Once you understand the key objectives of the managers you are dealing with, you can ensure that you position your own company's value proposition in terms that will mean something. You can show how your proposals will impact their business model to the good. You can demonstrate that allocating more of their resources to your products and services is good for both of you, and that attacking the segments in which you want to grow is going to deliver a higher return on investment for them. Equally, you can defend your corner when asked to concede margin or increase market development funding, by pointing out how little this will benefit their overall performance. We aim to increase your confidence to go high in your account relationships by understanding the overall business model and taking the conversation up to the strategic level.

Part Three focuses on what we term the final-tier trade channel players – the ones that touch the customers, and often are only accessible to suppliers through the intermediaries covered in Part Two. There is a huge variety of final-tier trade channels, yet the one thing they almost all have in common is that they provide the services that fulfil a supplier's brand promise. In this section, we focus on the unique characteristics of service provision. These players can make or break a supplier's success in the market, yet are often ill-served and supported by their suppliers. To help you avoid repeating this mistake in the way you design and manage your sales and marketing channels, we use the same structure as in Part Two: the roles of the players; how their business models work; the measures that matter; and, finally, how to get the best from these players.

At the end of this book, we have provided all the useful quick reference material you may need and a glossary of technical terms. Although we encourage you to read the entire book to learn what a powerful resource it can be for you with its hundreds of examples and insights, we also encourage you to dip into the book when confronted with specific challenges or new situations. Some of the more technical elements of the business models will not make compelling reading until you are dealing with a real issue and then you will welcome the detail of the explanations and the depth of the examples.

Although we aim to educate you through this book in the general and specific aspects of sales and marketing channels, with lots of practical, real examples, every so often we will express a point of view. It often seems to us that there are still some lessons that have yet to be learnt and entrenched behaviours that defy commercial logic: market share leaders employing the tactics of the new entrant, distributors and resellers discounting products that are in short supply, capital wasted without any understanding of its true cost. We aim to give you the benefit of years of hands-on management and consulting insight to help you avoid these pitfalls. Take heed, or you could find your competitor is the first to break the mould and win the business from under your nose!

The business of   02
getting products
and services
to market

Marketing and sales channels, and distribution strategy

Marketing and sales channels are the means to engage with your target customer over the entire lifecycle of your relationship. The customer will experience many touch points with your brand, whether you sell simple items to domestic consumers or complex integrated solutions to large enterprises. These include initial awareness-building, through the consideration process, evaluation, purchase, experience, loyalty building and advocacy phases, as set out in Figure 2.1. Each of these phases, and the processes behind them, involve multiple marketing and sales channels and many key considerations.

Note that these channels include *your own* go-to-market resources such as direct-to-consumer marketing, e-commerce and marketing websites, tele-centres, call centres, out-bound sales forces, own-brand outlets and service centres. Often the term 'channels' is used, misleadingly, as a shorthand to denote only indirect (or third party) channels such as dealers, distributors, retailers and influencers such as specifiers, architects or professional advisers. (Parts Two and Three of this book explore the roles and engagement strategies for these channels in full detail.) Many businesses rely entirely or substantially on these indirect channels for their market access, and many operate blended channels strategies, combining direct and indirect channels to achieve their market access goals.

Distribution strategy involves deciding which channels to use to fulfil all the customer engagement roles required to reach the different segments

Figure 2.1   The customer lifecycle – distribution strategy considerations

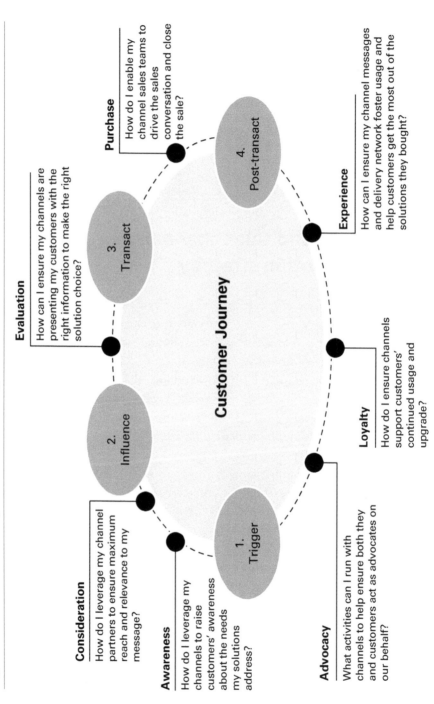

Consideration

How do I leverage my channel partners to ensure maximum reach and relevance to my message?

Awareness

How do I leverage my channels to raise customers' awareness about the needs my solutions address?

Advocacy

What activities can I run with channels to help ensure both they and customers act as advocates on our behalf?

Loyalty

How do I ensure channels support customers' continued usage and upgrade?

Evaluation

How can I ensure my channels are presenting my customers with the right information to make the right solution choice?

Purchase

How do I enable my channel sales teams to drive the sales conversation and close the sale?

Experience

How can I ensure my channel messages and delivery network foster usage and help customers get the most out of the solutions they bought?

Customer Journey

1. Trigger
2. Influence
3. Transact
4. Post-transact

of your target market and determining your channel value proposition to enable you to engage successfully with your chosen channels and channel players. It also includes defining your own internal organization structure and resources, competency frameworks, compensation plans and management metrics to be able to execute your chosen distribution strategy. An outline of the major steps involved in developing a distribution strategy is set out in Table 2.1.

Over the course of the book, we will bring each of these steps to life, providing insights as to the processes involved, giving examples of many of the deliverables, sharing illustrations of the trade-offs and considerations involved, explaining the economic fundamentals, and explaining the relevance of each step in building your strategy. For now, it is sufficient to realize that developing your distribution strategy is a complex challenge, involving considerations, such as:

- *Market access* – what reach and coverage of the target market can be achieved with each channel? Will you need different channels to reach different segments (eg large enterprises, small to medium businesses, micro businesses)?

- *Where and how customers prefer to buy* – it is extremely difficult, not to say expensive, persuading customers to change habits.

- *How well each channel will communicate or fulfil your brand promise* – you will find Rolex watches in up-market department stores, but not so much in discount warehouses.

- *The complexity of your offering* – how many interactions will it need with how many members of the customer's organization to tailor the proposition, price it and install it? How skilled and technically proficient will the customer-facing team need to be? How sure can you be that these skills will be up to date?

- *The loyalty of the channel to your brand* – many channels sell competing brands. Can you be sure that they will be willing to lose the sale by remaining loyal to your brand, and not switch 'your' customer to one of your competitors' offerings to win the sale?

- *Cost* – what compensation will the channel expect to fulfil the role you are asking it to play? What other costs will you incur in managing and servicing that channel (eg product training, co-marketing, account management, specialist logistics, etc)?

Table 2.1 Major steps in developing a distribution strategy

Target addressable market determination	Proposition development and channel landscaping	Go-to-market model development	Internal alignment, capabilities and resourcing
☐ Market space definition	☐ Customer value proposition	☐ Channel roles and activities	☐ Change management
☐ Market segmentation	☐ Channel capabilities	☐ Channel options and selection	☐ Organizational alignment
☐ Customer lifecycle and experience/ segmentation	☐ Channel capacity and costs	☐ Channel resources/ players	☐ Skill sets
☐ Customer buying behaviour	☐ Channel eco-system mapping	☐ Channel requirements	☐ Processes
☐ Market trend analysis		☐ Channel value proposition	☐ Systems
☐ Scenario development		☐ Business model	☐ Implementation planning
☐ Segment prioritization		☐ Rules of engagement	☐ Plan management
		☐ Measures and benchmarks	☐ Channel/partner performance analysis
		☐ Channel development plan	☐ Customer/ business performance analysis

- *Engagement* – will your ideal or preferred channel want to engage with you? If it does, how can you persuade it to give your brand the focus and attention it needs? What can you offer that would make it want to commit the resources and incur the cost and investment you expect? A large part of this book is devoted to answering this question for many types of channel.

It might be convenient to think of the output of your distribution strategy as an elegant architecture showing the channels engaged as a set of routes to market for each customer segment, defining the roles of each channel or channel player. If only! Usually your preferred channels overlap, interact, conflict, battle for brand dominance and can frustrate a vendor's intent. Smart strategy is needed to incentivize these channels to fall into line and do the job the vendor needs. Critically, every channel player needs to be commercially rewarded. Making this work is critical to the vendors' commercial and strategic success, which makes distribution strategy core to your overall strategy.

Distribution strategy matters

Typically around half the price paid for a product by a customer is absorbed by the activities involved in getting that product to the customer (and the customer to the product). This proportion has increased significantly over recent years as markets and media have segmented and fragmented and distribution channels have multiplied. Typically, this is the proportion of costs that is least well controlled and least well understood.

Markets are fragmenting as trends in consumer and business demographics create additional and more distinct customer segments. To make matters more complex, product and service innovations are multiplying the options available. Even simple, commodity-type products may now be distributed to multiple customer segments through multiple routes that differ by country or region. Many of these routes to market involve one or more types of intermediary, such as wholesalers, distributors, dealers, brokers, aggregators and retailers, or rely upon influencers who shape customer preference or act as specifiers or their behalf, such as architects or designers. Very few companies can tell you what it costs to sell through a particular route to market, whether that be direct (eg your own website, e-commerce site or salesforce), one-tier (eg supplier to dealer to customer) or two-tier (eg supplier to distributor to retailer to customer) distribution. Fewer still can inform you of the profitability of specific intermediaries. We have found wide variation in the costs and profitability of channels and specific intermediaries in every industry and distribution system we have investigated. Companies that have invested in analysing and understanding the business models of their distribution system have been able to take significant cost out of their own business, increasing profits or reducing prices to gain an edge over the competition.

Routes to market control access. Without the right routes to market, you simply won't reach your target market. Coca-Cola's brand goal is to make it easier and easier to buy a Coca-Cola. Just look at the result: there is virtually nowhere in the world where you are more than a few minutes from being able to buy a Coke at any time of the day or night. Many industrial companies are still struggling with access, unable to find the channels that will (note 'will', not 'can') take their products to market. Building market access can be expensive, requiring extensive internal systems and infrastructure to be able to sense market demand, gather and evaluate sales forecasts, deploy marketing programmes and promotions, or plan and execute complex logistics. It is a tough balancing act to increase access to the market while ensuring your network is profitable and capable of handling the growth you want. You look to your sales and marketing channels to generate demand for your products and services as well as fulfil it. Your market access depends on understanding the role you want your channels to play at a cost commensurate with the return generated.

Routes to market control brand. How can you deliver and fulfil your brand promise unless you manage your routes to market properly and control your sales and marketing channels? If your brand is built on quality attributes, you need your channels to execute on those attributes, not only at the point of purchase, but also if the product goes wrong or when the customer needs ongoing service and support. How well you incentivize and reward your channels will have a big impact on the ultimate customer experience and your brand. If your brand is built on low price, you need your channels to be aligned in eliminating every unnecessary activity that incurs cost.

Often, sales and marketing channels control product differentiation. You want your product or offering to be different from your competitors'. Channels play a vital role in enabling this. Often, the channel you use is the sole way of demonstrating that your product is different from your competitors'. Dell in the computer industry was a good example of this, selling a product that was over 95 per cent the same as all its competitors (with the chips and operating software coming from standard suppliers Intel and

Microsoft). Its channel – online direct – was its primary differentiator, offering price and flexibility advantages over its competition which, at that time, went to market through retail and dealer channels.

All the time, your chief finance officer wants more for less. Never have the costs and benefits of marketing and distribution come under such scrutiny. With a combination of significant costs, complexity, dependencies on external partners and variety by market, it is critical to understand and manage your distribution strategy and its economics.

Challenging business dynamics

Sales and marketing channels are complex economically. Any multi-channel strategy needs to engage multiple partners with differing business models, and your strategy needs to work for them as well as for you. Let's start with looking at the basic options available for going to market. In Figure 2.2 you will see that there are three structures for a distribution system:

- *Direct* – in this structure, the supplier owns and manages all the resources in the value chain through to the customer (or a particular set of customers). Companies employing this model have multiplied since the internet enabled online direct distribution. Examples include Dell in the

Figure 2.2 Typical distribution structures

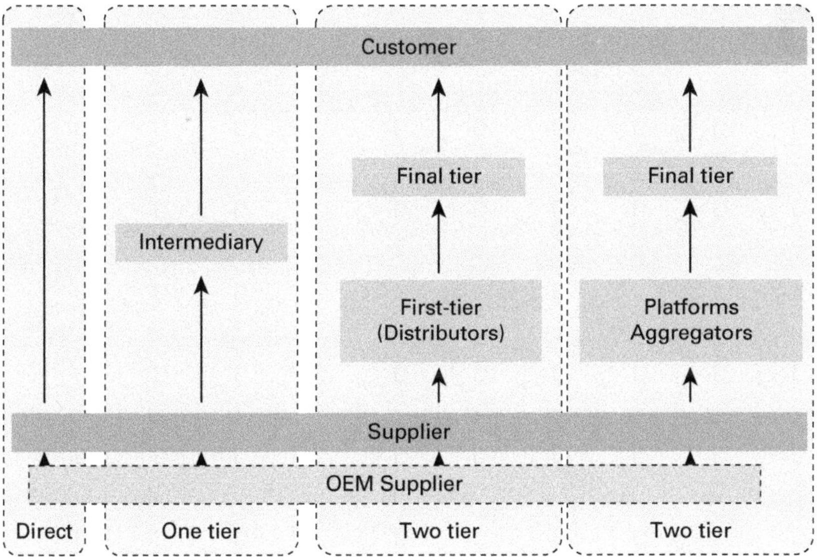

computer business, Southwest Airlines or easyJet in the low-cost airline business, Charles Schwab in securities and Lands' End in clothing. Each of these companies made a virtue out of increasing customer convenience or reducing cost, or both, by employing the direct model. In addition, they gained valuable customer insight through the direct interaction and can adjust prices and promotional offers instantly to respond to demand and supply issues. Now we see almost every consumer goods producer offering an online presence, which may include direct sales – a channel we will term 'vendor.com'. It is a model that also includes the direct sales force typically seen calling on the very large corporate accounts in most business-to-business sectors.

- *One-tier distribution* – this structure is defined by employing one set of intermediaries between the company and its customers to increase reach (such as overseas agents), provide special services to complete the customer offer (such as conservatory installers) or position the product within established channels for the customer (such as retailers), where it would make no sense for the supplier to try to persuade customers to change their shopping and buying habits. The benefits include easy and often immediate access to well-defined segments of customers or the leveraging of investments made by the intermediaries, such as overseas agents, warehouses and established sales forces. The disadvantages include the need to grant an acceptable trading margin to the intermediary and a degree of dilution of focus because the intermediary sells many brands, including potentially direct competitors (think how many varieties of soft drink or cereal are on offer in the average grocery store). In addition, the distancing of the customer by interjecting a layer of intermediaries can be a major disadvantage, depending on what information the intermediary is willing, or contracted, to share with the supplier.

- *Two-tier distribution* – in many markets there are potentially thousands of intermediaries who service the customer segments a supplier is seeking to reach. Each of these may handle only a few sales a month and the cost of finding them and managing a commercial relationship with them cannot be recovered from the margin on such a low volume of sales. Imagine yourself to be manufacturer of a particularly tasty chewy toffee. You need to reach the thousands of small boys and girls (and the odd parent and grandparent) across the country who would expect to find your toffees in their local newsagent, kiosk, station, airport, garage forecourt and sweet shop as well as the sweet aisle in the big grocery store. It would be prohibitively expensive in terms of sales people and infrastructure to sell to each one of the thousands of such stores across the country. Fortunately, someone has already done this for you, in the form of a relatively small number of cash and carry warehouses, where these stores go once or twice a week to replenish their inventory. To reach them, all you need is to get your product into these cash and carry operators (a challenge we address in Chapter 12), and you now have a two-tier distribution system: from you to the cash and carry to the newsagent to the customer. You will find similar models in the computer and telecoms industries where there are distributors servicing the many thousands of local dealers serving small and medium-sized businesses. The advantages are leverage and cost effectiveness, enabling the supplier to reach a wide, mass but low-volume market, but at the cost of further distance from the customer and market.

There are many variations on these basic structures, which evolve to meet the unique aspect of particular markets, industry sectors or customer segments:

- *Multiple-tiered distribution* – this is the same as the two-tier model but with additional tiers required to reach the end customer. In some challenging markets, perhaps caused by complex geography or economic conditions, there will be a number of players involved, such as for example the cigarette vendor in Zimbabwe who will sell a single cigarette at a time, having bought a packet from the local shop. In many emerging markets, Unilever sells soap in sachets containing enough for a single wash and these are bought and resold by several layers of dealers. In China, it is not uncommon to find five- or six-tier distribution channels moving products into the central areas, away from the burgeoning commercial centres ranged along the east coast.

- *Aggregators* – these are players who appear in some sectors and effectively force the vendors to do business with them. They are brokers who bring together the demand of customers or final-tier intermediaries so that they can buy in bulk, taking advantage of economies of scale. They can be disruptive, leveraging volume discount terms to secure the best prices and then selling on down the channel, retaining a small percentage of the revenue. They offer their customers a better price than the vendor is willing to give them because their margin is smaller than the volume discount break offered by the vendor. They do this because they rarely if ever actually touch the product – simply 'aggregating' orders. Because their business requires classic brokering behaviours, they tend to focus on a very restricted set of products – computer consumables or electricity supply contracts. For some vendors, aggregators can be a useful way to jump-start volumes or gain market access with limited resources. For others, engaging with aggregators is necessary (through their sheer size) but it distorts their channel strategy.

- *Platforms* – one of the greatest challenges facing small or niche online retailers is getting in front of their target customers, because they simply do not have the financial resources to build a visible brand presence. This is just as much a problem for the customer who has a niche need and knows that someone, somewhere is meeting it. This has led to the emergence of online platforms, the biggest of which are Amazon and Alibaba. There are hundreds of thousands of retailers finding their customers by leveraging Amazon's customer pulling power (virtual footfall) and search capabilities. Other platforms operate through offering a comparison proposition: Comparethemarket.com or MoneySuperMarket.com offer customers the ability to search for the best value car or home insurance, home utilities and other consumer services, clicking through to purchase. These platforms are moving into business services too. In the travel sector, we have seen an explosion of platforms like Hotels.com, Trivago, Kayak and Expedia. Many of these platforms operate in sectors where there are high fixed costs (like utilities, flights and hotels), where volumes are critical to profitability.

- *Original equipment manufacturer channel* – this is where one supplier, the original equipment manufacturer (OEM), makes a product that is embedded inside another. An example would be the electric motor inside a stair lift, or the silicon chip inside a computer. On their own the electric motor and silicon chip do not comprise complete products, so the route to market is first into the OEM channel (stair lift or computer manufacturers) and then as a part of a completed product into one of the other channel structures described above. Although this channel is primarily a direct connection between the OEM and its customers, Intel's well-known 'Intel inside' marketing campaign demonstrates that there is still an end-user marketing dimension even in the OEM route to market.

One-tier and first-tier intermediary businesses such as distributors or wholesalers offer the supplier efficiency and cost-effectiveness through leveraging their assets and infrastructure. This exposes them to the risky combination of long-term fixed costs and short-term visibility of revenues. To compound this, they are often critically dependent on a few major relationships, which can be changed with relatively little notice. They are usually fast-moving businesses that consume significant amounts of capital or people or both and, in many industries, have typically not delivered high returns. Very few make a return on capital above 20 per cent, the sort of rate you'd expect to compensate for the inherently risky nature of the business.

Final-tier intermediary businesses come in many forms. In the business-to-business sector they typically wrap services around the product, using special skill sets that need to be recruited, developed and retained. This means that these businesses can have relatively high fixed costs with lumpy, project-based revenues that can give rise to volatile profitability and awkward cash flow. To survive they need to be well focused on their offer to one or more defined customer segments, and to grow they need to invest in additional resources ahead of the sales curve. In the consumer sector, they need to juggle inventory levels against fluctuating (sometimes seasonal) demand to minimize over-stocking while avoiding empty shelves and missed sales. Allocating scarce retail space between distinct categories, competing brands and individual product lines has now become a data-driven process.

We go into these dynamics and how to manage the different business models in considerable detail in later chapters, but this introduction should be enough to convince you that these business models are challenging, whether you are managing them directly or need to partner with them as a supplier or customer. You should view this complexity as an opportunity, because it will give the advantage to the players who invest in mastering their channel partners' business models.

Many companies use a mix of distribution models to cover the market completely and to reach the different customer segments for which their ranges of products are intended. Operating with multiple distribution models and multiple channels creates the potential for channel conflict, where two or more channel players are taking the same product to the same customer. This is not always a bad thing (think of different retailers all offering Heinz baked beans for sale), but the multiplicity of channels can mean that some channels are given an unintentional advantage or that some are 'freeloading' on the work of others; this can be very damaging to your ability to get your products to market. For example, the specialist hi-fi shop that invests in sound studios and trained sales people to show the advantages of your brand of audio equipment will not be too impressed if the customer can walk around the corner to a Costco discount warehouse and pick it up 30 per cent cheaper. A solid understanding of the different economics of the major types of channel player will ensure an objective approach to the challenges.

Business models are key to value propositions

Although every supplier would like to think its products and services are world-beaters that virtually sell themselves, there are very few brands or products that ever achieve this status. As a result, it is rarely sufficiently convincing to tell your channel partners that your product has terrific customer benefits. The channel will regard your product's customer appeal as only one aspect of its business proposition, ie one that will shape its likely rate of sale. The intermediary will want to know all about your product's margin, what it will cost to sell and support, its probable lifecycle, the likely level of returns and warranty claims, the level of your promotional spend to build demand (both direct to the consumer and through them), stocking requirements, the opportunity to sell related products and services, and many other specific aspects of the business model. It is the composition of all the elements of a commercial relationship that determines whether a supplier can command advantage in the distribution system.

Take, for example, the suppliers of oil lubricants such as BP Castrol or Shell Lubricants. They both sell what are essentially the same products, the oils used for cars, marine engines and industrial and agricultural engines. Certainly, each company will provide detailed scientific justification of the technical superiority of its brands. But as a customer, do you really have a preference for which brand of oil is used in your car's annual service (Ferrari owners excepted)? Quite. So how do Shell and BP Castrol persuade their dealers and distributors to take their particular brand of products to market? The answer lies in understanding the business models of these dealers. Many of these dealers are small independent garages with limited cash resources. The oil suppliers compete to offer finance for major equipment purchases such as hydraulic hoists or diagnostic computers or even the storage facilities for their new and drained oil supplies in return for a multi-year commitment from the dealer to buy their brand. Their value proposition to the dealers has everything to do with the business model and almost nothing to do with lubricants.

If your role involves building business through your channel partners, it is critical to understand how their business model works to be able to communicate the value in your company's value proposition. You need to know what levers in the channel's business model are available to you and how to connect your proposition to those levers. As we have shown in the examples above, these levers can come from almost any aspect of the channel's business, not just the margins or rate of sale of your products. But this is only half the story; you also need to look inside your own business model and identify unique strengths that your competitors cannot match and then find ways to turn these into compelling value propositions for your channels. For example, if you are a market share leader, you should be looking for fixed-cost investments that you can spread over your higher unit volumes to give you a lower cost per unit. This might be in the form of a national media campaign that drives traffic or sales leads to your channel partners, or a supply chain initiative that increases the responsiveness of your logistics capability to fluctuations in demand experienced by the channel.

In the United States, the large grocery chains will major on Coca-Cola instead of Pepsi for the big holidays because they know that Coke can replenish the stores three times a day and as retailers they cannot afford to run out of stocks on 4 July or the days before the Super Bowl. Pepsi cannot match this, and no amount of additional discounting or rebates on each unit sold will win this business back. By owning all the major holidays, Coke dominates the category. In this way, Coke has used its unique strengths to the detriment of its competition.

Successful suppliers will go further and understand the 'business model inside' or how the business model for their products and services performs inside their channel's business model. They will know whether they are a drag on their channel's business or an enabler on all the key measures such as margins, volumes, stock levels, credit allowances and so on. As we show in the following chapters on each type of business model, there are many measures that can be used and it is important to identify the measures that matter, not just for the generic business type, but for the specific partner you are pitching to.

A structured approach to positioning your channel value proposition

A key thrust of this chapter has been that as a supplier you need to understand the business models of your downstream (ie nearer to the customer) channel partners to develop and communicate a compelling value proposition – just as the final tier needs to understand its customers' business to make the most effective offer. You need to adopt a structured approach to positioning your value proposition to ensure that you apply a well-grounded and logical approach to gaining advantage.

Table 2.2   Structured approach to positioning your value proposition

Analyse channel's business model	Identify own unique strengths	Identify opportunities	Develop and sell value proposition
• What are the channel's business objectives?	• What are your unique assets and strengths?	• How can you help the channel achieve its objectives?	• What are the core thrusts of your value proposition?
• What are its primary business measures?	• How can these be deployed to the channel's benefit?	• What is the competition doing?	• What channel business measures does it impact?
• What is the channel's core business strategy?		• What gaps exist in the market?	• What are its unique advantages for the channel over the competition?
• How well is the channel performing?		• How can your position be improved?	
• What are its greatest threats and weaknesses?			

Table 2.2 sets out the key steps in the process and the important questions that need to be tackled. Note how it requires you to consider what the competition is doing as well as identify your own strengths in developing the proposition that best positions you in terms of the channel's objectives.

Many suppliers require that their partner account managers establish themselves as trusted business advisers to their key distribution partners. They are expected to develop the relationship to the level of a strategic partnership with significant interdependencies. This imperative demands excellent understanding and insight into the business model of their key partner. With this foundation, the account manager can recommend unique investments that his or her company should make to further differentiate its value proposition.

Those partner account managers who work with the broad mass of channel partners in a particular segment need to understand the fundamentals of the business model of the particular type of channel partner with which they work. This is essential to their ability to sell in new products, programmes and terms and conditions. We have found that channels in every type of industry respond very positively to the supplier that has invested in understanding their business. They will share information more openly if they believe the supplier will add value to their business as a result.

This business model insight needs to be applied throughout the supplier's organization, not just at the front line, for maximum competitive advantage. In every industry examples abound of programmes and promotions that were conceived in innocence of the channel's business model and the amazement expressed when the channel fails to take up the programme. Even worse, the channel may take the programme even though it harms its business because it fears for the impact on its supplier relationship if it refuses. An obvious example is the type of end-of-quarter, 'channel stuffing' incentives that encourage dealers to take large amounts of product into stock to help the supplier to achieve its quarter-end targets. We show in Chapter 5 why this is so disastrous for the supplier as well as the channel, which often ends up having to discount heavily to clear the over-stock, diluting margins to the point where it may not even cover the extra cost of financing, stocking, damage, etc. This is before taking into account the distortion of its trading practices, impact on positioning and all the longer-term implications of pushing these bulges through the channel's business. This type of error could be reduced if product and programme managers as well as senior management understood the implications of their actions, through a solid understanding of the business models of the channels through which they go to market.

Major trends and developments in market access 03

Introduction

The challenge of gaining market access is one of the most demanding and fast changing aspects of any business. The combination of advancing technology, changing buyer expectations and behaviours, growth of social media, increase in competition from globalization, increasingly fragmented segmentation and virtualization of location means that every business is having to work harder than ever before to find and connect with its customers. Amidst all the rapid pace of change across multiple industry sectors, it is possible to pick out some underlying trends and developments that will affect almost any business, and which should be considered in developing a distribution strategy. In this chapter, we highlight these factors and show that there are some core principles at play that can enable you to navigate the complexities and focus on what really matters in managing your sales and marketing channels.

The myth of disintermediation

The majority of distribution strategies make significant use of third party, indirect, multi-tier marketing and sales channels to achieve their market access goals. For as long as we can remember, the distribution layer (or middle tier) has been under the supposed threat of immediate extinction through disintermediation – the removal of intermediaries. Telephone, telex, automation, internet, cloud have all been held out as the means to connect businesses with their customers directly, removing the need for the 'middleman'. These new technologies have often been cited as the impending death knell of intermediaries such as distributors, aggregators and brokers, but in practice have served only to empower them.

A more stringent examination of the effect of these technologies shows why they are unlikely ever to be the cause of disintermediation. The underlying rationale for the distributor/aggregator/platform middle tier is the need to bring multi-vendor solutions to the marketplace efficiently. This is reinforced by new technologies, not undermined. Very few products or services work in isolation. The increasing need for the final tier to specialize in one area of integrated solutions (horizontal focus) or a defined set of customer segments (vertical focus) means they cannot afford to seek out all the multiple vendors they need to offer their customer-facing proposition. This is especially true if new suppliers with new offerings are coming to market all the time. Equally, suppliers cannot afford to reach the myriad of final-tier specialists that address the customer segments and geographies they need to reach. They depend upon the economic leverage of distributors/aggregators/platforms that can spread market access costs over hundreds or thousands of suppliers, to be able to do this cost-effectively. The final-tier players also look back up the supply chain to outsource back-office activities, functions and processes to the middle tier to leverage scale advantages, enabling the final-tier players to focus downstream on their customers.

A good example of this is the latest threat of cloud-based supply chains, where we are seeing distributors playing an ever-increasing role. It's not hard to find the reasons why. The eternal needs of buyers and sellers to be able to find each other efficiently, continue to play out, whether in the real or the virtual world. In the IT sector, the top dozen or so distributors collectively passed a billion dollars of cloud-based sales in 2016. Their core competencies of providing instant availability across multiple vendors, pre- and post-sales advice, credit management, account management, transaction processing (including rebates), promotion management and segment targeting remain just as critical to suppliers in the cloud era as they ever did. The array of services offered downstream to the final tier has expanded hugely too. In Table 3.1 is an example of the huge array of services offered by distributors in serving cloud-based supply chains in the IT sector.

In developing your distribution strategy and defining your marketing and sales channels to gain market access, it would be risky to assume that the middle tier is going to disappear. In fact, we are seeing a more general trend for suppliers to increasingly outsource their own internal distribution capabilities to the middle tier, to gain their economies of scale and efficiencies of scope and to plug into the sourcing strategies of the final tier. It is likely that you will see consolidation in the middle tier as the larger, more economically powerful distributors, aggregators and platforms buy up smaller, possibly more specialized, distributors. This has the combined advantages of

Table 3.1   Services provided by IT distributors

Well beyond the days of pick, pack and ship		
• Engineering and design	• Cloud solutions/ programs	• Project management
• E-business integration	• Logistics	• Application engineering
• Vertical market solutions	• Credit/leasing	• Government/GSA services
• Demand generation	• Technical support	• Field application engineers
• Managed services	• Education and training	
• Licensing	• Authorizations	• Thermal management
• Config and assembly	• Account management	• Power supply modification
• Channel marketing	• Solution selling	
• Mobile device management	• Customer packaging	• Asset tagging and labelling
• UCC, telecomm, VOIP	• Electronic data interchange	• Software services consulting
• Reverse logistics	• Network assessments	• Sustainability measures
• Kitting	• Global certification	
• Device programming	• Hosted solutions	• Software/firmware updates
• Lifecycle management	• Site preparation	• Installation and deployment
		• Annuity management
		• Specialized communities
		• Asset disposition

SOURCE 2016 Global Technology Distribution Council Research

increasing their own economic efficiency, making them more competitive to the final tier and broadening their market reach and coverage, making them more attractive to the supplier tier, and more powerful in negotiating terms upstream. Your distribution strategy will need to include the development of compelling first tier channel propositions to ensure you command the attention and resources of these powerful market access channels. Part Two of this book is focused on helping you understand how to do this in depth, based on the commercial dimensions that dominate this type of proposition.

From products to services

One of the meta trends reshaping many industry sectors is the shift from selling products to selling services. Consumers and companies are buying functionality rather than assets. As an example: computing, printing and networking rather than software, computers, printers and networks. In other words, customers seek to pay only for the utility they need, when they want it, at a volume that fluctuates to suit their needs. This model, often termed the 'consumption model' has been around for quite a while in the business-to-business (B2B) world (think of Xerox selling photocopying to offices 'by the click') but is now becoming mainstream in the consumer world (B2C) too. Why is this, and what are the implications for distribution strategy?

Let's look at the B2B sphere first. Businesses love to turn fixed costs and up-front investments into variable costs that scale with growth (both up and down). For example, buying a major asset like a server farm is a big bet economically, consuming capital and requiring a forecast of capacity requirements that could prove to be wildly over- or under-optimistic, with challenging consequences either way. It also runs the risk of becoming technologically obsolete long before its working (and assumed economic) life is up. Cue the offer of 'Infrastructure as a Service' (IaaS). With IaaS, the business can purchase the utility of a server farm, pay only for actual consumption, scale up or down as needed, be assured of always having the latest technology and functionality on tap, increasing its own agility, and it can pay monthly instead of committing the capital up front. In addition, the business can integrate any number of its enterprise applications, like ERP, CRM, supply chain management, management reporting and data visualization systems onto the platform, replacing annual licences with consumption charges, thus buying its Software as a Service (SaaS) too, with similar advantages.

Where this model would once have applied only to large enterprises, it is now available to the smallest of businesses: Microsoft's Office 365 offers access to normal desktop applications, virtually anywhere, with additional cloud productivity services to a micro business for a monthly charge to a credit card. Many accounting, payroll, billing, payment and CRM applications can be bought singly or as integrated bundles of functionality in the same way, and in all cases, scope can be changed (adding users or additional functionality) with a few clicks. For small businesses, husbanding their cash flow and wanting to look bigger than they are, this is perfect.

In the B2C sphere, consumers are increasingly recognizing the benefits of buying the use of, rather than owning, assets. Many millennials are not concerned with acquiring possessions. They think nothing of renting a car for an hour, a single trip or a weekend and much prefer to avoid all the hassle of car ownership – insurance, servicing, financing, taxing, etc. This has opened the way for Zip Car, car clubs, City Car and the like to offer the opportunity to find the nearest available car, unlock it, return it somewhere else and walk away, all through an app. Once these services become more widely available, non-millennials will quickly take advantage too. Other services are gaining ground. Instant ink from HP will enable you to forget about needing to buy ink cartridges (plus a spare) episodically, by having your printer track your consumption and organize replacement cartridges before you run out, for a monthly fee. Streaming services such as Spotify, Apple Music, Netflix, etc are displacing the outright purchase of CDs and DVDs, offering enormous libraries of music and movies on demand. Amazon's Prime does the same for books, offering its lending library instead of book purchase. Its aggressive bundling of other services and marketing of Prime may have attracted more attention and may cause higher than wanted customer churn (rapid gain and loss of customers), but it is gaining ground. This consumption model smooths expenditure for the consumer, removes or reduces ownership burdens, and increases convenience, flexibility and responsiveness.

For many of the middle-class consumption segments, lives are supersaturated with possessions, fostering a general trend away from buying stuff to enjoying experiences. The growth in travel, cruise lines, short breaks, live performances, cinemas with bars, sports events, dining out, chef's tables, music festivals, and extreme experiences all reflect the underlying trend of service consumption rather than acquisition of possessions.

What does it mean for the supplier, in either B2B or B2C, and its distribution strategy? Probably the biggest impact is that it potentially changes who the customer is. In some of these examples, the customer is no longer a single consumer or business, it is now the platform, aggregator or service provider that is the customer, potentially buying large wholesale volumes (eg of cars, licences, servers, capacity) to be able to offer the business or consumer a retail service. Now your channel strategy will need to ensure that you are accessing all the customer segments through these service providers, and your proposition and channel strategy need to focus on accessing the service provider. A big consideration here must be how this affects your brand, its positioning, price point and presentation. Not all of this will be in your control, as the major events have found when their tickets find their way onto the secondary markets or ticket touts. The same can happen when brands are suppressed under the brand of the service provider. Do City Club users care whether the car they use for a short trip is a VW Golf or GM Astra? Do users of Amazon Web Services care what brand of servers are running in the data centre?

Many services are predicated upon convenience, which has raised customer expectations for convenience in everything. Your channel strategy needs to look at offering more convenient ways of delivering your product or service. Almost every grocery chain now offers delivery, despite having spent the last decades building shops in every local district. Restaurants are finding that offering carry-out or take-away options is no longer enough. They now need to up their game and offer delivery and, in some markets, such as the Middle East, delivery is a mandatory channel. Even that's not enough. The growth of digital channels means that customers expect to be able to order online, through an app or a bot, and then choose whether to pick up or have it delivered. Convenience is a virtual play that needs to be integrated into your physical channels.

Your distribution strategy needs to become multi-tier, making your aggregating service providers into essential channel partners, while you continue to communicate your brand values to the ultimate consumer via other marketing channels and through the service providers themselves. You'll need to demonstrate to the service providers that you are generating demand for them, and that partnering with you is commercially valuable to them. You will be simultaneously selling to them, with them, through them and around them. We cover the techniques to do this in Part Three and take a deep dive into the insights available from the service sector in Chapter 23.

Emergence of the cloud, apps and microtransactions

A related but different trend is the emergence of microtransactions, driven by the increasing consumption of services and underpinned by the technologies of the cloud, apps on all types of device and digital wallets. We have become familiar with paying for the use of telephone networks by the minute or second, and this microtransaction model now extends to include in-app purchases (not just in games), the consumption of IaaS and SaaS functionality by the plug-in, bits consumed, storage capacity used, seats or hours online and many others. Within two years of launch, revenues from online TurboTax users nearly doubled the revenues from desktop users; the Google Adwords model bills by the click, digital rights to images and content are charged by the media, location, channel, and several other variables.

The generation of new streams of microtransactional revenue opens up both new markets and new types of channel engagement with consumers but holds many challenges for suppliers, with risks to their market access, revenue stability and ultimate profitability. The incredible complexity of tracking, reporting and billing billions of microtransactions across millions of customers, gives power to the player that has that billing relationship. For in-app purchases, this can be the platform such as Apple Store and Google whose revenue share of each transaction is 30 per cent (reducing to 15 per cent after the first year of subscription). That's a 30 per cent cost of distribution in a digital channel – pretty steep and non-negotiable. For many consumer services the network provider owns the billing relationship: mobile phone network providers bill for purchases made involving data; cable and satellite networks bill for media, TV app and in-app purchases; utility providers bill for add-on services related to home emergency cover and insurances. The reason the billing provider holds the power is not only because it owns the billing relationship, but because it is a full route to market, providing a marketing communication platform too. It can highlight fast-growing options, support promotional campaigns and lend its own brand credibility to give customers, who have never heard of a new, upstart service provider, the confidence to buy.

For IaaS and SaaS types of solutions, the service provider has the option to spend aggressively on brand building through marketing channels to attract demand direct to its own server supply channels or leverage an aggregator platform or distributor. If the service is often consumed along with other related services, there could be real advantages to going to market through these platforms. The final tier does not want to build multiple supplier relationships, with the complexity of managing multiple billings, payment cycles all using different processes; they would prefer to go to one platform that can aggregate all the services they wish to bundle for their customers and receive one aggregated bill aligned to their own billing schedule.

The supplier's distribution strategy needs to be designed back from the customer and ensure that there is as frictionless a consumption process as possible, including initial subscription, ongoing consumption, service scope enhancements and issue resolution. Difficult trade-off decisions are involved between paying intermediaries for market access while gaining instant massive market access; between building and operating owned channels and outsourcing to third parties; between customer acquisition costs and customer life-time value. One critical point is that many service streams take longer to reach breakeven compared to old product revenue streams, so aligning costs to scale with revenues can be very attractive.

Multi-channel (omni-channel) challenges

Buyers now expect to flit randomly from one channel to another as they browse, consider, choose, buy, receive, consume and dispose of their products or service relationships. And they expect their providers to enable this, seamlessly across all the channels they choose to use, with price consistency, brand consistency and the ability to pick up using a completely different channel to where they last left off.

Complaints, comments, demands for help with problems can no longer be channelled directly into customer services channels; they are just as likely to be posted in full public view on Twitter, Facebook, Snapchat and all the other social media channels, possibly complete with a video record of the whole saga. A customer service issue can go viral globally before the local manager is even aware of it. Verizon's refusal to close a dead customer's account without his PIN number, Chipotle's food poisoning incidents, and United Airlines' forced physical off-loading of a passenger from an over-sold flight, all went viral and caused massive reputational damage with consequent economic impact to brands that had millions of satisfied, but silent, customers.

Market access channels now include the huge array of virtual channels, such as apps, websites, mobile access devices, social media in all its forms, bots, comparison sites (Comparethemarket.com), review sites (TripAdvisor), market places (Amazon), as well as traditional real channels, such as retail outlets of all types, warehouse clubs, dealers, etc. Your distribution strategy now needs to be designed as an omni-channel strategy from the start. It's no longer acceptable to simply address the question, 'Where does the customer want to buy?' Rather, the question is: 'What are all the channels where the customer may want to be present?' followed closely by responding to these questions:

- What would the customer expect of us in each channel (communicate offers, enable a purchase, be listening out for comments or complaints)?
- How do we substantiate our brand values in each channel?
- How can we differentiate ourselves in each channel?
- Which channels are best for customer acquisition, retention, up-selling, cross-selling, introducing new products or services?
- What is the cost to our brand and revenue of avoiding certain channels?
- How do we encourage our customers to engage through, or migrate to our lowest cost channels?
- How do we avoid our proposition being reduced to price comparisons?

Any supplier used to going to market through a multi-channel distribution strategy will be familiar with the problems of channel conflict. This is where different channels compete against each other to win business, often compromising the supplier's brand and pricing strategies without growing the total revenues for the supplier. The net effect can see customers pulled towards channels offering the lowest price to make their actual purchases, undermining the total value proposition and removing revenue from the higher-cost channels. These higher-cost channels could be critical to the supplier for creating brand awareness and preference in the mind of the customer, communicating the brand values and bringing the customer to the point of making a purchase. If a supplier allows such a situation to continue, with low-cost channels stealing revenue away, the higher-cost channels will cease to carry the brand, damaging sales for the supplier. Channel conflict can be tough to manage, with legal limitations on the supplier's ability to control street prices, and global sourcing enabling unintended avenues of supply in any given market. In an omni-channel distribution strategy, the risk of channel conflict is magnified, and in today's transparent market places, price and proposition differentials are rapidly brought to customers' attention.

The underlying principle of managing omni-channel distribution strategies is to compensate each channel only for what is of value to the supplier. For example, if a supplier needs a higher-cost channel to position its products, promote the brand to key customer segments and explain its differentiation, then it must find a compensation model that rewards this activity. This can be tied to space provided on display (real and virtual), communications made, investments made to promote the brand to the right customers, promotions conveyed and so on. Note, none of these are tied to actual sales. One example of such a strategy in both the B2B and B2C space is the provision of demonstration centres where customers can interact with the products in a variety of realistic environments (these can be both owned and third party centres). Many new software applications have been positioned in this way by leading system integrators, often shown operating in conjunction with complementary applications and solutions. By co-investing in such a facility, the supplier profiles its products in an expert-enhanced context, while the system integrators show off their leading-edge credentials and hope to land the installation engagements from customers exposed to the opportunities and business case. We deal in detail with functional compensation models, as this conflict-management strategy is termed, in Chapter 22; the insights supplied there apply to any sector faced with this challenge.

Consumer channels: more than just retail and e-tailer

Perhaps always the most fickle of buyers, consumers now enjoy more control in their purchasing than ever before: from where and how they source their information, to what products they opt to buy, what price they are prepared to pay, where they prefer to buy and what they choose to share about their ownership experiences, they are very much the centre of everyone's attention: manufacturers, distributors and retail. Any one of us considering a purchase today has access to some immensely powerful tools. Let's take the purchase of a smartphone as an example:

- At the tap of a trackpad or the swipe of a finger, we can access detailed information on any aspect of the smartphone: specifications, unboxing videos, who else has bought it, what they think of it.

- We can compare prices – across the globe if we wish using Google translate – or see price trends by outlet over the last few weeks.

- We can identify where we want to buy, view live stock levels of the phones that interest us, and choose between buying immediately online for rapid delivery (as rapid as within the hour) or opt to visit a store to touch, feel and try the different phones on our shortlist.

- Even as we stand in front of the phones on the shelf, we can be browsing other places to buy the same item, learning about other buyers' answers to questions potential buyers have raised, their experiences of customer service, or we can seek the opinions of friends on whether to buy a particular make and model.

- With our decision made, we can choose between buying the phone outright, or signing up for a monthly pay-as-you-go contract that lets us enjoy all the benefits of the latest flagship with none of the up-front cash outlay.

- We can choose to have the phone delivered to our homes, to a nominated store, to a network of collection points, even in some cases directly into our hands.

- We can share our delight about our new purchase instantly with our friends on Facebook or Instagram, and learn about other products like cases and headsets that complement it or improve its usefulness.

- As we start to use the product, we can shoot videos of our own experience with it, including how to fix it ourselves (or if not we can learn how others have fixed it).

- We can voice our opinion about the entire experience and broadcast it across the globe in a single tap or click.

If consumers are now hugely empowered by the above, it has provoked dramatic change in consumer channels. For many years market access for consumers was dominated by the major retail store chains. Channel choice used to be simple – mass, multi-specialist or specialist – and the rules of the game well-established: defined assortments, pricing negotiations, listing fees, paid-for communications and display, inflexible delivery slots... and maybe some exchange of consumer data. Online retailing was the first wave of disruption to this model, providing a lower-cost alternative route to market; the addition of pervasive information and social media into the mix has made for further complexity. Your consumer distribution strategy now needs to answer some very different questions:

- What are we doing to maintain dialogue with our consumers and customers throughout their journey with our products: who exactly are they, how are they finding out about our products, what are they buying, where are they buying and how are they getting value from using our products?

- How can we shape the ways in which consumers become informed about our products and offerings?

- Where would we prefer our customers to buy? What is the role of stores in our mix: online and offline? What other channels do we require to maintain an effective dialogue with our consumers?

- How much should we invest in stores as a marketing medium? What should our compensation model be for retailers that have diminishing footfall, earn very little profit on our products but do a fantastic job of showcasing them? How do we manage our pricing through such varied channels?

- How should we engage and enable a constantly churning store staff of millennials to explain and promote the benefits of buying and using our products?

- How should we respond to the demand for pay-as-you-go consumption models and what role should our channel play in their delivery?

- Whose logistics capabilities must we leverage to handle the complexities of envelope-level, in-the-hand delivery... and returns? Who should be building our return logistics capability?

- How do we orchestrate our response to customer service issues and returns across our own and our partners' supply chains?

- How do we manage social media with and through our channel partners to maximize net promotion and minimize brand damage?

With the consumer now genuinely king (or queen), your omni-channel strategy needs to encompass much more than multiple purchase channels.

In Chapter 22 we provide insights and examples of how to devise an effective consumer channel approach.

Commercial channels and ecosystems

One of the key characteristics of today's B2B space is that products and services are rarely ever sold as stand-alone items or transactions. The nature of businesses as customers is that their needs require more complex, tailored solutions with multiple vendors' offerings needing to be integrated in some way.

Here's a simple example to show how this works: retail premises requiring site security. A solution would typically involve the supply and installation of various types of CCTV cameras, one mounted over each till or cashpoint, to capture the activity every time a sale is rung up, with other cameras dotted around the store, the stockroom, the delivery bay and focused on the customer entrances. These cameras all need to be connected to some form of internal network for monitoring, recording and integrating with the cashpoint system and alarm system and then connected to an external network for offsite or retrospective monitoring. All of this needs to be maintained, serviced and updated periodically, and may initially need to be financed. There are a lot of fixed and moving parts, and this is a relatively simple solution.

Solutions of any complexity generally need a complete ecosystem to deliver the full value proposition to the customer cost-effectively. From a distribution strategy perspective, an essential first step is to map out the ecosystems available, ideally from the customer's perspective. The players in the ecosystem will be the array of service providers, solution integrators (that assemble all the different elements into a bespoke solution tailored for each individual customer and coordinate all the suppliers and distributors to provide their elements in the right specification so that the whole thing will work together as required), specifiers, sources of advice, etc.

Some players of the ecosystem will be able to influence the brands purchased, others' roles will be to simply fulfil at lowest cost of supply, and some players exist to integrate and install the solution. The challenge for the supplier is to find the players in the ecosystem that can provide a cost-effective route to market for its part of the solution, conveying its brand proposition to the end customer. A strong brand can generate a brand 'pull' that sucks products or services through the ecosystem because the end customer demands it. James Hardie, a provider of fibre-cement sidings for houses, employed this strategy so robustly that it effectively forced the ecosystem players to serve as its routes to market, or risk being shut out of a substantial share of the market. Other suppliers may see that they simply need to market their proposition to the service integrators, making great play of their products' ease of installation, universal fit with other components of the solution, and high return on working capital investment for the service integrator. This can be considered a 'push' distribution strategy and, if employed well, can level the playing field for the smaller niche player alongside the brand behemoths.

In recent times, ecosystem thinking has become an essential approach to addressing the complex challenge of ensuring market access, reach and coverage at an effective cost. In Chapter 19 and throughout Part Four, we provide more insights and examples as to how to embrace this approach.

The 'gig economy' channels

The term 'gig economy' refers to labour markets characterized by the prevalence of short-term contracts or freelance work as opposed to permanent jobs. Examples include the taxi service Uber, the private room or home rental service Airbnb, the restaurant food delivery service Deliveroo, many courier services, pop-up stores and restaurants, etc. For each of these headline brands there are many lookalike players that may operate on a more localized basis.

Look closely, and you will see that many of the new players in the gig economy are playing a distribution role, improving market access for suppliers, and increasing choice and convenience for consumers. In many cases, these players are platforms offering much of the utility of a virtual market place or distributor, bringing customers and suppliers together through intuitive, immediate and efficient interfaces. They have succeeded because they address unmet, or ill-met needs:

- Deliveroo, Just Eat and UberEATS expand the market, enabling consumers to eat almost any type of cuisine at home (not just the cuisines that normally offer carry-out or take-aways).

- Uber reduces the cost of a taxi service while removing many of the bugbears: finding a taxi in a low-traffic area, not knowing how long you will have to wait, paying in cash, working out how much to tip, collecting a receipt, being able to redress a bad experience, even choosing what standard of taxi car you want.

- Airbnb provides attractive rooms or homes at a fraction of the cost of an equivalent standard hotel or aparthotel offering, often in very attractive locations, with accommodation of a quality that would be out of the price bracket of many of its customers. There are also higher-end alternatives such as Onefinestay.com and lower-end alternatives such as Couchsurfing.com.

- Similarly disruptive, although slightly different in the nature of its (more regulated) market is TransferWise, the peer-to-peer money transfer service launched in 2011. Its two Estonian founders, both suffering from the heavy fees levied by banks for transferring funds abroad, spotted the opportunity to arrange international transfers... by avoiding them! Combining an algorithm that matches transfers going in opposite directions with disruptive marketing techniques, a message of transparency and the promise to pass savings on to its consumers, TransferWise has carved out a successful position against the traditional distributors of foreign exchange products – the banks. The company currently serves over two million customers who transfer a total of £1 billion every month over more than 750 different currency 'routes', recently expanding its offering to include a 'borderless' current account.

In most cases these new players are also prompting new suppliers to come into the market. Deliveroo has turned many higher-end restaurants into carry-out/take-away places that previously would never have engaged in this potentially brand-demeaning, complicated offering. Now they can increase their visibility, broaden their awareness and make quiet periods earn revenue, all of which complements their core in-dining offering. Uber has pulled thousands of drivers into the taxi service business by letting them choose their own hours, enabling supplementary income opportunities. Airbnb has pulled millions of available rooms into the travel sector, creating a whole new market in travel.

Pop-up stores and food wagons were an occasional phenomenon, usually found only at events or at market days. They could not count on finding a market outside of these few high-traffic locations, until social media, apps and universal internet access enabled them to communicate their locations, offerings and customer ratings to potential customers. They can achieve word of mouth-type buzz in minutes.

As with any disrupter play, the market incumbents are squealing loudly and recruiting the regulatory authorities to rule some or all the disruptive practices illegal. In many countries, Uber, Deliveroo and others are defending the case that their drivers are self-employed, avoiding minimum wage, holiday pay and other employment burdens, a critical component of their ability to undercut competitors. Some they win, some they lose. Not every gig economy player gets it right all the time, leaving trails of frustrated and disappointed customers with booking failures (or scams), missing meals and failed pick-ups. However, the market incumbents should accept that the gig economy is a real threat and has created a whole new kind of competitor leveraging the power of market access that is tough to match with a traditional distribution strategy. One sector among those most disrupted by the gig economy is the hotel, restaurant and catering sector; almost as badly affected is travel. In Chapter 24 we look at how these markets' incumbents are fighting back, by harnessing their direct-to-consumer channels and propositions.

There will be many other trends affecting whichever sector you are involved in, and there is a good chance that many of the more significant changes will include a marketing and sales channel dynamic. Even if it doesn't initially appear so, you should run through this short checklist before dismissing it as a temporary trend. A 'yes' to any question denotes it will affect your distribution strategy:

- Is this trend going to change my customers or change my existing customers' expectations or buying behaviours?
- Is this trend going to change the ecosystem that determines my market access?
- Will there be new players engaging with my customers, or influencing their preferences?
- Will existing players be engaging differently with the market (eg moving to more direct channels, or moving to more indirect channels)?
- Will my customers be engaging with new media, new platforms, new apps, new venues, new players?
- Will my customers want to consume utility in different ways, pay for it in different ways or shift their consumption patterns in any way?

Often the guidance for how to build a distribution strategy response will lie in another industry sector that has already faced the challenges you anticipate affecting your own. We encourage you to read Part Four of this book and the online additions to this section that will appear from time to time, as a strategic resource for just this situation.

PART TWO
Distributors, wholesalers and intermediaries

The role of the distributor for sales and marketing channels

Distributors, wholesalers and intermediaries

For the purposes of this book, we will consider distributors, wholesalers and other 'first-tier' intermediaries to be the same and, certainly in terms of business model, they *are* the same. The distributor is an intermediary that services the final tier that serves the end user customer; for example, the cash and carry (wholesaler) serving small independent retailers, or the builders' merchant (distributor) serving people in jobbing trades such as plumbers, builders, etc, or the broadline technology distributors serving thousands of computer or electronics dealers and retailers. This means that distributors as we are defining them are to be found only in two-tier (or three-tier) distribution models and it is worth considering their role in terms of both their customers and their suppliers.

Customer role – core functions

For their customers, distributors fulfil a number of core roles, many of which are aspects of being a one-stop shop for their (final-tier) customers of smaller, independent traders, dealers, retailers and so on. These final-tier players cannot afford the complexity and cost of sourcing their products from the hundreds of suppliers that are integral to their own offer to end-customers. It is more efficient to be able to go to a limited number of distributors with whom they can establish trading relationships that meet most or all of their needs. For the distributors, there are a number of services they can provide that leverage their own scale advantages either as an integral part of their core offering or as discrete services their customers can opt to use (see Table 4.1).

Note that the one-stop shop does not necessarily mean that the customer is buying hundreds of different items at the same time. In fact, across a surprisingly wide number of industries, the average number of different line items bought at a single time or on a single invoice is around two (ie bricks and plaster, not two bricks). It really means that the customer expects to be able to go to the distributor for anything and buy it without needing to wait or to place it on back order. The customer is likely to shop around for price and availability, trading off convenience and cost. Core to the distributor's role is the ability to provide products on demand, saving or minimizing the stocking burden on the part of its customers. Typically, the distributor will offer many thousands of SKUs (stock-keeping units) to be able to promise universal availability of virtually every 'standard' and many not-so-standard products. For example, automotive parts distributors hold many thousands of individual parts ready for 24-hour delivery to garages and workshops servicing and repairing customers' cars, some of which may have been out of production for several years.

Table 4.1 Typical core offering and optional services offered by distributors to their customers

Typical core offering	Typical optional services
• One-stop shop – range and availability	• Sourcing of products • Back-to-back ordering • Simplified supply logistics
• Bulk breaking	• Consignment stocking • Repackaging
• Credit	• Extended credit, project finance
• First-level technical support (pre-sales)	• Second-level technical support (post-sales) – effectively acting as an outsourced provider of support • Technical training
• Logistics – delivery	• Logistics – drop shipment to ultimate customer
• Order consolidation	• Project management – coordinating the supply of several suppliers and shipping to multiple locations
• Product information collateral	• Marketing services – effectively acting as an outsourced provider

Implicit in the distributor's offer is also a proposition that has value to both the distributor's customer and supplier – breaking bulk. Most distributors break bulk to quantities nearer that required by the end-customer, such as case-quantities for wine and spirits in alcoholic drink distribution. Many distributors do very little genuine 'wholesaling', ie in large volumes, but sell in ones and twos, as their customers effectively trade back-to-back in the volumes required by individual end-customers. This does vary by industry sector, but as dealers and traders do not wish to carry stocks of anything but the most essential supplies, they regard the ability to buy in retail quantities to be an essential aspect of the distributor's offer.

The provision of credit is a core benefit enabling customers to be able to supply, install, or fit the products without having to finance their entire work-in-progress and end-customer receivables. This liquidity is often multiplied in a market with traders and dealers sourcing from three or more distributors to maximize the credit facilities available to them. The distributor uses its local market and trading knowledge to set sensible credit limits and can spread the risk of any bad debts over thousands of trading relationships.

Most distributors provide some level of technical support, usually on a pre-sale (and therefore free) basis. This is an integral part of the selling-in process, especially for new products and technical innovations, and varies from simple 'Does this do the job or work with other components in a system?' enquiries through to what can be quite sophisticated configuration activities in the high end of technology-based industries. This role may extend to include post-sale support in a troubleshooting mode to resolve mis-supply or configuration issues. As an extension of this selling-in to the final tier of the channel, distributors will often provide product marketing collateral for the trade to use in selling-in new products to the end-customer and support the overall marketing communication process.

Different industries and markets will have different norms for the provision of delivery logistics. In some industries, distributors may provide this free, in others distributors may charge on orders below a minimum amount and in others distributors may expect the customer to collect. Where a distributor is out of stock or does not carry a particular item, it will order it from the supplier and then ship it out to the customer when it arrives. Typically, as industries mature, costs become more transparent and so delivery charges will be shown separately from the core product price. Distributors rarely know the true delivery cost and their shipping charge supplements tend to be arbitrary and designed not to alienate customers. Closely related to this is order consolidation, enabling customers to minimize their delivery costs by waiting until an entire order of different products from different suppliers is ready to ship.

All the elements above (with the possible exception of delivery charges) are built into the price paid by the customer for the product. All the additional optional services that can be offered go beyond this core proposition and therefore are charged in addition to the product price, either as a service charge on a fee basis or as an addition to the transaction cost per item. These services typically emerge as an industry matures and the margin on the core value proposition becomes increasingly squeezed and the distributor needs to find new sources of profitability. The same competitive pressures apply to the final tiers, who look to eliminate any activities that are not core to their differentiation and turn to the distributor to provide these functions on an outsourced basis, taking advantage of their scale and depth of capabilities. These can be related to product supply such as consignment stocking (see box) of specialist products or the project management of complex multiple shipments across multiple suppliers to multiple locations, or logistics as in drop shipments, where the distributor delivers direct to the end-customer, on behalf of the final tier. This can be enhanced to include packaging and delivery notes that appear to be from the final-tier player and even invoicing, all saving costly handling events and activity in the value chain. Provided the distributor is efficient, savings can be shared between the distributor, the final-tier player and the customer (through lower prices).

Consignment stock

In developing markets, where finance and distributor capital are tight, consignment stock is often used to finance market expansion and penetration. For example, in the years immediately after the fall of the Berlin Wall, many companies scrabbled to secure market share in a 'land-grab' situation. Many US and European companies used consignment stock to finance distributors, fill shelves and block access to competition. BAT, for example, took the risk of setting up a consignment stock for its distributor, Brodokomerc, in Croatia. This risk, given the unstable nature of the market, was doubly surprising as the agreement to operate a consignment stock did not make any reference as to who was liable for any bad debt that might arise! This is a good example of taking a risk-positive approach to securing market access in the early stages of market development.

Bespoke services that are not directly attached to transactions include sourcing of new suppliers or products and outsourced marketing, where the distributor acts as the marketing services supplier to the final-tier players who do not want to in-source this activity. This enables the final tier to run more intensive marketing activities at key points in the year without bearing an overhead cost at other times. They are also able to access a depth of specialist marketing skills they could never justify on their level of sales. In technical sectors this can blend with the provision of second-level and post-sales technical support, which again the final tier may not be able to afford in-house but can subcontract to the distributor.

Supplier role

Distributors can play a wide variety of roles for suppliers as we describe below, depending on the maturity of the product category, product lifecycle stage, market share of the supplier and density of the final tier in the distribution system. But in every case, the distributor's primary role is as a route to market for the supplier and its effectiveness will be critical to the supplier seeking to reach a segment or the entire market.

Alternative models

This range of distributor types can be characterized in terms of their business model (see Figure 4.1):

Figure 4.1   Spectrum of distributors defined by business model

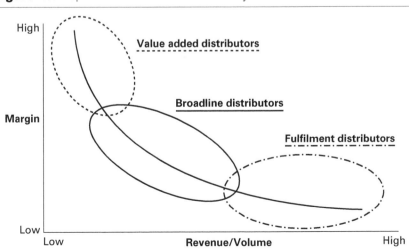

- *Value added distributors* – these distributors are focused on products where there is limited distribution, ie very few or only one distributor operates in the market. This could be for reasons of small market size, or that the suppliers are new to the market, or the technology of the products is at an early stage of the adoption lifecycle. In each case, the supplier is looking to the distributor to be highly proactive in recruiting and developing the often specialist final-tier players who can reach the right segments in the market. Market development is their core offering to the supplier. The distributor is tasked with building the demand for the product through marketing and proactive sales activities, which can include extensive training for the final-tier channel players, co-selling and the provision of extensive pre-sales technical support. To be able to do all this, the distributor needs to invest its own time and resources in fully mastering the product from a technical and marketing perspective. All this work does not come cheap, so the distributor expects to earn a rich margin to compensate for its investment in each sale and for the fact that initially sales will be relatively low in volume.

- *Broadline distributors* – as indicated by their name, these distributors provide the mainstream market coverage, both in terms of the product range they carry and the proportion of the market they service. Market access is their core offering to the supplier, covering most or all of the channels a supplier needs to reach through established trading relationships and with long-standing marketing and communications tools (catalogues, mailers, websites) with proven response rates. There will usually be several distributors competing in the market, creating a more price-competitive environment, leading to lower margins on product sales. Suppliers can expect to pay for placement in the marketing tools or for running sales promotions as these costs cannot be absorbed by the normal trading margin. As a result, market share leaders tend to be better served by the broadliner as their scale of business ensures high visibility and share of mind among the distributor's sales and marketing teams. Some brands, however, will go further and may seek greater influence over the distributor's resources, such as by financing a dedicated product manager. Smaller suppliers tend to have to work hard to ensure there is sufficient focus on their products and may have to offer one distributor in the market exclusive distribution rights in order not to dilute their focus. As markets mature, consolidation among broadliners reduces the number of distributors available to suppliers, increasing the distributors' power in extracting significant discounts and rebates from the supplier (at industry conferences it's interesting to observe whether the distributors are paying court to the leading suppliers or the other way around!).

- *Fulfilment distributors* – these distributors operate in markets where products are 'bought' rather than 'sold', such as aftermarket products and consumables. No marketing is involved in respect of the products, and sales are driven by price, availability and convenience. In effect these distributors are logistics engines for the supplier, who will have to make all the running to create brand awareness and preference in the end-customer market. Margins are very low, so the distributor runs a high-volume, highly efficient operation, doing all it can to eliminate unnecessary activities and complexity. The distributor needs massive volume at these tiny margins to be able to cover its infrastructure and operating costs. Orders are increasingly received through the website rather than the call centre and warehouses are highly automated central-ized operations. How do these distributors differ from the pure logistics companies such as FedEx or UPS? In two major ways: first, they bear a stocking risk, balancing demand and supply through their inventory management skills; second, they bear the credit risk, leveraging their local market expertise. Suppliers may compensate fulfilment distributors either through the trading margin or, more recently, by negotiating a fee per transaction as the cost of distribution tends to be the same regardless of the selling price. This ensures that smaller-ticket items are not subsidized by big-ticket items as would happen through a trading margin.

Supplier role – core functions

Given the description of the different distributor models above, it can be seen there are two core functions provided by distributors to suppliers: demand generation and supply fulfilment. Additional functions include providing market information and serving as an outsourced front office, representing the supplier in a territory, or as an outsourced service and support function, providing warranty and technical back-up and support services to the final tier or even end-customer in certain circumstances.

As suppliers increasingly move to focus on their core activities, they have turned to distributors as the logical partners to whom non-differentiating activities can be outsourced. As these activities themselves have varying investment, cost and margin profiles, distributors are segmenting their busi-nesses to offer specialized services from discrete divisions. This enables them to align their pricing and business models and avoid unplanned cross-subsidization of services and to be more competitive. The nature of these services varies by industry; some typical examples are given in Table 4.2.

Table 4.2 Typical core offering and optional services offered by distributors to vendors

Typical core offering	Typical specialized services

• Demand generation
  – Channel recruitment
  – Channel accounts and database
  – Marketing fund deployment
  – Special pricing management
  – Teleweb outbound and inbound sales
  – Regular marketing mailings
  – 'Spiff' sales promotions
  – Channel conferences
  – Channel training
  – Channel financing through credit provision
  – In-market product management
  – Frontline technical support
	• Demand generation
	  – Channel account management
	  – Programme management
	  – Co-op fund management
	  – Special channel financing and credit offerings
	  – End-customer marketing and lead-generation programmes
	  – Conference and exhibition services

• Supply fulfilment
  – Bulk breaking
  – Outbound logistics
  – Reverse logistics
  – Channel credit risk
	• Supply fulfilment
	  – Consignment stocking
	  – Vendor managed inventories
	  – Vendor stock warehousing

• Market information
  – Sales out reporting
  – Channel intelligence
	• Market information
	  – Channel research
	  – End-customer research

• Outsourced services	• Outsourced services
	  – Warranty management
	  – Break-fix operations
	  – Second-level and post-sales technical support
	  – In-market representation
	  – Trademark registration and protection

Note that many of the activities listed under 'Typical core offering' will be charged for in addition to the trading margin or distributor discount, especially the provision of sell-out information and participation in sales spiffs (short-term promotions involving incentives for the sales staff) and marketing collateral and catalogues. In many distributors the marketing function is a profit centre, attracting marketing development funds from its suppliers by offering innovative marketing tools and activities.

Depending on the product or the territory, the distributor may play an active role in demand generation, actively building up awareness and selling capability among its customers, who in turn promote sales among the end customers. Typically, suppliers negotiate targets for sales levels for a year and reward distributors with either higher levels of discount related to volumes or pay for results through rebates or other incentives for passing the target.

Suppliers can have a range of products requiring distribution that can number a few tens of SKUs or many thousands. Typically the sales volumes of these products are subject to Pareto's Law, ie 20 per cent of the SKUs account for 80 per cent of the revenues. For reasons of margin and customer service, the supplier expects the distributor to carry the full range, or a significant proportion of it, to ensure supply fulfilment. Contracts may specify the inventory-holding requirements of each class of product, or there may be a fee or incentive for stocking a proportion of the range. In many cases, it is in the distributor's interest to hold some inventory as the uncompensated costs of handling a back order for a one-off SKU can outweigh the costs of stocking.

By acting as the supplier to potentially thousands of local trade customers, the distributor takes the credit risk on these sales, requiring it to have excellent credit control and credit insight to minimize the exposure and cost of bad debts. This is of real value to the supplier, which would otherwise bear the cost of the credit management function as well as the bad debt risk.

To manage their channels, suppliers need good information about their distributors' sales and inventory levels and are prepared to pay to get it. This is either built into the margin allowed or is an explicit element of the discount. The latter approach enables a supplier to withdraw the margin in the event of a particular distributor failing to provide information of appropriate quality or in the right format. In mature industries, this is typically provided on a weekly or even daily basis through EDI links or internet-based automatic reporting. This market information may be augmented by other data such as competitor activity, customer recruitment reports, lost sales reports and so on.

The distributor also acts to a greater or lesser degree as an outsourced front office for the supplier, providing the channel development function: recruiting new partners, the supplier's local or territory representative and providing services such as warranty or pre- and post-sales support. All these functions are determined by contract and can be the subject of intense negotiation, the outcome of which usually reflects the relative balance of power between the supplier and the distributor. The agreed levels of distributor compensation are paid either through the margin allowed through discounts or as specific activity-based fees. In some cases, the fee will be partially or wholly dependent upon customer feedback on service levels and quality.

How distribution improves the supplier's business model

The distribution model, if executed well, can deliver substantial benefits to the supplier in terms of cost structure efficiencies and balance sheet leverage (see Figure 4.2). We are constantly surprised at how poorly these economic advantages are understood at the highest level of even the most sophisticated suppliers. We hear constant complaints as to the way 'we are giving away margin to the distributors' or 'this extra (distribution) layer moves us further away from the market or the demand signals'. However, in the projects we have undertaken on whether distribution should be insourced or outsourced, it has become clear how important it is to articulate the full, business and strategic case.

Figure 4.2　Distribution impact on supplier business model

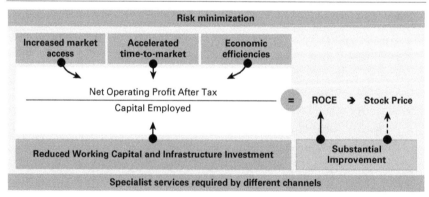

The better understood aspect of this business case is internal cost structure efficiencies. These include the simple leverage equation of the larger volumes handled by distributors. A single supplier handling its own distribution can amortize the cost only over its own volumes. Distributors can amortize their costs over the larger volumes of many hundreds or thousands of suppliers, gaining significant economies of scale. Less well understood is that by working with distributors, the supplier can convert what would be its own internal fixed costs (fixed asset depreciation and payroll costs) into variable costs (the margin paid to the distributor). Distribution infrastructure requires substantial investments in warehousing, racking, management systems, logistics equipment, delivery fleets, as well as the employment of a substantial payroll to operate it. A supplier can pay for this 'as it goes' by using third-party distributors, and even participate in the scale benefits of larger volumes as it grows if it negotiates its terms effectively.

In most established markets, distributors accelerate time-to-market for suppliers entering the market or launching new products or categories. Distributors will either already have existing relationships with relevant final-tier partners or the capability to recruit them. The supplier can simply plug into this established route to market, bringing forward sales and profits.

It is the balance sheet leverage aspect that is particularly poorly understood by suppliers. The best way to articulate this is to consider what would happen should an established third-party distribution model be brought in-house. We looked at this for a global consumer product company and showed that there would be a one-off multi-billion dollar hit to cash flow that would destroy its results for the period in question. Why so? The established distributors held billions of dollars of inventory and financed further billions of final-tier credit. These far exceeded the receivable balances due from the distributors. To bring the operation in-house would mean the supplier would have to take these assets onto its own balance sheet – a massive cash outflow (depressing return on capital, earnings per share and other reporting horrors the chief financial officer could not imagine in her worst nightmare). The reality is that working with even a small number of distributors gives a supplier access to their collective balance sheet power, leveraging up its own balance sheet power. Additionally, the supplier needs operate only a small credit management function, dealing with the small number of usually highly credit-worthy distributors. These distributors are experts in managing the credit function that deals with tens of thousands of smaller final-tier customers, and bear the bad debt risk should it get its credit risk management wrong. The supplier bringing distribution in-house would need to gear up its capabilities substantially, and take over the bad debt risk, not an undertaking to delight the CFO.

Each case is different and there will be situations where in-house distribution makes better economic sense than going to market via third-party distributors. However, the strategic and business analyses we have undertaken over the years have almost always shown that the case for distribution is compelling, especially when fully developed.

How the distributor business model works

05

What do we mean by business model?

Throughout this book we refer frequently to business models, so we had better explain what we mean by the term 'business model'. A business model is how a business makes money from its activities. It is the financial expression of the role, positioning, strategy and execution of a business plan of a specific player in a specific industry. It is the logical financial result of the economics of the structure of the industry and its distribution infrastructure. It is both static – in the form of certain cost structures, margins, capital turns and the like, and dynamic – in the way that costs behave, key ratios change with growth or margins behave under increased competition. So, the business model of, say, a distributor of plumbing supplies will have some predictable similarities and some predictable differences with that of a computer products distributor, and further predictable similarities and differences with a sheet music or a cream cake distributor. The same can be said of different players in the same channel eco-system, with their role, balance of power and strategy determining where and how they will make profits, where they need to deploy capital and the scale of both these factors relative to the size of business being done.

In this Part and the next, we will show you the connection between these forces and the impact they have on the structure of the business model. We will help you to understand the inherent constraints and continual trade-offs with which the managers of each business model are wrestling. We will take you into the ways to improve the business performance of each type of player, whether you are managing it or negotiating with it. These constraints are also opportunities. For example, many retailers cannot hold much inventory on their premises owing to size or cost constraints (attractive retail locations attract a fearsome rent). An enterprising supplier with an efficient distribution logistics capability can offer to supply just in time or manage the inventory on behalf of the retailer, gaining share of category over other suppliers without this capability. The retailer knows it can't afford to be out of stock, so will give up some of its demands for a better margin in return for assurance of full and replenished shelves. Being able to put these two aspects into proportion – or quantifying them – might not seem like selling or marketing, but it will have a much longer-lasting impact on doing business together than offering a short-term product promotion to gain share.

We will aim to teach you to fish, so to speak, rather than catching fish for you. We will point out the major breeds of fish, ie the dominant business models and their inherent characteristics, but more as a way to making you the complete angler. This way you should be able to assess the situation of any business model in any distribution system in any market from any perspective (managing the player or buying from or selling to it), work out the issues and opportunities available and identify the strategy that will best help you achieve your objectives.

We do not aim to teach you how to read balance sheets and profit and loss accounts or how to explain depreciation... though we expect you will probably be able to do these things by the time you have finished it. We will help you to understand:

- Why working capital management is critical to distributors.

- How to address the demands for more margin from your retailers or distributors if you are a brand leader.

- How to secure the resources you really need from a supplier to achieve your growth targets.

- How to increase your share of your partners' business even if they claim that you are not as profitable to them as your competitors.

- How to punch above your weight in the distribution system if you have a tiny market share.

- How to ensure you are allocating scarce resources to the channels that will generate the highest returns.

- How to increase your leverage over partners that may not even sell or distribute your products, but whose recommendation is critical to customer preference.

Role defines business model

The roles fulfilled by the distributor for both customer and supplier define the business model of the distributor and its key characteristics. The first of these is that the distributor's business model is capital intensive, driven by the need to hold stock and finance trade customer credit, less any supplier credit received. Second, as essentially a high-volume, low-value-add business, the distributor trades on thin margins, and thus needs to be a low-overhead business. This is a challenging model, requiring the ability to manage both profitability and asset efficiency or productivity.

Let's look a set of typical distributor financial statements to see this in action (Figure 5.1). You may want to note this figure, as we will be using the numbers from it throughout this part of the book. The first thing to note is that the balance sheet, on the right, is dominated by three numbers:

1 inventory (products held for resale);

2 accounts receivable (from customers for sales made on credit); and

3 accounts payable (to suppliers for products bought on credit).

These three items are the constituent elements of working capital (inventory plus accounts receivable less accounts payable). A balance sheet shows the

Figure 5.1 ABC Co distributor financials

	$m			$m
Sales	19,316	**Fixed assets**		423
Cost of sales	18,308	**Current assets**		
Gross profit	**1,008**	Inventory	1,408	
Overheads	952	Accounts receivable	1,897	
Operating profit	**56**	Cash	401	
Interest	12	**Total current assets**		**3,706**
Profit before taxation	**44**	**Current liabilities**		
Taxation	16	Accounts payable	1,550	
Profit after taxation	**28**	Other	764	
		Total current liabilities		**2,314**
		Net current assets		**1,392**
		Long-term liabilities		59
		Net assets		**1,756**
		Shareholders funds		**1,756**
Income statement		**Balance sheet**		

situation at a moment in time, so it is effectively showing us a snapshot of the working capital cycle frozen in action. The other items such as fixed assets (land, buildings, warehousing systems, IT systems, etc) and other balances are relatively immaterial. It is mainly the net total of the working capital items that determines how much capital the distributor needs to raise to finance its business. It's a fine balancing act; too little and the distributor runs out of inventory ('stock-outs') or cannot pay its suppliers in time while waiting for payments from its customers; too much capital and the cost of the capital required drags down the profitability of the business.

Profit is a very small number between two very big numbers

Looking at the income statement, on the left of Figure 5.1, we can get a sense of just how tight the margins can be in some sectors of distribution. The gross profit is the difference between the price the distributor pays for its products to suppliers (= cost of sales) and price it gets for them when sold to customers (= sales). It's a very small number between two very big ones. The distributor must pay for all its overheads and interest out of this gross profit, leaving whatever is left over as its net profit – which is an even smaller number compared to the two big numbers, sales and cost of sales. After tax is deducted (assuming there is a profit), whatever is left is available to be paid out as a dividend or retained in the balance sheet to finance a bigger working-capital balance (needed if the distributor intends to grow in the next trading period).

It gets even more interesting when you compare the gross profit made in the year of \$1,008m in our example with the working capital of \$1,755m (= \$1,408m + \$1,897m – \$1,550m). This means that our distributor has tied up over \$1.75 billion for a year to earn just over \$1 billion in gross profit... and \$44 million in net profit. Seems like a lot to lay out for not much return. The slightest hiccup in buying, say, some products that need to be written down in value because they don't sell, or incurring a few bad debts, would have hit profits and turned even that profit into a loss.

Managing working capital is a balancing act

This balancing of the profitability and working capital profile of the product range is at the heart of the distributor's business model. Each of the types of distributor profiled earlier (value added, broadline and fulfilment) has a balance that is right in the context of its value proposition and business model. All of them are striving to get higher margins and reduce their working capital while offering the best range of products and in-stock availability to their customers in the market. The role of product managers in the distributor is critical and their incentives should be tied to *both* margin and working capital (or at least inventory) management.

The smart distributor knows that margin management is critical to its success, using a portfolio approach to blend fast-turning, low-margin products with slower-turning but higher-margin products. Even tiny improvements in margin make for a big impact in the operating profit. The challenge is to balance the product range and stocking depth with what customers are demanding and the suppliers are insisting on with what makes sense financially. The 80:20 rule applies everywhere in distribution, with 20 per cent of the products accounting for 80 per cent of the volumes, but a *different* 20 per cent may account for 80 per cent of the profits. To make things more complex, distributors are vulnerable to offers from suppliers to take lorry loads of extra stock into their warehouses for an additional discount (usually near the end of a quarter or a supplier's financial year). These discounts initially appear attractive, but as the deal is being offered to all the distributors in the market, any cost advantage often ends up being passed on to the customer as a discount incentive to ensure the extra stock moves out of the warehouse. The net result is happy customers and suppliers but often not much more profit for the distributors, with the extra sales putting more pressure on their infrastructure. However, the distributors cannot afford to be out of line with the market on high-volume items so they often feel that they have no choice but to take the extra discount available (and extra volumes) to protect their market positioning and customer base.

Controlling overheads is equally important, with many of the costs being essentially fixed in nature, ie they do not vary directly in line with sales volumes. Distributors looking for growth need to time their investments in additional capacity carefully to avoid getting too far ahead of the curve and pushing up the cost base before sales have grown to cover it. This can be trickier for IT systems, which seem to take years to deliver their promised productivity, than for warehouses, which can be thrown up in less than a year. Increasingly, distributors are looking for ways to make more of their costs variable by outsourcing elements of their essential infrastructure, including transport, warehousing and even sales call centres. Each of these involves tough trade-offs between the benefits of improved cost flexibility and lower costs and the risks of loss of control and potential impact on customer satisfaction. Another challenge is whether to put more sales through web portals, reducing the costs of order taking but losing the chance to up-sell or cross-sell to the customer on a call or the opportunity to respond to a competitor's pricing to keep a valued customer.

For distributors, working capital management is all about recognizing that they are dealing with a finite and expensive resource – capital. Money tied up in product A is not available to invest in stocking product Z. Credit extended to (or stretched by) one customer cannot be used until the debt is paid. Supplier credit limits, once used, need to be paid off before more products can be ordered in. In order to grow, the distributor needs to increase its working capital to match the bigger trading volumes or accelerate the cycle of cash to cash: money paid out to suppliers for inventories that are sold to customers on credit who eventually pay for them. Distributors that fail to plan for growth find that their cash situation deteriorates rapidly despite sales and profits growing healthily. Often called 'overtrading', it has been the cause of more distributors getting into trouble than falling sales. The speed at which it happens is startling. Taking ABC Co's financial statements as shown above, a 20 per cent growth in sales volumes would require a similar increase in working capital, which in cash terms means $351m (ie $1,755 × 20%), almost eliminating its cash balances of $401m and leaving it with just $46m. Another 20 per cent the following year would require an overdraft of nearly $400m (ie after a further $351 × 120% = $421m has left the building). So, in just two years, ABC Co would have traded its way from a cash balance of $400m to an overdraft of the same amount. Even if ABC Co applies all its after-tax profits to funding working capital, these would make barely a dent in the overdraft: $28m × 120% in year one equals $34m, plus $33m × 120% in year 2 equals $40m, making a total of $74m. This is less than 10 per cent of the $800m change in the cash balance, and assumes no cash is used to replace fixed assets or repay long-term liabilities, etc.

To increase its capital, the distributor needs to retain more profits (assuming it's earned any), borrow more or go back to its shareholders and ask for more capital to be invested. Both borrowers and investors will ask tough questions about the business plan and the distributor's ability to service the investment (pay the interest or dividends) and either repay the principal borrowed or grow the capital value of the business for shareholders. Any investor will want to know what sort of return he or she will get on his or her investment. In our example above, the net profit of $44m is the return generated in a year on capital invested of $1,756m which is a return of about 2.5 per cent, ie some way short of the rate available by leaving the cash in short-term deposits. ABC Co is unlikely in purely financial terms to command a high price for its original investors if it were to be sold with that level of profitability. (It may secure a premium for some strategic market positioning.)

The alternative is to accelerate the working capital cycle, which means tightening customer credit, reducing stocking levels or asking suppliers for extended credit terms or credit limits. Each of these has implications for the distributor's key trading relationships and may conflict with its growth ambitions. All in all, the distributor is faced with a challenging business model, one that requires exceptional day-to-day management control as well as a clear business strategy and well-defined market positioning.

The measures that matter and how to manage with them

The measures that matter in a distributor reflect the way the business model works, with margins, working capital management and productivity measures (combining margin and working capital management) being especially powerful. We have devoted a chapter to each of these types of measure (Chapter 6 – Margins and profitability, Chapter 7 – Working capital and Chapter 8 – Productivity), explaining how and why distributors should use these types of measure to manage their businesses. In Chapter 9 we show how to assess sustainability – the long-term business health – of a distributor and set out a recommended template or dashboard for monitoring the entire business. Finally, in Chapter 10 we focus on the challenge of managing growth and show how to define the safe level of growth for a distributor without overtrading.

Managing distributors – margins and profitability

06

Multiple margins

The first point to note about margins is that although the basic concept is to measure the profit of the business, there are as many ways to calculate a margin as there are distributors, certainly when measured on an internal basis. Even with national and international accounting standards, there is still plenty of room for the exercise of judgement as to what can and can't be included in a margin calculation. So never assume that you can compare margins between distributors (or any business) without first asking what is and is not included. Even the most qualified of accountants would have no hesitation in asking, 'How are you calculating your margins?' so neither should you. Let's start with the basic types of margin and what they tell you.

Gross margin and value-add

The gross margin is a measure of the distributor's value-added as it is the purest measure of the difference between the price paid to suppliers and the price obtained from customers. The higher the margin, the greater the value added by the distributor. In our example distributor, ABC Co, the gross margin is $1,008m/$19,316m × 100 which equals 5.22 per cent. There are several things to note for even this simple measure:

Gross margin %
$\text{Gross margin \%} = \dfrac{\text{Sales} - \text{Cost of sales}}{\text{Sales}} \times 100$

- Neither sales nor cost of sales should include VAT or sales taxes.

- Cost of sales (sometimes called cost of goods sold) includes all costs incurred in getting the product to its state and condition necessary for sale. So, it will include any shipping inbound costs but *not* costs incurred in shipping the product to the customer.

- Cost of sales includes any work done on the product such as testing, processing, configuration, assembly and packaging. If these costs are internal to the distributor, they should include a fair allocation of labour and overhead costs.

- Any discounts, rebates or other price reductions received from suppliers should reduce cost of sales and therefore increase gross margins.

- The cost of writing down inventories for obsolescence, shrinkage or stock losses, deterioration and so on is added to cost of sales, reducing margins as soon as the loss is recognized.

- Costs of selling the product or sales commissions are not included in cost of sales but discounts given to customers are deducted from sales.

- Prompt payment discounts received from suppliers are generally not deducted from cost of sales nor those granted to customers deducted from sales. However, in some industries these discounts are so significant that they have become part of the normal discounting mechanism used by suppliers and are deducted to present a fair picture.

Note also that the gross margin is the gross profit expressed as a percentage of sales. If it were expressed as a percentage of cost of sales it would be a mark-up (in our example the mark-up is 5.51 per cent, ie $1,008m/$18,308m). It is not uncommon in talking to distributors to find the terms gross margin and mark-up used interchangeably, and incorrectly, so do not assume that the term has been used correctly – ask the basis of the margins you are being presented with.

Gross margins can be applied to the entire business, as we have just done for ABC Co, as well as to individual SKUs, product lines, product categories, suppliers, business divisions, customers and customer segments. It does not

Figure 6.1 Comparison of gross margin % and gross margin $ earned on different brands

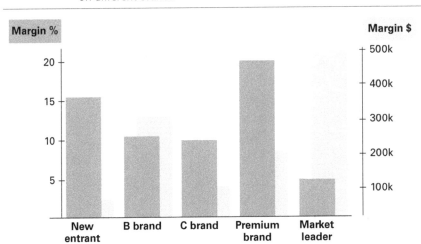

matter whether it is calculated for a year or for a day's trading, so long as the sales and cost of sales are for the same period.

One point to watch is that percentages can be used or interpreted in misleading ways because they convey no sense of the size of business done. For example, which is better: a gross margin of 12 per cent or one of 7 per cent? Well, if the 12 per cent margin were earned on product A with sales of $1,000 and the 7 per cent margin earned on product B with sales of $5,000, the distributor would have earned a gross profit (or 'money margin') of only $120 on product A but $350 on product B. This might seem obvious, but it is a key point that is often overlooked. It is important because most distributors' overhead costs are usually fairly fixed so they need to earn a fixed amount of gross profit before the business can earn an operating profit. In managing their business model, distributors need to beware of incentivizing their product managers just on gross margins expressed as a percentage as the profit measure, as the chart shown in Figure 6.1 illustrates. Dropping the market leader to focus on the new entrant could wipe out gross profits of $500,000 that the other brands' sales would be very unlikely to replace, as relatively few customers would be switch-sold. There is more than one global distributor which, in seeking to increase its gross margins, has focused on products with higher margins at the expense of its high-volume, low-margin products. This has led to lower overall gross profits, and in one case caused operating losses for several months before it was able to turn the situation around.

Margin mix or blended margin

For distributors handling the brand leaders in a market, the margins will tend to be lower, but the volumes higher if they are getting their fair share of the brand's market-leading volumes. Attempting to increase margins by dropping the top brands damages not only gross profits but also the distributor's market credibility if customers expect to find the major brands stocked at their usual distributor. The answer lies in managing the margin mix or blended margin.

Consider the example shown in Table 6.1. The blended margin of these products is 7.6 per cent ($34,900/$461,000). The options available to the distributor for improving its blended margin are:

- Reduce sales of products D and E, which have margins below the blended margin, but this would put the money margin at risk. These two products account for $21,900 of the total gross profit or money margin, almost two-thirds of the total money margin of $34,900.

- Increase sales of products A, B and C, which would increase overall gross profits as well as strengthening the blended margin.

- Add a higher margin product into the mix, which would dilute the impact of the existing products in the blended margin, and increase the blended margin so long as the new product's gross margin was higher than 7.6 per cent.

- Increase sales prices of any of the products or negotiate better discounts from the suppliers.

In practice, many distributors can often increase prices for products that are lower volume because they do not represent price-benchmarking items.

Table 6.1 Example of blended margin calculation

Product	Sales price	Cost price	Gross margin	Gross profit per unit	Volume	Sales revenue	Gross profit
A	$500	$450	10.0%	$50	100	$50,000	$5,000
B	$400	$352	12.0%	$48	50	$20,000	$2,400
C	$350	$322	8.0%	$28	200	$70,000	$5,600
D	$300	$279	7.0%	$21	500	$150,000	$10,500
E	$180	$168	7.0%	$12	950	$171,000	$11,400
Total			7.6%			$461,000	$34,900

One famous example from the IT sector is that the distributor can make such a high gross margin on the carrying case compared to the laptop computer that it makes more money margin on the case! Even within product categories, there will be SKUs that are less price-sensitive than others and these can be eased upwards without impacting sales volumes. Smart differential pricing within a category and across categories is called 'portfolio pricing', enabling the distributor to achieve its targeted blended margin by continually tuning its pricing and making more effort to cross-sell from its high-volume products that are priced to drive volume and meet customer demand.

Making some minor improvements to the pricing and volumes of products A, B and C in our example could achieve a new blended margin of 8.7 per cent, up from 7.6 per cent (see Table 6.2). Note that not only has the gross margin percentage increased, but revenues are up by 8 per cent and the money margin is up by almost 25 per cent. Unfortunately, it sometimes takes a crisis before a distributor can be persuaded to make these types of moves with its pricing strategy, but there is much to be gained by experimenting with price changes and finding out which products will bear higher prices and which will not. The rewards available justify taking some carefully controlled risks and, where volumes are adversely affected, prices can be quickly adjusted back again. Good product managers should be able to identify most of the safe products and SKUs that can bear price increases but it requires excellent coordination with the sales teams to make sure that the cross-selling is driven through to maintain and build volumes in the right SKUs.

Sales management is a key discipline in distributors' margin management and one that needs constant attention and monitoring. In most distributors,

Table 6.2   New blended margin calculation

Product	Sales price	Cost price	Gross margin	Gross profit per unit	Volume	Sales revenue	Gross profit
A	$525	$450	14.0%	$75	120	$63,000	$9,000
B	$420	$352	16.0%	$68	70	$29,400	$4,760
C	$355	$322	9.0%	$33	240	$85,200	$7,920
D	$300	$279	7.0%	$21	500	$150,000	$10,500
E	$180	$168	7.0%	$12	950	$171,000	$11,400
Total			8.7%			$498,600	$43,580

there are multiple discounts that can be applied by a sales person to allow for the size of the order, the loyalty or spending power of the customer, the need to defend against specific competitors or to support current promotions. Wily sales people can usually find a way to play these rules to the customer's greatest advantage to ensure they maximize their sales. The distributor's sales people don't see an additional 1 or 2 per cent discount as a big hit to their margin objectives. The result of this mindset is potentially very damaging to the economics of the distributor's business model. Take the extra 1 per cent discount given away and put it into context. For a distributor making, say, 8 per cent gross margin and 1 per cent net margin on sales, that extra discount knocks the gross margin down to 7 per cent and wipes out the net margin. As highlighted earlier, profit is a small number between two very big ones, so a small reduction in the sales line (without any impact on cost of sales) becomes a very big hit on the profit line – in our example 100 per cent of the net profit! Sales people need to have this in the front of their mind when negotiating the last few points to clinch a sale.

One way distributors attempt to manage this is to ensure that the absolute floor or 'low ball' on pricing is still profitable, so that even the most aggressive sales people cannot discount their way into a loss. In countless distributors examined, the effect of this is to produce a gross margin percentage–volume chart that looks like Figure 6.2. This chart shows the volume of sales closed at each level of gross margin in bands of a half

Figure 6.2   Illustration of sales volume by margin where there is a 'low ball'

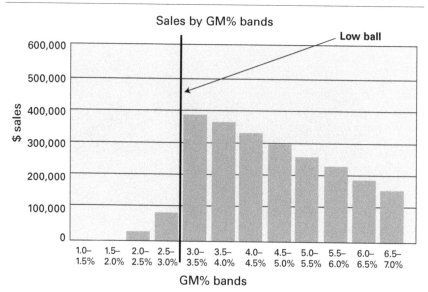

per cent, so for example $300,000 of sales were closed at between 4.5 and 5 per cent gross margin. The 'low ball' is the lowest gross margin at which the sales team can make a sale by applying all the discounts allowed according to internal rules. This margin should be possible only when selling to the distributor's best customer, buying its on-offer products in a single large order and claiming that it can get a better price from the competition... obviously a fairly rare situation. But look at what the analysis (taken from a real case) shows. More business is done at this 'minimum' margin (ie maximum discount level) than at any other. Rather than being a floor, the low ball has become a leaning-post propping up the majority of the sales. What does this do to the blended margin? It pulls it right down to around 4.5 per cent. Even worse, there is something over $100,000 of sales closed *below* the low ball, something that shouldn't even be possible under the distributor's own rules. The lesson is clear: sales people will find ways over, under and through any rules controlling discounts if there is a sale to be made. Regular analysis of this type is needed to track the situation and to take control.

Interestingly, the far right of the chart, out of sight in Figure 6.2, will often show a few pockets of business closed at very high gross margins. Investigation of these sales, in terms of which products have been sold to which customers, can uncover some interesting niche opportunities that are worth developing into bigger business activity. Indeed, taking a customer perspective often throws up a picture of opportunities to improve the way

Figure 6.3 Illustrative distribution of gross margin % by customers' sales revenues

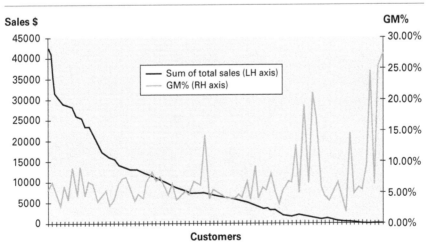

discounts are applied to improve margins. Figure 6.3 shows customers ranked from left to right by sales volumes (left-hand axis) and the margins earned from them (right-hand axis).

Applying the normal rules of giving better discounts to the best customers would suggest the margin curve ought to slope smoothly up to the right in a mirror image of the sales curve. Instead, what we find (taken from a real case) is that there are some customers at the far right-hand side with the smallest level of business delivering margins as low as the distributor's best customers. Some of these dips may be caused by the particular products bought but, on investigation, the random pattern of the margins owed much more to the random pattern of customer discounts awarded by the sales team. It also suggested that the distributor was not doing enough to take care of its best customers.

Contribution margin

So far we have focused on the gross margin, but how do you account for the fact that some products require a lot more pre-sales support, take more time to sell to customers, require special handling or attract a higher level of returns involving expensive reverse logistics? Or that some customers demand more account management, require shipments to go to multiple drop-off points, quibble over every invoice and take twice the credit period to pay? These customers may deliver the same gross margins as ones that don't behave in this way but they certainly don't deliver the same level of profitability for the distributor. The measure that reveals the impact of these types of factor on profitability is contribution margin:

Contribution margin %
$\text{Contribution margin \%} = \dfrac{\text{Sales} - \text{Cost of sales} - \text{Variable costs}}{\text{Sales}} \times 100$

This margin deducts variable costs as well as cost of sales so that it reflects all the factors illustrated above. There is no definitive list of the items that make up variable costs, so the contribution margin is not one that can be compared between distributors. It is up to the individual distributor to decide which costs it deducts in striking the contribution margin. In some distributors they will strike a series of contribution margins, working down the profit and loss account to bring in additional factors and costs and savings ('contribution margin 1, contribution margin 2, contribution margin 3'), which will be used for different analyses. In order to allocate costs to the specific product or customer, distributors use some form of allocation algorithm or mechanism, which means that the contribution margins are less accurate than the gross margin. For example, it may be easy to allocate the sales commissions paid to the sales team and the rebates and allowances provided by suppliers to specific products, but it may be harder to allocate the pre-sales or returns costs.

Earlier we highlighted the fact that market-leading brands tend to have lower gross margins, but equally they require less marketing and selling activity on the part of the distributor than a new brand for which the distributor is building up a market presence. The contribution margin is one way to quantify this impact if it includes some allocation of sales and marketing costs. Good distributors run frequent contribution analyses of different cuts of their business, by product category, by supplier, by customer or customer segment. Typically these analyses show that the best performers are earning contributions 20 per cent higher than average and the worst 20 per cent below. This is a significant range (ie 40 per cent) and smart distributors use this insight to make decisions about the mix of products, suppliers and customers in their business and identify the opportunities to fine-tune the contributions earned.

Fire the biggest customer

The need to understand the economics of a distributor's different customers and customer segments was made very clearly in the case of one distributor which, in sales terms, was successful but struggling to make an operating profit. Its cash flow was sinking to the point that action was needed to save the business.

Analysing the contribution by customer showed that the distributor's biggest customer, which accounted for over 25 per cent of its sales, was in fact making a negative contribution. In other words, the distributor was paying for the privilege of serving its biggest customer – not a healthy way to run the business.

Action was taken to identify the cost drivers that were hitting the contribution (extended credit, multiple ship-to points, pre-sales support) and the customer invited to change its demands or to accept that it should pay for them. These were tough negotiations but the distributor management team's backbone was stiffened by the thought that failure to confront the situation would leave them without a viable business. The customer refused to accept new terms so the distributor bit the bullet and terminated the trading relationship. The sales, management and other resources in the distributor that been focused on its previous biggest customer were rapidly redeployed to build up other, more profitable customers and find new ones. Within a month, the distributor's profitability improved and cash flowed back into the business. To put the icing on the cake, its fired customer returned with requests to supply (lower-volume and higher-margin) products that it had been struggling to source reliably elsewhere, making it now one of the distributor's more profitable customers. It was a salutary lesson, but it had taken a cash flow crisis before the management team were prepared to take the right action.

It is vital for a distributor to have a customer view of its business and to understand the economics of its different customers and customer segments. All too often the situation is left to continue because the distributor does not do the analysis or is afraid to lose the business by getting tough with costly customers. Rigorous analysis shows just how expensive this approach can be and highlights the fact that the best customers are often subsidizing the worst customers, putting long-term success at risk. The differential costs of serving customers can be classified under a number of headings:

- *Marketing-driven costs*: relationship management; allowances; programmes (eg loyalty programmes).
- *Sales-driven costs*: discounts/rebates; promotions; sales person time required; sales cycle times and conversion rates; sales channel used.
- *Transaction-driven costs*: order complexity; size of order.
- *Logistics-driven costs*: ship-to points; returns.
- *Inventory-driven costs*: inventory levels; product mix required.
- *Finance-driven costs*: credit limits; credit period taken.

Mapping these graphically would look like Figure 6.4, giving a complete profile of the cost to serve one customer or customer segment. Comparing these charts between customers (or between customer segments) will reveal which costs are the most differentiated and thus should be tackled. Customers

Figure 6.4 Cost to serve profile of one customer or customer segment

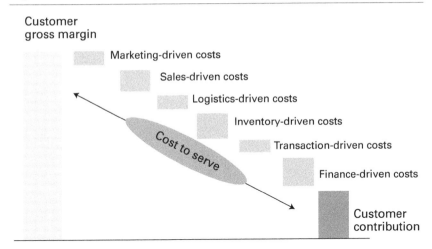

with a high cost to serve can be incentivized to reduce the costs they impose on the distributor, eg offering a discount for moving from dedicated to non-dedicated sales people or, better yet, ordering online. Alternatively, discounts could be offered for less frequent but larger average orders. Clearly these discounts need to be less than the costs already incurred, but customers will change behaviour for surprisingly small incentives or, if preferred, penalties. Most distributors will either set a minimum order size or charge extra for multiple ship-to points.

A word of caution: some distributors have got carried away with analysis and installed full-blown activity-based-costing (ABC) systems to allocate every cost in the business. The test to apply is: are you able to measure the cost driver – for example the number of ship-to points – and does it vary significantly by customer or product? If you cannot answer yes to both, then do not bother allocating the cost. It wastes your time and adds complexity and confusion rather than clarity and insight.

The contribution margin takes account of the variable costs in the cost structure, leaving the fixed costs, which need to be less than the contribution if the business is to make a net profit. Fixed costs are defined as costs that do not vary directly with unit volume. They aren't really fixed, of course, but in the short term they are relatively fixed and certainly are not affected by incremental sales. They tend to be related to infrastructure such as warehouses and storage racking or the IT systems, call centres and payroll. Distributors monitor their cost structures by comparing either individual elements or the total to their sales. In our ABC Co example, overheads are $952m/$19,316m or 4.9 per cent. Over time, as the distributor grows, it would expect this percentage to go down as it gains the benefits of economies of scale. In some industries that are experiencing declining average selling prices (ASPs), such as in the high-technology or telecommunications sectors, at times falling by up to 40 per cent over a year, stable revenue will hide a significant increase in volumes, putting the cost structure under pressure. The extra activity will mean more orders, more picking and packing, more invoicing, etc, but for the same amount of revenue. Distributors faced with this challenge try to up-sell their customers (encourage them to buy bigger-ticket items) or increase the cross-sell rate (number of customers who buy additional products) to counteract the effect of falling prices. Two key measures used by distributors to track their effectiveness is the average order size and the average cost of processing an order. Both are key profit drivers, with even small increases in average order size or small decreases in costs per order processed having a big positive impact on the bottom line.

Net margin and operating margin

The best measure of a distributor's overall profitability is net margin as this shows the level of profit made from the business as a percentage of sales. As with gross margins, care needs to be taken as to exactly which net margin is being used. As there are several profit lines struck in the profit and loss account (operating profit, net margin before tax, net margin after tax), each of these can be used to calculate a net margin. Internally, management teams will focus on operating margin as they may feel that the interest costs, which are ignored in this margin, are not their responsibility because the capital structure of the business is given to them. However, the executive team may focus on the pre-tax net margin and benchmark this against other competitors or industry norms. Tax is ignored in this margin as the vagaries of the tax system, timing of allowances, use of brought-forward losses or group tax reliefs may distort the picture and are not really a measure of the business's performance. All of these margins are calculated as a percentage of sales. In our ABC Co example the operating margin is:

Operating profit of $56m/Sales of $19,316m = 0.28%

and the net margin is:

Net profit before tax of $44m/Sales of $19,316m = 0.23%

Operating margin %

$$\text{Operating margin \%} = \frac{\text{Sales} - \text{Cost of sales} - \text{Overhead costs}}{\text{Sales}} \times 100$$

Net margin %

$$\text{Net margin \%} = \frac{\text{Sales} - \text{Cost of sales} - \text{Overhead costs} - \text{Interest}}{\text{Sales}} \times 100$$

Where the distributor is part of a corporate group, the corporate management will focus on the pre-tax net margin as the measure of the operational management's profitability performance. Tax management will be a group-level responsibility. In some corporate groups the treasury function is also centralized, which effectively removes from operational management the responsibility for the funding structure of the business. However, the cost of capital achieved by the treasury function should be applied to the capital employed in the business by each operation. Distributors are capital-intensive businesses and controlling the capital requirements is very much an operational management issue. We would be very wary of any distributor management team that only focused on the operating margin and absolved themselves from the interest charge and net margin before tax lines. Certainly changes in the cost of capital and interest rates will be a factor in the level of interest costs, but a much bigger factor will be the amount of capital required and this is very much in the hands of the operational management team, as we will see in the next chapter.

ABC Co is effectively trading at break-even with an operating margin of 0.28 per cent and a net margin of 0.23 per cent. Break-even means that the volume passing through the business is generating just enough gross margin to cover the overheads (or, more accurately, just enough contribution margin to cover the fixed costs) and so is making neither a profit nor a loss. Taken in isolation, this is not good. But if the previous year's results have been loss making, then getting the business back to break-even could represent a major achievement. The problem with operating at or close to break-even is that any slight hiccup in operations, slight changes in the market or even interest rate changes can push the business into making a loss. It is a precarious position to be in and, without profits, the business is not generating any cash with which to finance the capital needed to grow and move up and away from break-even. Given overheads are relatively low in a distributor, there is little mileage in cutting overheads as the basis of moving the business into profit, so sales growth and margin improvement are the only real strategies to move above break-even. ABC faces a tough challenge in the next year.

Investors in an independent distributor will use the net margin after tax as their key measure, as they can only participate in these distributable profits after deduction of tax. They will expect management to include the minimization of tax costs as part of their overall fiduciary duty to the shareholders. As investors, they will be comparing the after-tax returns on their investment in the distributor to other investment opportunities.

As we have shown, the net margin is usually a very small percentage of sales and can be significantly influenced by changes in the gross margin. Distributors' overheads are relatively stable and, being a small percentage of sales, fluctuations in the cost structure do not have such a dramatic impact on the net margin. Over the longer term, management are expected to ensure that net margins are improved by ensuring that sales growth feeds through to the gross profit at a faster rate than the overheads. This is more easily achieved in mature sectors where prices are relatively stable, but can be extremely challenging in fast-growing and technology industries where average sales prices continually move downwards.

Managing distributors – working capital

07

Working capital management

Working capital is an excellent descriptive term for the capital tied up in the trading cycle of a distributor. It represents the capital needed to fund the cash-to-cash cycle, ie the time taken from cash leaving the business to pay suppliers until it comes back in from customers when they pay for their products after the period of credit given to them and includes the time the products spend in inventory in between. The shorter the cash-to-cash cycle, the less working capital a distributor will need. It is, however, a confusing term because 'capital' is normally a term applied to a *source* of funds and in this context, it is describing an *application* of funds.

Managing the three components of the working capital cycle is of paramount importance to a distributor, both individually and as a system, and the whole emphasis is on time. The speed with which a distributor can turn its working capital back into cash, having made a margin on the products passing through its hands, determines how much cash it needs to have tied up. So all the measures of working capital management convert the financial amounts into days – how many days the inventory will be on the company's books, how many days it is taking for the customers to settle their debts and how long the distributor is taking to pay its suppliers. Put all these together and you know how many days it takes for the distributor to turn its cash through the working capital cycle (see Figure 7.1).

Figure 7.1 The working capital cycle

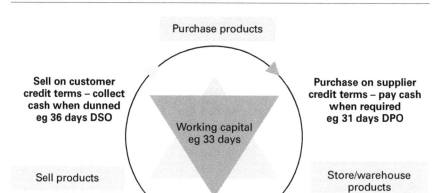

Supplier credit

Taking the components in turn, the time taken to pay the suppliers is known as days payable outstanding (DPO) or sometimes 'supplier days' or 'creditor days'. It is calculated by working out the average accounts payables balance divided by cost of sales as a fraction of the year:

Days payable outstanding (DPO)
$DPO = \dfrac{\text{Accounts payable}}{\text{Cost of sales}} \times 365 \text{ days}$

Technically, accounts payable are the result of making purchases on credit, so the calculation should use accounts payable divided by purchases. However, the purchases number is not disclosed in published accounts, so cost of sales is often used as an approximation. In practice, as long as inventory levels are not volatile, there will be very little difference between purchases and cost of sales. In our ABC Co example, DPO is:

Payables of $1,550m/Cost of sales of $18,308m × 365 days = 31 days

How do you interpret this? Usually by comparing it to standard supplier terms, which are typically 30 days, or by making comparisons to prior periods to see whether the distributor is stretching its supplier credit. In this case, ABC Co seems to be paying its suppliers almost exactly on standard terms, though of course this is an average number and within it there will be a range of payment terms taken. Some suppliers offer attractive prompt payment discount incentives that justify early payment by the distributor (reducing its DPO) and some suppliers will be so dependent upon the distributor for market access that they will cede generous payment terms and credit limits up to 90 days or even beyond. Regional variations will also apply, with longer credit terms generally applying in southern Europe, for example. Distributors use all the usual strategies of querying items or demanding credit notes before paying invoices in order to legitimately delay payment beyond the official credit terms, and the actual DPO will be the outcome of the power struggle between the accounting departments of the distributor and its suppliers.

Inventory

Once purchased, the products go into the distributor's inventory waiting to be sold to customers. The time spent in inventory is known as 'inventory days' or 'days inventory outstanding' (DIO) and is calculated in a similar way:

Inventory days or days inventory outstanding (DIO)
$$DIO = \frac{Inventory}{Cost\ of\ sales} \times 365\ days$$

Note that cost of sales is used, as both inventory and cost of sales are valued at cost (sales would include a margin on the product and so would distort our calculation). In our example, ABC Co, inventory days is:

Inventory of \$1,408m/Cost of sales of \$18,308m × 365 days = 28 days

This means that on average the inventory is spending just under a month in the distributor's warehouse. Is this good or bad? Well, it depends on the nature of the products. If they are strawberries or cream cakes, this is very bad indeed! If they are electronic components or computer products, this would probably be acceptable though risky, as prices seem to fall rapidly in that sector. If they are steel or brass bars, tubes, pipe connectors, etc, this is probably acceptable. The reason any distributor holds inventory is to be able to offer instant availability when customers enquire. If demand is relatively stable and suppliers can be counted on to deliver reliably within a few days of orders being placed, the distributor need hold only enough inventory to cover sales in the order-to-delivery period plus a safety buffer, a total of, say, 10 days' worth of inventory. However, delivery is an expensive activity for suppliers so they will want to deliver in bulk to minimize their costs and pass on the cost of breaking the bulk (and holding it) to the distributor. If the products move in large volumes, this will not inflate the inventory levels, but for slower-moving items, the distributor will find itself with three months or longer of inventory of these products.

Should you take the prompt payment discount incentive from the supplier?

Many suppliers will offer credit terms along the lines of '2 per cent 15, net 45', which means that should you choose to pay them within 15 days you will be given a 2 per cent discount off the invoice value, but otherwise you must pay the full amount within 45 days. Is this a good deal and should you take it?

At first glance, it appears that you are being offered a good deal as you can earn 2 per cent for paying 30 days early, which equates to an annual rate of interest of 24.3 per cent ($2 \times 365/30$), which is probably better than the rate you are paying on any loans or overdrafts. However, there are two other factors that you should consider: the market and the impact on working capital.

In terms of the market, this prompt payment discount may in fact be a disguised trade discount if all your competitors are taking it and using it to lower their prices to the final-tier trade players. In effect, you have no choice but to pay up early and take the prompt payment discount to be able to offer competitive prices yourself. Where this is the case, we have seen distributors account for the discount as part of their gross margin because they consider they have no option and so cannot treat it as a financing issue, but simply a pricing issue.

In terms of working capital, by paying early you are effectively sucking 30 days of working capital out of your business and, if you are capital constrained, this could have a much higher cost than you might realize. Effectively you are constraining the sales levels of your business by 30 days' worth of trading. What contribution margin could you earn on that? If you are earning, say, a 10 per cent contribution margin on sales of that supplier's products of $3.65m, then another 30 days' sales would generate a contribution of $30,000 ($3.65m × 30/365 × 10%). The annual value of the prompt payment discount is $65,700 ($3.65m × 90% × 2%), so it would still be worth taking the prompt payment incentive. But if your contribution margin is 20 per cent, look again... the value of 30 days' lost sales is $60,000 and the annual value of the prompt payment discount is $58,400 ($3.65m × 80% × 2%), so the lost sales are worth more, although with such a small difference other factors may come into it.

It is a vital lesson to remember that averages can hide a wide range, so ABC Co's average of 28 days' inventory can include products that spend a few days in inventory right up to some that will be in inventory for over a year. Many distributors operate sophisticated product management systems to control their inventory levels and match depth of stock to the volume shifted. To determine target inventory levels, these systems employ some key parameters such as volume (or 'run rate' or 'rate of sale'), marketing support for the product, volatility of demand, order-to-delivery time from suppliers, minimum order quantities and reliability of supply.

An additional factor that can be taken into account is where the product is in its lifecycle. Early in the lifecycle a distributor may 'take a position' in the product to ensure it has plenty of availability for when demand kicks in, and towards the end of the lifecycle, may run down inventories to ensure it is not caught with obsolete product when it is superseded.

Typically, the inventory will be stratified into an A to E classification with 'As' being fast-moving products with daily or twice-weekly replenishment, allowing stocks to be kept in single figures in terms of days of inventory. 'Bs' will be slightly slower-moving products with possibly weekly or 10-day replenishment, and so on. The 'Es' will be service parts and spares that the distributor stocks as a service to its customers (and for which it should earn a high margin as compensation for the value of this service). One of the many balancing acts the distributor must manage is the mix of products across the A to E range as this will be the way that it can manage its inventory days to minimize its investment and the risk of stock-outs. Another complexity is seasonality, with distributors needing to increase stocks ahead of the peak season and ensure that they exit the season with stocks run down to lower levels. In judging the inventory days, it is important to bear in mind the date of the balance sheet in relation to the seasonal profile. Usually distributors' financial year ends are set just after the peak season has ended to enable them to present balance sheets with low inventory days, which is a sign of good management.

Some distributors narrow the bandwidth of their business model, for example stocking only the fast-moving products in their industry and avoiding the riskier, slower-moving products. In office products, there are distributors selling only the paper, printer supplies and consumables products, who seek to compete on price against the one-stop-shop convenience of the broadline, catalogue-based distributors. These specialist distributors work with thinner margins, but do not incur the costs of inventory write-downs or big warehouses and complex systems and they can capitalize on volume discounts and logistics efficiency incentives from their suppliers.

Even with sophisticated inventory management systems, Pareto's Law bites hard in inventory, with 20 per cent of the products accounting for 80 per cent of the volume. This can mean that the majority of the inventory is held in the 80 per cent of the products that account for only 20 per cent of the sales. In the next chapter on productivity measures you will learn how to judge whether a product justifies its inventory investment. For many distributors, the effect of constantly adding new products and suppliers to their portfolio creates a kind of creeping malaise in its inventory profile that only a periodic audit can address, to help reduce the inventory days.

Customer credit

Products leave inventory when they are sold to customers on credit, creating a receivable balance. The time customers take to pay is called 'days sales outstanding' (DSO) or 'customer days' or 'debtor days'. It is calculated by working out the average accounts receivable balance divided by sales as a fraction of the year:

Days sales outstanding (DSO)
$$DSO = \frac{\text{Accounts receivable}}{\text{Sales}} \times 365 \text{ days}$$

Note that sales is used, as both the numerator and the denominator are valued at sales prices. In our example, ABC Co, DSO is:

Accounts receivable of $1,897m/Sales of $19,316m × 365 days = 36 days

This means that, on average, customers are taking just over five weeks to pay for their products. As with DPO, this number should be compared to the terms that apply, in this case the standard customer credit terms. In practice, different customers may be offered different terms depending on their importance, track record, credit-worthiness and market practice. Some customers may have to pay cash with order, so a proportion of sales won't generate any accounts receivable. But if the normal terms are 30 days then ABC Co is doing a pretty good job of getting the money in, given that at any point in time a certain proportion of its invoices will be the subject of disputes and so on.

Drivers of inventory levels

Stock levels of companies are not only set by 'industry norms' but are often influenced by cultural differences and market maturity. In some countries, such as Turkey and to a lesser extent Greece, historic high inflation and currency devaluation have had a great bearing on how inventory was viewed. Even today in Turkey, long after the worst of the hyperinflation has gone, Turkish distributors hold considerably more stock than, say, their German or British equivalents. In the automotive lubricant and chemicals industry it is not uncommon for distributors to hold six to nine months' stock, whereas in the UK a similar distributor of those products will typically hold six weeks to two months.

Market maturity often brings increased pressure on business to control costs in the face of squeezed margins. As price pressure and competition grow, companies respond by driving down the most visible business cost-driver: stock levels. This reduction is supported by the investment of suppliers in ever more sophisticated supply chain technology that gives the security and service previously only deliverable with high stock levels. Stock levels in many mature sectors are now around half what they were only 10 years ago, with the consequent saving in cost, but increased risk of business disruption if transport logistics are affected by weather, strikes or unforeseen changes in demand (for instance when a product is suddenly put under the spotlight as when Delia Smith exhorted the use of cranberries in one episode of her cooking programme, broadcast nationally – the shops were emptied within hours).

As with DPO, it is useful to track DSO over time to make sure that the credit control function is not slipping or that there has not been some shift in the overall mix of credit arrangements that is giving rise to an increase in the distributor's investment in customer credit.

DSO in seasonal businesses

In some sectors where sales vary significantly by month, such as fashion or garden products, a more accurate way to calculate DSO is the 'count back' method. An example illustrates this:

Receivables at 31 December: $480,000
Monthly sales: December: $385,000   31 days in month
                       November: $325,000   30 days in month

The receivables balance is assumed to be built up from all of December's sales (31 days), which leaves $95,000 (ie $480,000 – $385,000) that came from November's sales. This represents nine days of November's sales, calculated as follows: $95,000/$325,000 × 30 days. So, the total DSO is 40 days, ie 31 days from December plus 9 days from November.

Working capital cycle

Putting these three elements together gives the working capital days: ie inventory days plus DSO less DPO. In the case of ABC Co, its working capital days equals inventory days of 28 days plus DSO of 36 days less DPO of 31 days to give 33 days. This means that ABC Co takes 33 days to cycle its cash through working capital and back into cash again. Another way to think about this is in terms of how fast it is turning over its working capital a year. In the case of ABC Co this is 365 days/33 days, which is 11 times per year:

Working capital turn
$$\text{Working capital turn} = \frac{365 \text{ days}}{\text{Working capital days}}$$

The faster the capital turns, the less cash is needed to finance the working capital cycle and the more efficient is the distributor. Small improvements in the elements of working capital can lead to a significant change in the overall efficiency of the distributor and reduce the cash needed to finance the business. The box 'Unlocking the cash' shows how this works.

It was mentioned earlier that some distributors operate a narrow-bandwidth business model to keep inventories low. We have seen distributors that exploit their focus on high volumes with a few suppliers to negotiate extended trading terms up to 60 or even 75 days' credit. This enables them to operate with negative working capital: inventory days of 20 plus DSO of 35 days less DSO of 75 days gives working capital of *minus* 20 days. What does this mean? It means that the distributor has 20 days of sales worth of cash in its business, sometimes termed a 'cash float'. The bigger the business grows, the more cash it holds in its bank accounts. By putting the cash on long-term deposit and earning a decent rate of interest, the distributor can either make a super-profit or cut its prices to increase its competitiveness and attract more business. This option is available to any distributor that has the clout to negotiate advantageous trading terms and as a result use its suppliers to effectively finance its inventories and customer credit. As we have seen, the lower the working capital balance, the more efficient the distributor and the more it can grow without needing additional finance.

The ability to manage working capital efficiently is a core competence for any distributor. As we have seen, it has a fundamental impact on the amount of capital needed in the business and thus the distributor's ability to finance its own growth without having to raise more capital or increase borrowings. Typically, in a distributor, the day-to-day management of the three key measures we have covered in this chapter are the responsibility of different departments or functions: DSO is managed by the credit control team, DPO by the bought ledger or purchasing team and DIO by the product managers. Each of these roles can be incentivized to improve the performance of these measures, though care should be exercised to avoid the law of unintended consequences.

Unlocking the cash

Take a distributor with sales of $20m and cost of sales of $19m with the starting and improved working capital profiles shown in Table 7.1. By improving each working capital element by five days, the reduction in working capital is 15 days (down from 60 to 45 days). This means that the investment in working capital falls from $3.25m to $2.45m, an improvement of $0.8m. This is very significant in a business with sales of $20m.

Table 7.1 Example working capital profiles

| Working | Starting profile | | Improved profile | |
capital	Days	$ value	Days	$ value
DIO	40	2.08m	35	1.82m
DSO	45	2.47m	40	2.19m
DPO	−25	−1.30m	−30	−1.56m
WC days	60	3.25m	45	2.45m
WC turn	6 times per year		8 times per year	

If this distributor is looking to grow but has been strapped for cash with its old working capital profile, it has unlocked the cash to reinvest in working capital at its faster cycle:

$0.8m free cash × 8 turns per year => $6.4m extra, taking sales up to $26.4m.

This is a growth rate of nearly 40 per cent and all this expansion can be financed without extra capital or loans. If the distributor was not looking to grow but trying to avoid a cash flow crisis, the cash freed up would appear in its bank accounts within 45 days, keeping the bank at bay!

None of these measures should be driven beyond a certain limit or range. For example, attempting to drive down DSO to the formal credit terms would wipe out a lot of the distributor's business as large and loyal customers would resent such aggressive dunning behaviour and move their accounts. However, an incentive to keep DSO within management's view of an acceptable benchmark can be effective if applied by a smart and commercially aware credit team manager. The same applies to DPO, where some key suppliers should be paid on time, every time, but not all suppliers are equal and renegotiating extended terms from lesser suppliers may prove beneficial. We will look at the way product managers should be targeted in the next chapter as they need to balance the 'earn and turn' priorities across their portfolio in tandem.

However, all the working capital measures are framed by the strategic choices made by the distributor's management team. The markets and customer segments chosen to be served will determine both product requirements and typical DSO terms. For example, many distributors aim to serve the largest and most successful final-tier trade players, but here the competition is often the most intensive so there may be an unwillingness to exercise credit control too aggressively for fear or losing these premium customers. However, those distributors that focus on the 'B' and 'C' players may find that they can earn better margins and effectively charge higher prices to those players to whom no other source of credit supply is available. With this positioning will come the ability to apply assertive credit control practices reducing DSOs (and reducing bad debt risks). Other distributors may choose to serve final-tier players servicing the public sector and the provision of liquidity to the channel may be a competitive weapon. But it will mean that the DSO will be much higher than for those players servicing the commercial sector. It may also impact DIO as the public sector often makes demands for supply availability. In a similar way, the strategic choices as to whether to distribute only well-known major brands or to focus on new and emerging brands will determine the length of credit a distributor can secure from its supplier base.

Managing distributors – productivity

08

Earn and turn

So far we have looked at measures that help distributors manage the profitability and working capital aspects of their business separately, but there are a number of powerful measures that combine both aspects in one metric. These measures, sometimes called productivity measures, combine both the 'earn' and the 'turn' aspects of the business as well as of individual products, categories, suppliers or customers.

The simplest of these measures is gross margin return on inventory investment (GMROII):

Gross margin return on inventory investment (GMROII)

$$\text{GMROII} = \frac{\text{Gross profit}}{\text{Inventory}} = \frac{\text{Gross profit}}{\text{Sales}} \times \frac{\text{Sales}}{\text{Inventory}}$$
$$\text{'Earn'} \quad \times \quad \text{'Turn'}$$

This measure, which can be expressed as either a money amount, or as a percentage if multiplied by 100, shows the amount of gross profit earned per year per dollar invested in inventory. In the case of ABC Co, GMROII is:

Gross profit of \$1,008m/Inventory of \$1,408m = \$0.72 per \$ or 72%

This needs context to be interpreted, for example the average figures for the industry sector, but by most benchmarks this is likely to be low. As we have already indicated, for ABC Co the gross margin (earn) was low and the inventory turn was average. Some examples will bring this to life (see Table 8.1).

Table 8.1   Example product 'Earn' and 'Turn' combinations

Eg	Sales	Gross profit	Inventory	'Earn'	'Turn'	GMROII %	GMROII $
A	15,000	1,500	1,500	10%	10x	100%	$1.00
B	25,000	1,250	1,250	5%	20x	100%	$1.00
C	20,000	2,400	1,667	12%	12x	144%	$1.44
D	25,000	2,500	1,500	10%	17x	170%	$1.70

Product A has generated $1 of gross profit for every $1 invested in inventory for the year. It has achieved this with a gross margin ('Earn') of 10 per cent and a sales-to-inventory ratio ('Turn') of 10 times per year. Distributors refer to this as a GMROII of 100 and, as a very rough rule of thumb across most industries, a product needs a GMROII of 100 to justify its place from a financial perspective. Products can have very different profiles with the same GMROII. Compare product B to product A: its margin is half that of product A at a lowly 5 per cent, but it earns that 20 times a year to deliver the same return on inventory investment.

All distributors have products with a range of profiles from low-earn, high-turn products like product B to high-earn, low-turn products. Note how relatively small improvements in both factors multiply up to deliver a very attractive GMROII, as in the case of product C compared to product A. Product C has a slightly better margin and slightly better turn to give a GMROII that is close to 50 per cent better. This is significant because it means that the distributor has earned considerably more gross profit with product C than product A, an increase that will have a much bigger impact on the bottom-line operating profit. Against that, it's possible that as product C is turning faster than product A, it is driving more transaction activity, but then it's spending less time in the warehouse.

Most distributors have a natural rhythm to the business and 80 per cent of their products will fit within a reasonable range of earns and turns. Products outside this range have a distorting effect on the whole business model and make it harder for managers to tune the business. Distributors can increase their productivity and capital efficiency by setting a minimum threshold for GMROII and either eliminating all products that fall below it or changing one of their earn or turn characteristics. By definition, such products have low margins and low turns, but product managers tend to trot out arguments for retaining these below par products such as 'it completes the range' or it is necessary to continue to list the product for 'credibility in the category'. This may be so, but it is no justification to make a low margin on a low-turning product. If it is retained in the category for reasons of category credibility or customer service, it is fair to ask for the service to be paid for through the margin. Generally it is easier and cheaper to improve the margin on these types of product by increasing prices than it is to accelerate turns by increasing rate of sale.

The reason GMROII is such a powerful measure is that it can be applied up and down the business, from an individual SKU to the product line group, the category, the vendor and so on, right up to the business as a whole. It is an ideal performance measure for product managers as it encompasses both dimensions of their role in a single, intuitive measure and, by splitting out the 'earn and turn' dimensions, it is easy to identify what action is required to improve business performance. It is often used as the measure on which to target and incentivize product managers.

Contribution margin return on inventory investment

One refinement that should be adopted, if at all possible, is to replace the *gross margin* with the *contribution margin* to establish contribution margin return on inventory investment (CMROII):

$$\text{Contribution margin return on inventory investment (CMROII)}$$

$$\text{CMROII} = \frac{\text{Contribution profit}}{\text{Inventory}} = \underbrace{\frac{\text{Contribution profit}}{\text{Sales}}}_{\text{'Earn'}} \times \underbrace{\frac{\text{Sales}}{\text{Inventory}}}_{\text{'Turn'}}$$

This provides a more effective measure for the same reasons that the contribution margin is a more effective measure than a gross margin, ie it allows for all the costs and allowances that are directly attributable to the product. In general, managers should use contribution margins and profits instead of gross margins and profits when making decisions such as which products to promote over others, or in allocating scarce working capital resources across categories and product lines.

Continuing with the theme of using a product's earn and turn characteristics, product managers can profile their entire portfolio against the category averages using volumes and contribution margins (Figure 8.1). In this chart (taken from a real case, but simplified), each dot represents a single product SKU. The axes are positioned at the category averages. Those

Figure 8.1   Product portfolio profiled in terms of 'Earn' and 'Turn' characteristics

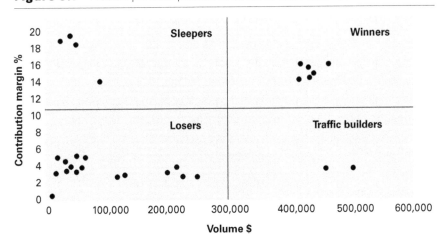

products with above-average contribution margins and sales volumes are termed *winners* for obvious reasons and there will tend to be relatively few products that exhibit this high-earn, high-turn profile. Products with a low-earn, high-turn profile are termed *traffic builders* as these tend to be the strong brands that customers buy in volumes but which distributors know they need to discount aggressively to compete in the market and use as a price-positioning signal.

The most interesting products are the *sleepers*, which generate high contribution margins but sell in relatively low volumes. Some of these may be the service-type items that are bought rather than sold. However, there may be products here that are perhaps early in the lifecycle and less prevalent in the market and would respond to sales stimulation efforts. It is likely that the suppliers of these products will share the aim of accelerating sales growth and make a financial contribution to sales and marketing efforts, protecting the distributor's own contribution margin. The real opportunities lie in finding ways to connect the traffic builders to the sleepers, as there is usually a very poor connect rate. An analysis of sales invoices or sales by customer will show the connect rate. Given that the average number of sales lines on a distributor's sales invoice (ie the number of different SKUs) is less than two in many industries, it is easy to see that the connect rate will be low. Where distributors have put real incentive and education into the sales force to improve connect rates, they have seen dramatic improvements in profitability as traffic builders are leveraged effectively.

Active portfolio management

In one distributor, portfolio analysis was turned into an active management discipline, with the segments termed BMWs (winners), Fords (traffic builders), Ferraris (sleepers) and Ladas (losers) with matching green, blue, red and grey colours to pep up the interest and attention of the sales force and product managers. As customers requested products, the order system's colour coding highlighted the segment of the product and stimulated a conversation to either change the customer's preference or cross-sell an additional higher-contribution product.

Customers' recent purchasing history was also analysed to identify those whose contribution was below average. Account management campaigns were run to understand all the needs of high-volume customers and ensure that they were aware of the full range of products available. The order entry system was programmed to highlight low-volume customers whose purchases were exclusively traffic builders. When these customers called to enquire about prices and availability, they were aggressively cross-sold other winners and sleepers. If this failed to make an impact on their purchasing profile, prices on traffic builders to these customers were marked higher. The distributor took the view that if the customer was only buying its traffic builders, then the customer was going elsewhere for the rest of its business and should not be retained.

Over the course of around six months, the distributor was able to improve its contribution margin by over 30 per cent and reduce working capital by 20 per cent while increasing sales. It took a combination of incentives and training for both the sales force and the product managers to drive home the changed approach as well as some minor IT programming. The return on these investments was excellent.

The final group of products are called *losers* as these drag down overall business performance with low volumes and low contribution. Product managers should review these products at least every quarter and either raise their prices (and contribution) or remove them from the category to free up cash for higher-performance products. Simply removing these products will have a marked impact on average contribution earned. See the boxed material on 'Active portfolio management' for an example of how one distributor applied this approach.

Returns on working capital

The two productivity measures, GMROII and CMROII, are powerful because they can be used within the business, but they take into account only the inventory component of working capital. To optimize the business model, measures are needed that include the other two elements of working capital – accounts receivable and accounts payable:

Gross margin return on working capital (GMROWC)

$$\text{GMROWC} = \frac{\text{Gross profit}}{\text{Working capital}} = \frac{\text{Gross profit}}{\text{Sales}} \times \frac{\text{Sales}}{\text{Working capital}}$$

Working capital = Inventory + Accounts receivable – Accounts payable

---

In the case of ABC Co distributor GMROWC is:

Gross profit of $1,008m/Working capital of $1,755m = 57.43%

This would generally be regarded as a very average performance, like its GMROII measure, but possibly improved by its good management of DSO.

This is probably the best measure for product managers, but it does require good IT systems to be able to allocate all the working capital elements to the category. In the absence of this, some spreadsheet work done on a periodic basis will reveal the productivity of one category in comparison to others. Working capital is always scarce in a distributor and should be allocated to those products and categories that can generate the best return. Tracking GMROWC performance for a category over time is an excellent way to target and incentivize product managers' performance as it requires them to fine-tune the balance of earn and turn characteristics of the possibly hundreds of products in the category. As with any percentage or ratio measure, GMROWC does not indicate the scale of the business so it should be used in combination with sales volumes and dollar values.

The final version of this measure is contribution margin return on working capital (CMROWC), which replaces the gross profit with the contribution profit but is the same in all other respects:

Contribution margin return on working capital (CMROWC)

$$\text{CMROWC} = \frac{\text{Contribution profit}}{\text{Working capital}} = \frac{\text{Contribution profit}}{\text{Sales}} \times \frac{\text{Sales}}{\text{Working capital}}$$

The CMROWC measure is probably the single best indicator of a distributor's performance in the short term as it includes all the costs and allowances directly related to products and customers and the complete working capital cycle. It is also possibly the best guide to supplier productivity as it builds in all dimensions of its economic performance.

Return on brand investment – another name of CMROWC

Some distributors and their suppliers use the term 'return on brand investment' instead of CMROWC as a rather more snappy term. Using the same framework, they can compare results for one brand inside distributors (or within just one distributor), which can be very revealing (see Figures 8.2–8.5).

Figure 8.2   Components of return on brand investment

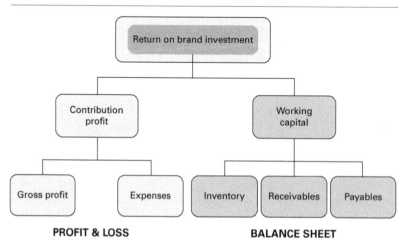

Figure 8.3 Example of return on brand investment by country

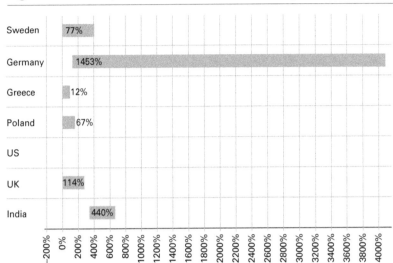

Figure 8.4 Example of contribution margin by country

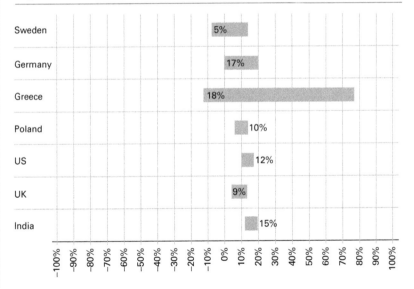

Figure 8.5   Example of working capital turn by country

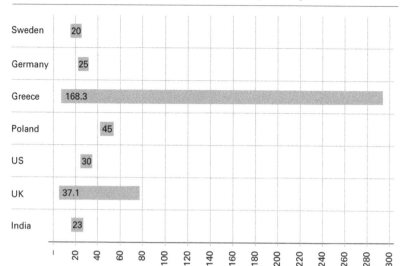

These charts (from a real supplier) show just how differently the same supplier is performing within its main distributors in its international markets. By doing this analysis the supplier's international management team were able to focus their account managers on the ground on addressing the right issues with appropriate targets. Previously they had set one benchmark for all international markets with little credibility.

Drilling down further, the supplier investigated how well its own two brands performed on return on brand investment in its main distributors and how these compared to the competitor brands (see Figure 8.6). The analysis showed that, while its own brands compared favourably with the distributor's overall business measures, the supplier was underperforming against its competitors in the category. Further analysis showed that the supplier's own average hid a disparate performance between its own brands A and B. Brand A is clearly underperforming against any benchmark and needs to be either transformed or withdrawn. The good news is that Brand B outperforms against the competition and can be used to anchor the relationship with the distributors while Brand A is sorted out.

Figure 8.6 Example of return on brand investment benchmarked against competitors

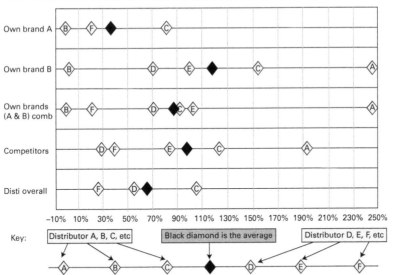

In this real example, the supplier was the first to run this type of analysis and was able to convince its distributors to act on its recommendations. Many of the distributors had not been aware of how the different brands they distributed performed for them and were very impressed by a supplier that was able to show them how to improve their own business performance.

Managing distributors – sustainability

09

Sustainability – longer-term business health

Given that the distributor's business model is predominantly tied up in moving products through working capital as fast and profitably as possible, we have focused on the measures that help monitor those aspects of business performance. In the short term this is all that really matters, but it is also important to monitor the other, longer-term aspects of the business, which include fixed assets and long-term liabilities such as loans as well as the capital structure of the business. These factors matter when it comes to measuring the management team's performance in delivering good returns on the assets they are accountable for or on the capital with which they are entrusted.

Return on net assets and return on capital employed

There are two measures that are similar and are often used to track the business's overall performance: return on net assets (RONA) and return on capital employed (ROCE). We will look at RONA first:

Return on net assets (RONA)
$$RONA = \frac{\text{Operating profit}}{\text{Cash} + \text{Working capital} + \text{Fixed assets}}$$

RONA measures the return on the assets employed in the business, so is useful when applied to the distributor's business units, subsidiaries or divisions, where assets can be clearly allocated, as well as to the overall business. In the case of ABC Co the RONA is:

$$\frac{\text{Operating profit of } \$56m}{(\text{Cash of } \$401m + \text{WC of } \$1,755m + \text{FA of } \$423m)} = 2.2\%$$

This would be regarded as a woeful performance, delivering a return of just over 2 per cent on net assets of over $2.5 billion. Either the management is asleep on the job or there is something seriously wrong with the business model. It may be that competition has found ways to drive down costs or is much more efficient in its management of working capital; it would be instructive to compare its earn and turn characteristics with competitors to see where the disadvantage is greatest. Let's see if its use of capital is any better, using ROCE:

Return on capital employed (ROCE)

$$\text{ROCE} = \frac{\text{Net profit before tax}}{\text{Total assets} - \text{Non-interest-bearing liabilities}}$$

ROCE for ABC Co is:

$$\frac{\text{Net profit before tax of } \$44m}{\text{Shareholders' funds of } \$1,756m} = 2.5\%$$

This is slightly better, but this is the return that investors would compare to other investment opportunities and, in most economies, this return would be well below that available from simply putting the money on deposit.

Table 9.1 lists a set of performance measures for a sample of distributors from different sectors, which shows that very few make a return on capital above 20 per cent, the sort of rate you'd expect to compensate for the inherently risky nature of the business.

Table 9.1   Returns on capital for distributors from different sectors

Sector and distributor	Gross margin	Operating margin	Net margin (pre-tax)	Return on capital employed
Building supplies				
Travis Perkins	N/A	1.6%	0.2%	0.4%
Boise Cascade	13%	1.8%	1.1%	3.8%
Wolseley	29%	4.6%	2.8%	9.2%
Chemicals				
Ashland	32%	6.5%	−1.3%	−0.8%
AM Castle & Co	23%	−9.5%	7.1%	−26.6%
Electronics				
Arrow Electronics	13%	3.6%	2.2%	7.3%
Avnet	13%	3.1%	1.5%	4.2%
Electrocomponents	43%	6.1%	8.8%	13.8%
Information technology				
ScanSource	10%	2.4%	1.8%	6.5%
Tech Data	5%	1.1%	0.7%	5.5%
Pharmaceuticals and healthcare products				
Henry Schein	28%	6.7%	4.8%	14.3%
AmerisourceBergen Corp	3%	1.2%	0.8%	13.1%
McKesson Corp	6%	3.6%	2.7%	24.0%
Cardinal Health	5%	1.8%	1.0%	9.4%
Office supplies and business products				
Spicers	21%	1.1%	0.4%	1.1%
Weyerhaeuser	23%	15.0%	7.7%	2.6%
Multi-sector				
Genuine Parts Co	30%	6.9%	4.4%	15.7%
Financial services				
Charles Schwab	N/A	39.9%	25.6%	10.8%
TD Ameritrade	N/A	39.1%	24.9%	11.9%
Travel				
Flight Centre	N/A	11.9%	7.6%	14.3%
Coporate Travel Management	N/A	23.0%	17.2%	16.8%

Return on invested capital

Now it gets more complex. Some of the world's largest and most sophisticated distributors use return on invested capital (ROIC) as a purer measure for management targets and incentives:

Return on invested capital (ROIC)

$$\text{ROIC} = \frac{\text{Operating profit after tax}}{\text{Invested capital}}$$

$$= \frac{\text{Net profit after tax} + \text{Interest}}{\text{Total assets} - \text{Excess cash} - \text{Non-interest-bearing current liabilities}}$$

This measure focuses on the operating components of the business model and relates them to the relevant portion of shareholders' funds. Note that the top line is operating profit after tax (sometimes called *net operating profit after tax* or NOPAT), which means that although it uses an after-tax profit number, it should not have had interest deducted. Here's what this looks like for ABC Co:

NOPAT ($40m) = Net profit after tax ($28m) + Interest of ($12m)

$$\frac{\text{Invested capital}}{(\$1,414\text{m})} = \frac{\text{Total assets} (\$4,129\text{m}) - \text{Excess cash} (\$401\text{m})}{- \text{Non-interest bearing liabilities} (\$2,314\text{m})}$$

This gives an ROIC of $40m/$1,414m = 2.8 per cent. How do you interpret this number, which certainly looks a lot better than the RONA or ROCE returns? The test of ROIC is whether it is higher than the weighted average cost of capital (WACC), because this determines whether the management team have created any value with the invested capital allocated to it for the year. Think of WACC as interest paid on the capital invested at a rate that's adjusted for the risk in the business (it's more complex than that because the capital will be a mix of equity and debt and WACC calculations are a somewhat technical specialty. The WACC for a start-up with a new business model would be higher than for a long-established distributor with a proven business model with the same mix of debt and equity). So, the following applies:

ROIC   >   WACC   →   Management has created value
ROIC   <   WACC   →   Management has destroyed value

In other words, management should demonstrate that it should be entrusted with the capital invested because it can generate a better return with its business model than by leaving the capital in the money markets, and the money markets are exactly where the largest distributors must go for their multi-billion dollar funding requirements, through rights issues to tap the equity markets or the issue of bonds to raise debt. As we saw at the start of this Part of the book, distributors are generally capital absorbing and the bigger the distributor, the bigger the capital requirement. So it makes good sense for the executive team of the distributor to ensure that their direct reports in charge of the operating subsidiaries in each of the markets in which it operates are measured and rewarded on their ability to drive ROIC upwards.

The argument for adopting ROIC is just as applicable for smaller distributors, regardless of whether they are publicly accountable quoted companies or privately owned companies or subsidiaries. In all sizes and types of distributor the management team should be rewarded for creating value above the cost of capital allocated to its business. However, care should be exercised in the way management teams are incentivized, as ROIC is vulnerable to short-term optimization. An unbalanced focus can encourage management to ignore growth possibilities and damage long-term value creation. Also, as we have highlighted before, it is a percentage measure, which means that it ignores the scale of the business and dollar dimension of the value created or destroyed.

Value creation

The concept of value creation (VC) is powerful and quite intuitive (though the maths behind some of the calculations can be somewhat technical). It requires management teams to make not just a profit, but a profit in excess of the cost of the capital they used to make that profit. As we have seen with ROIC, it is possible to determine whether a management team is creating or destroying value in comparison to its WACC.

The VC measure (otherwise known as economic value added or EVA) uses this concept but establishes a dollar value, which is more intuitive than a percentage and reflects the scale of the business. It also has the advantage that it can be applied in managing components of the business, as we shall see later on. Let's start with the basic value creation measure:

Value creation (VC)
VC = Operating profit after tax – (Invested capital × WACC)

To calculate value creation for ABC Co we need to know its WACC, something that is usually possible only for quoted companies, but these public rates can be used as a guideline for private companies (possibly with an uplift for additional risk). Taking a WACC of 6.2 per cent for the sector average, and the values for operating profit after tax and invested capital calculated earlier, gives:

Operating profit after tax of $40m – (invested capital of $1,414m × 6.2%)
= value destruction of $48m

This is not an enormous sum given the scale of the business (with sales of almost $20 billion) but it is a negative number, which means that some value has been destroyed, ie the management has been unable to generate a profit in excess of the opportunity cost of the capital invested, a result that is consistent with what would be suggested by the RONA, ROCE and ROIC measures.

There is much evidence to show that VC is the performance measure most closely linked with the creation of shareholder wealth over time. It can be used as a measure for targeting and rewarding managers within the business and indeed it provides a single framework for measuring and guiding the performance of managers in functional areas as well. With a good training programme and useful tools, managers can use VC in their everyday decision making as they understand how each part of the business model influences whether value is created or destroyed using the value creation 'tree', which links all the elements we have covered. The VC tree is like a map of the business model showing how all the different dynamics interact. Every decision taken within the business will impact how the business performs and the VC tree shows how these effects cascade up the tree to impact the overall value created or destroyed.

Figure 9.1 shows the value creation tree for ABC Co. To the right of each of the profit numbers is their related margin as a percentage of revenue (eg gross margin of 5.2 per cent is next to $1,008m). To the right of each of the working capital elements is their equivalent in days (eg DSO of 36 days is next to $1,897m). The best way to understand the value of this VC tree layout is to watch the impact of changes dynamically ripple through to ROIC and VC. If we look at how ABC Co has performed in the following year (year 2), we can compare the two years and see the changes.

In year 2 ABC Co managed to grow the business in a tough market so its aggressive discounting shows up in a lower gross margin. However, on the plus side the management team achieved tight overhead control and some small improvements in working capital management.

Figure 9.2 shows the balance sheet and profit and loss account in the traditional format. What has happened to the key measures of the business? Do these changes mean that the business has created or destroyed value in year 2 (Figure 9.3)? Starting from the top of the tree, we can see that ABC Co has in fact managed to create $2m of value compared to destroying value to the extent of $48m in year 1. While this is a small amount in the context of the scale of the business, it is a considerable improvement. Which changes have contributed to this achievement? Working down the tree, ROIC has made a dramatic improvement from a paltry 2.8 per cent to 6.4 per cent (which is higher than WACC, hence value is created). This is the result of doubling the NOPAT from 0.2 to 0.4 per cent on a reduced invested capital base.

By working on both elements simultaneously, the management team have effectively multiplied improvements in the business model. Had they only managed to improve NOPAT on the same invested capital base, ROIC would have been 5.5 per cent, which is still below WACC, and ABC Co would have suffered another year of destroying value. This is a critical lesson: management needed to fine-tune its performance in *both* profitability and the management of capital to create value. Improving either side of the business model on its own would not have been sufficient.

The key to reducing invested capital has been the improvement in DPO or payables days. The extra two days on average that ABC Co is taking to pay its suppliers has shifted the burden of financing the extra working capital from the shareholders to the suppliers. (Note that this could be the result of negotiating better terms or shifting the supplier mix, rather than merely becoming a slow payer.) In addition, the one-day improvement in each of inventory days and DSO or customer days has reduced the total

Figure 9.1 Value creation tree for ABC Co – Year 1

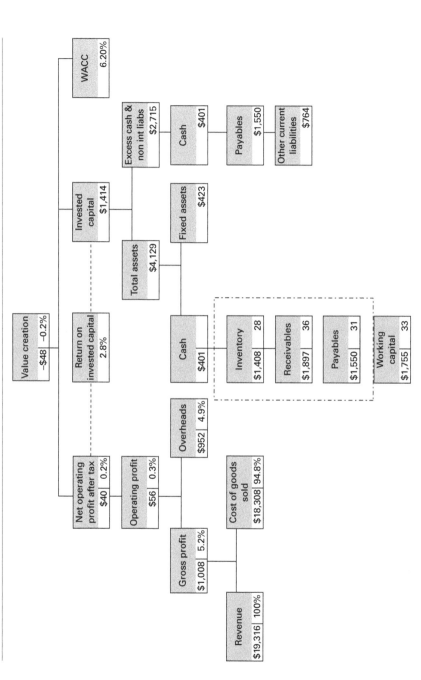

Figure 9.2 ABC Co balance sheet and profit and loss account for Year 2 compared to Year 1

	Year 1 $'000	Year 2 $'000
Sales	19,316	21,248
Cost of sales	18,308	20,158
Gross profit	**1,008**	**1,090**
Overheads	952	980
Operating profit	**56**	**110**
Interest	12	24
Profit before taxation	**44**	**86**
Taxation	16	32
Profit after taxation	**28**	**54**

Income statement

	Year 1 $'000	Year 2 $'000
Fixed assets	423	434
Current assets		
Inventory	1,408	1,492
Accounts receivable	1,897	2,011
Cash	401	376
Total current assets	**3,706**	**3,879**
Current liabilities		
Accounts payables	1,550	1,814
Other	764	902
Total current liabilities	**2,314**	**2,716**
Net current assets	**1,392**	**1,163**
Long-term liabilities	59	75
Net assets	**1,756**	**1,522**
Shareholders funds	**1,756**	**1,522**

Balance sheet

Figure 9.3 Value creation tree for ABC Co – Years 1 and 2

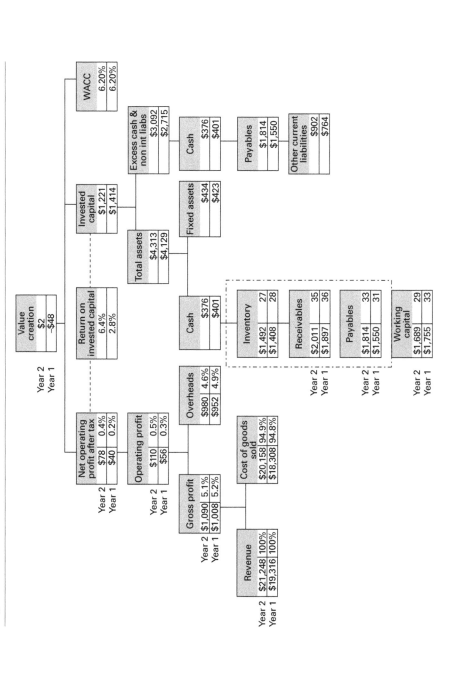

working capital needed, so there has been an overall improvement in working capital of four days. Is four days really all that significant? Well, in this distributor's case, it's worth about $230m, which accounts for most of the reduction in invested capital. This shows the power of the logic of using invested capital in these measures, because although ABC has grown its net assets year on year in the balance sheet, the capital invested in the trading operation has gone down, thanks to management's skilful handling of its business model.

Managing value creation on an operational basis

Value creation is an excellent overall measure, but how can operational managers relate to it? At a very basic level, every manager should be able to consider the implications of his or her decisions in terms of the income statement and balance sheet dimensions that drive value creation. Senior management has a key role here in communicating down and across the organization the major value drivers on which it wants operational management to focus.

However, more sophisticated suppliers and distributors are looking at value creation at an individual customer level, and distributors are looking at the value created in their own business by the major suppliers whose products they distribute. Most businesses can measure customer (or supplier) profitability at a gross margin level and many go further to contribution margin. Some businesses now are allocating their major working capital assets and liabilities across customers and even including the impact on their fixed assets, such as distribution systems and factory utilization (for example, a customer that places orders in line with forecasts will drive efficiency through the factory compared to one that fluctuates wildly, distorting factory production). By factoring all these elements into a value creation measure, and applying the cost of capital inside your own business, it is possible to look at whether an individual customer (or supplier) is creating or destroying value. Figure 9.4 shows a real example from a distributor's analysis of its customers. The size of each circle represents the amount of value created and each has been positioned on the axes of Contribution margin and Cost to serve, as these represent the two primary value drivers. The arrows and dotted circles represent the distributor's objectives for each account. The implications of the analysis shown in the figure are:

Figure 9.4 Illustrative analysis of value created by different customers mapped on axes of contribution margin and cost to serve

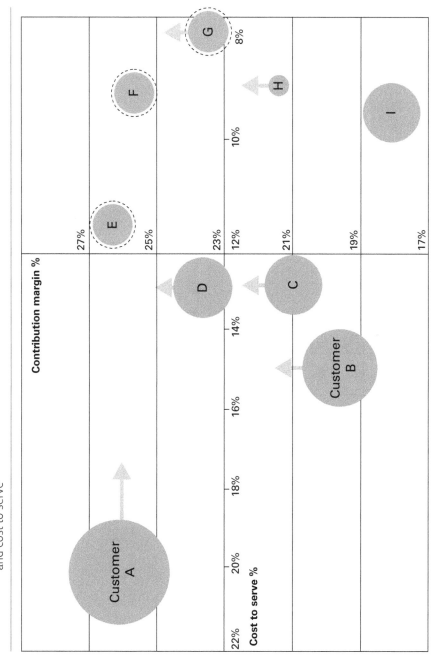

- Account A is creating the most value, through its substantial contribution margin, which is more than covering its high cost to serve. The account team looking after this account will be tasked with addressing the cost-to-serve drivers next year and moving the account to the right, which should increase the value created for the distributor. By sharing the rewards generated, both customer and distributor will benefit.

- Account B by contrast is creating value through its low cost to serve, but needs to improve the contribution margin generated.

- Accounts E, F and G are all in excellent positions: high contribution, low cost to serve, and just need to be grown, with G possibly moving up its contribution.

Each account team will be tasked with drilling down further to understand the factors driving the position and size of their account's circle on the chart and then to partner with their account to improve in the direction required. Regular meetings of all account teams together will be useful to share best practices and insights that all accounts can share. This type of analysis may look difficult, time-consuming and expensive to commission, but in fact this is usually only true the first time it is done. Once the cost and revenue allocation algorithms have been developed and the data feeds from the company's information systems established, the analysis models can be run pretty much at any time. It probably does not make sense to run the analysis more frequently than quarterly as the types of changes needed to make an impact can be significant and take multiple quarters to plan and implement. Clearly a distributor managing its strategic relationships using value creation is going to be at a competitive advantage as it will be taking the conversation to real value drivers that both sides can benefit from improving. This is quite a different game from the traditional confrontational approach where both sides are fighting over the same, possibly shrinking, margins.

Managing distributors – managing growth

10

Growth dynamics

Managing growth in distributors is a demanding management challenge because the hundreds of buying, pricing, selling and stocking decisions taken every day affect the margins and costs reflected in the profit and loss account. As we have seen, there is very little room for slippage – a couple of points off the margin and a couple more points on the costs and the profit turns into a loss. The market context plays a big part in the challenges of managing growth, because it's one thing to grow with the market but quite another to fight for market share against the competition to grow faster than the market. The challenge is even more severe if attempting to grow in a shrinking market.

Overcoming these challenges requires some form of competitive advantage such as product exclusivity, more (or more effective) advertising and promotion, or better prices, service and availability, or more responsive delivery speeds. Each of these competitive advantages comes at a cost, so what are the advantages of growth that more than compensate for these costs? What economies of scale can the distributor gain? There are two major benefits available: cost structure efficiencies and working capital efficiencies. However, there is also a limit: growth means that increased working capital is required, and that absorbs cash. How fast can a distributor grow before it overtrades and runs out of cash? We start with working out the limits and then explore how to realize the economies of scale.

Internally financed growth rate formula

We have already seen how the size of the distributor's business and the efficiency of its working capital management determine how much cash is needed to fund the business. The same principles apply in determining how much growth a distributor can finance from its own internal resources – called its potential growth capacity:

Potential growth capacity % (internally financed growth rate)
Potential growth capacity % = Net margin after tax % × Working capital turn

In other words, assuming the distributor is trying to maximize its growth, it will apply all the profits it generates to funding its increased working capital requirements. This assumes that no dividends are paid out of the after-tax profit, but that everything is retained and therefore added to retained earnings in the balance sheet as additional shareholder funds. The distributor can of course choose to apply the capital in other ways, such as buying fixed assets, but we are looking for the theoretical maximum growth rate here. This means that all the increased capital is invested in working capital to support the increased sales. The working capital turn is the number of times the capital is used each year (ie sales divided by working capital), so multiplying the extra capital by the working capital turn gives the extra sales that are possible. Applying the formula to ABC Co (year 1) gives the following:

$$\frac{\text{Net margin after tax of } 0.15\%}{\times \text{ WC turn of 11 times}} = 1.6\%$$

This means that ABC Co can grow at 1.6 per cent in year 2 with its own resources and with the same business model. If it grows faster than that, it will run down its cash balances and push them into overdraft or will need to increase its third-party borrowings, or a combination of the two. We know (from the accounts shown in Figure 9.2) that sales in year 2 were actually 9 per cent bigger than year 1, so how did ABC Co achieve this? It did two things. First, it improved its working capital turn from 11 to 12.6 (ie 365 days/29 days). This slightly increases the growth capacity to 1.9 per cent (ie the net margin of 0.15% × 12.6 turns). Secondly, it allowed its cash balances to be reduced (and absorbed into working capital) from $401m down to $232m. This difference of $169m is partly used to increase fixed assets (net of the increase in long-term liabilities) and the rest ($152m) is also cycled through the working capital turn 12.6 times to fund a sales increase of $1,915m or 9 per cent of year 1 sales.

In other words, because its potential growth capacity was so low at the end of year 1, ABC Co has had to run its cash reserves down to fund the growth it achieved. This will be fine for a couple of years but no distributor has inexhaustible supplies of cash in its balance sheet. It will run into the buffers after another couple of years and that source of growth funding will no longer be available to it. In many industries, the bigger distributors have become public companies with access to the capital markets to fund both their organic growth and their acquisitions to bolt on growth. The price of tapping the capital markets is the high cost of adhering to listing require-ments and the extraordinary level of public (ie analyst) scrutiny, which demands the highest standards of management to optimize the business model. The returns generated by ABC Co would not pass muster, with its returns on capital (ROIC) below its cost of capital (WACC) and its ROCE below that generally available from putting the funds in the bank. If ABC Co wants to grow in the next several years, it needs to continue improving its business model, especially its net profitability. Perhaps growth will bring its own profitability rewards as economies of scale kick in.

Economies of scale – profitability

There is considerable evidence that the activities of a distributor benefit from economies of scale as the fixed costs become spread over a larger volume of business. Some of the costs of a distributor vary directly with sales – which accountants term 'variable costs' – that is, costs such as sales commissions. However, most costs are fixed costs, which is really an accountants' misno-mer for stepped costs. Virtually all the IT systems, warehousing, logistics, product management and marketing costs are costs that increase in steps as investments in additional capacity are made. The key to realizing economies of scale is to make sure that capacity is fully utilized before incurring the additional costs of increasing it. Even a delay of six months in stepping up capacity is six months of operating at or near to maximum capacity, which is where the economies of scale lie.

Figure 10.1   Profile of how contribution margin and fixed costs interact as sales increase

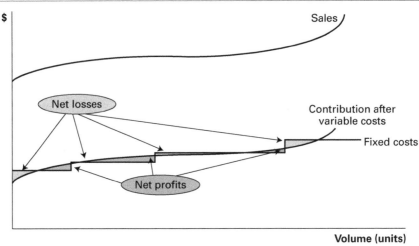

Take a look at Figure 10.1, which shows fixed costs stepping up as volume increases compared to the smooth increase in contribution from revenues after deducting variable costs. The interaction of these two profiles is the generation of alternate net losses and net profits as the contribution moves above fixed costs and then is overtaken as fixed costs step up again. This example, which is a simplified version of a real distributor's experience, suggests a business model that is fluctuating above and below break-even. Every time the business looks as if it has moved into profit by growing revenues, management invests in increasing capacity that incurs another set of fixed costs that swing the operation back into a loss. Look at what could happen if management were to operate the business with a delayed investment strategy, as shown in Figure 10.2.

Apart from the initial period, the business model remains in profit with the same stepped increases in fixed costs. The key to this strategy is delaying making the investments that increase fixed costs until *after* revenue growth has pushed up the contribution to above the new level of fixed costs. This means that the business may need to operate under stress for a while as it runs at close to capacity for a number of months (or years), but management needs to see this as the way to generate the returns on previous investments. Most management teams naturally tend to focus on the future, building the business case for growth and increased investment. But in distributors, management teams need to be just as focused on the past, ensuring that they deliver on past promises of improved returns. This is a vital strategy in

Figure 10.2   Profile of how contribution margin and fixed costs interact with delayed investment strategy

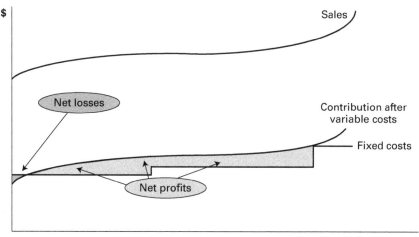

the low-net-margin business model that typifies most distributors. We have seen net profitability jump dramatically from less than 1 per cent of sales to over 2.25 per cent of sales through the disciplined operation of the delayed investment strategy.

It requires management to have a good strategic sense of how fast the market is changing, sound forecasting of the speed at which the distributor can grow, and a steady nerve to get the balance right. Taking this strategy too far could put a distributor at a competitive disadvantage through under-investment that might take years to recover from because of the negative effects on customer experiences.

Probably the hardest area in which to get the balance right is in committing to major IT system upgrades with their long lead-times, complex implementations and initial negative impacts on productivity. In some cases, we have seen more changes of position among the top three or four distribution players in a market caused by their relative successes (and failures) with complex integrated system implementations than by any difference in their price/availability/service-level propositions.

Interestingly, management teams find that they can learn some useful lessons from operating their business under the stress of working at or near full capacity. They find out which members of their teams thrive under high pressure and which wilt and let performance suffer. Often, valuable innovations are developed to enable the business to go the extra mile with the current resources and capacity; inventory turns a little faster, resources are allocated more carefully to optimum suppliers or product categories or customers, and poor-performing products and categories are terminated earlier. We have seen processes become more streamlined by the order processing, warehousing and product management teams as they work to cut out activities that waste their own time, in efforts to relieve pressure on themselves.

However, management needs to be able to recognize the symptoms of burnout and ensure that the new investment or additional capacity is on stream before the pressures put high performance into reverse. In addition, management needs to judge how much effort the investment is going to require in terms of change management. We mentioned earlier the impact that systems implementations can have and these often impose huge burdens on process teams when they are implemented or upgraded. The benefits of these investments often lie in the fact that they require fundamental changes in processes, with steep learning curves, accompanied by shifts in the burden of work from back office to front office teams. Changing systems and processes while operating at full capacity is not to be recommended and can be compared to changing the engines on an A380 while in mid-flight!

Indeed, managing growth dynamics can be seen as a continuous exercise in change management and it is often the 'softer' human aspects of change that are the hardest to get right. One of the critical success factors in managing change is to inculcate a solid understanding of the business model and the planned impact of changes among the people directly affected. We have seen too many instances of teams undergoing significant changes in their roles and working practices without any real understanding of the objective. Equally we have seen the real benefits of involving these same people in exploring ways to achieve the step change in performance required and gaining both commitment to the change and the additional insights and innovations that could come only from those people that have first-hand experience. People are invariably the critical factor in realizing economies of scale and giving them an informed role in achieving business improvements will usually achieve more than simply 'managing by the numbers'.

Economies of scale – working capital management

There are some significant advantages to working capital management in operating a larger-scale operation. In inventory, buffer stocks can become a smaller proportion of the inventory-holding requirement as the larger distributor benefits from priority in stock replenishment from its suppliers. For the A and B lines (the high-volume lines), orders from large distributors will comprise one or more truckloads, which make for easier and faster scheduling for suppliers than part truckloads. These factors combine to enable the larger distributor to run at higher sales to inventory ratios, which is another way of saying that it can operate at higher inventory turn ratios for the same or lower risk of stock-outs.

In managing all the elements of working capital, increased scale increases the likelihood that investments in IT and operating systems can be made to pay out. For example, it is only the largest distributors that can generate a return on 'warehouse in the dark' operations. These are highly automated facilities where the physical placing and retrieval of product is handled by robots (ie with no need to have the lights on) governed by sophisticated algorithms that decide where to put each SKU according to the frequency and volumes of orders to be picked. These systems constantly appraise when it is worth moving SKU items around as demand for them rises and falls, and can rely on computer memory rather than a system for layout organization. (Imagine the chaos if 30 pickers were working in a warehouse that is reorganized several times a week – but this is effectively what a robotic system can do.) Other systems can be deployed to increase the efficiency of credit control, credit management and billing to improve the management of accounts receivable. Equivalent systems can improve the management of payables balances, ensuring that all credit notes are claimed, vendor credit balances are maximized and promotions are exploited to the full.

These systems are expensive capital investments that can only be justified if amortized across hundreds of millions of dollars' worth of business, but they can generate significant efficiencies in working capital turns. Such systems do not completely replace the need for human judgement and management experience. We have seen several instances where the lack of these human skills has negated the benefits of some major investments. For example, the power of these systems can tempt the distributor to increase the number of vendors, product lines and SKUs in its efforts to promote growth. However, each additional SKU brings a dimension of cost and working capital that dilutes the overall efficiency of the distributor's business model. In our turnaround projects, one of the first areas in which we can find quick wins is to eliminate the bottom 10 per cent of products and vendors. This can release working capital and other resources that would be more effectively redeployed to the 'sleepers' and 'winners' discussed earlier.

The number of locations at which a distributor holds inventory is another factor that can undermine financial scale. Each separate inventory location multiplies the number of buffer stocks required and can render the biggest distributor little more efficient than the local player of equivalent size. There is a constant shift in the balance of costs between shipping and storage, reflected in the trend to centralize or localize distribution operations at any one time. This is a complex calculation, but the distributor seeking to grow should be wary of using additional locations as a key plank in its growth strategy. We would need compelling evidence that sales could not be serviced from a central location before allowing an additional stocking point to be added to a distributor's operations. Vendors are wise to the costs they incur of serving multiple ship-to points and will penalize a distributor financially if it has to drop to more than one distribution location.

Risks of growth – diseconomies of scale

Growth brings its own complexities, which can become diseconomies of scale. These are related to the coordination and control of an operation that is handling millions or even billions of individual transactions. Complexity can hide the issues in the distributor that are holding it back. Answers to key questions such as which customers and which products are delivering the best returns become elusive, hidden in the mass of data and information about thousands of products and customers. Layers of managers are needed to coordinate teams within acceptable spans of control. Each additional SKU, product, product line, supplier, customer, customer segment, service offering and location adds another dimension of complexity as well as incremental growth.

Managers of distributors that have grown successfully keep their focus on the basics of the business model. They use the measures we have covered in this Part of the book and they make sure that each of their subordinates understands how his or her actions can affect the performance of the business model. Success in distribution comes from understanding the dynamics of running a business in which profit is a small number between two very large numbers and that managing both earn and turn is equally important.

Understanding the distribution landscape

11

Introduction

In every sector, suppliers are challenged to define their optimal go-to-market model – one that maximizes market access at the lowest cost and harnesses the most responsive distribution partners, willing and able to support brand building while able to execute on strategic and tactical plans. Among the many decisions involved in achieving this channel nirvana is determining the right number and combination of distributors for the supplier. The first steps in resolving these issues are to understand the distribution landscape and take an informed view as to how that landscape may evolve over the medium term. The distribution landscape maps the relevant distributors in terms of the brands, volumes and categories handled and the final-tier partners and segments serviced, ideally with related volumes. The landscape defines the marketing, sales, logistical, financial and operational capabilities of these distributors and evaluates their likely level of engagement and degree of fit with the strategic intent of the supplier.

As we have seen over the preceding chapters, just because the supplier wants to do business with a distributor there is no guarantee that this interest will be reciprocated by the distributor. It will take a compelling distribution partner value proposition to secure market access via the preferred distributors, and part of that proposition is the well-rationalized answer to the question, 'How many and which other distributors will be appointed?' While we cannot provide a definitive guide to addressing these issues for every sector and situation, we can point out some reasonably consistent patterns in the way distribution landscapes evolve that should help you.

Typical landscape evolution

Distributors typically exist in sectors to meet the capacity requirements of the major suppliers and respond to the needs of the final tier serving the market. Once the volumes in the market's major categories can deliver economies of scale, distributors emerge. This can be because existing players move in or across from adjacent sectors and categories, or because the volume players in the final tier, which may have already been servicing the smaller players, establish a distributor focus. Where the supply side of the sector is relatively concentrated, distributors also tend to be relatively low in number.

Suppliers tend to want to deal with the fewest number of distributors that can assure them of market access to all the segments they intend to reach. This bias is driven by the need to ensure there is enough business going through each distributor to motivate high levels of focus and attention on that supplier's brands and products. For example, if a supplier has around 15 per cent market share and appoints eight distributors, each distributor will have less than 2 per cent share, and as shares will not be equal, some distributors may have well under 1 per cent. At these levels of business, none of the distributors is going to regard the supplier as strategic and will not allocate much resource, sales focus, marketing attention or management interest to it. However, if the supplier limits its distributors to, say, three, then each distributor will have something around 5 per cent share of the market. It may be that the supplier will be able to access the bulk of the market through these three distributors, but will not be accessing some of the more specialist final-tier players. The options are to find a specialist distributor, allocate those segments uniquely to one of the three distributors (with support to ensure they address that part of the market) or to serve those players direct (which may or may not be an economically feasible option). It can help if there are specialist products for this part of the market, and these can be restricted to only the distributor that's focused on the segment. Without this, the supplier may need to steer specific accounts to that distributor and establish some form of accreditation criteria to qualify that distributor to service them (such as requiring dedicated product management or sales resources).

It is rare for a supplier to want to appoint only a single distributor, as this effectively hands considerable relationship power to that distributor. The supplier would be entirely dependent on the performance of that distributor for its own market volumes and penetration – not a healthy situation. An exclusive distributor can also abuse its power by setting final-tier prices that suit its margin goals, but may not suit the supplier's volume goals. Appointing even two distributors will dramatically improve the supplier's ability to keep them both in line, and offer its final-tier partners a healthier supply chain. Appointing three distributors improves the situation further and can protect the supplier from one of its distributors losing focus or generally underperforming in any way. The other two distributors can carry the run rate while the situation is addressed or a new distributor appointed.

As the business grows and segments, drawing in new distributors, a supplier will need to manage its market access by ensuring that it is always working with the best of breed distributors, capable of delivering growth, responsive final-tier service and able to manage the capacity of business expected. From time to time, suppliers will need to groom their distributor set, removing poor performers and appointing others that have demonstrated stronger potential. This process is not entirely in the hands of the supplier, as distributors may make strategic choices as to the final-tier segments served or categories carried on their line card, which could conflict with the supplier's intentions. There may also be merger and acquisition (M&A) activity, possibly affecting two of the supplier's appointed distributors. Left unaddressed, the supplier will find it has too much of its market access concentrated in the hands of the newly merged entity, forcing a move to appoint a new distributor. It is not unusual for a supplier to be aware of the possible M&A dynamics in the market and move to influence the outcomes to suit its own goals, brokering the right conversations and threatening not to renew distributor contracts should the parties act in a way that is counter to the supplier's goals. Most contracts contain a provision that it would be terminated should there be a change of ownership, to give real teeth to such threats.

Consolidation in the distributor tier tends to accelerate when sector growth slows, margins decline or categories and final tiers sub-segment, increasing the complexity of the business and destroying the economies of scale at current volumes. At this point, you may see increasing specialization from the existing distributors, looking to increase margins through a focus strategy, and possibly buying up the relevant parts of other distributors. Suppliers find that this aligns with their own strategy, ensuring they have distributors with the critical mass to reach key segments of the market. Alternatively, suppliers may find that their distributors are now too concentrated and one or more additional distributors are required to ensure no one player has the whip hand.

The supplier will need to be close to the distribution landscape to ensure it understands the capabilities offered by each distributor with which it works, and the rate at which they are differentiating themselves from each other. With distributors building platforms and automating processes to enable the final tier to configure, specify, check availability, etc, the final tier may limit themselves to the fewest distributors that can best meet their needs.

Be prepared for appointed distribution partners to constantly complain that the supplier is 'over-distributed', which is an expression of their desire for their suppliers to limit the number of distributors with which they are competing for share of each supplier's volumes. In our experience this accusation will be made whenever there is more than one appointed distributor!

How to get the best from distribution strategy 12

Building and leveraging distribution partnerships

As an important route to market, distribution provides access to the final tier of partners (dealers, resellers, retailers, etc) that supply the end-user market. Each distributor represents a strategic relationship, one that is built up over time to become a genuine partnership. Many suppliers use the term 'customer' when thinking and talking about their distributors. We believe this to be a mistake as it oversimplifies the value exchange between supplier and distributor – any vendor that thinks its job is done when it has sold products into a distributor will not keep its distributors for long. It is essential to adopt the mind set of 'sell through' rather than 'sell to'. Both parties share in the process of moving products to the final tier. In fact, the supplier wants more than just market access: it wants the distributor to help build sales, develop brand awareness, grow market share and embed its positioning in its targeted final-tier partners. It needs the distributor to focus on its products and actively promote their sale through whatever combination of market education, product management, marketing, promotion and competitive selling is required. The supplier may also want the distributor to take on one or more of the activities mentioned in Chapter 4 on its behalf. The supplier needs to build deep relationships with its distributors to achieve all this and grow their mutual business. While there may appear to be obvious goal alignment in this mission, building the relationship requires the supplier to think widely about all the aspects of the commercial relationship it wants to build with its distributors.

To the distributor, the supplier and its products are not remotely interesting in or of themselves. The distributor sees them simply as a means to its strategic and commercial ends, which we know are earning and turning products to create value. The salient attributes of the product as the end-customer sees them are only of relevance to the distributor in persuading it that your end-customer demand will be higher than for your competitors' equivalent products. In other words, the better mousetrap is only better to the distributor if that means customers are going to be demanding more of it from the distributor's final-tier customers. Even if you don't have the best mousetrap, you can still be the distributor's preferred mousetrap supplier if you can convince the distributor that it will make the most money doing business with you. This may be because, as the supplier, you are prepared to spend more on stimulating customer awareness and brand preference to drive higher revenues, or you are prepared to allow the distributor to make a higher gross margin, or maybe fund a dedicated sales person on its team. Perhaps you'll allocate consignment inventory or extended credit terms so that the distributor doesn't need to invest in working capital for your products, or you'll grant it an exclusive distribution deal so that it doesn't have to compete with other distributors. Perhaps you only go to market through 'the channel' and don't have a direct sales force competing for the same business, creating channel conflict. Maybe you'll commit to this model so that the distributor knows that any investment it makes in you will be protected. Any of these propositions could be very powerful in persuading the distributor to stock and promote your particular brand and products. However, they all come at a cost to you as the supplier. You need to make sure that every cent you invest in the relationship is valued by the distributor. This is essential: you are selling a commercial relationship; you are selling your distribution channel value proposition; you are not selling your products.

The engagement process

All good commercial relationships start with understanding the other party. You must take the time and effort to find out their needs. What are their business objectives? Which objective is the greatest challenge to them? What are their points of pain? What threats and weaknesses do they face (and do they recognize them)? These questions are just as valid whether you are looking to gain a listing or to build your business with a distributor. They form the first stage of your engagement process (see Figure 12.1).

Figure 12.1 Distributor engagement process

It is essential to understand and analyse your intended distributor partner's strategy. You must be able to position your relationship in that context, showing how you are going to help it achieve its objectives. We have seen countless suppliers waste their time by failing to grasp this simple point and act on it, for example:

- suppliers basing their pitches on enabling the distributor to broaden its range just as the distributor declares its intent to rationalize its ranges and offer best-of-breed to its customers;

- suppliers focusing on sales volumes (of their low-margin products) when the distributor is struggling to get above break-even;

- suppliers failing to mention the potential of their higher-end products to sweeten margins;

- suppliers only mentioning in passing the enormous end-user marketing campaign they are about to unleash;

- distributors with capital constraints looking to grow and failing to understand that the supplier is offering extended credit as part of the standard terms and conditions;

- suppliers burying in the small print of their contracts any distributor-friendly terms such as price protection (protects the distributor in the event of the supplier reducing the prices in its price list) in fast-moving industries.

Most distributors are happy to share their intentions and the strategy by which they plan to achieve them. Good questioning by the supplier will uncover where the distributor feels vulnerable or under pressure: which customers are switching business to other distributors, which categories are not growing as fast as required, which are not delivering the margins expected, which markets the distributor plans to attack or develop next. You may also learn which existing suppliers are damaging their relationship with the distributor by increasing channel conflict (by selling direct, for example) or adding new distributors in the same territory.

CASE STUDY   Edrington

In the late 1980s, the Edrington Group (then Robertson and Baxter) sought to find a distributor for its premium Scotch single malt brand, Glengoyne, in France. Edrington knew that Taittinger, a major Champagne house and distributor of wines and spirits, had recently lost the distribution for Glenmorangie. For Taittinger, Glengoyne would be a margin generator and a valuable addition to the catalogue. However, Edrington was not the only suitor of the distribution power of Taittinger, and needed to be sure it could beat the other contenders. The Edrington Group quickly learnt that what Taittinger lacked and desired most of all was an upmarket Scotch blend as their own private-label brand that would be a cash generator for the company. At that time, private-label suppliers were mostly producers of low-quality cheap supermarket brands and could not deliver the quality Taittinger required. The Edrington Group quickly developed a proposal to supply Taittinger with Defender Scotch, a quality product, as part of a comprehensive distribution rights proposal that included Taittinger distributing the Glengoyne malt, which was accepted.

The Edrington Group had successfully analysed the distributor's strategy and needs, identified the opportunity to tie Taittinger to the company, developed the strategy to produce Defender and sold Taittinger a business proposal based on its total business needs rather than the narrow item, price and volume discussion on the Glengoyne malt.

The insight gained from the strategic dialogue should serve as the bedrock of your response. You now know how to position your own strategy and make the connections in terms of markets, opportunities and shared goals. You should think of the business objectives of the distributor as the coat pegs on which to hang your bespoke business case. Each objective represents a potential opportunity for you to do business together. What investments are you making or actions are you taking that will address these opportunities and how do these create value for the distributor? Are you opening new market spaces, developing new types of channel, generating new service opportunities? Are you generating additional market pull that will increase volumes or promoting some form of differentiation that will improve margins? Can you offer a more attractive distribution strategy (fewer distributors) than your competitors? Will you be reducing the inventories needed or lowering the cost-to-sell for the distributor? All these actions are potentially of interest to the distributor, but you must hold them up against the coat pegs of the distributor's objectives and make sure they are relevant.

For those opportunities that measure up, develop the strategy and tactics of your relationship plan. This is the bit that most suppliers do well. It is important to make sure that it is obvious how the strategy and tactics advance the distributor's objectives. That is the bit that most suppliers do badly. We hear all about what they are going to do, less about how it delivers the distributor's objectives.

Now you are ready to prepare and pitch your business case. This includes both the strategic and commercial dimensions. Even the most tactical distributors need to know if they should regard you as someone simply bringing them a deal or someone with whom they can partner over a sustained period to achieve their objectives. Show the distributor that you know which of its business objectives you can help it with and on which of its business measures you can help it move the needle. Use the distributor's business model as a checklist in your preparation, and mark up the impact of your proposals, for example as shown in Figure 12.2. Note that there are eight measures that the supplier is claiming will be improved for the distributor by adding its product line. Using all these in the pitch would swamp the conversation with accounting jargon. Select the one or two measures that the distributor's management team themselves focus on to make the most compelling case. ABC Co's management team would be impressed by a supplier showing how it could improve return on invested capital, their priority measure, especially if that was the key measure in their bonus plan.

CASE STUDY   Uniroyal

At one time, the Uniroyal tyre brand was distributed in Italy by a network of 22 regional distributors. Uniroyal was a premium brand competing with Pirelli and Michelin, while other, less well-known brands made up the sales in the mid and price-fighter segments. As all distributors were multi-brand, they needed well-known brands to complement their offering in the bottom two segments. Uniroyal management recognized an opportunity to secure a disproportionate share of the distributor's time, energy and resources. They sourced a cheap no-name brand and badged it as Uniroyal to sell to the distributors, shutting out competition from the low-price, high-volume end of the market. Although the margins on these products were very much lower than could be expected on the Uniroyal brand, the company gained a bigger share of the distributors' revenues, strengthened their position in distribution and protected their higher-margin products.

Figure 12.2   Example impact on a distributor's business model of adding an additional product line

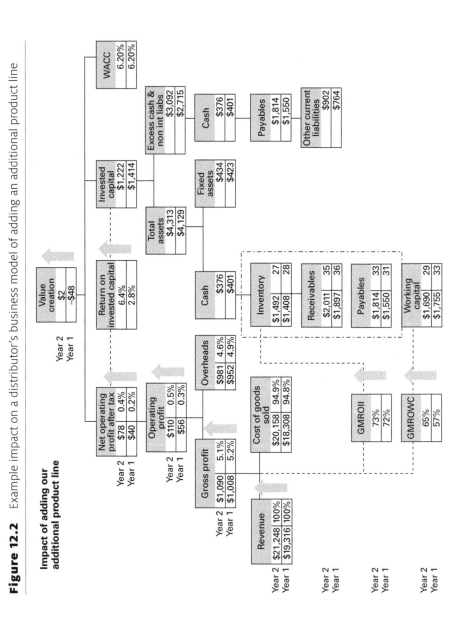

Impact of adding our additional product line

Managing the account relationship

Most distributors expect to sustain long-term relationships with their suppliers. They recognize that there is a high cost to them of switching key suppliers and will only fire a supplier if things have really broken down, both commercially and in terms of relationship management. However, there is a world of difference between being a key strategic partner, leveraging the full capability of the distributor's market access, and being just a make-weight supplier barely commanding the attention of the category manager. Some suppliers can command distribution attention simply by virtue of their market share, but without active account management, even the most strategic supplier can waste the potential of the relationship. Smaller suppliers can differentiate themselves significantly by the quality of their account management. This involves many skills, including those involved in multi-level selling, relationship building and so on. The key differentiator though is a laser-like concentration on the commercial dynamics of the relationship based on understanding the key measures that matter for the distributor and fed by good visibility of how these measures are performing on a day-to-day basis.

Managing the relationship with a distributor is a portfolio management challenge. Some products or product lines will deliver volumes, others growth and yet others high margins (see winners, losers, sleepers and traffic builders in Chapter 8). The key is to position products to deliver the measures that they are capable of impacting positively. You will never get a high-market-share product to deliver good gross margins because it will be widely distributed and frequently used to signal the distributor's own price positioning (ie that it is price competitive). However, it will draw traffic and, by working together, you can develop strategies for improving the connect rate to higher-margin products (be open-minded to building traffic for a non-competing complementary supplier if necessary).

With strategic relationships between supplier and distributor, it is helpful to apply what is known as the 'reverse bow-tie' or 'diamond' model to achieve the degree of alignment necessary to drive real mutual economic benefit. Look at Figure 12.3, which shows the ways the two organizations can line up: on the left is the traditional model, looking like a bow-tie, where everything is channelled through the two primary points of contact (the respective account managers), with the very high potential for bottlenecks and miscommunication. On the right-hand side is the reverse bow-tie model where the account managers' role is to orchestrate the alignment of the key

Figure 12.3   Supplier–distributor relationship models

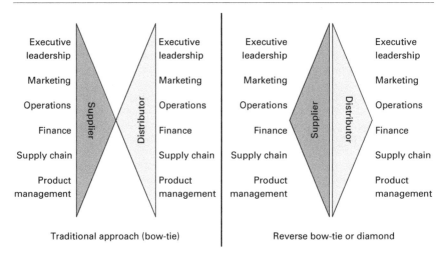

Traditional approach (bow-tie)   Reverse bow-tie or diamond

functions in their two organizations, so that operations talks to operations, supply chain to supply chain, etc. The account managers act as facilitators and coordinators, ensuring the top issues on both sides are being addressed by the right people, stepping in only when needed.

Making compelling business cases

There is no substitute for tailoring your business arguments to the unique situation facing your distributor and your own position. There are some rules of thumb that can give you a head start.

If you are a market-share leader

Being a market-share leader can apply to either the supplier as a brand or a specific product or product line. There are several elements to the business case that normally apply in this situation:

- Focus on the gross margins in terms of cash (GM$s) that a market-share leader will generate, even on the relatively low GM% (gross margin as a percentage), from its high level of unit sales. Make the case that these 'bankable' GM$s are valuable in covering a significant proportion of the distributor's fixed overheads. This argument may not cut much ice with the category buyer whose performance measures include hitting a target GM%, but as a market-share leader you should have a relationship higher up the distributor's management structure where there will be recognition that this is a valid argument.

- Switch the focus from gross margins to contribution margins (% and $s). As a major brand in the category, the cost of selling your product will be lower than for a less well-known brand. The trade channels will be benefiting from your end-customer marketing activity and ordering familiar products from the distributor, which requires very little sales time and marketing effort on its part. This should be reflected in the notional contribution margin if not actually in the way any one distributor measures its contribution margins. Similarly, the larger volumes of well-known brands and products typically have a lower cost-to-ship from a logistics perspective and incur lower rates of return and associated (expensive) reverse logistics costs. The same business argument extends to pre- and post-support, with few if any demands being made by the trade channels for help on products with which they are very familiar. Even the costs of new product introductions will be amortized over the higher volumes, reducing the cost-to-sell per unit to negligible costs.

- Switch the focus from return-on-sales to return-on-asset/capital. The high volumes of market leaders usually mean that their asset turns are good, giving them above-average returns on working capital. This is the critical combined measure of 'earn and turn' for any distributor. Those products that dominate their revenues in a category need to deliver on these returns on asset/capital measures for the distributor. Many distributors set some form of turn target on their category managers, and more are now setting targets using the return on working capital measure.

These three elements will form the backbone of your business case with a distributor, so before you go in to make your case you need to do your homework. Analyse just how your portfolio of products is performing across both the measures the distributor uses today and the ones that you want it to recognize. Be able to answer for yourself questions such as:

- In each category, are our products pulling up or dragging down the key measures?

- Overall, is our brand a puller or a dragger on the distributor's business model?

- What is the value of the GM$ (or contribution$) that our brand is generating for the distributor, and what proportion of its fixed overhead costs does this represent?

- Can we show that the contribution from our products is comparatively better than our gross margins?

- What evidence can we provide of the level of connected sales and margins resulting from the traffic generated by our brand?

- How fast are our products moving through the distributor? Can we show an above-average rate of return on working capital?

- Which are our 'problem' measures and which our 'star' measures?

- Which measures matter to our distributor's senior and junior management?

If you are a smaller vendor or new entrant in a category

Smaller vendors often struggle to get attention from the senior management of the distributor, so they need to concentrate on the category manager and show just how good a job they can do of hitting the measures that matter at this level:

- Focus on the GM%. Typically, as a smaller supplier your products will be less widely distributed and you will be looking to the one or few distributors appointed to be doing more to create a market for your products. Your distributors' category managers will be struggling to hit their GM% targets, and one possible way to achieve them is to increase the proportion of sales of higher-margin products... such as yours. Few distributors are proactive in this regard and active account management will be well received if it drives up margins by putting some of your key products in the spotlight. Even the limited amount of marketing dollars you will be able to apply will have an impact if tightly targeted on the highest-margin products in your range, building revenues for you. Most categories will have one or two market-share leaders on which the distributor makes very small margins, so it looks to its third and fourth brands to make up the margin it seeks. To do this, the distributor needs to sell these second-tier brands in sufficient volumes to be able to improve the blended margin for the category. This is your opportunity. Emphasize the degree to which you have given the distributor (full or near) exclusivity on your products so it will benefit directly from all your end-user and final-tier marketing spend. Build up the support for switch-selling the top-tier brands and provide the evidence that your products are just as low cost to sell and support. If you are very small, you may need to focus on one part of the final-tier channel and concentrate your marketing (and direct the distributor's efforts) to gain traction.

- Emphasize the growth rate, especially in percentage terms. All category managers look for growth in their category and, coming off a small base, it will be easier for you to demonstrate relatively high growth rates.

- Highlight the connect rate opportunities. Most distributors make more money on the accessories than they do on the core products they attach to. But how many accessories do they sell per core product? Often less than 1 in 50. Certainly not all deals will be for end-users who require accessories, but we have seen many distributors uncover and exploit some very profitable connect rate opportunities. Your role is to help the distributor see the potential of connecting your products to the traffic builders and build some sales force and trade channel incentives around these proposals.

Summary of Part Two

Distributors are a key route to market for many sectors. Although they seem to fulfil only a few basic functions such as breaking bulk, providing credit and offering one-stop convenience to the trade channels, their pervasive presence in emerging and mature markets is testament to the value they deliver.

The distributor business model is highly challenging to get right, with its very small margins on massive volumes across tens of thousands of individual SKUs, each requiring decisions on stocking levels and reorder quantities. On top of that, the distributor needs to ensure it sells only to creditworthy customers and then get them to pay on time. It needs to find products that the final-tier channels want and then extract the best possible terms out of its suppliers, ensuring that its marketing and sales costs are predominantly covered by marketing funds from these suppliers. By doing all this, the distributor must create more value than its investors would have earned in an investment of equivalent risk.

Traditionally, distributor management controls the business by breaking the business model down into its 'earn' and 'turn' elements, but it is the combination measures (such as GMROII and GMROWC) that reveal the true financial productivity of products, categories and customer segments. More sophisticated managers are now applying the principles of value creation both to measure and to motivate their teams to focus on the levers of value in the business.

Suppliers looking to engage effectively with distributors need to develop a thorough insight into their partner's strategy and recognize that they are selling a complete business model. This model needs to deliver positive forces on the distributor's economics. The successful supplier will be able to analyse where it can deliver commercial advantage to the distributor and make the business case for commanding more of the distributor's resources. The prize for those suppliers that get it right is a cost-effective route to market that can build and sustain profitable market share across a large number of final-tier channels.

PART THREE
Managing final-tier sales and marketing channels

The roles of the final-tier channel players 13

The final-tier channel players

Although the generic term, 'final-tier channel players' may not mean anything to you, this Part focuses on the players that interact with the end customer. This can be in any capacity, including straightforward product supply such as dealers or retailers as well as the whole array of service-related players who install, set up or integrate products for the end customer. It includes the players who don't touch the product at all but can have a major influence on the customer's choice, such as architects who specify the fittings in a new house or building, or the accountant who recommends the bookkeeping package a small business should use.

Every industry uses its own language to label its different types of player, reflecting tradition, the role or simply industry jargon. Table 13.1 shows just a small selection by industry of the types of player we are covering in this Part, which may help you to recognize the players you are interested in.

You can see even from this limited selection that there is a huge range of types of players and that they can range in size from a one-person independent trader through small and medium-sized businesses up to global enterprises. Despite this large degree of variation, there is a surprisingly high degree of commonality in terms of the roles or activities that types of partners fulfil in the value chain. Because of this commonality, their business models also reflect some standard characteristics.

There are bound to be some players that are extremely specialized, and you will find that their business is simply a very pure version of the one of the models we will explore. Many of the players in any industry are, to some degree, hybrids, to meet customer demand or expectation. For example, shops selling car hi-fi systems and car alarms have found that they need to operate a service bay (usually round the back of the store) to fit systems

Table 13.1 Types of final-tier trade channel player by industry

Industry	Final-tier trade channels	Typical activities
Automotive – cars, spare parts, consumables (oil, screen wash, tyres, accessories, cleaners, etc)	Dealers	Sell, service and support cars, bikes, vans, trucks
	Workshops	Service and repair cars, bikes, vans, trucks
	Specialist repair shops	Supply and fit tyres, exhausts, brakes, clutches, etc
	Accessory shops and retail motor factors	Supply (and possibly fit) spare parts, accessories and consumables
	Garage forecourts	Supply consumables, some generic parts and cleaners
Information technology and telecommunications – hardware, software, components, switches, etc	Resellers, dealers, corporate resellers, independent software vendors (sell hardware on which their software runs)	Sell and support computers, software, telephones, etc
	Value-added dealers, value-added resellers, solution providers, service providers	Install, set up, configure IT and telecoms systems, possibly using their own specialized software or solutions
	System integrators	Specify, design, install and integrate complex IT and/or telecoms solutions
Building and construction – windows, pipes, taps, switches, boilers, radiators, burglar alarms, wood, paint, glass, tools, specialist clothing, etc	General tradespeople (such as plumbers, carpenters, decorators, glaziers, electricians, heating engineers, etc)	Supply and fit new or replacement products or systems, service and repair existing installations
	Specialist tradespeople (such as window installers, kitchen fitters, alarm installers, etc)	Design, install and integrate windows, kitchens, alarm systems, etc
	DIY superstores	Supply wide range of products
	Hardware or specialist stores	Advise and supply products, can sometimes provide or broker installation services

into customers' cars to be able to sell these aftermarket products at all. The same is true in the business world, where many businesses do not have the specialist skills to install and configure new unified communication systems.

This need to customize, install and integrate products is a major driver of the role of final-tier trade channels, whether selling to consumers (B2C) or to businesses (B2B). Once installed, most products and systems need maintaining, servicing, repairing and upgrading. Very few products, beyond fast-moving consumer goods, can be sold as stand-alone items.

The common thing we have established about the final-tier trade channels is that they play a vital enabling role in the sales process through their skills and expertise in making the product work for the end customer, ie making it a solution to the customer's needs. Let's look at their role in more detail so that, no matter which industry, you can identify the implications for either managing or working with these businesses.

The possible roles of final-tier channel players

One key point to note about the final-tier channel players is that they fulfil different roles for each of the other components of the ecosystem in which they work. For example, to a small or medium-sized business customer (let's call it 'Acme Widgets'), its IT provider ('Advanced Computing Co') may be a solution provider. Advanced Computing Co helps to work out what combination of servers, computers, storage, switches and other hardware Acme needs to run its office, network, e-mail, accounting systems, management applications and so on. Each time Microsoft upgrades its operating system, Advanced will advise Acme on whether it makes sense to upgrade or move to the cloud, and then installs and integrates the systems to work seamlessly. Advanced may also provide day-to day support and troubleshooting. It possibly won the relationship with Acme in the first place because it offers a specialist production control software that is built on Oracle's database product. So, Advance Computing Co is simultaneously:

- a customer advocate to Acme Widgets;
- a solution provider to Acme Widgets;
- a service provider to Acme Widgets;
- a reseller for various hardware suppliers like Hewlett-Packard, IBM and Cisco;

- a value-added reseller for Microsoft;
- an independent software vendor for Oracle;
- an influencing partner for the accounting software supplier.

In another example, Mr and Mrs Smith decide to do a loft conversion to create an extra bedroom with en-suite shower room. They contract with Easy Lofts to do the job for them and choose the shower and bathroom fittings that they prefer. Easy Lofts draws up a loft design and does the plans for the project. It orders in the three special loft windows, heating pipes and radiators, and subcontracts the bathroom installation to a specialist fitter, Pipes and Co. Pipes and Co points out to Mr and Mrs Smith that their first choice of fittings isn't suitable for the loft conversion and recommends an alternative that they accept. It also recommends the extractor fan and trunking required by building regulations that are installed by Easy Lofts. So Easy Lofts has been:

- a master contractor for Mr and Mrs Smith;
- a specifier for the windows, pipes and radiator vendors;
- a trade installer or reseller for the windows, pipes and radiator vendors;
- a master contractor to Pipes and Co;
- a trade reseller of the timber, plasterboard, floorboards, plaster, paint, etc.

Pipes and Co has been:

- a specifier for the shower and bathroom fittings;
- a trade installer or reseller for the shower and bathroom fittings;
- an influencer for the extractor fan and trunking vendors.

In the background, there are one or more local builders' merchants who supplied the timber, plasterboard, floorboards, plaster, paint, etc, and the shower and bathroom fittings as first-tier distributors for the suppliers of these products.

To cut through the complexity caused by the myriad of different labels used in each industry, we are going to suggest some generic roles that you should be able to recognize and apply, no matter what terminology your industry uses. We believe that there are five discrete roles (see Figure 13.1) that final-tier trade channel partners can chose to fulfil:

1 *Extension of a vendor* – essentially some form of outsourced capability, usually handling logistics or back-office processes. The partner can take on some of the business risk in the activity, such as providing financial

Figure 13.1   Roles for final-tier trade channel players

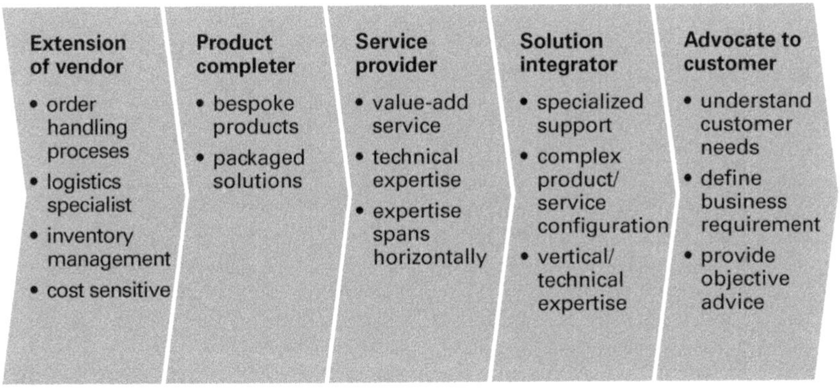

Extension of vendor	Product completer	Service provider	Solution integrator	Advocate to customer
• order handling proceses • logistics specialist • inventory management • cost sensitive	• bespoke products • packaged solutions	• value-add service • technical expertise • expertise spans horizontally	• specialized support • complex product/ service configuration • vertical/ technical expertise	• understand customer needs • define business requirement • provide objective advice

credit insurance for large capital purchases, or simply be paid a fee for operational activities such as for freight forwarding or logistics.

2 *Product completer* – providing some degree of customization of the supplier's product for individual customers or for whole customer segments. The product completer role can be as simple as opening the box and adding the local type of power supply cable and local language manuals, before shipping to the end customer.

3 *Service provider* – providing any of a huge range of services such as design, pre- and post-sales support, installation, onsite configuration, maintenance, financing and so on. Depending on the product, the service provided can be minimal, such as helping to select the right product for the customer's needs, through to fundamental such as constructing the conservatory base for the prefabricated windows and doors provided by the conservatory supplier. We tend to characterize the service provider in 'horizontal' terms, that is, its skills and capabilities are related to the product rather than the customer. This is in contrast to the...

4 *Solution integrator* – which applies customer insight (vertical skills) and knowledge to render a solution fit for the unique needs of the customer. A large solution integrator can cover a wide range of customer types, perhaps with different divisions or sections within its business, whereas a small integrator may specialize in just one type of customer. The critical difference between the service provider and the solution integrator is their orientation, with the latter often helping the customer to make several products and services work as a seamless whole (think of a master contractor commissioning a new production line in a customer's existing

factory) in comparison to the service providers ensuring that their particular products work (the electricians installing the control systems and the riggers setting up the conveyor belts and operations stations). The service provider needs to make the product work to the specifications agreed; the solution integrator has to make the whole solution work for the end customer.

5 *Advocate to customer* – is the role that has a bigger impact the more its skills and knowledge are needed to specify and select solutions. These are players whose roles have become highly specialized and as a result are needed only intermittently. Examples of this role include the independent financial adviser, which helps its customers choose the best life insurance and pension plans to meet financial objectives and risk tolerances; the strategic consultancy that helps its customers select the best IT systems to support its strategy; the doctor who prescribes the best pharmaceutical remedy for an ailment; and the accountants who recommend the best accounting package for use by its small business customers.

You will have detected that there is shift in orientation across these roles, from completely supplier-oriented at the extension of a vendor end through to completely customer-oriented at the customer advocate end. This has a very big bearing on the business models associated with these roles. You can think of these roles being defined in terms of the knowledge value chain or core competencies that they require to be effective in their role (see Figure 13.2).

In most sectors, partners can fulfil several of these roles seamlessly and, in some cases, may fulfil all but one of the roles – it would be too great a conflict of interest to encompass both ends of this value chain in the one player. Most often the divide comes between: 1) the product completer and service provider, where the service provider role is essentially 'on the customer's side'; or 2) the service provider and the solution integrator, where the service provider role is 'on the supplier's side'.

Note that even in the first of these situations, such as, say, an automotive workshop (like Halfords), where the service provider is working to give the customer the right parts at the right price, it is very much in the parts suppliers' interests to train and support the service provider in the correct installation of their products. The smart supplier would want to make sure that the service provider understands its product range and how its products are differentiated from those of its competitors. It may even want to offer the non-brand-specific training needed to become a competent

Figure 13.2 Final-tier roles defined in terms of the knowledge value chain or core competencies

These roles...

| Extension of vendor | Product completer | Service provider | Solution integrator | Advocate to customer |

...are defined by the knowledge value-chain or core competencies

| Knowledge of the product's market and supply chain

Process management knowledge | Knowledge to configure the product | Knowledge to make the product work and to get the best out of the product | Knowledge to make the product work with other products and to make the product work within the customer's organization | Knowledge of the customer's requirements and which products meet those needs |

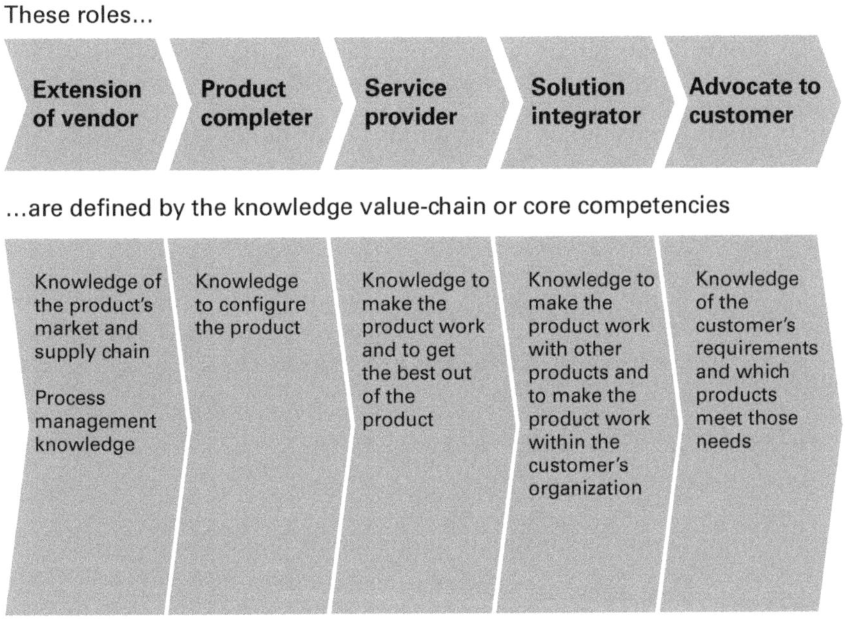

mechanic in an attempt to win share of mind and, with it, share of recommendation. The big pharmaceutical companies seek to influence prescribing doctors with seminars on the latest techniques in treating, say, cardiovascular thrombosis.

Matching channel roles to channel players

As we explore each role you will probably find that you can quickly map the roles to the types of partner in your industry. Be prepared to find the customer fulfilling some of the partner roles; this is especially frequent in the B2B context. For example, in the small and medium business sector, very few information systems are properly integrated. Customers are left to work out for themselves what systems they need (they are their own advocate) and rarely get the best out of what they pay for. Some computer dealers have recognized the opportunity and positioned themselves to fulfil the customer advocate and solution integrator roles, usually by selecting a particular segment of customers in which they can specialize and become expert. The two market structures look something like those shown in Figure 13.3.

Figure 13.3   Traditional and new final-tier roles in the computer products market

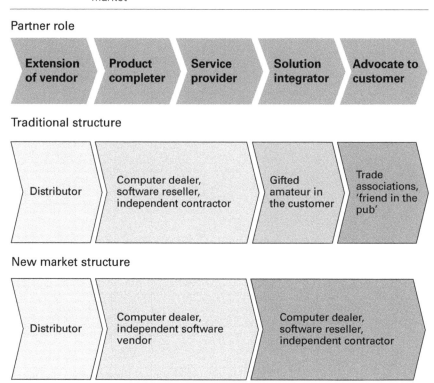

In many industries, channel players have had to 'switch sides' (from the supplier side to the customer side) like this to survive. As the industry grows and matures, two things happen: the number of service providers multiplies and customers start demanding a lot more integration in exchange for their custom. The service provider finds it is stuck in the middle, with declining margins for what have become almost commodity services and suffering from a lack of ability to compete for the higher-end work demanded by customers. The service provider either has to become the price-leader in commodity services (through scale efficiencies) or 'switch sides' and become specialized enough to be able to command compensation from the customer for higher-value-added integration work, ie become solution integrators. Compensation becomes highly or entirely customer determined through negotiation of the scope of the work and the degree of expertise required.

Different roles command different compensation models

Although ultimately all final-tier compensation is paid for by the end customer, the structure of partner roles in an industry can appear to fly in the face of this obvious fact. Take the example of 'trade discount', where a supplier gives the trade channel a discount off its list price to end customers. Many suppliers operate a 'Preferred Partner Programme' in which partners that meet certain criteria have access to direct and indirect discounts (such as higher levels of pre-sales support) that other partners do not.

In large distribution structures, with perhaps many thousands of trade channel players competing for business with few differences between them, these trade discounts become the basis of differentiation. Bigger players with bigger trade discounts (secured through their greater volumes) can afford to pass on part of their discount to the end customer – known as 'passing it to the street' – and win business through offering lower prices. Smaller players are unable to match these prices and may abandon that supplier as uneconomic. Note how the whole emphasis of this compensation conversation is between the trade player and the supplier.

Suppliers have found that this situation, if left unchecked, will damage their distribution network by eliminating all but a few price-led partners. Their ability to launch new products and install their products in specialist segments of the market is destroyed by this. Their response has been either to make it harder for the trade channel to pass its discount on to the street or to move away from volume and recognize accredited skills and competencies as the basis of discounts.

The typical approach to making the trade discount 'stick' in the channel (as margin) has been to make part or all of the discount uncertain, so the trade cannot afford to give too much away in case it doesn't earn it in the first place. Sometimes called 'black box' discounts, there are all sorts of ways suppliers have found to create uncertainty:

- Giving the trade channel discount in the form of a rebate or 'back-end margin' rather than built into the price as 'front-end margin'. The rebate has to be earned based on hitting some targets during a period (annual, half yearly, quarterly, etc), so unless the target is achieved the trade player cannot be sure it has earned the rebate. These targets can be sales volumes, but can also be end-customer satisfaction scores or quality ratings.

- Awarding bonuses after the end of a trading period. These bonuses can be pre-announced with a scheme of rules, or simply announced after the end of the period as a 'reward' for exceptional performance. Care must be taken not to become too predictable or else the trade will start factoring the expected bonus back into its street prices.

- Ranking partners based on performance in a period and giving different discounts to the different tiers. Performance can be defined in many ways other than sales volumes, such as accounts opened or quality and customer satisfaction ratings. Partners will not know until after the trading period into which tier they have qualified, so cannot afford to give away the higher-level discounts.

The accreditation model is where the vendor compensates the final tier for investing in the competences and capabilities necessary to implement solutions (thus enabling sales of their products). In low-tech sectors, the accreditation can apply to factors such as compliance with operating guidelines, health and safety compliance, basic technical qualifications, adherence to trade association business practices, etc. Even the most straightforward of products will benefit from the sales and installation teams being trained in how to sell and install the product. In high-tech sectors, the need for accreditation is more obvious. Cisco led the way in the IT sector by identifying a small number of strategic capabilities (networking, unified communications, etc) allowing its partners to secure trade discounts on relevant products provided they had the required number of trained engineers to qualify under its tiered partner programme. This meant that size no longer had any price advantage and it enabled Cisco to promote its channel as the one best qualified to serve customers' business needs.

The alternative approach to these models is to pay for functions or activities performed by the final tier. At a very basic level, this may simply be in the form of the supplier paying an extra 0.5 or 1 per cent discount for receiving 'sell out' data, reporting in some prescribed level of detail about the sales made to the end customer. In some sectors, this approach has evolved to cover many functions and levels of performance in a blend with more traditional discount structures, as shown in the box, Fee for function.

Fee for function

For many years, a major film and home entertainment distributor had compensated its channel partners in Germany, the UK and Spain by giving discounts and rebates based entirely on sales volumes. These

Figure 13.4   Illustrative compensation structure in a 'fee for function' model

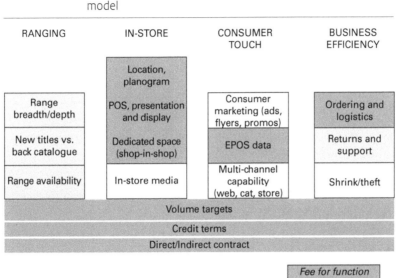

were either in the form of on-invoice discounts or applied as month-end, quarter-end and annual rebates. Although the distributor had tried to persuade its channel partners to carry out a series of activities to the best of their ability, it had no mechanism for recognizing and rewarding such performance.

The distributor took the bold move to change its approach and decided to reallocate the available compensation by paying partners for discrete activities based on the partners' ability to deliver on four dimensions: Ranging, In-store, Consumer touch and Efficiency, in addition to the basic compensation model (see Figure 13.4):

- Although volume targets remained, they would be flexible to reflect individual partners' performance rather being a set unearned percentage.

- Other elements such as the partners' merchandising, display of products and point-of-sale displays would be rewarded on a fee-for-function basis.

- Some activities, such as consumer marketing, would remain outside the normal terms and conditions and be paid for through discretionary marketing development funds that were allocated based on the merit of the activity.

- The final group of activities, the hygiene factors, were considered so fundamental to the role of the distributor that no remuneration would be offered or indeed needed.

The effect of this approach is to give the film and home entertainment distributor much more control over its channel, paying for what it wants the channel to do and pulling compensation away from partners that simply choose not to deliver. These hybrid types of compensation arrangements will become more common as the spotlight increasingly falls on ensuring that all distribution expense is making a positive contribution to business performance.

However, even this approach still positions the whole compensation negotiation between the supplier and the trade partner, with the customer excluded. Why is this? Well, the answer lies mainly in the fact that the supplier needs the final-tier channel to 'complete' its offer. The final tier is fulfilling all those needs we highlighted earlier, making the product available when customers want it, where they want it, configured the way they want, working the way they want in their business or home. These activities come at a cost and the supplier recognizes that it needs to compensate the channel for doing essential work in taking its products to market, so we can expect the supplier to define that part of the compensation in some way. However, this is not the complete offering the final-tier channel provides to the customer. Each sale is a project and, as such, the customer should define the scope of specific services that it wants from the final-tier channel.

What if the customer does not know what to ask for? For example, would you know what should be done to service your car after two year's ownership? Here the supplier (Ford, Nissan, GM, etc) steps in and defines the two-year, 20,000-mile service that is required and encourages its dealers to offer a prescribed price. So, what we have is the picture of compensation shown in Figure 13.5. At the top of the picture are our familiar partner roles. Below these, the business model shows the progression from supplier-related activities, defined by contracts between the supplier and its trade channel, to customer-defined activities where the customer is seeking to outsource work and risk to secure a certain level of performance. The price paid by the customer is directly related to the value and performance received or risk defrayed. Continuing our car example, you pay more at a franchised (or authorized) dealer than a workshop around the corner, because you know that the people working on your car are technically bang up to date on your model and should something go wrong after the service, you can take it back and expect them to sort it out, no questions asked. You are also sure that your warranty is not invalidated. You will get the car back from the service with a free valet and the use of a car while yours is with the dealer. You, the customer, are paying for all this and if you don't get it, you'll go to another dealer. At some point in the car's life, however, your performance and risk-management requirements might change. The owner of an older car needs someone who can pop round and get it started on the first frosty morning of winter because he is only around the corner and doesn't expect you to book it in two weeks in advance. This is a different performance requirement and it comes at a different price. Note that the customer is in control of the value/compensation equation now. This is shown in the bottom part of Figure 13.5, with the supplier paying for those activities it needs the channel to fulfil and the customer defining bespoke packages of value and risk management.

Figure 13.5   Business model and compensation model for different partner roles

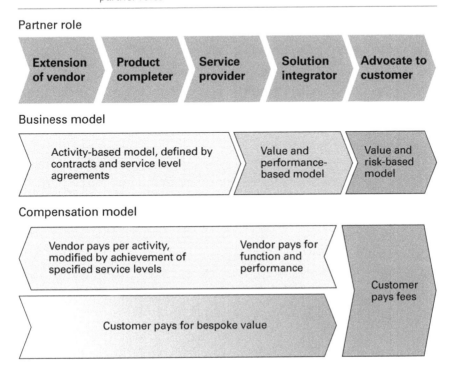

Partner role

| Extension of vendor | Product completer | Service provider | Solution integrator | Advocate to customer |

Business model

| Activity-based model, defined by contracts and service level agreements | Value and performance-based model | Value and risk-based model |

Compensation model

Vendor pays per activity, modified by achievement of specified service levels

Vendor pays for function and performance

Customer pays fees

Customer pays for bespoke value

Customer advocates and sell-with players

We have hinted earlier in this chapter about the role of 'sell-with' players, particularly in the role of advocate to customer. This terminology is, of course, that used by suppliers as it defines the role in relation to taking products to market. As the name implies, these players do not handle the product or play any role in getting the product physically from the supplier to the customer, work that is done by the sell-through players. However, these sell-with players can be crucial to the selling process in some sectors. This is usually the case where customers are ill-equipped or even incapable of defining what they want. You might think of it as a technical purchase and this applies in both the business and consumer markets. Architects and interior designers specify the products and often the brand of product to be installed in their designs. IT consultants specify the hardware and software architecture needed by businesses and are often asked to specify the products and brands required to build and implement it.

So, if the sell-with partner doesn't 'touch' the product, how does its business model work? In Figure 13.5, we indicate that the customer pays fees, which is the dominant compensation model, because it is the customer who has initiated the purchasing process and gone to the player it believes best understands its needs and budget. This creates a challenge for the supplier who is now dependent on the customer advocate to recognize and specify or recommend its products over those of its competitors. The supplier's opening comes from the customer advocate's need to be sure it knows of the best-of-breed alternatives, new technologies and materials, etc, and to be sure it knows which problems each of the alternatives is best configured to solve. So, the door is open to credible suppliers to inform and educate the customer advocate and suppliers should manage these relationships in much the same way as a key sell-through account. This means that the supplier should establish regular meetings, promote discussion of current projects and prospects, provide strong information flow in the form preferred by the customer advocate and generally do all it can to ensure that it is positioned in the customer advocate's thinking as top of mind, best of breed and a useful source of answers to technical problems.

All of this can be described as influencing sell-with partner behaviour, but can the supplier go further and reward the customer advocate, to create a commercial influence on recommendation? Care is needed to avoid compromising the customer advocate and placing it in a conflict of interest (see the case study on the financial services industry). Bearing in mind that reward can be both financial and non-financial, the answer is almost certainly yes.

Familiar strategies are to provide resources that are valuable to the customer advocate, such as:

- free technical help, demonstration and 'extra' products that enable the advocate to do its job at a lower cost;
- training that goes beyond simple product knowledge, which displaces cost for the customer advocate;
- broker introductions and leads sourced through the supplier's own networking, marketing and sales activities;
- conferences and other events at attractive locations that serve as reward and motivation opportunities to the people of the customer advocate at no cost to its own business.

In some sectors, suppliers have provided direct compensation for introductions or referrals that have led to sales. Here, there are enormous challenges in measuring the degree of influence of the sell-with partner and even attributing a sale to a partner at all if the influencer is not in an existing relationship.

CASE STUDY   Financial services industry – who pays the final tier?

The financial services industry is an interesting case, with many financial advisers (ie the trade channel) working for the customer but compensated through commissions paid by the suppliers (the pension funds and life assurance companies) on the products the advisers recommend and sell. This has long been recognized to be a situation open to abuse as there is clearly an inherent conflict of interest. Some advisers have solved this conflict by acting only in return for fees paid by the customer. Others have tied themselves exclusively, and overtly, to the supplier they believe to offer best-of-breed products – their compensation comes in the form of commissions earned on the products they recommend. It tends to be the more sophisticated customers who prefer to pay the fees to an independent financial adviser, as they need sound advice and expect to source their products from a wide variety of suppliers. However, surely it is the unsophisticated customers who need even more advice? Quite possibly yes, but they are unwilling to pay for it when it is made an overt fee. They do pay for their advice, but because it is wrapped up in the overall price of the product, they believe it comes to them free of charge. As a result, many people are horrified when they try to exit from a policy part of the way through its term and find that most of the money paid into it for the first 18 months has gone on commission payments and the policy is worth much less than the monthly payments made to date. That's rather late to find out the price of the advisory service they have received.

Applying this framework to your industry sector or channel

You may find the terms 'service provider' or 'solution integrator' hard to relate to the particular types of channel player with which you are familiar, and it can seem rather over the top to describe the classic trades of plumber or kitchen fitter, etc, in these terms. Don't be put off. Remember these are *role* descriptions, not *player* descriptions, and they are deliberately set in terms of the customer's context, not the supplier's. In our experience, it is very helpful to think in terms of these roles as it can help suppliers clarify their channel strategies or go-to-market models. Indeed, Hewlett-Packard overhauled its entire European distribution model for its computer and printing products for business customers using this framework and improved its market position and distribution efficiency by so doing.

How the business model works for final-tier channel players

14

Role defines business model

As we have seen in the previous chapter, the business model of a final-tier trade channel player usually comprises a mix of product resale and service provision. This mix can vary widely, from players where service provision makes up next to nothing as a proportion of sales, to players where it can represent up to 100 per cent of the sales with no product resale at all.

Typically, the proportion of services increases as you move from left to right of the partner types we have profiled in Figure 14.1. This reflects the higher value added and greater level of customization of the offering required to be competitive and effective in each role. We will examine the implications of this later in the chapter.

The general trend across most industries as they mature is for the final-tier trade channel players to grow the proportion of their sales coming from services. There are several reasons for this:

- As markets mature and growth rates slow down, final-tier players need to compete harder for their own growth. They find that service provision is a basis for increased differentiation.

- Better differentiation tends to drive higher margins from services.

- Product resale wrapped up inside a service proposition can generate higher margins than just reselling a product without service.

- Many types of services need not be capital-intensive, so making it easier to grow the business from a limited capital base.

Figure 14.1 Typical product/service mix across the spectrum of partner roles

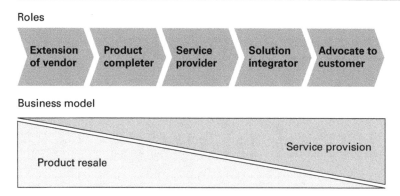

Roles

| Extension of vendor | Product completer | Service provider | Solution integrator | Advocate to customer |

Business model

Product resale

Service provision

Although few of these players manage their businesses by splitting their 'product' and 'service' business models apart, it is helpful to focus exclusively on the service-provision model for this Part of the book to understand its special challenges, which are quite different from those of the product model.

Service-provision business models – people and platforms

It is helpful in understanding service-provision business models to think of them as either a people-based model or a platform-based one. Many services are delivered by people applying their time and skills in activities such as configuring, installing, servicing, fixing, advising, training, project managing and many others. The alternative way to deliver services is through the provision of a platform that enables customers to travel, dine, stay, access information, receive media, content, make or update reservations, execute transactions, change consumption profiles (add a user, extend functionality), diagnose issues and many others. Common to both these models are a number of features that differ markedly from the product-based business model:

- *Volume sensitivity* – both people- and platform-based business models rely on a cost structure that is predominantly fixed in the short to medium term (in the long term all costs are variable). These are costs that need to be paid for each week or month.

- *Time dimension of capacity* – most services consume capacity in the moment, creating the need to manage capacity utilization. The time of people, unsold seats or rooms, bandwidth, etc cannot be inventoried to match demand, so demand must be managed to fit supply.
- *Contract-based value delivery* – the unit of sale is usually a contract with a large number of variables, all of which can affect delivery time, cost and quality and require sophisticated control, accounting and billing processes to ensure that value delivered turns into revenue.

In the following chapters in this Part, we explore how these features are managed and leveraged differently by people-based and platform-based service providers. The overall result is that the business models reflect somewhat different architectures, as summarized below.

Special features of the people-based service business model

The logic tree approach to setting out a business model can be applied to the service-provision model in exactly the same way as the product-based model we have explored in depth in Part Two, when examining the distributor tier. Figure 14.2 shows the people-based business model together with its primary drivers. You can see that the core structure is the same as the product-based business model with margins and overheads feeding up into ROCE and ROIC on the left, and with working capital feeding up from the right. What is not immediately apparent is the dynamics of how revenues, costs and margins behave as the business scales. The most significant factor is that cost of sales is relatively fixed because it comprises people costs (mostly those of employees), and will be incurred regardless of sales volumes. In Chapters 15 and 16, we will dive into the detail of this, showing how it impacts on the measurement and tracking of margins in this context.

Managing people is not a simple numbers game, however. People are tough to manage, and expect their managers to pay attention to the variety and mix of their work experience, work/life balance, morale, training and development and offer them career progression, etc. In many ways, the demands of the people responsible for delivering the services are at odds with the demands of the customer and even those of the service provider itself (see Table 14.1).

Figure 14.2 People-based business model drivers

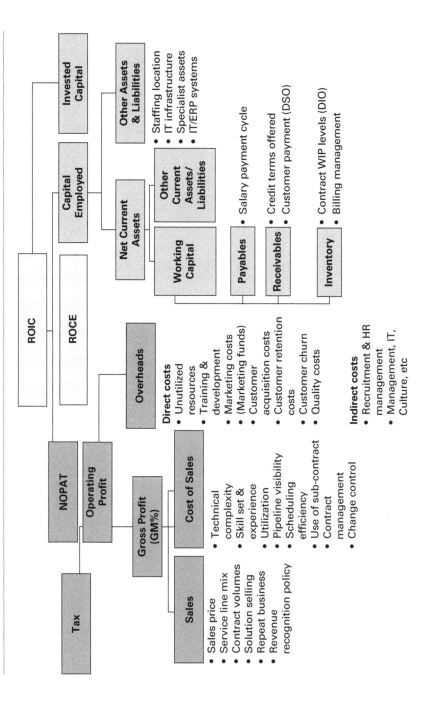

Table 14.1 Conflicting expectations of the service provider's stakeholders

Dimension of work	People expectations	Customer expectations	Service provider expectations
Match of experience to requirements	Variety of work that offers fresh challenges and personal development to increase 'personal capital'. Do not want to be doing the same type of work all the time	Highly experienced and expert people that have done this type of work many times before and can deliver faultlessly every time	People expert enough to deliver the work on time, on budget and to the required quality, without being over-qualified and thus too expensive, or too inexperienced and thus requiring intensive supervision and allowance for learning curve
Scheduling	Steady work without too much pressure involved in meeting the deadlines. Time off for vacations when convenient for family commitments, etc	As quickly as possible, with plenty of time allowed for client sign-offs. Resources available to meet demanding deadlines without interruption	Steady full-time work scheduled over a fixed period with no downtime or breaks
Continuity of staff	A reasonable period spent working on one customer followed by the opportunity to move on to bigger, more prestigious customers Opportunities to be involved in putting together bids for new work at new clients	Same staff all the time, so no requirement to orient the service team and minimal distraction for own staff. Can be expected to understand client expectations without these needing to be spelt out No distractions or absences	Flexibility to rotate and assign staff to where there is the best fit. Need to move best performers to highest-risk or most valuable customers Able to assign best staff to bidding for new work and new clients

Each time the service provider generates an opportunity to win a new customer, bid for new business or start a new project, it needs to balance these potentially conflicting demands in the way it allocates its people to contracts and customers. Each individual decision will come out in favour of one of the three stakeholders and to the possible detriment of the other two, but over time it must maintain a fair balance. It is too easy for weak management to succumb to the 'squeaky wheels' and concede to the most demanding customer, most strident contract manager or most disaffected member of staff. Strong management requires the ability to assess the business dimensions of long-term customer value, development of service team capabilities and managing the career development of individual members of staff. Management also needs to be able to explain the basis of its decisions and persuade everyone involved of their merits. This requires interpersonal skills on the part of managers, strong team management skills across the company and excellent communication and selling skills to make the case for resourcing and scheduling decisions.

Larger service providers invest heavily in their people management infrastructures to ensure that all members of staff experience best-in-class training, personal development, feedback, evaluations, and pay and benefits so that they want to stay and build their careers with the service provider. In return, the service provider secures a loyal, motivated, appropriately skilled team, seasoned in customer service and the provider's offerings and differentiation, who can be called on to go the extra mile when needed. The best service providers have the mechanisms in place to track performance, identify the good, poor and non-performers and address problems early if necessary. Good talent management systems will give transparency to the availability of staff, the depth and relevance of their experience and the staff's own expressed preference for future work experience.

The more 'high end' the services being offered by the service provider, the more critical the ability to retain and develop the specialist people that deliver them. The departure of a single person, or worse, a team of seasoned specialists, could be catastrophic for the service provider and this often goes hand-in-hand with client defections and further staff departures, possibly to a direct competitor. It may take months to recruit replacements, if it is even possible, and once on board, it may take up to a year for the new people to reach full productivity as they master the unique approach of the service

Figure 14.3 Platform-based business model drivers

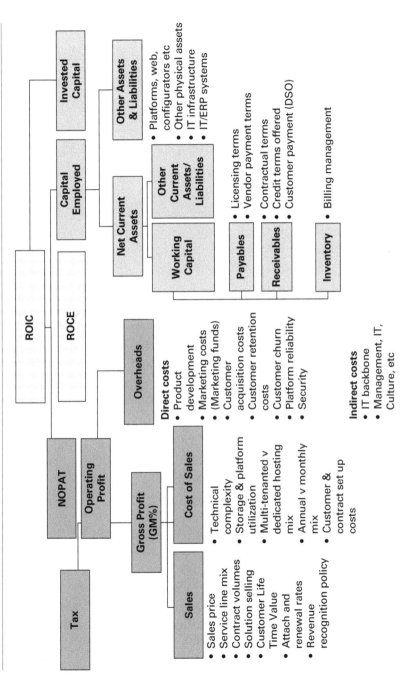

provider. A service provider can spend thousands on expensive training and skills upgrading for its people and it should regard this as an investment that needs protecting to secure the expected return. Service providers offering even basic services will feel the impact of high staff turnover, as it will impact customer service, team continuity and general experience levels that enable service teams to handle the hundred and one issues that arise in service delivery.

Special features of the platform-based service business model

The platform-based service-provision model has several similarities to the people-based one, with a high dependency on the technical skills of its people and a more extreme version of the rigid cost structure. The difference lies in the fact that the technical skills are leveraged for the design, execution and evolution of the platform that delivers the services. Set out in Figure 14.3 is the logic tree of the platform-based business model.

One major feature of the platform-based model is that the entire platform needs to be built and tested before it can be released to the market. This is in contrast to the people-based model, where it is potentially possible to be up and running in business terms with a single person. The implications of this feature for the platform-based business is that a substantial up-front capital investment is required before the first revenue can be realized. Depending on the cost of customer acquisition, there may be a period of negative cash flow during which operating and customer acquisition overheads exceed any initial cash-in flows. This problem is exacerbated if the platform is providing services that are paid for either on a consumption basis (pay-as-you-go) or an annual contract basis.

As a side-bar, one of the more interesting aspects of the platform-based service model is that it often passes work back to the customer. Customers are willing to spend time filling in online forms, searching for the best deals, assembling their own packages (for instance, flight, hotel and car rental instead of asking a travel agent to do this), configuring their own reports, specifying their own products by selecting from options and scheduling delivery times or locations. Customers have shown that they are willing to do this work in return for the benefits of convenience, responsiveness, flexibility and control.

Managing final-tier channel players – sales and utilization

15

People-based service business model

Revenue recognition

The level of sales revenue in any week or month has a critical impact on the overall profitability of a people-based service provider, given that so many of its costs are fixed. However, the matter of what constitutes revenue or, rather, when to recognize it, is much more complicated than for a product business.

Recording sales or revenue recognition in a service business is surprisingly one of the most subjective areas in a service provider's financial statements and is quite open to abuse or manipulation. Why is this area so complicated? Let's look at XYZ Co and ask some questions.

XYZ Co has three types of service income streams:

1 large contracts with multiple phases spread over periods of up to 15 months;

2 small contracts that typically take around three months to complete; and

3 fixed-term service, support and maintenance contracts.

Now, in the case of the large contracts, when might you consider a sale is made? Is it:

A When the customer calls to commit to the contract?

B When the customer signs the contract?

C When the first consultant arrives at the customer's site?

D When the first month's work is completed?

E When the first month's work is signed off by the customer?

F When the first month's work is paid for by the customer?

G When all the work is completed?

H When all the work is signed off by the customer?

I When all the work has been paid for by the customer?

These options have been laid out in an order that accountants would recognize as having the most 'aggressive' at the top and most 'cautious' at the bottom. Few people would be comfortable recognizing all or even some of the income on a contract at point A and equally few would think the company should wait until point I before recognizing any income. Fifteen months is what accountants call a 'long-term' contract and under international accounting standards, revenue and the related profit should be recognized as the work is carried out, *provided the outcome can be assessed with reasonable certainty*. In simple terms this means that options D and E are the most widely accepted revenue recognition points, depending on XYZ Co's practices. Note the words in italics, which mean that as the revenue is recognized and the associated profit is booked, XYZ Co must look at the way the contract is going and be sure that it will not make a loss at the end. If a lower than planned profit or even a loss is looking likely, then it must reduce the profit it books accordingly.

Revenue recognition practices will depend somewhat on the rigour with which XYZ Co controls its contracts and the way it records the activity of its billable staff (ie the ones that work for customers to earn income). At the high end and increasingly towards the low end of the service spectrum, timesheets are kept to allocate hours to specific customer contracts. Extending these timesheets by the billing rates for each grade of staff will give a 'gross revenue' that can be recognized. Taking note of the words in italics means that the progress of the contract should be assessed against the time charged and a judgement call made as to what proportion can be recognized as sales for the period. The same principles apply to small contracts, though here there is less scope for error and it may be acceptable to divide the revenue over the number of months of the contract to keep things simple.

The third type of income is from fixed-term service, support and maintenance contracts. These can be fixed- or variable-price contracts or a blend of the two, with a fixed and a variable element. The fixed-price contract is effectively like an insurance policy for the customer, where the contract price is the insurance premium and XYZ Co takes the risk on the number of 'claims' or call-outs it will have to service. A low number of call-outs will result in a healthy profit and a high number of call-outs can generate a loss for XYZ Co. Typically, service providers simply divide the contract price by the number of months covered and take the same amount to income each month. The costs then fall in the month incurred. Over a large number of contracts and months, this evens itself out and results in a fair revenue treatment. Only if the service provider knows something different should it adjust this approach.

Pipeline visibility

Given the nature of services, almost all service providers make their sales in advance of the time they book the revenue. As we saw above, lengthy sales cycles require service providers to make their sales as far ahead of actually booking the revenue as possible. This visibility of revenue, the sales pipeline, is a critical success factor and the service provider must be able to measure it effectively and consistently. The most effective tool available to the service provider to measure its pipeline is a schedule of the revenue booked and visible, by time period, either weekly or monthly. An example of a sales pipeline is shown in Table 15.1. Note that the date of the pipeline is shown as mid-July, so the sales schedule shows actual sales (in $000s) for the first six months of the year and an up-to-date projection of sales in each of the months for the second half of the year. It is vital that the pipeline is updated on an event-driven basis, ie every time there is news of a sales win or an expected slippage.

In the example shown, sales have been running ahead of the business plan for the first six months (which is why the 'to convert' numbers are shown darkened and negative). However, in mid-July, there is still some work to be done to win business for July ($5,000 short) and an increasing amount to be sold for the other five months of the year. This is very typical of a service provider with, say, a one-month sales cycle, but of course would be rather worrying if the sales cycle was, say, three months – unless of course there's lots of business about to be closed.

The sales pipeline above is called Category 1, which for this particular service provider means actual confirmed sales (which can still slip even after confirmation). It defines Category 2 as work that has been bid for or a price quoted and a bidding document or quotation submitted to the prospective customer or client. Category 3 is used to denote opportunities that the sales team have identified and are hoping to be the subject of either a bid

Table 15.1 Example of an order book shown in a sales pipeline

Sales Schedule – Category 1

Sector	Client	Description	Job No.	Jan	Feb	Mar	Apr	May	Jun	Jul	Aug	Sep	Oct	Nov	Dec	Total
									Current year							
Auto	ABC Co	Technical project	ABC342	11	10	10	10	10	10							61
Manf	DEF Co	Strategy project	DEF001	22	22	10	16									70
Ret	GHI Co	Investigation project	GHI233		25	17	17	15	5							79
Ret	GHI Co	Second phase	GHI234					5	15	15	15	15	15	15	15	110
Auto	JKL Inc	Technical project	JKL040					30	20	25	25	30	35	30	5	200
Manf	MNO Co	Technical project	MNO002	10	15	15	15	15	15	15	15	15				130
Airl	PQR Co	Strategy project	PQR027			15	15	15	15	15	15	15				105
Com	STU Co	Investigation project	STU004	25	25	20	10	5								85
Com	WXY Co	Technical project	WXY112													0

Total CAT 1	68	97	87	83	95	80	70	70	75	50	45	20	840

	Jan	Feb	Mar	Apr	May	Jun	Jul	Aug	Sep	Oct	Nov	Dec	Total
Business plan	65	75	75	75	75	75	75	80	80	80	80	80	915
To convert	-3	-22	-12	-8	-20	-5	5	10	5	30	35	60	75

or quotation. To qualify for Category 3, the service provider has decided it must be able to quantify the likely value of the work and estimate the likely schedule for the work. Calculating the pipeline from these numbers is usually done using some variation of this formula:

Sales pipeline
$$\text{Sales pipeline} = \frac{\text{Booked sales plus profitability of expected sales}}{\text{Average monthly targeted sales}}$$

It is up to the service provider to decide how stringently it applies the test of probability. Looking at the actual numbers in the sales schedule, the pipeline can be summarized as in Table 15.2. Comparing this to the average targeted sales by month of $80,000, as shown in the business plan (for the period August to December), produces a pipeline of 4.6 months (ie $369,000/$80,000).

Is this good or bad? The first factor to consider in assessing this pipeline is the typical sales cycle. If this company takes only a month to convert leads into sales, then a pipeline of almost five months is excellent. On the other hand, if the sales cycle is typically six months, then things are not looking nearly so good. As we can see from Category 1, there is still $75,000 of sales to make in the next five months to hit the business plan for the year as a whole. Looking at Category 2, the weighted probability of future bids is only $109,000, which, although it is higher than £75,000, suggests that there is still a risk that the company will miss its business plan, unless its

Table 15.2 Illustrated summary of sales pipeline

August Cat 1	$70,000
September Cat 1	$75,000
October Cat 1	$50,000
November Cat 1	$45,000
December Cat 1	$20,000
Total Cat 1	$260,000
Weighted Cat 2 (Prob total)	$109,000
Cat 3 (ignored as too uncertain)	$0
Total booked sales plus probability of expected sales	$369,000

probability assumptions are extremely accurate. While the overall pipeline number (4.6 months) is helpful, care must be taken in its use, as it grossly oversimplifies the situation. Probably of more relevance is how the pipeline is changing over time. If it is increasing, that is definitely good, but this increase may not be driven by near-term sales, so immediate revenues could still take a dip. If the pipeline is decreasing, then urgent attention is needed to ensure that opportunities to win more contracts are being generated. If the pipeline is shortening, this is a real problem. If management is doing its job it will be reviewing the full profile of the sales schedule every week or even more frequently, so the sales pipeline number is just an overall measure for the record.

To show how this works, we will use an example, XYZ Co, a people-based service provider with a value creation tree as shown in Figure 15.1. The sales in the current year have doubled over the prior year, which looks like a terrific result. But, and this is a very big 'but', its sales pipeline has fallen from six months in the prior year to two months in the current year, a real collapse. How could this have happened? It can't be very realistic, can it? Well, unfortunately, this example is an all too real illustration of one of the biggest issues facing service providers: 'feast and famine'. When (particularly smaller) service providers land some big projects, they become totally focused on delivery and take their eye off the sales pipeline. This is often exacerbated by the fact that the process of bidding for new business requires the time of the more senior billable people to scope the work, prepare the technical sections of the tender documentation and estimate the work effort. When the demand for their time is consumed in delivering current work, these resources are not spending time helping to win new work. In larger service providers with dedicated sales teams this challenge can be more easily overcome, but in smaller service providers, the sales effort is often headed up by one or more of the founders/key executives who lead on the technical front and thus are heavily involved in both sales and delivery. For these service providers, when one or two major contracts are won, the pipeline can suddenly shoot up to six or even nine months. This causes the company to heave a collective sigh of relief that sales are taken care of for a while and focus switches to delivering these big new projects. However, it's not easy to switch selling activity on and off, and once 'put down' the sales task is a hard one to pick up again. As we shall see from the other measures, XYZ Co is wrestling with so many challenges caused by the doubling of business volume that management can easily have become distracted from focusing on the pipeline.

Figure 15.1 XYZ Co (a service provider) value creation tree

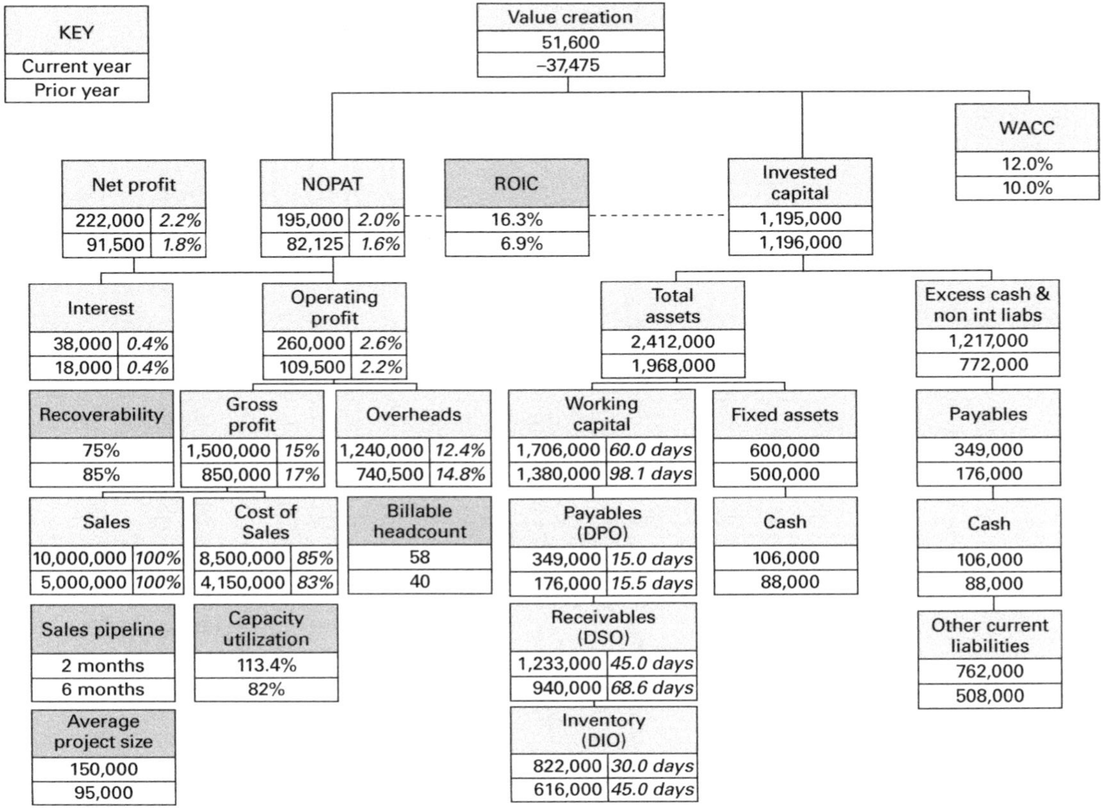

KEY
Current year	
Prior year	

Value creation
51,600
-37,475

NOPAT
195,000	2.0%
82,125	1.6%

ROIC
16.3%
6.9%

Invested capital
1,195,000
1,196,000

WACC
12.0%
10.0%

Net profit
222,000	2.2%
91,500	1.8%

Operating profit
260,000	2.6%
109,500	2.2%

Total assets
2,412,000
1,968,000

Excess cash & non int liabs
1,217,000
772,000

Interest
38,000	0.4%
18,000	0.4%

Gross profit
1,500,000	15%
850,000	17%

Overheads
1,240,000	12.4%
740,500	14.8%

Working capital
1,706,000	60.0 days
1,380,000	98.1 days

Fixed assets
600,000
500,000

Cash
106,000
88,000

Payables
349,000
176,000

Cash
106,000
88,000

Other current liabilities
762,000
508,000

Recoverability
75%
85%

Cost of Sales
8,500,000	85%
4,150,000	83%

Billable headcount
58
40

Payables (DPO)
349,000	15.0 days
176,000	15.5 days

Receivables (DSO)
1,233,000	45.0 days
940,000	68.6 days

Inventory (DIO)
822,000	30.0 days
616,000	45.0 days

Sales
10,000,000	100%
5,000,000	100%

Capacity utilization
113.4%
82%

Sales pipeline
2 months
6 months

Average project size
150,000
95,000

Revenue impact of capacity and utilization

As well as the issue of demand management, the service provider must manage the supply side, ie the service provider's own resources, with equal attention. The key to success is to have resources fully utilized for as much of the trading period as possible, maximizing the income generated from each person, without overdoing it and driving people too hard.

Managing capacity utilization requires many trade-offs, not least between short- and long-term capacity, permanent and subcontracted staff, home-grown and bought-in skills, and aggressive and cautious recruitment plans. In the short term, there are constant challenges on the supply side. These can include:

- sickness and absence of key staff;
- staff turnover with the loss of specialist skills as well as capacity;
- overruns on current projects requiring additional time of key staff;
- subcontractors failing to honour commitments;
- inexperienced or over-qualified staff being the only resources available, impacting either quality or cost of delivery.

Any or all these factors can change the service providers' capacity and availability of key resources, and if they are not available, they cannot generate revenue. Capacity and utilization planning requires a good understanding of the different technical skills and experience of each of the staff and teams as well as the requirements of each customer. This means that large service providers need to be able to classify and maintain a database of the skills of each of their people in such a way that as new projects or customer requirements come in, available resources can be identified and allocated.

Planning capacity for the longer term, ie for the next one to two years, to meet the business plan for revenue growth, requires some strategic vision. Decisions need to be based on an informed view of which services, offerings, skills and resources will be needed as the market and customer requirements change in the future. The service provider needs to decide how to ensure it retains its differentiation and must understand which skills underpin this. Decisions need to be made on whether to recruit from outside or develop people internally based on the degree of specialization of the service provider. Capacity planning needs to take into account recruitment and training lead-times given the availability of skills in the marketplace.

Service providers typically find it tempting to add to their headcount as soon as they see demand growing and the pipeline improving. Here the issue is one of when and how to expand the resource pool to match planned revenue and profitability goals. In making these decisions, the main considerations include:

- How many people will need replacing through staff turnover?
- Which specialty skills will experience growth in demand and which shrinkage?
- What new services or offerings are we planning to introduce?
- How many of each type of skill and depth of experience do we need to deliver our services at the requisite level of quality?
- How confident are we in our assumptions about growth and shifts in demand?
- How seasonal or volatile is our demand pattern?
- What is the right balance between generalist and specialist skills?
- Which skills are critical to our differentiation and should they be owned and protected?
- Which skills should we subcontract out and which should we hire in?
- How experienced are we at managing the types of skills we need?

People, or more specifically their hours, are the unit of production for a service business, so it is natural to want to grow the resource base because that underpins the ability to grow revenues. However, there is a real ratchet effect of adding to the headcount in that it may take three months to recruit and induct a new productive resource but, once added, there are legal (and human) barriers to removing that person if the demand does not materialize. Excess products can be sold off to realize cash (albeit at low or negative margins), but excess people may involve many months of unproductive employment costs and the softer impacts of low morale, disaffected staff and the related impacts on quality and customer relations. Any decision to add to the capacity of a service provider is almost always a long-term decision and should not be made simply to resolve short-term staff shortages.

Managing people utilization

Different service providers will have adopted different ways to calculate utilization but in most cases, it will be along the lines of this:

Utilization
$$\text{Utilization} = \frac{\text{Billable time}}{\text{Standard time}} \times 100$$

Billable time is the time spent working on agreed customer contracts or projects, usually tracked by being recorded on timesheets by billable staff against specific customer projects. Standard time is the number of hours or days that a billable person should be available to work in the relevant period.

For example, a full-time person will work 52 weeks less, say, 4 weeks of vacation less, say, 2 weeks of statutory holidays = 46 weeks, or 230 days or 1,840 hours on an 8-hour day. Some companies may factor in a standard allowance for sick days or training days, so reducing the standard time further. Most companies will *not* factor any overtime into the standard time as this creates the wrong impression culturally – most employees need to understand how utilization is calculated and applied and they will not be happy to see overtime built into the measure.

Utilization is a sensitive number as it is often used in assessing individual or team performance and to judge personal productivity levels. Therefore, when calculating the measure on a month-by-month basis, the standard deductions of personal vacation and statutory holidays should be removed from the denominator. This is a calculation that needs to be done each month using the 'actual month', as shown in the example in Table 15.3.

Thus, even though this individual took two weeks off in July, his or her utilization will show as 100 per cent for the period he or she was available to work. Note that in February and September, this person's utilization was in excess of 100 per cent, which simply means that hours worked on customer contracts was in excess of standard hours, something that indicates a high level of productivity, which is good for the service provider's profitability.

Table 15.3 Example of utilization calculation

Month	Billable hours	Statutory hols and vacation taken hours	Standard hours	Adjusted standard hours	Utilization
	A	B	C	D = (C – B)	E = A ÷ D
January	160	0	160	160	100%
February	160	8	152	146	110%
July	80	80	160	80	100%
August	80	0	160	160	50%
September	172	24	168	144	120%

In some higher-end services, the service provider will pay its more senior staff a fixed salary without overtime (which is effectively built into the worker's compensation level). In these companies, high utilization translates into super-profits because the hours represented in excess of 100 per cent utilization are revenues with a zero cost of sales.

The calculation works for groups of people, teams, divisions, etc, as well as it does for the individual. Simply aggregate the total hours of each billable person and calculate using the aggregated numbers. In our example service provider VC tree (Figure 15.1), XYZ Co is showing utilization as 82 per cent for prior year and 113 per cent for current year. What do we make of these figures? Is the increase in productivity always a good thing? Could this measure be increased further? Given we are dealing with people here, there is a natural limit to the amount of utilization that can be sustained over time without suffering a fall-off in quality, burnout and increased staff turnover.

Over several months, the pattern of an individual's billability may look like that shown in Figure 15.2. Note that the employee does not have the same number of hours/days each month. December and January suffer from the seasonal holidays and February is known in the trade as a 'short month'. Generally, as a very crude rule of thumb, utilization levels need to be kept in the range 85 to 115 per cent. Less than 85 per cent means low revenues per billable person, with the knock-on effect in terms of profitability. Sustained levels much above 115 per cent tend to lead to problems over time of quality through tiredness or burnout on intellectually or physically demanding work, and ultimately people will leave, increasing rates of staff turnover.

Figure 15.2   Example of an individual's utilization pattern for a year

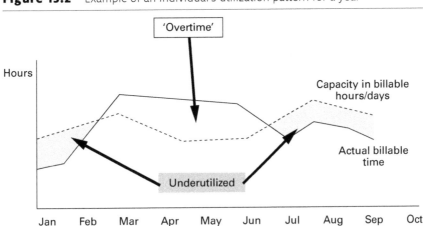

Like all measures, a simple number does not give the whole story. One of the keys to success in a service business is finding ways to put people to work for large chunks of time without distraction. That way, every hour of every week of every month for several months is billable. All the things that people find to fill their days when they are not busy, such as personal admin, keeping up to date on technological or industry developments, etc, somehow get squashed down and absorbed into the hours billed to customers.

Average project/contract size drives utilization

The single most effective way to achieve the service provider nirvana of deploying lots of people full-time on single customer projects is to sell big projects or contracts. Not only that, but each project tends to have a certain 'overhead' in terms of selling and negotiating effort, project set-up and button-up, project management and so on, which must be repeated for every single project. Selling fewer, bigger projects reduces this overhead in proportion to the revenues, increasing productivity and margins, as shown in Figure 15.3.

In scenario A (dotted line), our worker is employed full-time on one big project through to the end of June, takes some holiday in July and then ramps up on another big project from August onwards. In scenario B (solid line), a different worker is deployed across a number of smaller projects of

Figure 15.3　Comparison of utilization under two project size scenarios

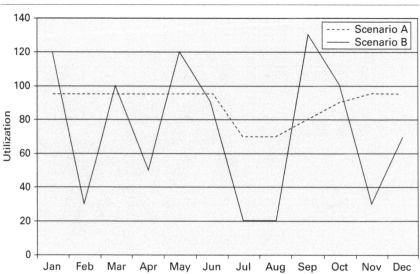

one month or less, some of them quite intense and others that do not require much time at all. Smaller projects rarely dovetail neatly, which means that there are gaps between projects of zero utilization, which kill the overall average. In this example, the worker in scenario A is 22 per cent more productive (higher utilization) than the worker in scenario B, even though not an hour of overtime was worked, compared to well over 100 hours of overtime for the poor worker in scenario B.

Smart service providers have learnt the lesson that bigger projects drive productivity and margins and use it to increase their chances of winning such projects. Average project/contract size gives a good indicator as to how well the service provider is doing in improving this 'effectiveness' measure over time:

Average project size
$$\text{Average project size} = \frac{\text{Total (project) sales}}{\text{Number of projects}}$$

In the case of XYZ Co, it has substantially increased its average project size from \$95,000 in the prior year to \$150,000 in the current year. It would be interesting to investigate whether this is the result of most of its projects increasing or if it is the effect of one enormous contract distorting the overall picture. When this happens, the major project often sucks up all the best resources, consumes senior management's exclusive attention and other projects and customers suffer, impacting longer-term sales. As we have already seen, the management team have taken their eye off the pipeline and now we find that they may have stretched the business, with utilization up at the ceiling of sustainable levels and the average project size up by 60 per cent in one year. Maybe that doubling of sales year on year wasn't such a great achievement after all...

Platform-based service business model

Volume sensitivity

The platform-based model is like the people-based model in its volume sensitivity: its cost structure is mostly fixed in nature, meaning that its profitability is entirely dependent upon revenue levels. Hotels, airlines, rental car fleets are all examples of this model, with the key utilization metrics of occupancy, load factors and usage respectively determining profitability. The platform is built for scale so the ramp-up rate for revenue levels matter greatly. The quicker revenues ramp up, the quicker the platform model will pass its break-even point and start to make a positive operating profit. Seasonality plays an important part too, as the platform's capacity cannot be reduced to match the seasonal volumes, so one particularly good or bad high season can have a significant impact on annual profitability. Many airlines run at an operating loss for the first six months of the year and rely on the second half to turn the situation round and deliver a profitable year overall. Bad weather, strikes, etc in the second half of the year will have a bigger negative effect than in the first half.

Where platform-based models usually gain some advantage over people-based models is in their ability to scale up capacity as volumes grow, especially if they are technology-based platforms (internet service providers, cable or satellite TV, cloud-based applications, etc), less so if they are capital asset-based platforms like airlines or hotels where lead times can be lengthy.

Customer retention and growth

Given this revenue dependency, platform-based service providers work hard to retain customers through a variety of strategies, including contracts, service level agreements, penalties for cancellation, teams dedicated to saving customers threatening to leave, and providing attractive inducements and rewards to customers for loyalty or referrals to new customers.

Contracts and service level agreements aim to balance the value exchange between service provider and customer, committing the service provider to deliver defined levels of service over the period of the contract in exchange for the customer's commitment to use the service for a fixed period. To demonstrate the commitment to the contract or service agreement, it is common for there to be predefined penalties for either side failing to keep their side of the deal. Refunds are due from the service provider in the event of a service failure or below par delivery, and cancellation penalties apply should a customer wish to walk away before the end of the contract term. Exercising these terms is an indication that the relationship has either broken down or is at risk of doing so. They do not generally save the relationship, but seek to mitigate the economic impact of its termination. Far better to offer a carrot than a stick.

Rewards and incentives for customer loyalty are the positive way to retain and grow customer volumes. We explore the role of customer loyalty schemes in the travel and hotel sectors in Chapter 24, and most readers will no doubt be member of at least one such scheme. The key economic characteristic is that the service provider seeks to turn its otherwise unused capacity into customer rewards that have minimal marginal cost. For example, the free flights offered to loyal airline customers are carefully restricted to ensure that they do not cannibalize revenue-earning seats. Hotels offer room upgrades, *if available*, car rental companies offer preferred customers the option to pick a better car off the line of cars available (you can have your pick of convertibles any time... except summer).

Platforms are embracing more subtle strategies to stimulate customers to do more on their platforms, leveraging FOMO – fear of missing out. They do this by sharing stories in their customer communications of how other customers are exploiting the capacity and higher functionality of the platform to their benefit: cue video clips showing a group of customers just like you having an amazing time on the beach/shopping/travelling while keeping track of their team or favourite series with a voiceover saying, 'Did you realize that you can access your cable channels on your mobile phone or tablet (if you upgrade to the superior service contract)?' Airlines or travel platforms invite you to explore destinations, book the entire vacation, including experiences, all on their platform, with emphasis on the time you'll save and the convenience of having to go to only one site.

Platform service providers aim to increase the 'stickiness' of their platforms by delivering an engaging, relevant experience, convenience (of purchase, access and use), and reducing the need for you to visit any alternative provider. Their entire business model is built upon high volumes driving revenue from long-lasting customers and ensuring their expensive platforms are running at very high levels of utilization for as large a proportion of the year as possible.

Managing final-tier channel players – gross margin and recoverability

16

People-based service business model

Calculating gross margin

One of the primary drivers of the increase in services provided by the final-tier trade channels is the potential of earning higher margins than is possible simply by reselling product. However, the potential to mismanage margins is also higher, underpinned by a lack of understanding of how margins are measured in service businesses. In Chapter 14, we showed how the cost of sales is virtually fixed in a business where service is provided by in-house employees who are on fixed salaries (ie not subcontractors). This means that as sales fluctuate, so gross and net margins fluctuate, or in economists' terms marginal revenue becomes marginal profit, dollar for dollar. In other words, once a business moves above break even, the next $100,000 of sales goes straight to the bottom line as $100,000 of gross and net profit. Although this is somewhat of a simplification, it is an accurate representation of the dynamics of margins in a fixed cost of sale business. This means that if the management takes care of the sales, it is also taking care of the margins and overall profitability of the business.

So how can we talk about the higher margins in services, if they are entirely driven by sales? The fundamental economics we have described above are helpful in understanding the dynamics of the overall business model, but not in managing the business on a day-to-day basis. Imagine you are the sales person who brought in that last $100,000 of sales as a single contract to take the company up and away from break-even. What was the margin on it? Surely, we have just said it was 100 per cent? Bonus please! Well, if you did claim your bonus on this basis, you would not be too popular with the other members of the sales team who have also sold some sizeable contracts to reach break-even for the period. Did they all make negative gross margins on their sales? Of course not. The answer lies in what accountants call taking 'a full costing' rather than 'a marginal costing' approach. In full costing, the resources consumed by a contract are charged against its revenues, just like product cost of sales is matched to the product sales revenue. In this way, every contract sold shows a positive gross margin (assuming it was priced above the sum of the resources required) and margins of different projects can be compared on a like-for-like basis.

Note that under this accounting approach, a service provider could sell four projects in a period, all at substantial gross margins, and still make a loss. Look at the example shown in Table 16.1 for a service provider with a total payroll cost for its billable people of $600,000. The key line is clearly the 'Unused resources', sometimes call 'unallocated resources'. This is the payroll cost of the time of people for whom there were no projects on which to work in the period. It is vital in managing a service provider to understand the impact of unutilized resources on the overall profitability as well as to know how to maximize the profitability of the projects that are sold.

It is not easy to tell what is happening in the business model of a service provider if you are reviewing the external accounts, because of the different ways of accounting for the unused resources. There are three alternatives:

Table 16.1 Example of project/contract and overall profitability

Contract	Sales	Cost of sales	Gross profit	Gross margin
A	$100,000	$50,000	$50,000	50%
B	$150,000	$90,000	$60,000	40%
C	$50,000	$20,000	$30,000	60%
D	$200,000	$120,000	$80,000	40%
Unused resources		$320,000	–$320,000	
Total	$500,000	$600,000	–$100,000	–20%

1 Treat the cost of all billable staff as cost of sales, regardless of utilization.

2 Do not charge any people costs into cost of sales and show it all as overheads.

3 Treat the 'used' time of billable staff as cost of sales and leave the unused resources in overheads.

Compare the accounts of the three companies shown in Table 16.2. All have achieved the same level of sales and net profitability. Company A has adopted the first of the three accounting options, treating the full cost of billable resources as cost of sales, giving it a low gross margin.

Company B has adopted the second accounting option, treating all its people costs as overheads, giving it very healthy-looking margins indeed. Company C has taken the third option, charged in the cost of the time required to earn the sales to cost of sales, leaving the balance of unused resources in overheads. None of these is wrong, though accountants would prefer the third option, as it adheres to one of their core principles of matching costs and revenues as closely as possible.

Recoverability

A key factor affecting profitability in a people-based service business is recoverability. This is essentially the proportion of the fully priced resources consumed by a contract or project that the customer agrees to pay for:

Table 16.2 Alternative accounting treatments of people costs

	Co A	Co B	Co C
Sales	1000	1000	1000
Cost of sales	300	300	300
People cost of sales	400	0	250
Gross profit	**300**	**700**	**450**
Gross margin	30%	70%	45%
Overheads	200	200	200
Salaries	0	400	150
Operating profit	**100**	**100**	**100**
Operating margin	10%	10%	10%

Recoverability
$$\text{Recoverability} = \frac{\text{Final contract price paid by customer}}{\text{Total resources used} \times \text{Standard prices}}$$

'Final contract price paid by the customer' is equivalent to the sales line in the income statement and reflects what was originally agreed at the time the contract was signed plus any variations agreed as the project or contract has progressed. 'Total resources used' are the time of in-house people and any external people or services bought in to deliver the contract. 'Standard prices' refers to the target prices the service provider has set for each of its resources to achieve the margin it should earn. This may or may not be made visible to the customer depending on sector, norm, or the service provider's own policy. For many service providers it is an internal pricing tool to set a starting price when estimating or quoting for a project, which the service provider may choose to discount.

In the case of XYZ Co, recoverability has slipped from 85 per cent in the prior year to 75 per cent in the current year. This is a little like discounts increasing from 15 to 25 per cent and, put in those terms, this is clearly an alarming shift in the business model and one that needs investigating immediately. We know that the business has exactly doubled its sales (which equals the final contract price paid by the customer on all its projects) year on year, but because the recoverability rate has fallen, XYZ Co has had to increase its resources used to deliver those projects, ie $200\% \times 85/75 = 226$ per cent. This is the amount of additional work deployed in the current year compared to the prior year.

Let's look at how it has attempted to cope with this on the supply side:

- Billable headcount is up from 40 to 58, an increase of 45 per cent, but this would have been spread over the year, so on average this would represent an increase to capacity of 22.5 per cent.

- Utilization is up from 82 to 113 per cent, an increase of 37 per cent.

- Combining the two gives an overall increase in in-house capacity deployed of 168 per cent (ie 122.5 per cent × 137 per cent).

How has XYZ Co managed to deliver 226 per cent extra work with an increase in deployed capacity of 168 per cent, a gap of 58 per cent? The most likely answer is that it has used subcontractors, and while this has plugged the gap in capacity, it has given rise to other issues. Subcontractors will almost always cost more per hour or day than in-house people, and this additional cost shows up in higher cost of sales, which has reduced the gross margin. Even the best and hardest-working subcontractors will take time to climb the learning curve of the service provider's internal methodologies and in-house ways of doing things, requiring more time and resource than an experienced employee. There is a risk with subcontractors that they will not bring the same level of commitment to the project as an in-house person whose future career prospects are bound up with the service provider's success, and quality may be a casualty.

So, it seems that XYZ Co has pursued the goal of growth taking on bigger projects, but paid a high penalty in terms of increasing its fixed cost base, damaging recoverability, reducing its gross margin and taking its eye off the ball in terms of maintaining a healthy pipeline. It could be heading for disaster as it now has to meet the payroll costs of 58 people but has just two months' of sales on its books. You can bet that the management team will not be sleeping well, assuming they can read the business model as well as you now can.

Improving people-based margins

What are the typical gross margins that can be earned for service? As a very crude approximation, low-end services look to multiply the fully loaded payroll cost (ie including taxes, insurances, etc) by a factor of 3 and high-end services by a factor of 5. This means margins (excluding the cost of unused resources) of 33 per cent for low-end services and 80 per cent for high-end services, a very wide range but one that reflects the potential to deliver value for customers as well as the degree of competition for the particular services on offer. Note that these factors are used for setting 'prices' or rates to price up contracts, and that the local market situation, length of pipeline, season- ality and the level of unused resources will all play a part in the final rates achieved in practice.

The more differentiated the service, the higher the potential margin that can be earned. Domestic trade services such as plumbers, electricians, deco- rators, etc, have recently seen their margins improve as their time-poor, cash-rich customers become more willing to pay for trustworthy, reliable workers, who clean up after themselves and can do the increasingly high-end and technical work required. Plumbers who specialize in installing luxury bathrooms complete with wet areas, power showers, self-demisting mirrors, etc, can demand very high rates, once they have established their reputation and can provide top-drawer references. Equally, the plumber who is prepared to come out at all hours of the day and night to unblock sewage pipes can also command high call-out rates, but only for the 'distress purchase'. It will not be able to command such high rates for regular plumbing maintenance and installation work unless it is operating in an area where there are few plumbers to meet everyday demand.

Similar examples can be found in all other service sectors, whether they be for consumer or commercial customers. Applying the framework of types of service providers helps to fix a pattern to the types of margins earned, based on role in the value chain and the level of value delivered (see Figure 16.1).

This should be taken as a very rough guide to target margins for service business models, but should help you to evaluate whether the intended role for a service provider is being borne out by its margins. In our experience,

Figure 16.1 Typical service provider gross profit margins by role

Roles

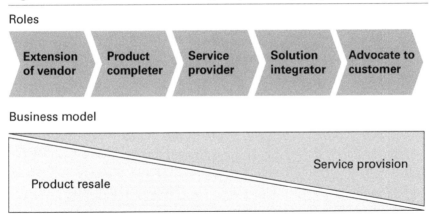

Business model

Margin model

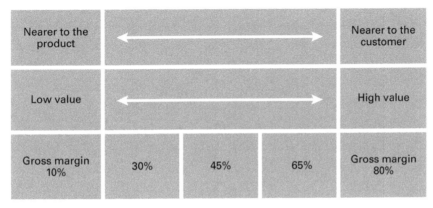

most service providers perceive themselves to be at least one role to the right of this model than they really are, and the actual margins earned expose the self-deceit. While moving to the right appears to be the best move possible, there are real challenges in achieving this, as discussed in Chapter 13. In terms of the business model, these high margins come with the increased risks of the specialization being eroded over time, fewer customers and opportunities that demand the specialist skills and more time needed by the service provider to remain current and to communicate its high-end capabilities through thought-leadership activities. On the other hand, the low-margin end of the spectrum needs to maintain extremely high levels of utilization to cover its costs and make a net profit.

Platform-based service business model

Capacity management and delivery

The key features of a platform-based service are its instant and constant availability (ie, 24/7), responsiveness, convenience, consistency, flexibility and uptime. Detailed, flexible planning is required to ensure the platform can consistently meet these customer expectations while delivering on business requirements such as scalability, low cost, robustness, security and peak-load management. The platform's gross margins will be highly dependent on being able to handle large volumes at a tiny marginal operating cost. The business model will move into an operating profit once its gross margins surpass its overheads. The most substantial overhead costs are likely to be the depreciation or amortization cost of the platform development costs and the cost of customer acquisition.

It is a tough judgement call as to the level of volumes to plan for, what rate of scaling up will be achieved, and what the cost of customer acquisition will prove to be. Underestimate these and the platform will need to be retooled during the ramp-up period, a highly risky undertaking. Overestimate and the platform will have higher depreciation costs that may not be recovered from the gross margins. Some of the key considerations that should go into capacity planning include:

- *Volumes processed* (revenues, transactions, customers handled), in total, by hour, by segment, etc. As well as driving the traditional measures of revenue and gross margins, volume measures are critical to assessing the degree of utilization of the infrastructure, enabling capacity to be added ahead of the demand curve (or downsized if necessary).

- *Customer browsing behaviour* – which pages customers used to enter the site (not always the home page and often special landing pages are designed to catch click-throughs from promotions and campaigns), which pages they arrived from (by type), how long customers spent on the site, which pages they visited, etc.

- *Customer buying behaviour* – average basket, proportion of purchases bought on promotion or from specific campaigns, use of redemption codes, payment methods, frequency of visit, recency (time since last visit) and many other aspects relevant to each specific business.

- *Downtime* – the length of time the service is not available to its users or customers, especially if it is due to some outage or failure without adequate back-up. Sophisticated systems can identify specific customers or groups of customers affected by downtime and calculate the cost in terms of money or customer impact. For large entities, an unplanned outage, such as British Airways suffered in 2017, can really harm the brand and affect the loyalty of customers, even if they weren't directly affected.

- *Customer transaction success/failure rates* – identifying at which stages in the transaction process the customer is lost. Although occasionally caused by technical issues (which are tracked), one of the great frustrations for online services is the abandonment of the process part-way through. This may be because the user is put off by the appearance of charges late on (credit card fees, booking fees, etc) or the request for too much personal information, confusing signposting, poor site design, or the customer simply finding a better offer.

- *Transaction processing times* or delays and connection speeds by region and by hour – these are factors that may throttle volumes or increase transaction failure rates.

You can see that many of these measures mirror those of the people-based service model, because the platform-based service model replicates the model of establishing a capability that delivers its highest margins when operating close to capacity. In effect, the measures of downtime, transaction failure rates, processing delays and connection speeds together measure the drivers of online recoverability.

Improving platform-based margins

After acquiring customers and keeping them engaged long enough to complete a transaction, the platform provider faces the challenge of driving up margins. There are five major drivers of platform-based margins available to work with:

1 *Migration up from entry-level proposition* – encouraging customers to consider higher value, higher margin propositions requires advanced sales skills in the face-to-face or telephone-based environment. It takes equally advanced merchandising skills to achieve this through an online platform. Most techniques apply some form of 'fear of missing out' (FOMO) and many sites now enable comparisons of three or more propositions across all the variables. These help customers answer the question as to what they get for the higher ticket service. Insurance propositions usually offer some variation of the Good, Better, Best array, encouraging customers to consider the risks if they merely choose the Good option. This may provide reimbursement only of the depreciated value of an insured item, rather than the replacement cost as under the Better option, and people may be able to claim for the cost of any matching items if one element of a suite is damaged under the Best option. The platform needs to tread the fine line between gently nudging the customer to the higher margin option without alienating the budget customer or making any customer feel manipulated.

2 *Attach rates* – margins can be increased significantly if the costs of customer acquisition can be amortized over multiple purchases, especially if they form a single basket. Many platforms offer customers suggestions based on the purchasing behaviour of other customers, encouraging the addition of contents insurance alongside house insurance, for example, or providing support for a complete array of software applications rather than just one. This needs to be done in a way that is seen to be relevant to the customer, and allows the customer the clear choice to opt in or out. Some low-cost airlines have suffered bad publicity for their technique of automatically loading various types of unwanted insurance and other add-ons to customers' orders, requiring an opt-out.

3 *Renewal and life-time value* – many services are sold for a year, requiring customers to renew their subscription. The ability to automatically renew a subscription is usually forbidden by law, unless it is necessary to avoid a lapse in something like car insurance. Thus platform-based service providers need to ensure they have built the processes and tools to minimize the risk of customer atrophy through apathy. They need to be actively managing renewal rates, analysing the reasons behind falling rates and instigating programmes to address the underlying causes. One of the biggest causes of poor renewal rates is the conflict between acquisition offers necessary to attract new customers, and the sense of value for loyal customers. How do you feel when your broadband provider

is offering new customers an introductory free or reduced subscription period, which is not available to you because you have been a customer for a year or more? This conflict can be reduced by adopting a well-defined customer lifetime value approach, measuring the margin earned from a customer, or customer segment, over the expected life of the customer relationship. Such a model factors in the cost of acquisition, retention and service delivery measured against the revenues over the same period.

4 *Platform reliability, contention rates, product development, security* – each of these technical attributes can influence margins, involving trade-offs between the cost of provision and customer value perceptions. Each of these requires investment on the part of the provider, but over-engineered solutions drive up costs for limited value-perception gain, and under-engineered solutions damage customer service delivery. Contention rates relate to the number of users contending for the service on the platform: more customers means more contention, and the risk of slower response times, for example. From the service provider's perspective, high contention rates mean high utilization but, once service levels are affected, that can quickly turn into customer accretion. Good margins depend upon being able to optimize the cost-value equation with high utilization, but remain below the point at which service levels start to decline.

5 *Cost of customer acquisition* – generally the more valuable and expensive the service provided, the higher the cost of customer acquisition. Customer life-time modelling helps determine how much can be spent acquiring customers, once the cost of service provision and expected margin levels have been deducted. However, the great unknown in the model is the expected length of the customer relationship. Retail banks have famously benefited from customer relationships lasting longer than most marriages. On the other hand, most internet and mobile network service providers have found their customers change provider almost every year, or two at the most, which clearly limits the budget available for customer acquisition. However, many platforms require high volumes of customers to run above break even (and make any kind of margin), so are forced into aggressive customer acquisition strategies to ensure they reach these volumes.

Given the challenges set out above, the platform-based service provider represents a potentially high-stakes business model. It involves a high level of up-front investment to initiate the platform and the ability to balance the variables in the customer lifetime value model. As the rule of thumb is that the model should break even in no longer than one year, that is a long time to be funding negative cash flow. A year is time enough for new competitors to come up with more attractive propositions that could pull customers away, just as the model moves into the black (assuming that customers even stick with their provider for the contracted period). All this means that most platform-based service providers tend to be well-funded entities, able to ride out the initial ramp-up period and sustain any financial shocks along the way.

Managing final-tier channel players – working capital management

17

The cash-to-cash cycle

Let's look at the elements of the working capital cycle for a service business: supplier credit, inventory/work-in-progress and customer credit. These are directly comparable to the product-business working capital cycle covered in Chapter 7, but with some very significant differences that reflect the nature of a service business.

In most service businesses, there are very few assets and liabilities in the balance sheet that are not part of the cash-to-cash cycle, or working capital of the business. You may come across the occasional exception – a long-standing highly profitable service business may choose to invest some of its accumulated capital in a property that houses its working premises, which we would argue is dipping into another business model altogether and nothing to do with running a service business. Indeed, one could argue that this is a risky move as the business may outgrow its premises. A call-centre-based business may invest in the IT systems that power its out-bound calls and control its telesales scripts, but generally these are small items on the balance sheet.

People-based service business model

The real investment required to underpin the long-term sustainability of a people-based service business is sufficient working capital to be able to pay its staff and subcontractors (and the 'overheads' suppliers) on time, while waiting for its customers to pay its invoices. In a well-run service provider, the level of working capital is relatively small compared to that of an equivalent-sized product business. In a poorly managed service provider, it can balloon alarmingly to levels that could be far higher than a product business.

The cycle starts with the sale of a contract in which key business arrangements, including the phasing of the work, a billing schedule and credit terms, are defined. Many service providers operate a project accounting system in which each contract is assigned a project account with a unique number or identifier to aid in accumulating charges and credits. Once this account is opened, the costs of time and of work done on the project are charged in, as (unbilled) work-in-progress. The largest item will be the time cost of in-house workers (using timesheets) and subcontractors (using either invoices or timesheets). Most workers and subcontractors expect to be paid monthly, taking cash out of the service provider's bank account. Many service providers use long-term contract accounting rules to recognize an element of attributable profit as the project progresses. At agreed points in the project, the service provider invoices the customer for the work completed to date, or for a predefined amount like 33 per cent of the contract, and this effectively removes that amount from the unbilled work-in-progress and puts it into customer receivables. At the end of the credit period agreed in the contract or whenever the customer decides to pay, the bill is paid and the service provider receives the cash back into its bank account.

Let's now turn to the balance sheet and see how well XYZ Co is managing its cash-to-cash cycle and if it might be able to weather the storm until more contracts can be booked into the sales schedule (for more explanation of the key ratios used in this section, see Chapter 7). The cash-to-cash cycle is shown in Figure 17.1 for XYZ Co in the current year.

Is this good or bad? Has XYZ Co improved its grip on working capital? Overall, the working capital cycle is now 60 days, or two months, which is often regarded as an average benchmark for people-based service providers – 'one month to bill and one month to collect' is the rule of thumb often heard. This compares to 98.1 days in the prior year, which is over a month longer and would generally be regarded as appalling. To put it into context, if XYZ Co had not improved its working capital cycle at all, it would have needed another $1 million of cash in the business by now (the extra 38.1 days ÷ 365 days × $10 million sales). Given it has total capital employed of $1.45 million, this might have been difficult to find! No bank would grant a loan or overdraft for this sort of amount, so it is just as well that XYZ Co has grasped the nettle and improved its working capital cycle in the way it has.

Figure 17.1 The cash-to-cash cycle for XYZ Co in the current year

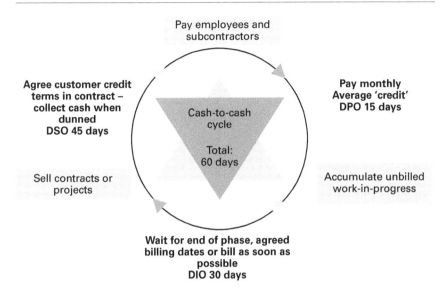

Improving working capital

Could XYZ Co improve its working capital further? Let's look at each element and see what scope there is to make improvements.

On payables, XYZ Co is taking 15 days' credit, as it is paying its workers and all those subcontractors hired in to meet demand at the end of each month. There may be some overhead suppliers where it can stretch its payment terms, but many of these will be utilities and services providers that it cannot afford to alienate and with which it is likely to have little bargaining power. It may be able to negotiate longer credit terms with its subcontractors if they are companies, but individual contractors cannot afford to agree to this. So, there appears to be little room for improvement on the days payable outstanding (DPO) measure.

XYZ Co has 30 days in inventory (DIO), which means that on average each contract is clocking up one month's worth of activity before it is billed to customers. Can this be improved? There are two ways to improve this measure, depending on the management and negotiation skills of the company and how the contracts have been defined. If XYZ Co has managed to agree that work on contracts can be billed at the end of each month, it will be removing the balance from inventory/work-in-progress and posting it into accounts receivable before the accounts are closed off for the month. In this way, there will be virtually no inventory at month end.

If XYZ Co cannot manage to negotiate monthly billing, it may try to secure stage payments or agree a billing schedule.

Its second strategy is to negotiate an up-front payment 'to secure the resources to be committed to the project'. This is the equivalent of taking a deposit to secure a hotel room booking and is quite reasonable if XYZ Co is effectively committing its scarce resources to a project. These advance payments can be for whatever XYZ Co can negotiate. The real advantage of these up-front payments is that they create 'negative inventory', because the invoicing takes costs out of inventory that haven't yet been incurred. In practice, accountants keep these negative balances separate on the balance sheet, call them 'income in advance' and put them in with accounts payable. The effect is to reduce the working capital cycle by the equivalent number of days' worth of advance payments received. Taking this principle further, XYZ Co can negotiate its billing schedule so that each invoice is an advance payment, with only a small proportion of the contract price to be paid after all the work is signed off on completion. Depending on the work schedule, some of these payments may be partially in advance and partially in arrears, but in every case where the billing is going out of inventory ahead of or in the same month as the work, the month-end balance will be close to zero or even negative. The best way to think of the effect of this is that the service provider has accelerated its cash flow by a month or more. Table 17.1 shows how the difference in terms negotiated will affect the end of month balances.

Table 17.1 Example of how differences in contract terms affect end-of-month inventory balances

Month	Beginning inventory balance	Work done on project	Invoices raised	Ending inventory balance
Contract terms agreed: Invoice monthly in arrears				
Jan	$0	$50	$0	$50
Feb	$50	$150	$50	$150
Mar	$150	$100	$150	$100
Apr	$100	$0	$100	$0
Contract terms agreed: 33% up front, 33% one month, 33% on completion				
Jan	$0	$50	$100	–$50
Feb	–$50	$150	$100	$0
Mar	$0	$100	$100	$0
Apr	$0	$0	$0	$0

Note how by negotiating the billing schedule shown in the lower half of the table, the business has managed to avoid any month-end inventory balance at all and even starts off with $50 of income in advance. This is a substantially better working capital outcome than results from accepting terms that state that invoices can only be submitted monthly in arrears. Using this approach, XYZ Co has plenty of potential to reduce its days in inventory balance further and should aim to reduce it to, say, 20 days initially and then see if it can go further. It will take time to implement this new strategy as it will only be able to negotiate better trading terms on new contracts and projects. XYZ Co may have to concede some margin in its pricing to secure these trading terms, and the merit of doing this will depend on how closely it is likely to bump up against its overdraft limits. There will often be customers who won't accept such terms, so XYZ Co will have to decide if it is willing to work with them or possibly to charge a (hidden) premium in its pricing to these customers to cover for the adverse impact on its cash flow.

From this analysis, we can see that there are some areas in which XYZ Co
Once the invoices are sent to the customer they become receivables and XYZ Co should aim to get them paid as close to its credit terms as possible. These terms will have been the subject of negotiation when the contract was set up, and powerful customers may be able to impose their 45-day or longer payment terms over XYZ Co's stated 30-day terms. Currently XYZ Co's days sales outstanding (DSO) are running at 45, down from 68 days in the prior year, which is a substantial improvement. Generally, higher-end services tend to go through more approval processes with higher levels of management on the customer side, which can slow down payments, whereas lower-end services get paid more quickly for the opposite reasons. Can XYZ Co improve on 45 days DSO? Possibly, depending on its customer base. If it is serving the public sector or very large corporate customers, the chances of improvement are slim. Optimal arrangements usually require a reasonable track record of working together and the customer to have built up a high regard for the accuracy and reliability of the service provider's contract delivery as well as its billing systems.

From this analysis, we can see that there are some areas in which XYZ Co can improve its working capital management and accelerate its cash-to-cash cycle (which is the sum of DSO and DIO less DPO), from the current 60 days down to something approaching 30 to 45 days. Shaving 15 days off the cycle at the current level of business would free up $410,000 of cash (sales of $10m × 15/365), which would help it to meet its monthly payroll until the pipeline of new contracts is built up. However, all the improvements we have discussed are more easily done when negotiating new contracts and much harder to introduce to existing contracts or customers.

Platform-based service business model

The working capital cycle for platform-based service providers is the balance of receivables and payables. There is no meaningful inventory in these types of business.

For some platform-based service providers in sectors such as travel, a high proportion of their income is paid for in advance of consumption, from sales of tickets, pre-paid room bookings, etc. These create a useful cash float, significantly reducing the need to fund working capital. Those platform-based service providers that derive income streams from licensing models, consumption models or fixed-term service, support and maintenance contracts will need to finance some level of receivables. These models are usually invoiced monthly, possibly with an element paid up-front to reflect the costs of setting up the contract initially. Added together, these up-front payments can represent a useful cash float, which helps to compensate for the typically lower margins earned from this type of income. Indeed, taking a portfolio approach to its income streams is a powerful strategic option for management, optimizing cash flow from the different models. However, management should always ensure that it is securing the best possible trading terms from each type of income stream, and not feel its job is done when the contracts are won.

Payables for a platform-based model are related to either the licences or third-party application consumption being resold, or to the operating overheads of the platform. Operating costs can vary from minimal (the costs of turning around a hotel room), to significant (the operating costs of a flight such as fuel, passenger meals, crew overnighting costs, etc). For the hosted application model, revenues are derived from the consumption of part of the platform's capacity so there is typically no related 'cost of sales' driving payables in the way there is for the resale model.

The cash flow trap of transitioning models

A major challenge for those providers making the transition from the traditional resale model to the hosted subscription or consumption model is the cash flow trough that the sector has had to bridge. Here's why: the sale of one annual $120 licence every month will generate income for the distribution value chain of $120 each month or $1,440 for the year. Selling the same number of subscriptions, or metering customers' consumption, at the rate of one per month will generate revenue for the value chain of only $10 (ie, one-twelfth) in month one, $20 in month two, $30 in month three and so on, giving annual revenue of $780 (the 'rule of 78'). It's not until year two, when annual revenue reaches $3,000 (as compared to $2,880 under the licence model), that cash flow moves back into positive ground and improves from then on. At that point, the model generates cash in increasing volumes, meaning that scaling up does not require additional working capital, in contrast to the product-, people- and resale-based models, which require working capital to scale with revenue. Capital will be required periodically to upgrade or grow the underlying capacity of the platform, and ideally this will be funded from the cash thrown off by the post break-even activity.

Managing final-tier channel players – value creation and growth

18

Value creation and improving the numbers

People-based service business model

Now we have looked at the two sides of the value creation (VC) tree of a people-based service provider separately, we can look at the way they come together and assess whether XYZ Co has done a good job overall of running its business in the last two years (notwithstanding potential troubles ahead!). In Chapter 9 we set out the principles behind value creation, ie that the operating profit generated should exceed the cost of the capital invested in the business to generate that profit. As we have seen, a people-based service business should not need much capital beyond its working capital, so it should be able to create value with a reasonable level of profitability. Figure 18.1 gives a reminder of the VC tree for XYZ Co.

In the current year XYZ Co has created value of $51,600, which is a tiny outcome for $10 million of business, but it is an improvement on the value destroyed in the prior year of $37,475. How has it managed to turn the situation around? If you look at the invested capital for both years, you will see that they are almost identical, but in the current year the larger scale of business has pulled the net operating profit after tax (NOPAT) up above the cost of that invested capital. Even so, the margin of error is very small and

Figure 18.1 XYZ Co (a service provider) value creation tree

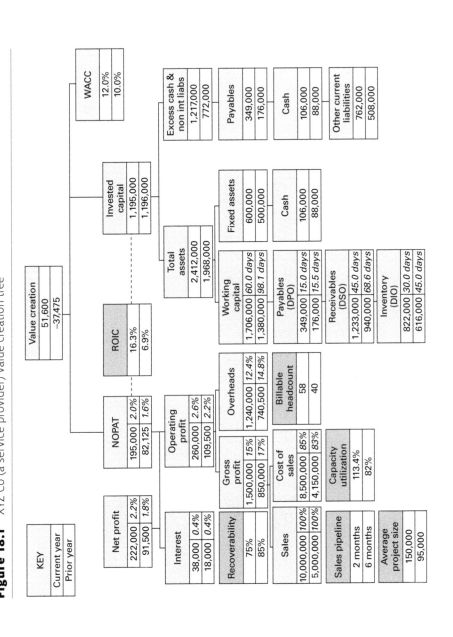

the real culprit here is the low gross margin, which barely covers overheads and leaves a very small operating margin of 2.6 per cent on sales (up from 2.2 per cent in the prior year).

You may have noticed that the cost of capital has increased from the prior year to the current year: up from 10 to 12 per cent. Remember that this is XYZ Co's cost of capital, not the general cost of money in the marketplace, and as such is a risk-adjusted cost of capital. This means that the providers of capital (shareholders, banks and other financing sources tapped by XYZ Co) have decided that the distinctly uncertain outlook for next year has increased the risk in the business and so have increased the return they want from their capital provision to the company. Thus, XYZ Co had to earn a higher NOPAT to create value to compensate for the extra risk it has built into the business. However, it needs to do much better, if it is to have a long-term future.

We have looked at various options for improving the business performance as we have reviewed each of the key measures in turn, but we need a strategic framework for sorting out XYZ's business model. Putting the issue of tight working capital control to one side (dealt with in Chapter 17), what are the options available to XYZ Co for improving its profitability?

The framework shown in Figure 18.2 focuses on the two key measures of profitability – gross and net margin – and is based on measuring gross margins after deducting the cost of time used on customer projects. Clearly, if the service provider is achieving high gross and net margins (ie it registers

Figure 18.2   Options available to service providers for improving profitability

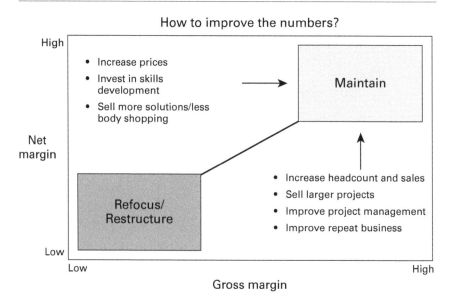

in the top right-hand quadrant), it should maintain whatever it is doing, as long as a review of the future prospects in the sales pipeline indicates that this situation will continue. Equally clearly, if the business is suffering low gross and net margins (ie it registers in the bottom left-hand quadrant) and the separate strategies set out in the other quadrants don't arrest the decline, it should review its whole proposition and consider refocusing or restructuring the entire business model.

The more interesting and challenging situations are if the business registers in the other two quadrants. In the top-left quadrant: net margins are adequate but gross margins are low, a combination that suggests there is no problem with utilization, but perhaps with commanding sufficiently high prices for the value delivered. It is not unusual for service providers to find that they are simply not charging enough. Management should experiment by increasing prices systematically to find at what point they start losing competitive bids. It may be that *some* prices for *some* services should be increased, for example any emergency call-outs or other crisis-response type services. Perhaps seasonal pricing may apply, with discounts for low season and premium (or normal, but higher) pricing for high season. Accounting firms regularly offer services at lower rates when not in the busy end-of-year reporting season (their busy season is the three months following 31 December and to a lesser extent the period following 31 March) and charge their partners and staff out at higher rates on more 'risky' work such as business valuation work or litigation support work.

The second factor to investigate is the skill set of the billable team. Is it up to date and fit for market? Could a greater investment in skills development command higher prices and does the team have the skills to sell the value it is really delivering to customers? Is the mix of skills aligned with market trends? What are likely to be the next services opportunities and how well do the current skills position the service provider to respond? It is better to implement a rolling plan of continuous technical and personal skills training if possible, but it may be appropriate from time to time to make a strategic investment in a major new area or technical development. The alternative to organic skills development is skills acquisition, in the form of either recruitment or acquisition of a company or business. This is a big, strategic, decision and should be based on a solid strategic assessment of the company's own situation, long-term goals and feasible options. A third way is to change the mix of business and sell more higher-end 'solutions' that deliver greater value. This will reduce the proportion of the business that comes from services that are more akin to 'body shopping', such as outsourced technical support, etc.

Let's examine the options in the other, bottom-right quadrant: high gross margins but low net margins. This suggests that there isn't enough volume to cover the unused capacity and overheads. Either the level of sales needs to be increased, absorbing the unbilled capacity, or, if utilization is already high and the business is capacity-constrained, possibly the billable head-count should be increased (healthy margins suggest a strong demand for the service provider's offering).

Closely related to increasing sales is the strategy of selling larger projects. Larger projects increase business productivity all round, with higher sales per sales effort and, once sold, higher utilization levels over sustained periods. It may be smart to trade off some of the strong gross margins through aggressive pricing to win bigger projects and increase net margins by eliminating the fallow periods in the 'feast and famine' cycle typical of shorter-term projects. Larger projects may mean changing the target customer or adding new capabilities to expand the range of service offerings, neither of which should be attempted without carefully weighing the considerations. Often, winning larger projects means targeting larger customers or the public sector. Is the service provider equipped for the longer, more demanding sales cycle? Can it meet the minimum requirements in terms of certifications, insurance, bonds or whatever other hoops it will have to jump through? Will it have credibility and an acceptable track record? Can it carry the greater risks associated with larger, often more complex, projects? This may mean a step up in project management skills and disciplines to control these risks and to ensure that the extra revenue generated improves the bottom line. Failure to invest in the right project management skills and experience could mean that all the larger projects deliver is larger problems and bigger risks, so that the extra revenues become absorbed in project overruns and fixes.

The final strategy, which all service providers should embrace at all times, is to increase the level of repeat business. There are many reasons why a service provider should do this:

- Repeat business is often not put out to competitive tender so there is a much lower sales effort required to negotiate the scope and terms of the work.

- Repeat business often follows on directly, enabling the team to remain in place with no downtime and no learning curve, induction time, etc. Even if the work does not follow on directly, the 'pick-up' time is greatly reduced, benefiting both service provider and customer.

- An invitation to repeat working for a customer is often accompanied by a greater level of trust placed in the service provider by the customer, widening the potential scope of services that can be provided and open-ing the door to higher-end services.

- Working within a familiar customer environment reduces the risk of unknowns, scoping errors, wrong assumptions, etc, improving the poten-tial for both higher margins for the service provider and keener scoping and pricing for the customer.

- New service offerings can be piloted with customers inside a strong working relationship where both parties can invest in the risk and return – the customer gets a potentially valuable service at a greatly reduced price and may gain a competitive advantage, though with more disruption over a longer period than is ideal; the service provider market tests the service offering and irons out the teething issues but possibly at a loss on the project.

Repeat business will be a key strategy for XYZ Co, with its dangerously short sales pipeline and overstretched resources. Existing customers are more likely to yield quicker sales cycles with less sales effort required. The projects are likely to be less risky as client environments will be familiar and client expectations more likely to be matched to XYZ Co's standards and performance.

As we have seen, the people-based service provider business model is just as challenging to get right as the product-based business model, with perhaps more of the 'softer' elements in terms of the people and team management dynamics. Applying this strategic framework should help most service providers to select the right strategy or combination of strat-egies to improve their business performance, while keeping a tight rein on working capital management, enabling the delivery of substantial value creation.

For more on how to manage the people-based business model, see the online chapter on this topic, which is available at: www.koganpage.com/SMC3

Platform-based service business model

For the platform-based service business, value creation improvement is almost entirely dependent upon growing the top line fast enough to exploit the period of above break-even operation before market demands require further investment in upgrading the platform's utility. Managing this stepped investment curve is all about getting the timing right and investing in the functionality and capability that customers will be demanding from the next generation of platforms. Underinvest or misread the market and the platform will not deliver a competitive value proposition; Overinvest and the platform will take longer to reach breakeven (due to higher depreciation costs) and generate lower profits over the cycle. This delivers a double shock to the value creation result: lower NOPAT and higher capital employed.

Managing growth – the integrated business model

Management needs to be able to identify and manage the product, people- and platform-based service business models separately, given the very different margins, working capital and specialist measures that apply to each model. In addition, it should be able to take an integrated view of each contract/project and each customer relationship. Most modern account-ing systems can support this two-dimensional view of the business for any size of final-tier channel player of any complexity. The rationale for this approach is further reinforced when contemplating managing growth, given the way the constraints work in the different models. In the product model, working capital is the key constraint on growth, whereas in the people-based service model, productive headcount and billable capacity will usually constrict growth before working capital (assuming the demand is there for both models). In the platform-based model, growth will be constrained by the ability to fund platform development and enhancement. The different models also tend to have different cycle speeds and reaction times needed – product businesses need faster responses in terms of changing the product lines listed and stocked; the people-based service business needs to be sure it is responding to an upturn in demand, not a 'blip', as increasing bill-able headcount is not easy to undo; and the platform-based model needs to exploit times of optimal capacity utilization for as long as possible before upgrading its capacity (and utility).

As we have seen with XYZ Co, the risks of taking on too much new busi-ness too quickly can overwhelm the business and the management team, leaving the business vulnerable to disaster. It is much more difficult to extri-cate XYZ Co from the situation at the end of the current year than it would be to turn around a product business facing similar consequences from over-expansion. The lead-times with adding and removing or even chang-ing people are measured in months and quarters, rather than days or weeks with products. These different 'rhythms', constraints and risks of the two business models are the fundamental reason why product and service business models should be kept separate and managed differently.

Managing growth is very dependent on being able to 'read' the sales pipeline and getting close enough to customers to be able to sense the level of demand ahead. It requires an ability to segment the market to be able to define offerings that meet the different needs of each segment and to gauge which offerings are going to experience the higher levels of demand. This places an onus on the management team to adopt a disciplined approach to business planning and to project the possible dynamics of the business models under their control. Sensitivity analysis (essentially modelling a variety of realistic alternative scenarios) should help identify which are the more and less risky options to pursue and how well the business can respond. We have seen several service businesses get caught up in the excitement of landing some new customers or major contracts and gearing up the business in terms of headcount and debt to finance the extra working capital, without considering the possibilities once the contracts are completed or expire. On the other hand, we have seen small players become very large players through careful assessment of the opportunities they have generated, positioning their offerings to be in the high-growth segments of the market and adapting their internal culture as they have grown. These are the businesses that have been able to finance growth through good net margins, a firm grip on working capital management and, maybe, just a little luck.

How to get the best from final-tier channel players

19

Introduction

Just as engaging with distributors is really about making the business case for a commercial relationship or for a particular product or category, so engaging with a final-tier channel player is about demonstrating how you can deliver business benefits from working together. The final tier is not the end customer, but a route to market to the end customer, and as such represents a critical element of your distribution model. You need to demonstrate that your value proposition is more compelling than the competition to win and retain share of the final tier's business.

To get the optimum channel value proposition, you need to apply your insight into how the final tier's business models work to construct a stream of commercial benefits that both meet their needs *and* exploit your unique advantages to the full. For example, as a leading brand you can offer a final-tier trade channel player the benefits of strong customer demand (sustained by a roadmap of new products or technologies and backed by substantial end-customer marketing spend), low cost of selling and a robust support infrastructure.

> **Keeping your channel value proposition in tune with the market**
>
> Smart suppliers run partner advisory boards that engage a cross-section of relevant partners in regular dialogue (say every six months) and use these boards to test their channel value propositions or planned changes. Partners are generally quick to say what they don't like about planned

changes, though are not so good at making proposals that suit the channel as a whole, restricting their suggestions to ones that will benefit them uniquely! Partners will sometimes volunteer what the competition is or will be doing with their channel value propositions, though often with some embellishment in an attempt to lever some improvements from the supplier running the advisory board. Experienced suppliers know they have to navigate this continuous 'negotiation' and keep the dialogue at a strategic level, parking the tactical stuff for partner account managers to deal with in one-to-one meetings.

If yours is a niche brand, you can offer exclusive dealership status with high margins and a high degree of account management (we shall explore both these positions later in this chapter). In the approach we proposed for engaging with distributors in Chapter 12, we advocated starting with an analysis of the distributor's strategy. However, in the case of the final tier, this is usually not feasible simply because of the numbers of individual final-tier players involved. Instead, you need to research the business models and objectives of the *types* of channel player you want to engage to define your channel strategy. This research will enable you to size and prioritize the business potential of each channel type and to determine the key elements of your channel propositions.

Segmenting the final-tier trade channel

Your final-tier channel value propositions should be the commercial expression of your channel strategy. It should set out a segmented approach to working with your different channels, showing how you plan to reach and serve each customer segment. It should spell out:

- What role you want the channel to play in terms of market access, demand generation and fulfilment.
- On which customer segments each channel player should be focused (for example, large global customers are addressed by the direct sales force, large national and mid-sized customers are served by Gold dealers and small-sized customers by Silver and Bronze dealers handled through distribution).
- What functions you, as their supplier partner, want to pay the channel for fulfilling, through margin or functional discounts or marketing funding.

- The standards of accreditation and resources you expect them to dedicate to your brand and the level of support and other benefits on which they should base their activities.

- What you expect them to deliver in terms of volumes of business and at what cost to you.

In return for these expectations, you can set out your channel value proposition, based on the economic needs of each type of partner. Segmentation enables you to allocate resources according to your business priorities, for example allocating greater margin rebate incentives to the dealers who recruit more mid-sized customers to your brand, or you can reward your Gold dealers for capturing new large-sized accounts from specific competitors or perhaps for achieving up-sell or cross-sell objectives. By segmenting your final-tier trade channel, you improve your chances of understanding your channel economics in terms of cost per lead, cost per sale and cost to serve for each customer segment.

What the final tier looks for in a vendor

In dealing with any vendor, all channel players look for a predictable source of commercial profit so that they can invest in the relationship with confidence in the return it will generate. This predictability is surprisingly difficult to deliver and many vendors have created a reputation over the years of 'dipping in and out of the channel', meaning that at one time they have established a 'pro-channel' strategy, working with indirect channels to drive their go-to-market strategy for a year or so, then they have switched emphasis to their in-house direct sales force, pulling (usually the largest) accounts and deals away from the channel. Partners that have invested in winning the account over time suddenly find the relationship ripped away from them by the vendor with little or no compensation. Why would vendors do this? Perhaps they are concerned about account control (fearing the channel could switch-sell to another vendor brand), or are responding to the customer's expressed desire to be managed directly by the vendor. Whatever the short-term reasons, the effect is to send a clear signal to the channel that the vendor is not serious about its commitment to working with channel partners over the long haul, and cannot be trusted. Even vendors that claim to have seen the error of their ways and are now committing to a long-term pro-channel strategy will find that the channel has long memories and will be slow to trust such promises, notwithstanding the attractiveness of the channel value proposition.

Final-tier channel players understand that vendors usually don't want to hand over the entire market to them. Most of their vendors will have a segmented approach and have allocated only part of the market to them. The channel players don't have a problem with this so long as they can see that their vendors have a clear channel strategy and well-defined rules of engagement that they can work with. The channel's perspective is, 'Tell us where we can make money and stick to it.' Even rules that say 'The top 200 named accounts will be served by our direct sales force' are acceptable so long as the channel understands the criteria that define 'top 200' and the process and frequency for moving accounts in and out of the list.

Long-term partnering with the channel is essential where the channel is required to invest in the relationship to fulfil its role. For more technical or sophisticated products, this investment can mean adopting a long-term positioning alongside the vendor's brand, dedicating significant numbers of marketing, sales and technical people to being trained up in the vendor's products, building platforms or dedicating part of their infrastructure. Examples of final-tier trade channels that have done this include information systems installers such as Accenture that have specialized in SAP's software; trade installers of specialist equipment such as stair lifts, conservatories and kitchens; dealers in earthmoving equipment such as JCBs or Caterpillar; and petrol stations that have a franchised shop or coffee station.

Once the groundwork of a consistent set of rules of engagement, backed by a sustainable channel strategy, is in place, the vendor's challenge is to sell the commercial relationship so that it can recruit and retain the right channel players as go-to-market partners. The vendor's channel value proposition needs to be cued into the specific pressure points on the business model normally experienced by the channel players it is selling to.

At the end of this part of the chapter, Table 19.1 shows the suggested areas on which to focus by channel player type. First, however, we provide a checklist of the key dimensions of an effective channel value proposition; these dimensions are growth, profit and productivity.

Growth

Most if not all the partners that you want to engage with your channel value propositions will have growth ambitions. Check the following for relevance and, wherever possible, quantify the value of the benefit stream:

- Brand
  - Do you have a commanding market share or can you demonstrate growth in market share (overall or within key categories or key segments)?
  - What investment in marketing are you making to sustain or improve your market share?
  - What impact is this investment having on customer awareness and preference ratings?
- Positioning
  - Are you positioned for growth in terms of the technologies, key market categories or segments?
  - Does your brand offer credibility that the channel can 'borrow' or leverage to strengthen its sales and marketing proposition?
- New markets
  - Do your offerings open up new markets for the channel, perhaps through a new price point or new functionality?
  - What market research can you share that shows the future direction of the market and where partners need to be positioned?
- New customers
  - Will your brand or offerings bring the channel new customers?
  - Where is your marketing activity focused?
  - Is your marketing spending increasing?
  - Do you have a lead-sharing capability backed up by lead-generation activity?
  - Will you send sales people to co-sell alongside the channel's own sales force?
  - Do you have an end-customer sales force that will pass leads on to the channel?
- Address new/unmet needs
  - Will your offerings help your partners increase their penetration and relevance to their existing customers?
  - What research and insights can you share about unmet needs or emerging needs to demonstrate the relevance of your offerings?
- Stream of new technologies and products – Can you demonstrate that you will be able to respond to future demand through a roadmap of new technologies and products?
- Revenue pull-through – Will your channel partners be able to generate additional revenues from installing, servicing and supporting your products (sometimes revenue pull-through can be many times the revenues from reselling the actual products)?

- Joint business planning – Can you jointly pursue new opportunities through focusing your combined sales and marketing resources?

Profit

Although partners will usually focus initially on gross margins and gross profitability, it will usually be in your interests to widen the whole business case to include all the elements of the income statement that come into net margin and net profitability. For example, as a vendor, many of your marketing funds will be taken as a reduction in the channel player's marketing costs, so will show up only in contribution or net margins. Check the following for relevance and, wherever possible, quantify the value of the benefit stream:

- Contract definition. Do you offer any aspect of a protected market space for a particular channel partner that will improve its ability to earn higher margins? This protection can be in the form of explicit exclusivity, such as a franchised territory, or implicit through restricted access through accreditation (by product range, size, resource commitment, certification, etc).

- Margins
  - What level of front-end discounts, back-end discounts, functional discounts, rebates, bonuses, volume rebates, etc, do you offer?
  - How does the timing of when margin is earned vary?
  - What targets and standards must the channel partner achieve to earn the different levels of margin?
  - What margin protection do you offer, such as price protection (against price changes), inventory protection (against loss in value of inventory), returnable inventory, etc?
  - What margin protection do you offer to those who have invested in the pre-sales process and capabilities (accreditation, authorization to sell technical products, etc)?

- Margin mix
  - Does your brand offer a richer margin than the competition because it offers higher-end solutions, more opportunities for cross-sale and up-sale?
  - What level of marketing support and positioning for the channel do you offer to reinforce the higher-end sales?
  - Does your brand require a greater level of service and support from the channel player, or command a premium for its skills? (Anyone who has seen the difference in servicing labour rates for an Aston Martin compared to a Ford will understand this point.)

- Soft funds and marketing funds
  - What funding do you provide?
  - How restrictive are the activities that qualify for your marketing funding?
  - What agency support and resources do you provide for the application of these funds?
  - How quickly do you approve and pay claims for marketing funds?
- Overheads. What infrastructure do you provide that reduces the overhead costs of your partners?
- Standardized systems and processes (perhaps made available online through partner portals).
- Technical back-up, knowledge bases, online documentation.
- Training (not just in your products, but in generic skills such as core technology, diagnostic processes, project management, integration, sales or interpersonal skills).
- Professional sales and marketing resources (ranging from artwork and templates to sales support and marketing services such as PR).

Productivity

This is perhaps the least well-exploited aspect of many vendors' channel value propositions and can best be thought of as the dimensions of doing business that the partner could not deliver itself (or not economically). For example, a regional dealer simply could not build a globally recognized brand that has customers walking in demanding named products. Nor could it afford to design and develop the rigorous training that its technical sales and support people will need to keep at the leading edge of technical developments. Check the following for relevance and, wherever possible, quantify the value of the benefit stream:

- Lead generation
  - Do you distribute leads to your partners?
  - Do you actively generate leads (either continuously or in promotions)?
  - Do you manage lead distribution, to your better-qualified or more responsive partners?
  - Do you facilitate partner lead broking, so that partners can team up to pursue a lead?
  - Do you provide lead registration, so that partners can pursue a lead on your behalf exclusively, or with your assistance exclusively?

- Co-branding
  - Do you provide access to other leading brands through co-branding or co-marketing brands?
  - Do you develop segment-specific marketing initiatives? (For example, Hewlett-Packard, Vodafone and Microsoft all teamed up to put together bundled deals aimed at the small/medium-sized business market.)
- Marketing. Do you provide (or provide access to) marketing services, PR, marketing services agencies, etc?
- Resource alignment
  - Do you provide resources or undertake activities that multiply the productivity of the partners' own resources such as sales training, business management courses, etc?
  - Do you integrate your technical support and sales support capabilities (so that you don't compete with each other)?
  - Do you provide some form of relationship management (eg partner account managers) who can help ensure the partner's strategy is aligned with the vendor and manage the vendor's processes and resources to the partner's benefit?
  - Have you lined up other strategic alliance vendors to provide preferred status for your partners (banking, insurance, legal, accounting, etc)?
  - Do you use your bulk-buying power to access resources and services that would not be available to the individual channel player (eg courses at world-class business schools) or to secure lower prices for the channel?
- Asset deployment

  - Do you provide consignment inventory (ie the channel only pays for the inventory when it sells it)?
  - Do you provide floor-plan financing (effectively cheap loans for inventory)?
  - Do you offer your own or a third party's trade receivable discounting service (so the channel can receive most of the cash from its trade receivables immediately and the balance when its customers actually pay)?
  - Do you offer schemes to help your channel partners set up or acquire the specialized equipment they need to run their operations?

(All of these options are effectively using the strength of the vendor's balance sheet or its cash resources to create advantage for its partners.)

You will need to tailor this list as you develop and refine your final tier value propositions, but an excellent approach is to challenge each of your internal business functions to set out all the ways they support (and could support) your partners. Not only will this bring forward opportunities to offer your channel partners some unique advantages from their relationship with you, it will encourage 'channel thinking' in the parts of your business that perhaps do not typically engage with the channel partners.

Table 19.1 shows which elements of a vendor's channel value proposition are more likely to appeal to the different final-tier trade channel types (using the different channel roles set out in Chapter 13). It is essential that, once you have determined your channel value propositions for each of your channel segments, your account managers who manage the relationship with your channels are properly briefed and updated regularly. Vendors that make the investment in explaining not only their channel value propositions but also the logic and data behind them usually secure a stronger position in their channels and can ride the storms of channel feedback from the occasional wrong turn or mismanagement with greater resilience.

It is often just as critical *how* a vendor deploys its channel value proposition as *what* it comprises. If the final-tier player sees a vendor account manager who takes the time and trouble to understand its business, and is exposed to the vendor's senior management who explain its strategy, and apparent breaches of channel strategy are pursued and resolved promptly, the channel will conclude that the vendor is serious about its channel relationships.

The best vendors regularly survey their channel partners to ensure they are tracking the competitiveness of their channel value proposition and the effectiveness of its deployment. Figure 19.1 shows an example of how well one vendor is meeting the expectations of its low-end value added resellers (VARS) in the form of a map. In this example, the vendor has broken out its channel value proposition by Business, Relationship, Marketing and Support. The black area charts how well it is doing on the individual dimensions of these elements.

It can also be very effective to ask your channel partners to rate your strongest competitor as well as yourself in these surveys to assess the gap between you. There is nothing better for fostering effective channel relationships than to constantly seek feedback as to how well you are doing and then to act on it. Business results are a lagging indicator of the competitiveness of your channel value propositions – by the time sales and share of account start to slip, the rot is well established and it will take time to reverse. Channel surveys are leading indicators, if well executed, and when done regularly can pick up issues or opportunities that can be dealt with before business performance is damaged.

Table 19.1 Relevance of a vendor's channel value proposition to different channel roles

Value proposition	Extension of vendor	Product completer	Service provider	Solution integrator
Growth				
Brand	✓	✓	✓	
Positioning	✓	✓	✓	
New markets	✓	✓	✓	
New customers	✓	✓	✓	✓
Address unmet needs	(✓)	✓	✓	✓
New technologies/ product	(✓)	✓	✓	✓
Revenue pull-through			✓	✓
Joint business planning			✓	✓
Profit				
Contract definition	✓	✓	✓	
Margins	✓	✓	✓	
Margin mix	✓	✓	✓	✓
Soft funds/ marketing funds	(✓)	✓	✓	✓
Overheads	(✓)	✓	✓	✓
Productivity				
Lead generation		✓	✓	
Co-branding			✓	
Marketing		✓	✓	
Resource alignment		✓	✓	✓
Asset deployment	✓	✓	✓	✓

What the final tier looks for in a distributor

Distributors compete with each other for their share of the different segments of the final-tier channels. Unlike vendors, they do not have their own end-customer brand pulling power to attract new channel players, but they do have other weapons, primarily their product range, which is multi-vendor based. The leading broadline distributors will have long-standing

Figure 19.1   Example vendor profile against low-end VAR channel value proposition

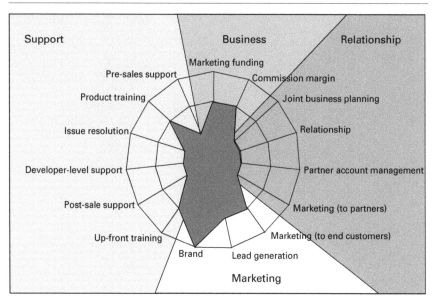

relationships with all the major brands and many lesser brands, making a one-stop shop a core element of their proposition. On top of range, they need to get the basics of availability, price, responsiveness and credit right. They may also offer services that leverage their scale, for example specialized logistics such as drop shipment (shipping direct to the end customer on behalf of the final-tier player), consolidation (assembling a complete assortment of products from multiple vendors for a single shipment to an end-customer) or special packaging (such as for retailers, who require bubble packs to prevent theft). Depending on the sector, they may also offer other services such as outsourced marketing services, project management and financing.

In most markets, you will find a handful of leading distributors competing for 'first call status' of the final tier – ie the distributor that the final tier will call first for 80 per cent of its requirements. Below these will be an array of distributors who can't secure a distributorship with all the leading brands, so will compete on some other basis, such as a brand or category specialization, better service levels (in some dimensions at least) or a commercial dimension such as offering credit lines to accounts that struggle to get sufficient credit from the bigger players.

For both the broadliners and specialized distributors, the same channel value proposition framework of final-tier needs applies and forms the basis for the checklist of growth, profit and productivity. Check the following for relevance and, wherever possible, quantify the value of the benefit stream.

Growth

- Brand
  - Do you offer all the brands necessary to meet the needs of your chosen channel segments?
  - How many brands do you distribute on an exclusive or semi-exclusive basis?
  - Are you increasing your share of distribution for any key brands?
- Positioning
  - What preferred distributor status do you have with vendors that will enable you to offer superior marketing or technical support to your customers?
  - Are you positioned for growth in terms of having distributorships with the emerging brands, technologies, product categories?
  - Do you publish a catalogue or product listing that serves as a reference guide for the end customer market?
  - Do you manage segments of channel partners on behalf of your vendors?
- New markets
  - Do your offerings open up new markets for the final tier, perhaps through securing new distributorships or being an early distributor for new technologies, categories or franchises?
  - Do you offer (better) training in the new technologies and products that will help your channel customer catch the next wave of opportunity?
  - Do you offer a higher level of technical support (pre- and post-sale) than your competition?
- New customers
  - Do you run marketing programmes and offer marketing services that will help the final tier recruit new customers?
  - Where is your marketing activity focused?
  - Is your marketing spending increasing?
  - Do you administer co-marketing funds on behalf of your vendors?
- Joint business planning. Do you help your final-tier players with their business planning?

Profit

- Margins

  - How many brands do you distribute on an exclusive or semi-exclusive basis?
  - What level of front-end, back-end or functional discounts, rebates, bonuses, volume rebates, etc, do you offer?
  - How does the timing of when margin is earned vary?
  - Do you charge for delivery in ways that improve the final-tier margins?
    - Free delivery for orders above a minimum order size?
    - Free delivery for back-orders?
    - Lower charges for multiple ship-to points than your competition?
    - Reward smart ordering behaviour on the part of your customers?

- Margin mix. Do you offer a range that includes brands and categories that offer a richer margin than the competition because it offers higher-end solutions, more opportunities for cross-sale and up-sale?

- Overheads

  - What specialized logistics services do you offer that minimize the costs for the final tier?
    - Drop shipments (to end-customer locations)?
    - Labelling, packaging and invoicing services (to the end-customer on behalf of the final tier)?
    - Multiple ship-to points (for final-tier customers who have multiple locations such as retailers)?
    - Delivery to desk (as opposed to back door)?
    - Consolidation (of multiple products to enable a single shipment of, say, all the elements of a project to an end customer)?
  - What marketing services do you offer that can save the final tier from needing to invest in its own marketing resources and can provide expertise that it could never afford?
  - What technical support and back-up do your offer your final-tier customers, pre- and post-sale, that saves them from needing to invest in these resources?
  - What infrastructure do you provide that reduces the overhead costs of your partners?
    - Standardized systems and processes (made available over the web through partner portals)?
    - Technical back-up, knowledge bases, online documentation?

- Training (not just in your products, but in generic skills such as core technology, diagnostic processes, project management, integration, sales or interpersonal skills)?
- Professional sales and marketing resources (ranging from artwork and templates to sales support and marketing services such as PR)?

Productivity

- One-stop shop. What proportion of each final-tier segment's product needs do you distribute?
- Resource alignment
  - Do you provide resources or undertake activities that multiply the productivity of the partners' own resources such as technical training, sales training, etc?
  - Do you provide some form of relationship management (eg partner account managers) that can help ensure your final-tier customer's strategy is aligned with that of the vendors that you distribute?
  - Do you use your bulk-buying power to provide resources and services that would not be available to the individual final-tier customers?
- Asset deployment
  - Do you provide advantageous credit facilities or credit terms compared to your competitors (perhaps for specific segments of the channel)?
  - Do you provide consignment inventory (ie the final tier only pays for the inventory when it sells it)?
  - Do you provide floor-plan financing (ie effectively cheap loans for inventory)?

You will need to tailor this list depending on what type of distributor you are and on which segments of the final tier you focus. Larger distributors will try to leverage their balance sheet strength by taking the big deal discounts and leading with price and/or credit facilities, whereas smaller distributors will try to leverage their specialization with customized support and service. Mature markets are characterized by fewer price-led propositions and stronger business-focused propositions, which do more for the final tier's efficiency and productivity.

Managing the account relationship

Whether you are a vendor or distributor, you will need to decide what level of account management is cost-effective for your array of partners.

Figure 19.2 Strategic account management process

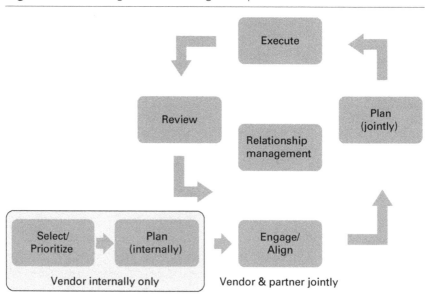

Key partners (typically the 20 per cent of your partners that deliver 80 per cent of your revenues or profits) should be managed on a strategic basis, sharing long-term plans and leveraging each other's strengths. There are two critical success factors: a strategic account management process, and a properly skilled strategic account manager.

The strategic account management process should engage the top-level management of both the vendor/distributor and the final-tier partner and ensure that there is sufficient alignment and focus in both businesses on helping each other achieve its business goals. Set out in Figure 19.2 is an outline of the process that should be driven jointly by the relationship managers of both parties.

Strategic account managers (SAMs) have one of the most demanding roles in business, sometimes termed a 'boundary role'. SAMs need to be able to establish themselves as trusted business advisers to their final-tier partners by virtue of their status in their own company (ie ability to command resources and influence priorities), commercial business skills, strategic insight and strong focus on shared business goals. It is essential that they understand the channel economics of their partners as well as how their partners impact the economics of going-to-market inside their own company.

In our experience, many vendors set up excellent account management processes, appoint their top managers to the SAM role with their key partners and then fail to recognize the damage inflicted by their short-term internal compensation and incentive structures. This often fatally wounds the ability of the SAM to engage the partner in establishing strategic programmes. Very few vendors tie meaningful compensation to the achievement of unique milestones developed in the joint strategic account plan. Instead, they impose a series of standardized growth volume, margin and logistics targets that can often run counter to the spirit of the strategic partnership they are seeking to build.

The real purpose of account management is to 'grow the pie' of business opportunity for both the vendor and its partners, rather than fight over the share of the pie – sometimes termed a 'zero-sum game'. To do this effectively requires joint business planning on an annual basis and some regular reviews during the year. Vendors can often bring market research and market-wide insight to the process to complement the more focused insight from the partner. By sharing their strategic goals, common objectives can be defined. The joint plan, leveraging the special advantages of their combined resources, should be signed off at high enough levels to ensure both organizations are committed to fulfilling the plan. Targets and incentives can be agreed for the personnel in both the vendor and its partner based on the plan. Wherever we have seen this approach implemented effectively it has always led to substantial gains in market share, profitability and competitive advantage.

Some rules of thumb for making compelling business cases

There are some generic strategies that vendors (or distributors) should employ to maximize the competitiveness of their channel value propositions. These strategies are usually differentiated by market share position as this fundamentally changes the economic viability of different strategies and creates different dynamics in the business models.

If you are a market share leader

If you are a market share leader, you usually have the strongest brand and you will be able to spread the cost of your end customer and trade channel marketing activities over a higher number of unit sales. As the (or a) leading brand, you should be leveraging the benefits of demand pull in your channel value proposition. The advantages of money margin, productivity and volumes should be highlighted to overcome the usual disadvantage of low margin:

- *Money margin* – or the gross margin in dollars will make a substantial contribution to fixed costs as most of the vendor's trade channel partners will see sales of the vendor's brand at something close to or above market share. These volumes would be hard to replace and even at low gross margin percentages will represent substantial gross profit.

- *Productivity* – usually a leading brand has done all the marketing needed to create demand for its products, so the trade channel's effort in selling them is greatly reduced. In addition, the burden of technical support is often reduced through greater market familiarity and higher customer knowledge. The greater level of business between a leading brand vendor and its partners can (and should) support more intensive account management, joint business planning and customized investments and activities, all of which should drive greater productivity and increased partner profitability.

- *Volumes* – depending on the category, carrying the leading brands denotes a status and credibility on the part of the trade channel partners that converts into higher volumes of business for them. This often brings 'carry-along' business from end customers as well as the opportunities to cross-sell and up-sell off a bigger revenue base. These benefits are multiplied for the senior tiers in a multi-tier partner programme.

- *Gross margin percentage* – the downside is that leading brands are, by definition, the most widely distributed, creating downward pressure on the gross margin percentage that can be earned on them by the final-tier trade channels. In many cases, the final tier will use benchmark products from key brands to articulate the competitiveness of its price proposition, dragging margins even lower. Vendors can exacerbate the problem by offering volume deals on their highest-volume products, forcing the final tier to pass these discounts on to the end customer ('passing it to the street') to make sure it in turn can offload its increased inventories.

If you are a small vendor or new entrant in a category

For vendors that do not command strong market shares or offer an end-customer brand with high awareness, the channel value proposition will be based on very different economics. Vendors in this position will be asking the final tier to actively sell their brand against the more established leading brands. The final tier will only do this if it can see an attractive economic return for its efforts, which will typically include high gross margins. Given the brand is not widely distributed, the final-tier players that do take it to market will not be competing with each other on price. It is likely that margins will be better than for the leading brands, provided the offering is competitive in terms of its end-customer functionality. Indeed it may well be that it is complementary to the leading brands and as such offers the final tier a high margin component of a solution that falls 'under the radar' from the end-customer's perspective.

An example of this is that retailers will often make a higher margin on the accessories than on the core product that is sold at the same time (sometimes even more money margin). It's not unusual for customers to have done their internet searching and found the cheapest source of the core product (because as a leading brand it is highly benchmarked), and then accept the retailer's suggested accessories without even pausing as they fish out their credit card. The result is that that unknown accessory vendor has delivered a very attractive channel value proposition by enhancing the overall basket (total paid by a customer), enriched the margin in both percentage and dollar terms and done so with a lower investment in inventory, shelf space commitment and with no marketing cost whatsoever.

As a market share minnow, you are offering your partners an open market landscape, but equally virtually no brand awareness or visibility. The key factor that your proposition must include is credibility for your offerings. Typically, this will be built around some high-profile reference sites or sales that borrow the credibility of the customer. In a business-to-business context this could be some early direct sales made to Fortune 500 corporations or a government department or agency. In the small to medium business context, you may need to seek approvals or certifications from relevant trade associations to demonstrate validity. In the consumer market, high-profile sport or entertainment endorsement is valuable, though it must be relevant to your target market. Alternatively, well-placed PR or editorial endorsement can be the difference between success and failure in convincing the final tier to take your products to market. Different channel types will have different concerns that the small vendor must anticipate and pre-empt:

- *Retailers* will be interested to know how fast production can be ramped up if the trial quantities of the product sell well. Going to a national chain of grocers may not be the best first-channel partner if it will expect you to be able to meet orders for several hundred thousand when the first order of 10,000 sells out quickly. You may need to start with regional grocers to give your capacity the chance to ramp up.

- *Trade dealers* will want to know what level of technical support and back up they can count on if the product requires specialist installation or fitting. Being told 'we can get back to you in 10 days' just won't wash with the channel if it has customers expecting the work to be finished on time.

- *Integrators* will want to know just how well you have tested your products across the array of permutations and combinations that they could be working with, for similar reasons.

If you can overcome these issues and offer a high margin on a credible offering, your channel value proposition's final ingredient should be the high degree of influence your partners will have with you as a vendor. This may not seem material, but many of your partners will value this, especially if they see you as a future winner, and their ability to position themselves with their customers will be enhanced.

Selling 'with' the final tier in an advocacy role

So far in this chapter we have dealt with the channel as 'sell-through' partners, ie they take your product to market on your behalf. However, there are many players in the final tier who do not 'touch' your product but can make or break your chances of building sales to end-customers. We called these players 'sell-with' partners in Chapter 13 and highlighted how critical it can be to include them in your channel strategy. Equally, it is important to define a channel value proposition for them to ensure that they are 'on-side' and will endorse your brand and products. Key to this is to help them do their job as customer advocates – they need to be experts in all new technologies, developments, market trends, etc. Their role, credibility and of course income depend entirely on really being experts with some degree of objectivity. You will enhance their capability and not compromise their objectivity by maintaining a dialogue with them through seminars, bulletins, briefings, conferences, relationship managers, etc. They will anticipate and filter your claims of market-leading innovations and product breakthroughs, but will listen intently to your technical updates, especially if you align your briefing teams with theirs. This means that if you have your technical people talk to their technical people, you will gain far more credibility than if you unleash your sales and marketing teams. Companies like IBM and Microsoft have hosted technical and consultant briefings for years. They have learnt to balance a few attractions (venues are often Venice, Monaco or Las Vegas) with the hard-edged technical symposia and throw in a few nice dinners. In the healthcare and pharmaceutical industries, there are now strict guidelines on what the drug companies can legitimately do to educate and brief their principal advocates – the prescribing doctors – but in most industries common sense sets the boundaries of what works before it becomes counter-productive.

Those vendors that deliver genuine technical briefings and updates build up a reputation over time that stands them in good stead with the advocate channel. Vendors do not always have to be the host and in many sectors independent advocates fill this role and seek to impress their clients with the quality and seniority of the vendor people they can get along to their customer conferences. In the IT sector, leading advocates like Forrester and Gartner will mount many conferences aimed at different communities and use the chief executives, chief technology officers, etc of some of the top brands to ensure they pull in a good audience. These provide the vendors with a double benefit: they get to put across their view of the world (with their products and technologies at the centre) to the end customer or sell-through partners and to influence the thinking and trend-spotting of the leading advocates in the industry. Smaller and emerging vendors will have to set their sights a little lower, focusing on more niche advocates and lower-key events and forums.

Summary of Part Three

The channel will take only relevant and competitive products and services to market so it is essential to pay attention to the basic offering from an end-customer's perspective. However, while necessary, a better mousetrap will not be sufficient to persuade the channel to take it to market. For that you need a compelling channel value proposition, which speaks in economic terms to your potential partners' business objectives. Segmenting your chan-nel enables you to segment your channel value proposition, so that it is relevant to the business model of each type of partner. For your more strate-gic partners you need to go even further and investigate their objectives and the pressures on their business model in designing a proposition that enables you to take best advantage of the unique combination of resources in your two organizations.

PART FOUR
Managing distribution in individual industry sectors

Introduction to managing distribution in individual industry sectors

20

In Part Four we share distribution insights from six diverse industry sectors. We believe these insights could be of real value in managing distribution in any number of other sectors. Each of the sectors chosen has overcome challenges in the distribution of their products or services that could be similar or analogous to the challenges you face in your role. In our consulting experience we have found that, to date, there has been very little read-across from one sector to another as to how distribution is done. Even one of the largest fast moving consumer goods (FMCG) brands could not believe how low the cost of pan-European distribution could be until we shared the cost structures in the IT distribution sector (below 4 per cent). This was quite significant in the context of a strategic decision as to whether to continue with in-house distribution or to outsource it. While it was not an exactly comparable distribution model, it was eye-opening for it to realize that substantial economies of scale could continue to be gained when aggregating even its large volumes with those of multiple other brands. This was the key lesson, and it brought credibility to the comparative business modelling exercise supporting the long-term distribution strategy project.

Many sectors have developed break-through distribution solutions, strategic capabilities, business models, techniques and technologies to achieve market access at economic costs. We have selected the six sectors that we showcase in the following chapters to encourage you to look laterally at whether any of their approaches could be relevant in achieving your business goals. In each sector, we provide a brief overview of the sector landscape, examine its specialist challenges and highlight the critical competencies it has developed to tackle them. Where relevant, we share any special metrics typically used. Here is a quick overview of why we selected these six sectors and the distribution insights you will learn:

Capital goods (Chapter 21)

The capital goods sector encompasses products used to produce consumer goods and goods for other businesses. This includes large machinery (such as found in factories), equipment (such as used in engineering, construction or mining) and transport (such as aircraft, trains, ships and automobiles). Given the potentially extremely high cost of capital goods, the sector has developed innovative ways of financing acquisition and use; built channel infrastructures that can keep these goods operating round the clock with exceptionally high uptime, often in challenging physical and remote environments; developed strategic selling skills to ensure multi-million dollar board-level decisions go their way; and the ability to specify and price what can be highly bespoke products, customized to each individual customer's requirements.

Consumer goods and retailing (Chapter 22)

All of us have direct first-hand experience of the retailing sector, which has undergone a recent revolution following the explosion of 'clicks' alongside 'bricks'. Consumer goods range from everyday groceries (FMCG) through fashion and apparel to brown goods such as hi-fi systems and white goods such as ovens, fridges, freezers and washing machines (Electrolux at one time defined its categories as Hot, Cold and Wet). Given the speed at which consumer tastes, buying habits and demand levels change, this sector has developed extremely powerful customer insight and segmentation tech-niques; integrated multi-channel propositions and brand presentation; built responsive supply chains to ensure products remain available on real and virtual shelves; and harnessed the sciences of anthropology, psychology, physiology and many more to the way it packages and merchandises its product, designs its stores and websites, and the influences they bring to bear on your customer journey.

Services (Chapter 23)

Services includes financial services such as personal and corporate banking, insurance, mortgages and pensions; healthcare provision; business services such as transaction processing, payroll, customer care and the whole world of advisory services. The sector has seen huge growth as economies develop and mature and needs become more sophisticated. Economics have increased the pressure to outsource non-core activities. This sector has learnt how to scale personal relationships and trust; adopted digital channels to provide responsive tailored offerings; combated commoditization of its brands across comparison platforms; expanded its scope by converting products into services; and offered convenience to personal and business customers that would not have been thought of even five years ago. It is at the forefront of the application of the consumption model and managing micro-transactions and has developed some powerful tools to run these business models.

Hotels, restaurants, catering and travel (Chapter 24)

Within the world of services, the provision of leisure, travel and dining experiences has evolved ever more rapidly. With increasing disposable income driving consumer demand, and globalization of business driving commercial travel, incentives, exhibitions and conferences, the sector has had to respond to some challenging threats. The greatest of this has been the growth of digital platforms and aggregators grabbing a huge proportion of customer search; the entire industry faced price-based commoditization through its primary market access channels. This sector's response through building compelling customer loyalty strategies to preclude iterant browsing should be relevant to almost any sector.

Intellectual property (Chapter 25)

Intellectual property (IP) is a vast arena, encompassing many of the world's newer industries. It includes copyright IP, patented inventions and trademarks or brands. Not all parts of the world recognize the creators' or authors' rights to profit from their work in the same way. Given IP's intangible quality and that value is created by exploiting the rights to IP, this sector has developed deep skills in reaching global markets through contracting with and licensing complex routes to market; learnt how to balance IP protection with market access and exploitation; and mastered techniques to combat piracy and fraudulent use. It has developed the processes and channel structures to sell IP rights into mass markets, into vertical niches and all types of market in between. Despite the inherently intangible nature of IP, this sector has mastered the means to limit parallel or grey marketing and to maximize revenue yields of short life (movies) and very long life (artwork) IP through cascades of accessibility.

Franchise systems (Chapter 26)

Although most familiar to us in the form of quick service restaurants, the franchise business model has penetrated many other sectors including cleaning, elder care, financial services and even technology services. Franchising offers the benefits of rapid growth without the need for capital (from the franchisor) and harnesses the inherent entrepreneurial energy that comes from working for oneself. While not all businesses can be franchised, the sector has mastered the standardization of operations, territory management, concept and new product development and international expansion of its market access.

You may be wondering why we have not allocated a section to insights from distribution in the IT or telecommunications sectors. There are many up-to-date references to these sector's insights throughout this book, and we have dedicated a whole book to this topic, *Technology Distribution Channels*, published by Kogan Page in 2014. Space constraints have limited us to the six sectors covered in the following chapters, so from time to time we will add insights from additional sectors to the online chapters available to complement this book.

> To read more about sector distribution insights, see the downloadable bonus chapters, available at www.koganpage.com/SMC3

Insights from managing capital goods distribution

21

Introduction

Capital goods are essentially large, expensive items of capital equipment. They fall into three major categories: structures such as factories and homes; equipment including consumer durable goods such as automobiles and producer durable equipment like machine tools and computers; and inventories including cars in dealers' lots. Our focus in this chapter is primarily on producer durables.

You will find some form of capital goods in almost every industry sector, as these examples illustrate:

- Construction and mining equipment for major projects, such as that manufactured by Caterpillar, Komatsu, Hitachi, Ingersoll Rand and JCB.

- Agricultural machinery, such as the combine harvesters, crop sprayers, specialized picking machines and high-end tractors, made by John Deere, CNH, CLAAS, JI Case, Massey Ferguson, and others.

- Manufacturing, including the machine tools, conveyor belt systems, packaging equipment, robots, control systems and kitting systems found in factories of all types. It can also include chilled or frozen storage, automated doors, extrusion equipment, kitchen equipment, high-control environments, R&D lab equipment, test and measurement systems.

- Transport equipment, especially in the aviation sector (Airbus, Boeing, Bombardier), shipping (Hitachi, Siemens), trains (high-speed passenger carriages and freight wagons), buses and trams, vehicle fleets and handling equipment.

- Construction materials, heating, ventilation and air conditioning systems, buildings, factories, distribution centres, IT server farms, wind and solar farms, and similar.

- Healthcare equipment, including diagnostic machines such as MRI scanners and X-ray, monitoring and analysis equipment such as ECG, and treatment equipment such as dialysis and life-support machines.

This extensive yet far from exhaustive list should give you a flavour of the category, as will a review of the particular challenges involved in the distribution of capital goods faced by suppliers.

Specialist challenges and how the sector tackles them

24/7 uptime

Capital goods are generally critical to the production capacity or operational performance of the business that buys them. Every airline aims to minimize the time on the ground of its expensive fleet, as an aircraft is only earning revenue when it is in the air. Production processes or extraction operations (mines or oil rigs) work best when operating round the clock, on a continuous shift basis. Building materials or air conditioning systems – once installed – will be expected to perform throughout the life of the building. The combination of a high purchase cost and operational business need usually leads to a customer requirement for 24/7 uptime from its capital goods; in some sectors such as IT, data centre and network engineers will talk about 'five nines' uptime, ie 99.999 per cent uptime (though if you are sitting on board a Boeing 777 cruising at 43,000 feet even that feels a little approximate!).

Part of the solution is to engineer this capability into the design of the machinery, with high fault-tolerance, but the rest of the solution must come from the supplier's support infrastructure. In most cases, capital goods are sold around the world, and for high-profile, high-ticket items the sale is frequently a direct one, but much of the influence network around the sale is linked to the channel, and much of the front-line support role falls to it. This means integrated manufacturer and channel support around the clock, seven days a week. This channel role includes:

- holding frequent service items and spare parts in stock near to the customer;
- operating an efficient supply chain for rarer replacement parts;
- maintaining a team capable of delivering technical support, both onsite and remotely;

- advising on and executing preventative maintenance schedules;
- providing replacement equipment or back-up solutions in case of breakdown or failure;
- ensuring business continuity throughout the product lifecycle;
- advising on and providing upgrade and enhancement services;
- operating telemetry (to monitor the operational health of the equipment).

A channel that can deliver a supplier's uptime guarantee is a key aspect of its value proposition and brand credibility.

Exposure to the business cycle

Performance in the capital goods sector is highly sensitive to fluctuations in the business cycle. Because the sector relies heavily on primary extraction or secondary manufacturing, it does well when the economy is booming or expanding. As economic conditions worsen, demand for capital goods drops off, leaving manufacturers and their channel under pressure.

Take the mining industry, for example. When copper commodity prices are high the pressure to maximize the output of a mine is immense, with vast resources deployed by mine operators, manufacturers and their extended channel to ensure that a mine is opened as quickly as possible, that the optimal rate of extraction is achieved rapidly, and that extraction continues at the highest possible speed and lowest possible cost. This generates peaks in demand for the huge and expensive excavators, trucks, conveyor belts and crushers that are required. Each part of the extraction chain also generates a vast requirement in consumables – fuel, lubricants, filters – which follows the peak in machine usage. Heavy duty cycles for the equipment also accelerate their requirement for maintenance services and replacement. In all, there is a whole series of revenue streams that are highly profitable to a manufacturer and its channel partners. Should the price of copper fall, however, the entire chain slows down: machines operate shorter hours or lie idle, requiring fewer consumables; maintenance intervals are stretched, requiring fewer personnel to keep equipment operating; and the demand for new equipment disappears, as mine operators sweat their existing assets. While this is a challenge for the operators, further upstream the whole value chain that was engineered for maximum uptime at peak demand is now left with redundancy: skilled staff from sales through to service; inventories of new machines; warehouses full of parts. Since this represents a significant cost and a high level of invested capital, it is crucial for the manufacturer and its channel partners to work closely together to build flexibility into the system to ride out such troughs in demand.

Extremely high cost

When buying trains, ships, aeroplanes, drag shovel excavators or factory production lines, the costs can run to hundreds of millions of dollars. At this level, 'buying' becomes blurred with leasing or even hiring – most aircraft are no longer owned by the airlines, but by specialized leasing companies, or even by the manufacturers themselves. Vehicle fleets, whether cars or trucks, are rarely owned by their operators. There are several considerations at work here: the initial high capital cost, the working life of the capital asset and the likely residual value when it is sold or scrapped (possibly incurring extensive decommissioning costs). Most capital goods manufacturers operate an in-house finance business to offer bespoke financial arrangements that suit the combination of these factors, the risk appetite of the customer and the strength of its balance sheet. Frequently operating as a profit centre, in its own right, it is not unusual for the finance business to deliver a better return on a customer deal than the manufacturing business. Usually there will be at least two major suppliers in deadly competition (eg, Boeing and Airbus) so headline prices and deep discounts may be needed to clinch the deal. However, offering to provide the finance, support and spare parts as package additions can enable the supplier to participate in multiple profit pools, and claw back the profitability it needs from the deal.

High prices are not limited to the equipment itself: although a Boeing 777 may have a list price of over $300 million, what keeps it in the air is a pair of the largest aircraft engines in the world, from General Electric or Rolls Royce. Just one of these will be at the high end of the $17–$35 million price range for aircraft engines. A lot to purchase, but also a lot of cash to have tied up on someone's balance sheet.

Shifting ownership and consumption models

Related to the previous point, given the high value of assets involved in capital goods distribution, ownership is becoming ever more complex. Since for the most part the equipment enables a business to deliver value to its own customers, but is not in itself a core competency, operators are more and more reluctant to acquire assets and, influenced by models from a range of industry sectors and even consumer markets, prefer to consume the benefits of the asset 'as a service'. This can have a profound impact on distribution networks and channels. For example, with data centres in the IT industry, as technology has shifted into 'the cloud' and customers no longer require them 'on the premises', the importance of manufacturer brands is diminishing and the expectation that vendors and their channel partners can realize a transactional sale is being severely challenged. This change has ramifications all the way through the value chain, as IT directors see their power base eroded by line-of-business managers who can rent functional services monthly with bundled IT, resellers frantically reconfigure to make sales of specialist vertically-focused contracts and fulfil on the linked service level agreements (SLAs), distributors focus on building the platforms to enable and track consumption, and vendors are left wondering how to explain the drop in their revenues and profits to the markets.

Difficult locations and extended supply chains

In some industries, like mining or transport, operational locations are remote or in hostile terrains, stretching the geographic distribution and support systems and requiring the extreme edges to be highly self-sufficient. It's not unusual for the suppliers of mining equipment or offshore platforms to station permanent maintenance teams on site. However, it can often be more efficient to have technical resources capable of servicing and supporting multiple types of equipment (rather than a team for the cranes, a team for the low loaders, a team for the excavators, etc), so the supplier engages a network of trusted local dealers. Their engineers will need to be familiar with specific local challenges (extreme heat, intense dust, even war) and any local regulatory or safety requirements. Channels come into their own in these circumstances, since channel players are typically closer to local conditions and better at adapting to them. They also have better access to flexible labour pools, and the benefit of being able to amortize costs over a portfolio of manufacturers' products. Of course, the trade-off here is whether the channel has the sufficient specialist skills required to maintain the equipment in question, as it becomes more technologically complex. The term 'channel' can also stretch to the highly informal, such as the specialist drill bit sharpener who will camp on the outside of a mine or drill a site perimeter fence in the Australian outback, ensuring that highly special-ist drill hammers and bits maintain their effectiveness without requiring a costly formal supply chain.

In other contexts, customers can be deep in city centres ('metro locations') where streets are narrow, parking restrictions limit physical and time access and traffic plays havoc with scheduling. Installing a crane in downtown Manhattan or central London requires an operator with good working rela-tions with the city fire, traffic, police and zoning teams, specialist techniques for operating in confined spaces and the ability to work to the tight hours allowed for shutting a street.

Political complexities

The global nature of capital goods markets, often related to the develop-ment of national infrastructure, can bring the supplier into the world of political complexities and economic risk. Selling mining equipment into Angola, refineries into Nigeria or ships to Iran is not for the faint-hearted or naive. Political considerations can distort the economic rationale. The deal will hinge on the ability to navigate local customs, a requirement to work through a local partner, the willingness to share intellectual property or know-how and a myriad of factors not normally encountered in devel-oped markets.

It can cut both ways. For many years, the United States has restricted the sale of high-end IT (such as provided by Intel or IBM) to markets governed by regimes not considered to be friendly; at the same time, Chinese Huawei was not allowed onto shortlists for supplying core network infrastructure to US markets. Considerations of security risk over-ruled any economic case. In some markets, the supplier is expected to extend its manufacturing or supply chain into the customer's market to secure the deal. Examples include the need to locate some sub-assembly, kitting or final assembly in the target market.

More and more mergers are taking place to secure the scale that is key to competitive advantage. A recent example is the merger of Germany's Siemens and France's Alstom high-speed train manufacturing operations to be able to better compete with China's CRRC. Merging such large-scale manufacturing is complex enough, but each player will typically have differ-ent channel structures and channel partners, so merging their channels will be both complex and time-consuming.

Critical competencies

Marketing to the C-suite

Given the strategic nature of capital goods to their customers and their extremely high cost, decisions as to sourcing, buying and timing will all be made by the 'C-suite', in other words the chief executive officer and other chief-level officers (operations, production, construction, etc). This means that the sales and marketing channels need to be able to operate effectively at this rarefied level. This will involve building deep, multi-level relationships across the customer's organization, and engendering a level of trust and confidence in the supplier's sales and marketing team, whether their own or their channel partners'.

Selling capital assets is a highly skilled and technical challenge, requiring consultative selling skills, excellent negotiation skills and processes, and the technical skills to ensure that specifications are right for the customer's needs. Often the financing of the asset is critical, enabling customers to balance risk and return in the way that best suits them, so mastering financial dynamics is essential for sales teams in manufacturers and channel partner alike. The customer will want assurances on the support infrastructure, its responsiveness, its proactivity, and capability around the world. Given the critical role played by these assets, the customer will also want to know that it will have the attention of the supplier's own C-suite at any time, while having 'one throat to choke' on a day-to-day basis. From the supplier's perspective, it needs to be able to manage lengthy sales cycles, orchestrating activity across marketing, sales, operations and service both within its own organization and with channel partners.

Given the complex nature of the sale, manufacturers often assume that only their in-house sales people can make and fulfil on a sale. For all the reasons outlined earlier in this book, however, it is important to assess the role channel partners can play in selling and delivering. It is critical to be able to take an objective view of this 'direct-indirect' debate, and avoid the temptation to rig the numbers and argument in favour of the status quo.

Buyers and users of capital equipment are no different from other sectors and are online with access to a wealth of information pre-purchase and the ability to share their experiences post-purchase. Ensuring that content about products and services is available, accurate and accessible is crucial, as is understanding how various white papers, brochures and web pages influence a final purchase decision.

Value proposition engineering

As should be clear by now, the sale of a capital asset is a complex process, requiring tailoring of a packaged solution that meets the customer's needs. It is expensive to tailor every solution from scratch for each sale, and difficult to present options for the customer's consideration if everything is possible.

It is a core competence to build and present a set of packaged value propositions that respond to the common needs of different customer segments. These can be fine-tuned in negotiation with the customer once they have been engaged. The supplier can design the value proposition 'packages' (deciding what's included and what's an extra for each package) only with an excellent understanding of core customer's needs. These provide the basis for modularizing the product – determining what needs to be core and what can be offered as augmented extra functionality or wrap-around service. For example, when Airbus presents a new aircraft to an airline it might offer either the standard model or the extended range one. It could offer up to three main seat configurations (that can each be further tailored at a later stage), a choice of three engine manufacturers with engines either purchased outright with the aircraft or leased by the flying hour. Various overall different operating cost envelopes could be guaranteed and the place in the manufacturing queue can be negotiated (this year, next year, option only). This over-simplification shows how Airbus needs to be able to help its customers to position the new aircraft against their planned operational requirements.

Once again, considering customer lifecycles can be informative here, both in terms of developing value propositions and in understanding the role for the channel in delivering them. Mapping out the lifecycle of a mine, for example, allowed a major manufacturer of mining equipment to identify how and when packages should be presented to the mine operators as well as where to position each product in its portfolio: drills and bits in the exploratory phase, earth moving equipment for the opening up of the site, mainstream excavators and trucks during the main operation, high-wall mining equipment to extract the last ounce of value from the main seams... and throughout the cycle a steady stream of parts and service opportunities (see Figure 21.1).

Financing capital procurement

There are many ways for a customer to procure the use of a capital asset, including financing options to enable a purchase, various leasing options, consumption models (pay as you use) and asset management models (the supplier manages a fleet of assets for the customer). In some sectors (usually

Figure 21.1 Mine lifecycle and equipment opportunity

CUSTOMER

HQ
- Output Potential
- Market Potential
- Environmental Review
- Forecast Operating Cost
- Investment Plan
- Exploitation Plan

	3rd Party Exploration / Exploitation Plan	Mine Exploration	Mine Feasibility	Equipment Sourcing	Mine Start-Up	Mine Operation	Service & Problem Resolution	Refurbish or Replace	Disposal	Mine Expansion	Seam Closure	Mine Closure
MINE	Exploitation Plan											
EQUIPMENT		• Drills • Down-the-hole hammers & bits		• Prime production equipment • Support equipment					Replace	Additional equipment	High-wall Mining	Transfer/Transport
		• Awareness • Literature & Information • Exploration equipment	Provide Options, Feasibility & Costing	Respond to RFQ	Equipment Commis-sioning	• Effective asset utilization • Product support • Efficiency/performance studies	• Service • Maintenance • Technical information • Problem resolution • Parts plan & distribution	Refurbishment & Replacement options		Feasibility & Costing	Equipment options, Feasibility & Costing	Transport/Transition
DEALER		Literature & Information	• Case studies/Input to feasibility • Equipment combos/options • Pricing • Lifecycle costings • Free Production Cost (FPC) studies	• Bid Support • Specification • Service/support proposal • Machine options • Financing options (Brand Finance)	Support for Commis-sioning Training	• Parts & support • Major & minor components • Preventative maintenance • Consumables • Customer & Dealer Training	• Parts & support • Major & minor components • Preventative maintenance • Consumables • Customer & Dealer Training	• Parts & support • Major & minor components • Preventative maintenance • Consumables • Refurb/Replacement financing options				
MANUFAC-TURER		Literature & Information				• Parts & support • Major & minor components • Preventative maintenance • Consumables • Customer & Dealer Training	• Parts & support • Major & minor components • Preventative maintenance • Consumables • Customer & Dealer Training	• Parts & support • Major & minor components • Preventative maintenance • Consumables • Refurb/Replacement financing options		Transition Brand financing	Input to Feasibility Supply options (Dealer/No Dealer)	Transition

lower-cost capital assets), the channel can handle the financing aspect of the deal, as a composite aspect of their sales and marketing role. For the higher-cost and more complex capital assets, a specialist financing channel may be needed to work alongside the sales and marketing channels.

Usually there is a need for the channel to offer trade-in capability for replacement capital assets. This can provide the channel with a useful profit stream as it resells restored equipment into the secondary market. Most suppliers need to remain vigilant that, when faced with a resistant customer, the channel does not proffer the used asset to close a deal rather than continue to fight to sell a new asset.

With large and expensive capital assets, even the spares and consumables can be very expensive. To maintain uptime, whole components are swapped out rather than serviced in situ. This can entail the channel holding substantial stocks of spare parts and accessories to meet the responsiveness and uptime demands of their customers. As an example, one of the parts essential to maintaining uptime for a Caterpillar excavator is its 'slew ring' – the rotational bearing on which the cab pivots. At close to half a million dollars for the largest models, measuring several metres across and weighing several tons, it is a challenge to find a channel partner who is happy to tie up that much cash in inventory on the off-chance that one might fail.

In these situations, it is common to see floorplan financing schemes, where a certain level of spare part stocking is financed by the supplier. Given the huge range of special accessories that dealers must stock in some sectors, this can have a big impact on dealer channel cash flow. In all cases, the risk for the manufacturer is that dealers do not focus on managing their parts inventories and so build up large stocks of parts that fill warehouses in disparate locations across the globe, and over time become obsolete but tie up cash and have a cost in term of space. At that point, the dealer can no longer finance the acquisition of new parts and typically turns to the manufacturer for (financial) help in clearing its warehouse.

Establishing global infrastructures

By their nature, many capital assets are bought and used by global businesses, operating in a huge variety of on- and off-shore territories. This puts the onus on suppliers to establish global infrastructures to sell, service and support customers, without risking brand image and equity.

This presents manufacturers with some core choices: which markets to focus on; where to manufacture and assemble to accommodate tariff and non-tariff barriers; what product portfolios to offer in which markets; how to price equipment, parts and service; what channels to use to communicate, sell, supply and support the value proposition. This last choice – establishing the right channel networks and designing the policies and programmes to drive customer value – is a key competency. Successful global capital goods manufacturers make clear channel choices on the blend between direct and indirect activity, and the role and value of their channel partners. As they expand into new markets and their offerings evolve into complex combinations of hardware, software and services, their use of channels is vital to the way their customers experience their brand.

This can throw up some difficult channel conundrums. For instance, there may be only one dealer operating in Outer Mongolia, and it already handles a major competitor, so what do you do? The solution may involve a degree of managing 'co-opetition'. Other challenges include keeping counterfeit spare parts out of the system and protecting intellectual property.

Even established market leaders can benefit from developing channel partnerships. As the markets of Eastern Europe opened up in the early 1990s, Hewlett-Packard made a significant investment in developing the business skills of its channel partners: mostly highly-skilled, technically expert systems engineers who had started selling equipment almost by chance. The relationships established over 20 years ago with distributors and dealers continue to bear fruit in today's revenues.

Providing a tiered value proposition

Many capital assets sectors have consolidated, with brands buying up other competing brands. For example, the mining equipment operations of Terex (excavators, drilling rigs and trucks) were bought by Bucyrus (drag shovels and underground equipment), which in turn was bought by Caterpillar.

At first glance this offers all sorts of potential synergies in the sales and marketing channels, with one network offering the complete range from all these businesses. However, in practice it can risk creating confusion in the marketplace. The challenge is to present a tiered value proposition, offering owned and competitors' brands. Broadly speaking, the channel would most likely want to be able to offer the full set of brands, but how well will premium brand customers accept premium pricing and trust the premium levels of support if they come from a dealer that also offers the discounted range? (It's why Volkswagen doesn't sell its Bentley and Skoda brands from the same showroom, although the showrooms may share common back-office functions.) Optimizing the channel structure to maximize efficiencies and economies of scale cannot be at the expense of brand presentation or quality of customer experience.

Tracking, telemetry and pre-emptive action

With asset value, operating costs and uptime all top-of-mind for customers, it is a competitive advantage to be able to plan and execute preventative maintenance to enable maximum operational uptime. The combination of tracking, telemetry and artificial intelligence is now playing a key role in optimizing service lifecycles and ensuring the parts supply chain has positioned spares and accessories where they are needed.

With a core driver being the number of cycles – take-off and landings for aircraft, pivots for excavators, metres x crawl road gradient for trucks, open-close cycles for high-performance door systems – the ability to track cycle times, ideally remotely, is a critical capability. For Rolls Royce and GE it requires continuous engine management of all engines in the air; for Caterpillar and Komatsu it means GPS and utilization tracking to monitor operational working loads, for ASSA ABLOY Group the requirement to build sensors into many of its door systems.

As the network infrastructure and technologies around the internet of things develops further, measurement will become all-pervasive, but data volumes and network traffic will be immense, requiring manufacturers to hire data analysts. Potentially it also offers a high-value opportunity to their vertically-specialized channel partners who can build dashboards, interpret their results, and advise on the business decisions surfaced.

Focusing on the full profit portfolio

The capital goods sector includes many highly-sophisticated industries with some of the most experienced salespeople on the planet. Even here, the dazzle of the sales commission on a multi-million dollar equipment deal can hide the real lifetime profit opportunity that equipment represents. In the focus to close the sale, it is still easy to forget that a door system with a life of five years is going to generate a rich stream of revenues over its life, including consumables, replacement parts and maintenance services. The key challenge for manufacturers is not only to focus on these revenue streams in the lean years of economic downturn or low commodity prices, but to make them central to sales targets and compensation schemes. What applies to their own sales force also applies to their channel partners, who too often fail to focus on these opportunities. Even where dealers push back on the service aspects, complaining that customers prefer using their own service personnel, there are opportunities to sell cycle-related, packaged services along with the equipment as part of a value proposition focused on customer 'peace of mind'. Worst case, the associated parts kits can be sold to the do-it-yourself customer.

Central to the extended portfolio opportunity is the 'installed base' or fleet of 'machines in field'. Tracking and understanding the evolution of this fleet is essential to targeting parts and service opportunities. Figure 21.2 shows graphically how fleet size is additive, but that fleet growth drives exponential growth in parts and service opportunities.

A number of factors will affect the real opportunity in parts and service. Parts volumes will be driven by machine utilization, availability, planned maintenance intervals and reliability. Where alternatives are available, parts volumes are also affected by the percentage of original parts sold (see Figure 21.3). Counterfeit parts are a key threat to parts volumes in all

Figure 21.2   Installed base, parts and service opportunity

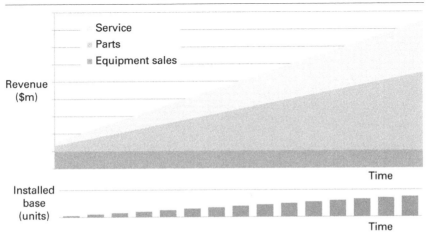

Figure 21.3   Drivers of parts revenues

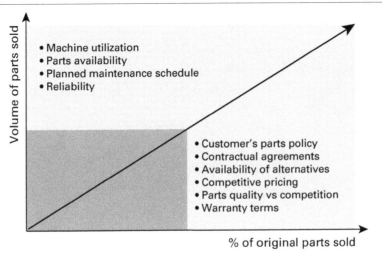

Figure 21.4   Drivers of service revenues

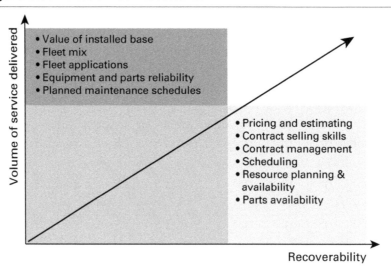

instances, but in high-risk environments such as aviation they can also have a massive impact on safety and, ultimately, brand perception.

The size of the service revenue opportunity has a number of drivers in common, such as service interval, but given the high costs of service delivery it is important also to factor in the *recoverability* of time and investment, ie what proportion of effort and value can actually be invoiced to the client (see Figure 21.4).

Channel and user enablement

Given the cost and criticality of capital assets, and the challenges and capabilities outlined above, it is essential that everyone who touches capital equipment is trained to operate, maintain and service it expertly and safely. Training, user enablement and channel enablement for complex, expensive, life-risking equipment are major aspects of channel design for capital asset suppliers. This is a challenge when standards and a safety culture need to be embedded across a global network, comprising multiple channel partners. Channel partner authorization, certification, banding and tiering are core components here, and a whole industry is devoted to providing the necessary enablement infrastructure, testing, certification and training to ensure partners can sell, install, maintain and – increasingly – dispose of capital equipment.

Once again, technology is transforming these aspects of the channel: old-style classroom training and operational manuals are giving way to virtual training, mobile on-the-job learning and certification. With a machine-tool operator able to control machining through augmented reality, from in front of the machine or from a table in the coffee area, it is no longer inconceivable that a partner mechanic diagnosing a hydraulic fault on an excavator in a deep mine in the wilds of Chile could be supported by similar technologies. Already, unified communications platforms are bringing engineers closer to customers without any requirement to travel.

Key metrics

The range of metrics used is as broad as the range of industries into which capital goods are sold and applications to which that equipment is turned. However, some key measures which distinguish capital goods channels are as follows.

Operations

- *Uptime* – Operating time vs downtime.
- *Owning cost per hour* – Links machine configuration, application and output to cost of ownership.
- *Operating cost per hour* – Links cycle times, burn rates and productivity to repair/maintenance costs and costs of consumables and parts.
- *Refresh cycle* – Average time to refresh.

New equipment

- *Sales* – Units sold, revenues, gross profit, inventory.
- *Installed base* – Machines in field, average unit age, application (eg materials extracted, distance flown, warehouse vs protective doors).
- *Cycles* – Tracking the duty cycle of the equipment, ie the key driver of wear and tear (eg hours in the air, bucket fills, open-shut cycles).
- *Refresh cycle* – Average time to refresh.

- *Residual value* – Residual value of equipment at the end of defined life (the trade-off here is whether it is best to take back as part of trade-in or whether to allow the dealer to sell into highly price-sensitive segments).

Parts and accessories

- *Sales* – Units sold, revenues, gross profit, inventory.
- *Fill rates* – Fill rate to shop, fill rate to customers.
- *Parts/machine ratios* – Units/sales ratios.
- *Parts freight cost.*

Service

- *Service/machine ratios* – Contracts sold per machine.
- *Average contract value.*
- *Sales* – Labour/parts ratio, sales mix.
- *Service recovery/utilization.*
- *Service workshop profitability.*
- *Service personnel costs as percentage of sales.*
- *Repair ratios* – Mean time to field repair, first-time fix rate.

Used equipment

Sales – Average sale of used unit as a percentage of new price, used equipment as a percentage of total sales.

Rental equipment

- *Average unit age* – Used equipment as a percentage of total sales.
- *Unrecovered customer abuse* – Cost of damage/depreciation that cannot be recovered from customers.

Insights from managing consumer goods distribution and retailers

22

Retailers and retailing

What distinguishes retailers from all other types of final-tier players? The generally accepted definition of retailing is that it consists of selling products and services to the ultimate consumer for private consumption. By and large that's whom retailers sell to, though not exclusively, as small business will also often use retailers for convenience (and sometimes for price). You will have noticed that the definition makes no mention of shops or stores. Retailers today go to market through many selling portals, including stores, catalogues, mail-order, the web and telesales. In some cases, players who started out as web-based only, such as Amazon, have opted to introduce stores into their channel mix. There is a general consensus that the long-term survivors in this sector will need to adopt an 'omni-channel' approach.

In consumer goods distribution, the goal of the retailer, whether physical, virtual or both, is to attract customers to its store, get them to 'shop' the store, get them to buy the best 'mix' (ie the most profitable lines) in the store and to get them to come back again. This very simple model (see Figure 22.1) underpins all the businesses in this sector, but the way it changes by channel provides insight into some of the pressures being faced by some major players.

Figure 22.1   Fundamental retail business model

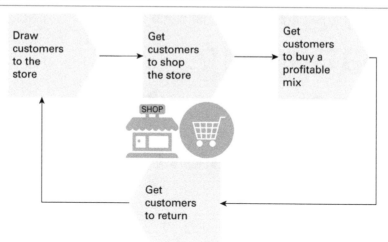

Store-based channels

It is easiest to start with the store-based retail selling motion, ie selling through physical retail premises, located in places that are convenient for the target customer. The core proposition of the store-based retail channel is convenience, product availability, choice and comparison, touch and feel, trial, advice, confidence through physical presence, the ability to return and the intangible dimensions of 'experience' such as image, entertainment, indulgence (why else would so many garments purchased on a Saturday afternoon in a glitzy store never make it out of the bag once they have been taken home?)

In store-based selling, the goal of the retailer is to select the best location, and as the store is built or fitted out, to communicate its presence and forthcoming opening so that it can hit the ground running. Once open, it must build up its customer base through aggressive advertising and promotion, refining its messaging and targeting as it learns more about the catchment area of the store. Depending on the store, the category and its competition, customers may be prepared to travel up to 100 miles to visit it or be unwilling to go further than a 15-minute drive (and with online availability for home delivery of goods from across the globe, 100-mile trips are becoming a rarity). Once customers are at the store, the retailer needs to draw them in through attractive window displays or good visibility of its most attractive products (which is why grocers always put fresh fruit and vegetables at the entrance of their stores). Alternatively, like the US clothing chain Hollister Co, the retailer may opt from a more intriguing, blind store front, using advertising and word-of-mouth to drive customers in through the front door. Once customers have been enticed inside, the retailer needs to draw them further in and around the store by smart layout and merchandising. Increasingly retailers are grouping items together in 'solutions' rather than simply by categories: clothing stores group polo shirts, chinos and pullovers in matching colours, with accessories like belts and shoes, while grocers group different types of rice, sauces, naan breads, curries, samosas, etc, with the other dips and accoutrements of an Indian meal in a 'recipe' display. Software stores merchandise the same product in multiple locations to catch the different types of shoppers in their stores: those who know what they want, browsers who could be tempted, novices who need help and the shopper who always wants what's in the 'top 10' list. The goal is to encourage customers to buy a bigger 'basket', spending more than they intended, and ideally to trade them up from the value to the premium range or from 'good' to 'better' to 'best', increasing both money margin and gross margin percentage.

The store-based retail channel is an increasingly high-risk channel: errors made in site selection may take more than a year to identify and correct; customer traffic can shift (for example if a mall is opened in a town or a major supermarket relocates); and competition can open up nearby, raising the bar for store fit-out and product range and lowering it for prices. New competition can also come from 'pop-up' stores, which have the agility to seize opportunities, profit from them and then move on. Once built and staffed, the core costs of a retail store operation are relatively fixed, putting pressure on the retailer to drive sufficient volumes and secure high enough margins to cover these costs. Most significant of all, the costs of staffing and display space are much higher than those of online competitors, who are driving ever-increasing customer expectations while offering a lower-cost route to market for manufacturers. Store-based retailers respond to these threats differently. US Macy's survived by rapidly building an omni-channel proposition, continuing brand boutiques in-store, but also aggressively closing stores... some profitable. UK's BHS was slower: maintaining own brands and space, failing to address competition, lacking omni-channel or consumer thinking all led to closure. To respond to these challenges, retailing has increasingly become a science, with software tools to support decision making, from site selection, through ranging (how many models and sizes to offer in each category and in what depth) to planograming (how to lay out the merchandise to maximize sales). Even the colours, lighting, background music and special odours pumped through the air conditioning are now chosen based on research into customer responses.

Given the pressures on the store-based business model, it is not surprising that retailers who ran pure store models developed a reputation for dealing with their suppliers somewhat brutally, demanding outrageously high margins, the right to return products that didn't sell (or didn't sell fast enough) and asking to be paid for just about every aspect of their operation – listing fees to include a product in their store, special payments for putting products in high traffic areas in the store, marketing fees for including products in their promotional brochures and even fines for deliveries that turned up late or errors in quantities or invoices. Many retailers became massive brands in their own right with the power to make or break a supplier's access to consumers through their presence in the market and share of a particular category. For example, at one time Dixons and MediaMarkt/Saturn electrical stores were present in every town and city of their home markets of the UK and Germany and they had a very high share of the electricals market. If you were an electricals vendor, you had to secure a presence in their stores to have any hope of making sales and you had to pay the corresponding price through very high discounts, fees and marketing funds as well as commitments to major communication campaigns aimed at drawing your customers into their stores. In return, you could count on high volumes and brand visibility, although in many categories they would compete with your products using their own-brand products at a lower street price.

Although many big store brands continue to have a strong position in the market, the advent of online retail has moderated their dominance since, as mentioned above, its lower cost allows it to provide a cheaper route to market, and its data-driven marketing models provide a more measurable return on channel and marketing investments. In addition, as store-based brands add other selling motions to their business, this makes them aware of some of the limitations of their historic model.

Online and catalogue channels

Online and catalogue channels offer a way of overcoming the constraints of the store-based business model. Where not part of a full, omni-channel model, these two selling motions are often integrated, with a combination of website and customer contact centre ensuring service levels meet consumers' needs. They enable retailers to:

- offer an almost unlimited range of products in breadth and depth that no physical store could match;
- increase convenience, allowing shoppers to browse and buy 'in the comfort of their own home' as expressed by so many retailers;
- increase opening hours to 24/7, making themselves available whenever the customer wants to buy, without the attendant cost in store and payroll costs;
- increase reach in terms of being accessible to any customer in the world with a phone, internet connection or personal device/smartphone, without needing to establish anything more substantial than a local language website;
- offer customization of the product before it is delivered, such as finishing, engraving, configuring, etc.

The number of categories sold online has continued to expand, with notable breakthroughs in fashion and general apparel, even shoes, despite early fears that shoppers would want to see and touch these products or try them on before purchase. Market-leading retailers such as John Lewis, JC Penney, Nieman Marcus and Nordstrom have led the way with websites that have become destination sites with genuine appeal. Packed with multimedia features, including advice on how to combine items, select the right size and add accessories, even try things on virtually with a personal avatar, these sites are pulling in more customers than their flagship stores ever could, round the clock. Vendors looking to be featured brands now must meet exacting standards of support for the retailer's digital production processes as well as excellent margins and responsive logistics. The catalogue selling motion now serves as a complement to its online cousin, with photography and production processes shared between website and catalogue. Digital printing enables highly-personalized, short-run versions of a catalogue to be sent to specific customer segments, reducing size, weight, cost and volumes sent out – as well as increasing relevance for the recipient.

For all its advantages, online selling has some severe disadvantages too:

- The challenges of drawing the customer to your online store, especially if you do not already have an established retailing brand, and the costs of maintaining top-of-mind awareness when the competition is only a click away.

- Making the online shopping experience as easy and intuitive as possible for the different consumer segments targeted.

- The challenge of up-selling and cross-selling customers to buy more than the specific product they have come online to buy.

- The inability to answer immediate questions or handle objections.

- Establishing trust in the mind of the customer in the absence of a physical presence and any tangible reputation.

- Competing with the 'manufacturer direct' and other online sellers, making for intense price pressure.

- Overcoming delivery logistics challenges, with many domestic customers requiring out-of-hours delivery slots (and dealing with the not-at-home problem).

- Overcoming payment logistics challenges with increasing risk and fear of internet fraud.

- The need to provide for 'reverse logistics' in the event the product delivered is faulty, not as ordered or simply not wanted by the customer.

Many of the original online-only retailers sought to dislodge the 'expensive and cumbersome' store-based retailers through the double play of price and convenience. However, with the notable exception of Amazon, few survived to the era of Web 2.0 and it is instructive to consider why. The primary reason is that they did not create sufficient awareness of their offer. Secondly, they were unable to engender sufficient trust with customers to overcome the barriers of adopting new buying and paying habits. Some survived through focus: since 2000, ASOS has grown into a thriving £1.9bn online 'fashion community', with close to 1.7bn website visits per year and an impressive 3% visit-to-order conversion. Their 2017 annual report explains: 'We operate in a world that's constantly changing – fashion, technology and 20-somethings themselves are in perpetual motion. So continuous evolution and innovation is fundamental to who we are as a business'. For newer players, barriers have been shrunk by marketplaces: with the top two business-to-consumer marketplaces, Amazon and eBay, registering over seven billion visits a month globally, problems of awareness and visibility have been solved for suppliers large and small. Couple that with protected payment options such as PayPal and consumers can confidently buy from a tiny supplier on the other side of the planet.

Multichannel and omni-channel

As the online retailing selling motion has matured, the major retailers have increasingly blended their channel proposition, allowing customers to browse in one channel, order in another and select either in-store collection or home delivery from any channel. This has led to some interesting pricing strategies with the online and in-store prices becoming more aligned and the emergence of smart ranging strategies as the faster moving lines are carried in store and the slower moving (but often more profitable) lines are made available online or through a catalogue, sometimes even through an in-store booth.

Similarly, the expectation of a physical presence from all retailers has driven even the purely online players to selectively open stores. Coolblue, a Dutch electricals retailer, which began life with an online offering, now has stores in five major cities in the Netherlands. Even Amazon is opening stores, with some interesting experimental dimensions such as checkout-free shopping (with payment done through an Amazon account by tracking a smartphone). Further east, Alibaba is experimenting with different store formats, both stand-alone and in partnership.

Of course, even within channel types retailers do not all fit one mould, and there are significant differences in approach that reflect their scale (national retailers, regional retailers, independents), core proposition (mass merchants, category killers, specialists) and price positioning (price leaders, service leaders), as shown in Table 22.1.

Table 22.1 Types of retailer customer value propositions

Type of retailer	Get customer to the store	Get customer to shop the store	Get customer to buy best mix	Get customer to return to store
National/regional retailers eg Tesco	Advertising in national/regional media, sponsorships, Stores everywhere	Standardized store layout & merchandising	Promotions, use of high spot locations in store	Loyalty programmes Store density (in region)
Independents ie local stores	Community-based marketing	Range and choice	Advice	Service and support
Mass merchants eg, Carrefour, Walmart, Auchan	Comprehensiveness of range	Store layout & merchandising	Promotions, use of high spot locations in store	Convenience of store location and coverage of weekly needs
Category killers eg Home Depot, Petco	Category-led communications, usually price-led	Choice and assortment	Promotions, use of high spot locations in store	Loyalty programmes, comprehensiveness of range in category
Specialists eg Barnes and Noble	Targeted communications	Advice, choice and assortment	Advice	Quality of service
Price leader eg Costco	Price-led communications	Store layout & merchandising	Drive volume through 2 for 1 type deals	Everyday low prices
Service leader eg El Corte Ingles	Service-led communications	Advice, choice and assortment	Advice, choice and assortment	Quality of service

(continued)

Table 22.1 (*Continued*)

Type of retailer	Get customer to the store	Get customer to shop the store	Get customer to buy best mix	Get customer to return to store
Major online player eg Amazon	Search Engine Marketing National media, PR, Word-of-mouth Membership (Prime) Day promos (CyberMonday)	'Introducing...' 'You browsed...' 'Recommended for you...' Brand boutiques Easy order/payment/ delivery	Accurate product specifications and comparisons for self-upsell 'People who bought this also bought...' Today's deals	Customer reviews Request for feedback EDMs by category New category introductions Loyalty programmes with benefits eg Prime delivery & content
Sole trader e-tail	Marketplaces	Standard website software merchandising Fulfilment by Amazon PayPal button View into distributor stock systems/drop shipment	Standard website software (Magento, Shopify)	Marketplaces Customer database and EDMs

One factor that has multiplied the impact of these channels has been the penetration of smartphones among almost every demographic segment. The key to understanding this power is to recognize the interactive dimensions they offer retailers:

- *Cell location*: enables the network to locate the user to a very local geographic area – such as within a street or two of their stores.

- *Wi-Fi connection*: enables the retailer to offer free Wi-Fi in the store – in exchange for discovering what sites the customer is browsing, even buying from, while shopping.

- *GPS location*: enables 'app' providers (with permission from the user) to identify exactly where they are, such as outside one of their outlets.

- *Content interest*: harnessing Google-type algorithms to relate messages to the content in which the user is interested.

- *Two-way communication*: fast ways for users to respond to messaging, such as ordering a product or booking a service, asking for a voucher or coupon on seeing a promotional message.

- *Peer-to-peer communication*: re-Tweeting a Tweet, forwarding a link, sharing a page or message can all be done in one or two clicks of a dextrous thumb, enabling viral marketing to take effect without the desktop or laptop and to flourish literally anytime and anywhere.

The focus of the 'multichannel' approach is nonetheless on sales. In contrast, true 'omni-channel' thinking recognizes the full customer journey before, during and after the shopping journey, with a focus on engineering and delivering the best possible customer experiences and on the lifetime customer value they can generate. As such, it leverages the presence and growth of social media such as Facebook, Instagram and Twitter, along with online behaviour tracking of smartphones, tablets and computers, to build a full picture of consumer preferences and behaviours beyond purchase, and uses these powerful communication channels to create and facilitate a degree of connection and immediacy that was impossible with earlier media.

More of a challenge, potentially, is going beyond communication to orchestrate activity across these complex channels to deliver satisfaction to an ever more demanding consumer. Pre-purchase, we are all now familiar with comparison sites as a first (instant) source of information for potential buyers. These sites have become another channel of significance, in effect acting as brokers. In each sector, you can now find sites that will help you make comparisons between multiple vendors using criteria such as price, features and benefits, enabling the user to configure the exact specification (for example in insurance, the level and quality of cover, the location of the car or house, the size of the excess, etc). Even in a market as associated with the elderly or infirm as stair lifts, there are now several comparison sites driving business to vendors in exchange for a commission.

Often comparison sites link to another extremely powerful channel: the peer-review sites, such as TripAdvisor (travel, hotels and restaurants), Open Table (restaurants), iTunes (music, films and videos), Amazon (books, gadgets) and many others. In the case of TripAdvisor, users are invited to provide their comments and feedback on places they have visited or experienced, including photos of rooms and facilities. Over time, these ratings and comments add up to a picture that influences prospective users to prefer or avoid specific places. You know when these channels are becoming significant when threats of litigation arise from places that have suffered from the comments made about them. Many sites offer the option to sort items by 'most popular' or 'top rated' as users increasingly prefer apparently objective peer perspectives to that of the retailer.

Cutting through the buzz around social media and its potential for reaching consumers through their personal devices, there are four daunting challenges both for retailers and their suppliers with social media:

1 *Staying up with the current trends*: there will be wave after wave of new developments that will soon render Twitter as old-fashioned as fax machines seem today.

2 *Selecting whether and when to engage customers through the new media*: typically, each of these channels requires regular and frequent contributions and once entered cannot be abandoned. This adds cost, but to avoid it can risk losing touch with the consumer. Capturing the right style and tone is not easy and it can take time to find the correct balance.

3 *Creating compelling content that engages its intended audience*: catching attention in a saturated environment, overcoming cynicism, fatigue and distraction.

4 *Keeping the messaging aligned* across multiple media with the core brand values and messages – and synchronized in time.

Addressing the challenges of omni-channel retail requires constant addition of new skills, entails a further dilution of the marketing funds available or requires additional resources. The old-fashioned virtues of keeping an eye fixed firmly on the business objectives and justifying expenditure in terms of maximizing its impact remain as valid as ever in this frantic, massively connected new world. Depending on your brand and its need to be seen to be out in front, it may pay to let others incur the costs of the learning curve, while being careful not to get left too far behind. However, sometimes the first mover secures an advantage that becomes very hard to shake.

CASE STUDY Distribution promotes whole new categories of products – the power of the iTunes store

When Apple designed its first iPod and needed some software to help users move their albums onto it, did it realize it was laying the foundations for a multi-billion dollar distribution business? From its launch in April 2003, the iTunes store has become the make-or-break market access channel for virtually all forms of digital products, be they music, films, videos, books or specialist software (apps). The numbers are mind boggling – with sales of apps, its newest category, reached $250 million in the month of December 2009 alone from 280 million downloads (many of which were free).

With Apple making 30 per cent gross margin, it clearly knows how to exploit its role as a route to market. In fact, this is an example of how the emergence of a new distribution channel has enabled the creation of a whole new category of products. It is unlikely that apps – many of which cost less than $1 – would have been commercially feasible without iTunes Store's ability to provide instant access to hundreds of millions of potential customers. Even highly specialized apps can find hundreds of thousands of potential customers through the powerful search tools and 'Genius' function that actively promotes products based on the 'If you like this, then you'll love that' principle.

Apple even appears to have broken the 'rule' that open systems should defeat proprietary ones, as other downloading sites and offerings struggle to fight back. The iTunes Music Store's intuitive ease of use when launched has enabled it to account for 70 per cent of worldwide online digital music sales, making the service the largest legal music retailer, reaching 35 billion song downloads by mid-2014 – in just under 11 years from opening. This equates to a lot of 'trained' customers who, after struggling with mobile phone interfaces for years, adopted the iPhone and later the iPad to drive extraordinarily fast ramp-ups of sales, happy to be locked into Apple's proprietary environment.

How can vendors hope to keep any pricing order for their products when they are simultaneously going to market through this blend of high- and low-cost channels? Price controls are illegal, yet if the situation is left unresolved, the lower-cost e-tailers will cannibalize the higher-cost retailers that provide valuable brand visibility and product merchandising, by undercutting them. The answer lies in compensating the higher-cost channels (web or store) for their value to the vendor. Additional discounts or marketing funds are granted to the retailers that provide shelf or web visibility, product advice, product demonstrations, carry the full range of products, achieve high connect rates on related accessories, etc. These rebates can also reward forward planning and disciplined ordering behaviours that help the vendor with its forecasting and planning. This multi-tiered rebate structure enables differential trade pricing to bring the street price from a price-led e-tailer nearer to that available from a full service e-tailer. It is unlikely to completely bridge the gap, but reduce it to the point where the customer will feel the experience of buying from the full service site justifies the price differential. We have seen some very sophisticated discounting and rebating structures from vendors containing up to 30 different elements. These structures allow street (close to) pricing parity to be achieved across the array of channel cost structures that they must deal with to achieve the market access they need. Figure 22.2 illustrates some broad principles of how to achieve this.

Finally, for vendors, a further complicating choice continues to be when to leverage the retail online channels and when to leverage their own. Bypassing the channel and engaging customers through a direct-to-consumer sales channel may appeal in terms of better margin retention and customer touch, but at what cost in terms of building and operating the myriad channels customers expect, and channel conflict?

To vendors or suppliers, the retailer's primary role as a channel is to deliver customer traffic to their products. More important, it is to deliver a well-defined set of customer segments with a predisposition to buy their products. In choosing to go to market through store-based retail, suppliers are engaging with a high-cost channel and need to ensure that they are geared up for the demands of servicing it, in terms of both the customer volumes demanded and meeting the demands of the retailers, financially, logistically, and in marketing support and account management. It is not a channel you dabble in. Retailers have long memories for suppliers that couldn't meet their side of the deal and will be reluctant to re-engage with those that have let them down in the past. Understanding the retailer's business model is key to negotiating your products onto the retailer's (best) shelves and staying there, and it is essential that you know what you want out of the channel before you go anywhere near it.

Figure 22.2 Vendor compensation programmes

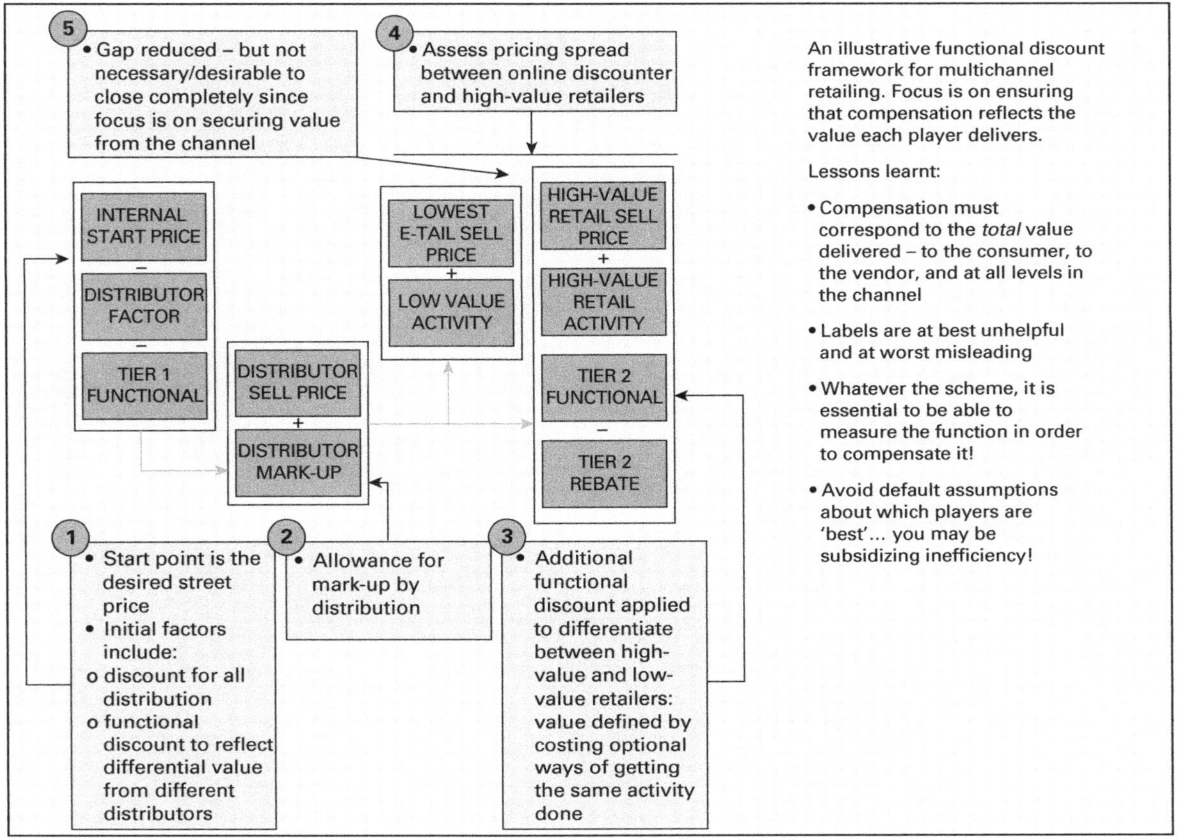

① Start point is the desired street price
• Initial factors include:
  o discount for all distribution
  o functional discount to reflect differential value from different distributors

| INTERNAL START PRICE |
| DISTRIBUTOR FACTOR |
| TIER 1 FUNCTIONAL |

② Allowance for mark-up by distribution

| DISTRIBUTOR SELL PRICE |
| + |
| DISTRIBUTOR MARK-UP |

③ Additional functional discount applied to differentiate between high-value and low-value retailers: value defined by costing optional ways of getting the same activity done

| LOWEST E-TAIL SELL PRICE |
| + |
| LOW VALUE ACTIVITY |

| HIGH-VALUE RETAIL SELL PRICE |
| + |
| HIGH-VALUE RETAIL ACTIVITY |

| TIER 2 FUNCTIONAL |
| TIER 2 REBATE |

④ Assess pricing spread between online discounter and high-value retailers

⑤ Gap reduced – but not necessary/desirable to close completely since focus is on securing value from the channel

An illustrative functional discount framework for multichannel retailing. Focus is on ensuring that compensation reflects the value each player delivers.

Lessons learnt:

• Compensation must correspond to the *total* value delivered – to the consumer, to the vendor, and at all levels in the channel

• Labels are at best unhelpful and at worst misleading

• Whatever the scheme, it is essential to be able to measure the function in order to compensate it!

• Avoid default assumptions about which players are 'best'... you may be subsidizing inefficiency!

Specialist challenges and how the sector tackles them

Any vendor contemplating the options for reaching consumer (and SME) markets is faced with a sector that is undergoing radical change. By way of illustration, Figure 22.3 sets out just a few of the key drivers of change in the consumer go-to-market for the IT and telecoms sector. From a vendor standpoint, the choice of channel is tough, so it is critical to be clear on overall objectives and how distribution strategy helps to meet them. There are a number of considerations that can help understand those dynamics and inform vendor decisions.

Consumer choices are evolving at a rapid pace

With a focus on the consumer, retail has always been exposed to changes in taste and fashion. Today's consumer, however, is both increasingly informed and demanding, and is influenced in store and shopping choices by factors that go way beyond traditional advertising and promotions. The significance of social networks as a mechanism for sharing the experience of using a product or service cannot be underestimated. Focus has shifted far more onto how consumers benefit from a product or service and away from how they buy it. In turn, this has influenced both a consumer's choice of how to buy subsequently and the choice of others in how and where to buy. The world of retail has moved from Procter & Gamble's first and second 'moments of truth' (the moment where a consumer is first confronted with a product in-store or in real-life, then the moment where a consumer purchases the product and is confronted with the experience of the product or brand) to the Google-defined 'zero' and 'ultimate' moments of truth (the moment where a consumer's online searching and experience shape a future purchase and the moment where a consumer shares his or her experiences of the product or brand with millions of others through Facebook, Twitter or their equivalent). The result is rapidly changing channel choices and a shift of power firmly to the consumer, who arrives in store or online highly-informed and with some very firm expectations about the availability of products and information about them.

Single-format retail has a limited life

With time-poor consumers looking to secure maximum value from every interaction, and with almost infinite product assortments available online,

Figure 22.3 Changes in the consumer go-to-market

Who are your customers and what experience do they want?

- Consumers are online: before, during (mobile) and after (social media) purchase
- Informed consumers' requirements have shifted from information to final choice and personal advice
- Poorer, older consumers visit stores: they tend to buy to last and look to get more from what they own
- Rich consumer data is available: but very little of it is exploited

What offers will deliver this experience?

- Price and Advice is now possible: instore focus is 'How will it work for me?'
- The real passion and excitement in products is about *owning and using*
- Consumers have been trained in subscription models by mobile operators and multi-play ISPs
- Convenience is in combinations: click and collect; brand and touchpoint
- Technology now enables cherry-picking, which can damage basket margin

Which channels, products and services make up those offers?

- Multi-channel, multi-format is required to maximize coverage and share of need
- Retailers are exposed to new competitors, especially utility billers of all types
- Partnerships are key: there is an increasing move to 'co-opetition'
- Every player needs to consider the 'ecosystem players': Apple, Google, Amazon

How should routes to market be configured and managed?

- There is increasing vendor concern about, and insight into, go-to-market cost
- There is currently a weak correlation between go-to-market cost and performance
- Channel conflict for vendors now translates into pressure to 'manage your channel'
- Historically poor relationships with traditional retailers shape a view that 'the boot is on the other foot'

How should your company be organized?

- Vendors still need to evolve their approach from separate 'retail' and 'e-commerce' into an integrated omni-channel strategy
- The old compensation schemes are inadequate to drive new performance: for example, how should vendors compensate for 'showrooming'?
- There is a multi-channel challenge: how can all parties preserve brand equity?
- Supply chain integration is crucial: forwards, backwards, sideways!

store-based retailers are opening in multiple formats. For example, as fewer and fewer French consumers make their monthly replenishment trip to the hypermarket, retailers such as Auchan and Carrefour, like their counterparts across the globe, are increasing their coverage of smaller-format stores, ranging from supermarkets through to convenience/proximity stores, while rolling out the 'drive' concept to make the hypermarket shop a less onerous experience. Consumers click and collect their replenishment products like milk, toothpaste and detergents, leaving them free to browse the more pleasurable sections of the store – which also happen to be the more profitable for the retailer. Even the multi-specialists such as Fnac Darty have been opening smaller outlets with limited assortments in stations and airports so as not to lose out to online competitors.

Distribution now extends to a 'live' customer location

Conditioned by the ever more specific times and locations for delivery by the online retailers, consumers now expect 'envelope-level' distribution in all aspects of their lives: if they make a trip to a store they expect to find what they are looking for, or to be able to access a touchscreen or terminal to order it for next-day delivery. If shopping online or in-store, whether for groceries or fashion goods, they expect to have the option to receive products at their home, workplace or other third location that ensures they have the product in their hands as quickly, and freshly, as possible.

If traditional store-based retailing was about breaking bulk from truckloads and pallets to shelves stacked with cartons, today's retailing is about configuring customer baskets for home delivery, or ensuring an HDMI cable is in the customers' letterbox almost as quickly as if they came to collect it in store. For fashion items in particular, but by no means exclusively, consumers expect to be able to return products not only if they are defective but also if they do not fit or are simply the wrong colour. Returns were already unwelcome in the store-based world, where they might typically run at 5–10 per cent. In online fashion retailing, returns can be three to four times that. Imagine if one third of products bought in a Gap store had to go back through the system! (Recent research by Barclaycard in the UK noted that 30 per cent of shoppers deliberately over-purchase and 19 per cent order multiple versions of the same item so they can make their decision at home.) The pressure on both manufacturers and retailer supply chains is acute.

Marketplaces now provide traffic to the smallest of online players

The historic defence for the store-based retailers against 'Fred-in-a-shed' (ie an online retailer with minimal costs, probably a sole trader with basic website backing onto a distributor's stocking system) was the lack of brand and marketing pull to the competitor site. Traffic was key. However, the advent of marketplaces has given visibility to even the smallest of start-up websites and removed that traditional barrier to entry. In a few clicks, any of us can sign up with Amazon and have an undreamed-of online presence and reach at a cost of £25 per month and less than 15 per cent in fees. With multi-specialist store-based retailers running at 25–30 per cent operating costs, there is still a wide margin between the price they need to charge and the price the start-up can charge and still make a healthy profit. While the Amazon marketplace paved the way, today many of the major multi-specialist chains such as Fnac Darty provide a window to consumers for websites which, to all intents, are their competitors.

It is no longer possible to address only the purchase part of the customer journey

Highly-informed consumers, a focus on use, sharing experiences of products and brands instantly online… the limitations of the historic store-based retailer model have been cruelly exposed. Its focus on acquiring customers, having them purchase, and then re-acquiring them as if they were new for every purchase has been shown to be costly and ineffective. Many of its exponents are no longer in business. In recent VIA research, many retailers highlighted that each store visit is a challenge to demonstrate value at the 'select and buy' stage of the cycle, or to lose the customer to online competition… potentially forever. If Apple has shown the way with its stores that focus on how products can be used (and which literally hide away the transactional aspects of the purchase) other retailers have started to address the sharing phase of the journey and entered a dialogue with their consumers post-purchase, actively encouraging them to share their experiences – good and bad – online, and rewarding them for their participation. The Xcite stores of Koweiti retailer AlGhanim have employed this technique with great success.

Stores are taking on a different role

As many of the traditional store functions – information, availability, purchase transactions, collection – are replicated or replaced by consumer online interactions, many are questioning the value of stores (in the case of some consumers by 'voting with their feet' and shopping online). However, stores continue to play a vital role in providing the opportunity to touch and feel products, to compare one with another, and to secure advice for a final choice. This is increasing the pressure on store-based retail to deliver on these promises: to provide a compelling, relevant assortment; to display products, increasingly in the settings consumers would expect to use or wear them; and to provide advice on 'how this will work for me' (rather than how it works, which we can all find out online). It is this last point that poses a particular challenge for some retailers, since a large share of their costs is related to store staff, who require re-skilling in consultative selling… an investment that is significant in any industry but which is doubly risky in an industry where staff churn is notoriously high. This is compounded by the cost of showing products, not least because a proportion of consumers in any store is 'showrooming', ie browsing the assortment with the intention of completing the purchase online or in a different store where the price is lower.

Manufacturers are already showing their impatience with store chains, with many exploring 'flagship' stores as a means of demonstrating how their products should really be experienced. Flagships are not just for the largest brands: Sonos, a manufacturer of multi-room audio – one of the most challenging categories to demonstrate – now has a flagship store in New York City featuring multiple living rooms, configured not only decoratively but also *acoustically* to optimize the listening experience for different tastes in music.

Competition from new sources – brands that can address the entire customer journey

Trained by the mobile phone operators and Internet Service Providers (ISPs), consumers have also taken a step further and are increasingly prepared to consume their products and services on a pay-as-you go consumption model. Even technically complex, highly personalized products such as contact lenses and spectacles can now be consumed on a 'sight as a service' basis – the French optical chain Alain Afflelou, for example, provides multiple pairs/sets for a fixed monthly fee. This has opened retailers to competition from any player that has a billing relationship with the consumer – from ISP to utility provider (who better than an energy company to supply any energy-consuming devices required and add the cost to a monthly bill?). So now a home security camera may be part of a security package rented out by your ISP, with installation rolled into the monthly charge, as the core offerings of connectivity and content become increasingly commoditized and ISPs seek to minimize customer churn.

Critical attributes and competencies

A glance through the challenges listed above might prompt any vendor or retailer to reconsider playing in consumer channels at all. However, few are in a position to turn down the opportunity that the consumer market represents, and nobody should ignore the trends and lessons from consumer markets, since they are increasingly evident in business markets, from small business, through commercial channels and into large enterprise. There are some core attributes and competencies that flag where a retailer or equivalent player is tracking with, or ahead of, trends.

Consumer insight throughout the customer journey

Successful retailers recognize the need to understand their consumers throughout the customer journey. At a simple level, this means mapping out the journey for given customer segments. Table 22.2 shows an example of the journey for a microbusiness customer for printing, showing the stages across the top and value factors that are important to microbusiness buyers down the side.

All players take their lead from online players, who can and do track every interaction with their consumers, from their search behaviours through their information sources, to which sites they explore before landing on the retailer's own site, to how they respond to customer reviews and what questions they ask their peers before making a purchase; then on to what else others typically purchase with the same item, through to repeatedly requesting feedback and review for weeks after purchase, tracking return rates and to EDMs offering accessories or components to increase the value secured from what has been purchased.

If replicating this detail in the physical store environment is tougher, successful players nonetheless push their consumers to subscribe to loyalty cards and analyse the insights purchase data can offer, from assessing choice of channel (online, large-format store or convenience store) to take-up of offers by communication type (catalogue, flyer, points statement, EDMs) through to developing bespoke promotions for specific customer segments and even individual customers. Probably the best-known example of this approach from a mass retailer is Tesco's Clubcard, a story extensively documented in the book *Scoring Points* by Clive Humby and Terry Hunt with Tim Philips. More specialist players will carry this insight through to

Table 22.2 Customer experience map – microbusiness printing

Journey stage / Value factors	Awareness Consideration Preference	Select and Buy		Use and Grow				Replacement and Disposal	
	Preference	Purchase	Delivery	1st 30 days	Use	Supplements/ Extend use	Maintenance/ Service	Replacement [Upgrade]	Disposal
Customer productivity	Inform me through my channels	Online and phone	Home or office delivery	Everything included	Reliability, minimum paper waste, printing speed	Accessories eg sheet-feeder	Post 1yr warranty options	Printer exchange	If functioning keep as second printer for kids
Simplicity	Clear presentation and messaging	Payment options	One call does it all	Plug and play	Ease of use	Easy to fit	One call, one destination	Knowledge of how to go about it	One call
Convenience	Clear info sources eg BrandX web and channel partner webs	Store location, web availability	Time of day and destination options	Install it for me/ Make it run on my network 'instant ink'	Driver info, ease of use, proactive interface	Broad distribution	24hr phone support, same day replacement	Regular, relevant promotions	Meets WEEE directive
Risk	Third party endorsement eg press evaluations	Return options, warranty, options	Guarantee delivery	Meeting expectations	Preventive service and emergency breakdown cover	Make scalable/ flexible/ upgradeable/ future proof	Warranty extension 24/7 'Critical incident' service	Proactive check to match printer to needs plus upgrade	BrandX deals with it
Fun and image	BrandX brand relevance to microbusiness	Brand confidence	Branded Packaging vs brown box	Congratulate me on my smart business decision	Make my business look bigger/more professional	Show me how to get more out of my printing Differing paper	Reassurance		BrandX is green
Environmental friendliness	Energy/ environmental standards		Minimal packaging	Efficiency	Easy return of empty cartridge	Easy returns of accessories		Meets WEEE directive	Meets WEEE directive
Connectivity	Universal standards, eg USB, wireless, bluetooth, network	Meet standards, future proof?		Fits with my network, does what it says	Always on	Wireless options			
Total cost of ownership/ use	Communication of TCO	Cartridge consideration with printer	Free delivery	Number of cartridges replaced	Right product for needs and cartridge POP	Cost of other options/ affordability	Warranty extension cost	Upgrade Incentive programme	Free cost of disposal

understand how their customers are using products and which of them are sharing their experiences online.

Orchestration and integration of brand and offerings across multiple channels

A coherent brand that operates across all the channels and touchpoints is essential to success in retail. This goes beyond simple branding of multiple formats in a consistent form: for example Carrefour's Market, City, Express, Bio and Montagne brands. The customer experience of the brand across and beyond formats must be consistent. For example, it would be reasonable to click and collect in any outlet of the brand, but with franchised or managed store models this is not always in the interest of the store used for collection.

Key factors to succeed across channels are now founded on true integration of online and offline environments. Some examples are:

- *Clarity of the values and role of each sub-brand in the mix* with a consistent experience across channels: this is especially important with franchised or managed stores.

- *Communication that operates across channels*: for example website promotions for instore activity, the option to book appointments online to get face-to-face advice from store staff.

- *Integration of online/offline transactions*: clarity and consistency of online vs offline pricing; online visibility of stock levels by store; options to 'click and collect' ie purchase online and collect instore, but also to browse in store and order for home delivery (for example if the required size/colour is not available); the possibility to browse the full online assortment from the store. Retailer Jack Wills has help points in store with the callout 'Can't find what you're looking for? Find it online. Free shipping. Free returns.'

- *Coherent and integrated after-sales policy*: option to return instore goods bought online, but also no requirement to return to a store to complete a return.

Ultimately this means that omni-channel retailers must invest in the strengths of each channel in their mix in order to differentiate against single-channel players. In the store, this means excellence in assortment planning, merchandising and staff training; online, the focus needs to be on outstanding purchase, delivery and after-sales service.

Responsive supply chains

In the world of integrated channels described above, the nature of success in supply chains is evolving. Retailers must ensure products are available on the real and virtual shelves, when and how customers prefer… and can be returned with equal ease. If direct store delivery drives a shift from truck and pallet to parcel and carton, then the new demands of consumers can require envelope-level delivery capability, within windows as short as one hour. Logistics operations must now support:

- *Click and collect*, ie order online and collect in store.

- *Third-party collection points*: consumers have now been trained to expect the option to return via convenient pick-up/drop-off points, such as their local dry cleaners.

- *Order in store for home delivery*: if consumers cannot have the product in their size and colour immediately, or if they do not want to carry it, it needs to reach their home within 24 hours.

- *Store and central inventory management*: with multiple channels, it becomes essential to track sales run rates across channels and to be able to move inventory to meet need.

- *Robust inventory tracking*: inventory now has to be visible not only to retailer management, but also to consumers: they want to avoid a visit to a store if the product they are looking for is not available.

- *Envelope-level, in-the-hand delivery*: the bar has been set high by Amazon and its peers, which can often offer one-hour delivery slots (at an extra charge, of course) for its Prime customers.

- *Reverse logistics for returns*: a returns system that accommodates a return to store or to/through third-party collection points.

Rigorous, scientific, algorithmic approach to every aspect of the retail business

The power of traditional retailers' brands with consumers has meant that they have been slow to invest in customer data. As an illustration, in two VIA studies into consumer channel trends, retailers of a category of consumer durables were asked what investments they had made in customer databases and data mining. In the first study, in 2003, they were exploring the options and looking at the example being set by Tesco's Clubcard. In the second, more than 10 years later, they confessed that they had made very little progress on the topic. It is now a core competency to be able to analyse customer behaviour throughout the lifecycle. Big data and artificial intelligence are being applied to retail consumers by many different parties from many sectors. Core retail capabilities must therefore now include:

- *Gathering data along the customer journey*: from what searches and influences shaped a purchase decision and choice of channel, to how consumers browse their store (combined with which websites they browse while in store), how they ultimately purchase (or contract) through to how they use and share their experiences of using. All of course, within the constraints of data protection legislation.

- *Mining the data to develop insights into consumer behaviours*: although Amazon, Google and Apple may appear to have a dominant position in this space, retailers need to understand the specifics of their consumers.

- *Applying the sciences of anthropology, psychology, physiology and many others to engineer an improved customer experience throughout the journey*: what information is provided for search, how products are packaged and merchandised, how stores and websites are designed, and how the post-purchase experience is managed.

Clarity of role in greater 'consumer ecosystem'

This data-driven insight in turn links to the need for retailers to have a clear strategy and positioning in the broader 'consumer ecosystem'. Stores, and even entire retail businesses, are only part of a greater ecosystem, so it is vital for them to 'know their place'. Some areas with increasing importance are:

- *Rich online content and advice*: 'unboxing' videos secure millions of views, providing rich information about what exactly a product contains and initial impressions; online reviews and questions provide an opportunity for users to self-help or to answer pre-purchase questions.

- *Display/showroom:* consumers still frequently need to see, touch and feel what they are buying; manufacturers also increasingly look to present their version of their portfolio in a flagship environment.

- *Social media as part of customer advocacy, pre- and post-sales*: leading retailers are making effective use of social media, for example BestBuy in the United States is using Facebook as a highly visible customer care tool; Toyota in France is going so far as to introduce prospective customers to existing owners of their hybrid vehicles.

- *Repair, replacement and disposal*: as more consumers opt for contracts and consumption models, there is an increasing requirement for services, from screen replacement on mobile phones to upgrades of spectacles or contact lenses; at a simpler level, legislation can require retailers to dispose of product they or others have sold, for example low-energy light bulbs.

Figure 22.4 Consumer journey core capabilities

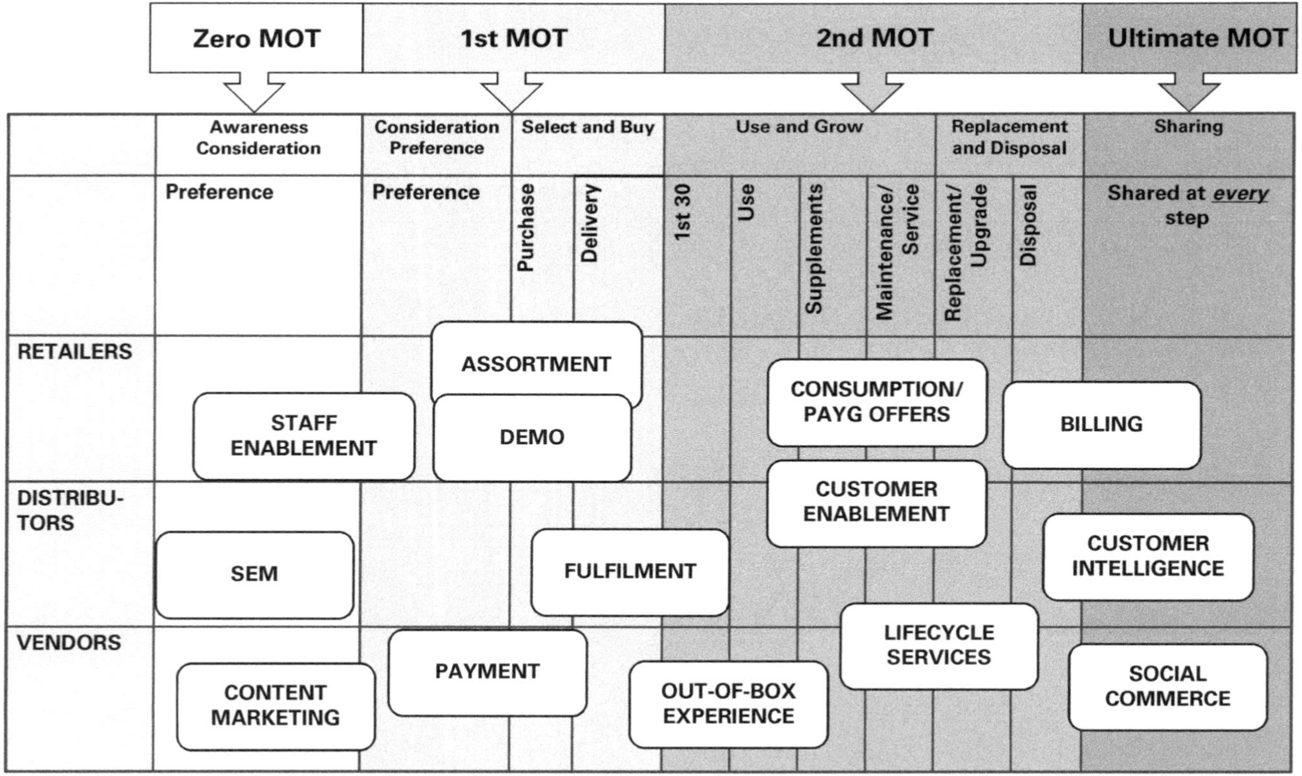

	Zero MOT	1st MOT		2nd MOT					Ultimate MOT
	Awareness Consideration	Consideration Preference	Select and Buy	1st 30	Use and Grow			Replacement and Disposal	Sharing
	Preference	Preference	Purchase / Delivery		Use	Supplements	Maintenance/ Service	Replacement/ Upgrade / Disposal	Shared at *every* step
RETAILERS	STAFF ENABLEMENT	ASSORTMENT / DEMO				CONSUMPTION/ PAYG OFFERS / CUSTOMER ENABLEMENT			BILLING
DISTRIBU-TORS	SEM		FULFILMENT						CUSTOMER INTELLIGENCE
		PAYMENT	OUT-OF-BOX EXPERIENCE				LIFECYCLE SERVICES		
VENDORS	CONTENT MARKETING								SOCIAL COMMERCE

- *Consumption billing capability*: with a switch to consumption models, a well-managed monthly billing point offers a powerful opportunity to maintain customer dialogue and to facilitate self-sell of add-on products and services.

- *Alliances*: all players in the ecosystem have high interdependency and very few can 'do it all', so a clear alliance strategy is critical, including collaborating with competitors in 'co-opetition' deals.

Figure 22.4 sets out one view of a capabilities landscape, showing that opportunities exist for partnerships between vendors, retailers and distributors to create and tap into profit pools throughout the journey. It highlights four 'moments of truth' (MOTs):

1 *Zero MOT* – what people search and find after encountering a trigger to action.

2 *First MOT* – what people think when they see an offering/product, including in-store, and the impressions they form when they read descriptions of it.

3 *Second MOT* – what people feel, think, see, hear, touch, smell and taste as they experience an offering/product over time and see how they are supported through the experience.

4 *Ultimate MOT* – shared moments throughout the experience that shape other people's zero MOT.

For readers interested in learning how to engage with consumer channels, there is a bonus online chapter available at www.koganpage.com/SMC3

Key metrics

Omni-channel operational metrics

These measure the fundamental retail concerns (see Figure 22.5):

- *Traffic.* Whether physical or virtual, a key indicator is customer traffic to a store. Store retailers will track footfall through the door and around the different zones of their stores. Online retailers as well as site visits will explore the source of traffic (whether the visit comes through referral, social media, organic or paid search, etc) using tools such as Google Analytics.

Figure 22.5 Operational metrics and factors driving performance

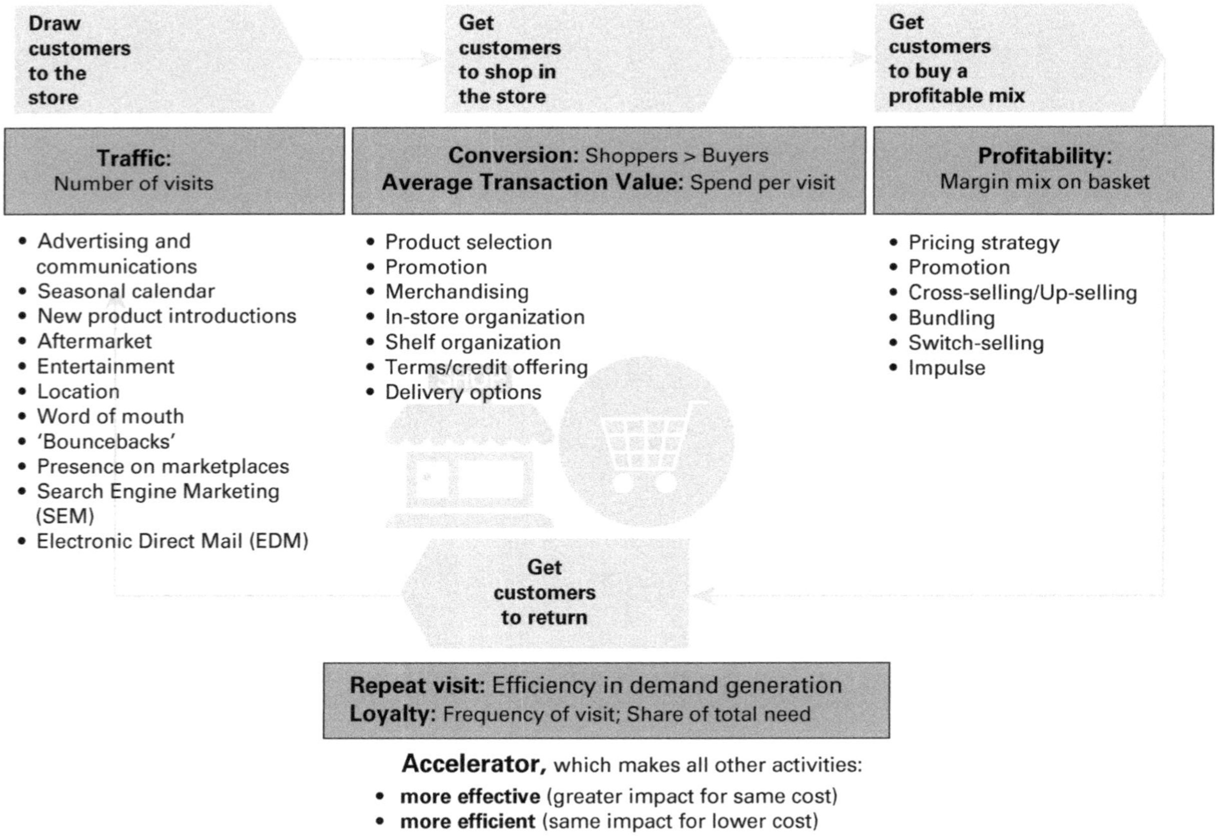

Draw customers to the store		Get customers to shop in the store		Get customers to buy a profitable mix

Traffic: Number of visits

Conversion: Shoppers > Buyers
Average Transaction Value: Spend per visit

Profitability: Margin mix on basket

- Advertising and communications
- Seasonal calendar
- New product introductions
- Aftermarket
- Entertainment
- Location
- Word of mouth
- 'Bouncebacks'
- Presence on marketplaces
- Search Engine Marketing (SEM)
- Electronic Direct Mail (EDM)

- Product selection
- Promotion
- Merchandising
- In-store organization
- Shelf organization
- Terms/credit offering
- Delivery options

- Pricing strategy
- Promotion
- Cross-selling/Up-selling
- Bundling
- Switch-selling
- Impulse

Get customers to return

Repeat visit: Efficiency in demand generation
Loyalty: Frequency of visit; Share of total need

Accelerator, which makes all other activities:
- **more effective** (greater impact for same cost)
- **more efficient** (same impact for lower cost)

- *Conversion.* A busy store or website is no guarantee of sales or profits, in particular in today's world of showrooming. Store retailers will track footfall through the door and compare with transactions at the till. Online players will track conversion from browsing to placing items in a cart, and then cart abandonment rates:

Shopping cart abandonment rate
$\text{Abandonment rate} = \dfrac{\text{Number of purchases not completed}}{\text{Number of shopping carts created}}$

- *Average transaction value.* A crucial measure of the effectiveness of all instore activity, since it measures the impact of store layout, display, cross-selling, up-selling and promotion effectiveness. Critical for physical stores (also called Average Basket Value or ABV) and for online stores (Average Order Value or AOV):

Average order value
$\text{Average order value} = \dfrac{\$ \text{ total revenue in period}}{\text{Number of orders placed in period}}$

- *Margin mix.* A blended margin across the portfolio of sales made, it reflects the success of customer, product and store strategies. It adds in the profitability dimension to the revenue-based metric of average basket value, reflecting the success of consumer, store, supplier and product portfolio choices.

- *Repeat visit.* Difficult for store-based retailers to track until the advent of smartphones and loyalty cards, now an essential measure of the effectiveness of the store experience and how well the retailer is avoiding the old challenge, and cost, of constant customer re-acquisition. Online, analytics and cookies allow thorough tracking of the percentage of returning customers or repeat customer rate (vital in a crowded e-commerce arena where ad impressions, clicks and conversions are constantly increasing in cost):

Repeat customer rate
$\dfrac{\substack{\text{Number of new customers in a given cohort/period who return and}\\ \text{make a second purchase within a specified time (eg 30 days)}}}{\text{Number of new customers in the given cohort/period}}$

- *Customer loyalty.* A combination of measures of frequency of repeat visit and quantification of share of total customer spend allows retailers to assess customer loyalty.

- *Customer lifetime value.* Increasingly significant to any retailer that hopes to compete in the world of 'everything as a service', retailers attempt to project the value of customers over the entire duration of their relationship with the brand. Lifetime is frequently abridged to five years, with this metric focusing on the profitability of the relationship to the retailer.

Sales metrics

- *Average store size.* Real estate is a cost, and most of it for retailers is selling space, so they need to know the average size of their stores. Some have larger formats than others, but all track average store size:

Average store size
$$\text{Average store size} = \frac{\text{Average sales space}}{\text{Average number of stores}}$$

- *Store openings.* A key measure of growth, store openings were traditionally a sign of retailer health. With hyper-efficient online competition, this is no longer necessarily the case.

- *Sales per store (or store productivity).* This metric shows the level of sales achieved on average across the store portfolio:

Sales per store
$$\text{Sales per store} = \frac{\text{Sales}}{\text{Average number of stores}}$$

- *Sales per square foot (or sales space productivity).* This is a crucial measure of how well store space is performing, used to compare stores within a portfolio, and one retail store network to another. Apple stores showed the world's highest sales per square foot in 2017, achieving an astonishing $5,546:

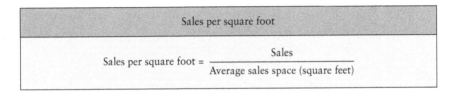

Sales per square foot
Sales per square foot = $\dfrac{\text{Sales}}{\text{Average sales space (square feet)}}$

- *Same-store sales (or comparable store sales or like-for-like sales).* Same-store sales include only sales from stores that have been open for one year or more (it takes time for a new store to ramp up to full productivity). Frequently referred to as 'Comps'.

Profitability metrics

The key metrics are gross margin and mark-up, as defined in Chapter 6. A distinction is made in retail between buying margin and achieved margin:

Buying margin %
Buying margin % = $\dfrac{\text{Expected retail price} - \text{Supplier cost}}{\text{Expected retail price}} \times 100$

Achieved margin %
Achieved margin % = $\dfrac{\text{Actual price received} - \text{Supplier cost}}{\text{Actual price received}} \times 100$

Since retailers in many sectors commit to buying decisions many months ahead of the products arriving in store for sale, in their negotiations with suppliers they make decisions based on the expected street price that the consumer will pay. By the time the product arrives in store, many things may have changed:

- Competitor retailers may be using that product as a 'loss leader' or to communicate their low prices to the market.
- Better or more popular products may reduce the price the market is willing to pay for the product.
- The product may not sell well, requiring the retailer to mark down its street prices to clear it off its shelves.
- The product may have gone into short supply, enabling the retailer to mark up its prices to capitalize on its good availability.

Figure 22.6 Retailer profitability levers – gross margin

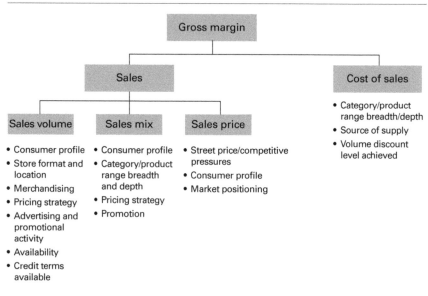

Figure 22.7 Retailer profitability levers – net margin

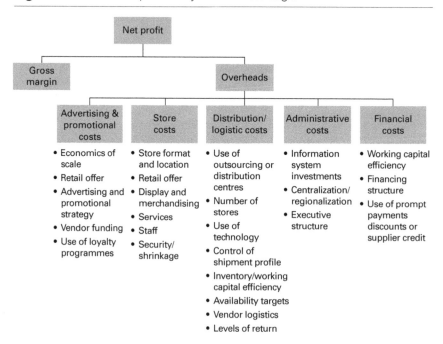

The major levers or decisions available to a retailer to manage its margins are set out in Figures 22.6 and 22.7.

Larger and more sophisticated retailers recognize that two products or two vendors with the same gross margin may not deliver the same contribution to net profit for a variety of reasons, such as size, weight and fragility or the shipping and invoicing accuracy of the products' suppliers. These characteristics drive what are known as direct product costs (DPC). The resulting product/supplier-driven costs are deducted from the gross profit to calculate a net product contribution, or direct product profitability (DPP); see Figure 22.8.

Figure 22.8 Components of direct product profit (DPP)

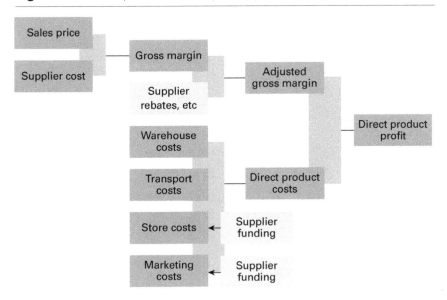

Figure 22.9 Application of DPP to segment products or categories

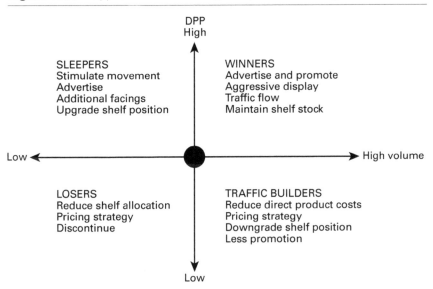

Within the store and category, retailers that use DPP-style measures can adjust the balance of product lines and products to their business model using a matrix such as the one shown in Figure 22.9.

Turns and productivity metrics

In addition to inventory days and inventory turns as covered in Chapter 7, retailers use sales per square foot and profit per square foot to round out their assessment of which products are earning their place on their shelves:

Sales per square foot
$$\text{Sales per square foot} = \frac{\text{Sales}}{\text{Average sales space (square feet)}}$$

Profit per square foot
$$\text{Profit per square foot} = \frac{\text{Gross profit or DPP}}{\text{Average sales space (square feet)}}$$

Retailers accept that different categories will have different productivity profiles, with some categories delivering good sales per square foot because of their high ticket prices but average profit per square foot because of relatively low inventory turns; other categories may deliver excellent performance across the three measures. Much of a retailer's skill lies in understanding the links and adjacencies between product lines and categories and not simply managing its product listings 'by the numbers'. For example, a photography retailer may find its leading brands of cameras turn over quite quickly, but competition on prices may mean that the profit per square foot is dismal. However, by stocking a fairly comprehensive range of the leading brands the retailer is validating its own customer proposition and attracting a good footfall in the store. Every camera sale represents the opportunity to cross-sell a range of lenses, accessories and consumables that deliver an excellent profit per square foot.

Insights from managing services distribution   23

Introduction

To give you an idea of the importance of the services sector, it represents over 40 per cent of Gross Domestic Product (GDP) in even the least developed economies. In the United States in 2015 it was 79 per cent; in Germany, a strong manufacturing economy, it was 69 per cent in 2016. In economies recognized as service-based like the UK it is just over 80 per cent and in the Euro area overall it is 74 per cent (all figures from the World Bank). The trend has been inexorably upwards with the Euro area climbing up from 66 per cent in 1992, with no real deviation from a steady upward trend throughout that period. It's easy to see why the services proportion is so high, when you consider just how broad the services sector is, across both business to business (B2B) and business to consumer (B2C).

We commented in Chapter 3 on the shift from products to services in the way that business consumes functionality, such as computer processing, rather than purchasing products such as computers. This has fed the explosion of 'everything as a service ('XaaS'), including infrastructure (IaaS), software (SaaS) and many types of managed services, such as networking or printing. Services includes call centres, facilities management, all kinds of business process outsourcing, logistics and shipping, marketing and advertising, finance and insurance as well as professional and advisory services. Some of the fastest growing corporate players include Accenture (everything from strategy consulting to business process outsourcing), Mitie (facilities management, project management and other services), Capita (administers a large variety of public sector services) and ADP (transaction processing services). In B2C the sector is just as diverse with utilities (water, electricity, gas, internet, media services such as cable, music streaming), financial services (banking, insurance, savings, investments, pensions, loans and mortgages), healthcare, senior care, home services, transport, education and many others meeting needs across every aspect of our personal and domestic lives.

Specialist challenges and how the sector tackles them

High- and low-touch distribution

The typical services provider business model is built on either scale, to achieve cost efficiencies, or specialization, to achieve deeper capabilities. Success in both cases is built on making customers feel their experience is tailored to their specific needs at the right price. Almost every service provider needs to contend with highly-segmented end user markets, and the need for customized provision at the point of delivery. To reach multiple end-user segments, larger service providers have developed complex, multi-dimensional distribution systems, providing the reach and access necessary to achieve scale. A critical factor in the design of these systems is assessing the degree of 'touch' involved in service delivery.

High touch is required where expertise or advice is needed to navigate the buying process. Examples include the Independent Financial Adviser (IFA) channel where the ability to understand the client's financial objectives and current situation to be able to safely recommend the right financial product is critical to securing the sale. Even the tied or in-house sales force channels will need to conduct similar levels of fact-find and needs assessment to be able to recommend a product. In this sector, there are often legal requirements for due process to protect the consumer in what is a complex, confusing area, open to abuse or worse.

Many financial services channels are high touch, including mortgage brokers, investment advisers, pension advisers, insurance brokers, etc. High-touch channels are expensive routes to market as the touch itself is time-consuming (and may involve an iterative process), and the expertise required is acquired through passing exams, gaining product knowledge, mastering legal and regulatory requirements and accumulating enough experience to be a confident adviser to clients of all types of sophistication and needs. Usually there is an ongoing burden of keeping up to date as tax regulations and other regulatory requirements change and new products continually emerge. High-touch channels are also found in the healthcare and senior care sectors, where the buyer is a novice, options are complex and services need to be uniquely tailored.

High-touch channels expect to be rewarded tangibly and have their investment in a service provider's brand protected. They will not want to see that, once they have acquired a client for a provider, the provider takes over the relationship. If they sense that is a risk, they will simply not bother to engage with the provider nor sell their products. If independent, these channels also expect intangible returns involving high touch for themselves. They need to be confident in the provider's strategy, ethics, direction and management. They expect to be courted by senior managers, nurtured through frequent updates, events, briefings (product changes, regulatory changes) and generally made to feel to be an integral and important part of that provider's market engagement. They will need regular product training, not only in the needs the product addresses, but also on how to match the product to the right customer, and how to sell against the competition.

Low-touch channels are required where the service is 'bought' rather than 'sold', usually simpler services, or for the parts of the customer relationship lifecycle where the buyers are simply browsing and learning what's available, or would prefer to be in control of the process themselves. Examples include customers using online channels to shop online, maintain their own account, receive bills and make payments, update their car insurance (eg when changing their car), add a channel to their cable subscription, buy travel insurance, or renew an existing service for a further period. Almost every major utility service company has now built online low-touch channels to enable customers to manage their service provision. They still need to maintain call centres to handle exceptional service adjustments, catch service failures, attempt to save customers (from leaving), and deal with the off-line customer.

In the B2B space, many managed services can be easily self-managed for the customer, adding new seats to a software licence, extending the usage of an application, signing up for technical and other training, booking travel and so on. The service provider's goal for low-touch channels is to migrate customers to the lowest cost channel consistent with an acceptable level of customer service functionality while providing a positive brand experience. To do this well usually requires a substantial investment up-front in channel specification, configuration, build or procurement, and testing and integration. Many brands are learning how to build-in an up-sell and cross-sell dimension to the channel, even in such a low-touch environment, and enable the customers to migrate across channels seamlessly to complete their self-service process. These aspects of providing effective low-touch channels mean they are generally seen in high volume contexts, where the service is relevant to large customer segments.

Many service providers have found that they need 'more than one bite at the cherry' to cope with the segmentation and modality of their target customers, which can create a fragmented distribution system. For example, a life insurance provider will need to deal with IFAs to reach (usually) high net worth customers who prefer to buy from a trusted adviser; their own tied salesforce to reach the mass market; banks and mortgage and loan providers to reach customers at the point of need; be present on portals (see below) to reach browsing customers; specialist channels to reach customers with specialist needs (older customers, customers in high-risk occupations, etc); and call-centres to service customers through the purchasing process and for after-care. Each of these channels will need active management to keep them up to date with product developments, regulatory changes, servicing requirements, etc.

Many of these types of channel are paid on a commission basis, creating a risk of channel conflict (from the 'two or more bites' strategy). Commission is essential to provide the incentive to the channel, and reward the right behaviours and performance. The design of commission structures, blended with other less-tangible rewards, is a core competence of the financial service industry. One of the risks of offering services is that an expected revenue stream can be curtailed if a customer cancels service, or ends a policy. Many commission structures provide an up-front payment to the channel, to reward the sales effort, but provide a 'tail' commission to encourage the channel to ensure the customer is reminded of the benefits of the service or policy and does not cancel it arbitrarily. Systems are usually put in place to ensure that, should a customer be 'poached' from one channel by another, such behaviour is not rewarded through the commission scheme, removing the incentive to poach, thus ensuring the focus is on new customer acquisition and retention.

Comparison sites and aggregators

Comparison sites like Comparethemarket.com, Etsy.com, Moneysaving expert.com and, in the travel sphere, Trivago, Hotels.com, Expedia, Kayak and many others have sprung up over the last few years in multiple sectors covering utilities, financial services, travel, healthcare services and, increasingly, business services. (We explore the specific insights from the travel, hotels, restaurants and catering sector in Chapter 24.) Aggregators like

Checkatrade, craigslist, Ratedpeople.com, Toptradespeople.com, Made. com, etc enable small players to raise their profile or integrate with other parts of the value chain.

Comparison sites promote themselves heavily as offering the customer the ability to shop the market to find the best deals available for the least effort. One of the reasons for the preponderance of these sites in B2C is that services consume a relatively significant proportion of a household budget and justify the consumer spending more time than usual on the browsing and selection process. Given the volume of traffic these sites attract, service providers need to make a strategic channel choice as to whether to engage with these players or not. Some insurance providers and airlines have actively made a play of not being on these sites, but usually they are highly visible brands in their own right and make heavy play of the need to visit them direct to gain the best deals. However, for smaller service providers, unable or unwilling to invest in building their own traffic, comparison sites and portals offer an immediate opportunity to put their proposition in front of potentially millions of customers who are actively searching for services.

The comparison site business model is based on compensation for the click-throughs provided to the service provider, creating a level of ambiguity as to whose interests are pre-eminent. Customers are becoming increasingly wary of the way offers are prioritized: are they in order of most attractive to the customer, or are they in order of most remunerative to the comparison site? These sites claim to be on the customer's side, loaded with consumer advice and advocacy, but the compensation model suggests otherwise. Any smaller service provider hoping to raise its profile through a comparison site will need to explore the algorithms at work, and evaluate how likely it is to appear on the all-critical first page of options presented to the customers entering a relevant profile of their requirements. The service provider may find that it is bidding for clicks, as it would under the Adwords model employed by Google. The search criteria may not necessarily play to the proposition or customer profiles that a service provider is looking to be matched to, and it may be bundled into generic segmentations that put it into competition with broader offers. By bidding aggressively for clicks it runs the risk of paying heavily for clicks that are too generic to be of real value (ie they do not lead to revenue). By not bidding enough, it may not receive any clicks at all. The real trade-off here is between highly visible comparison sites that draw substantial traffic, and smaller, less visible sites that draw smaller volumes, but offer traffic that is better matched to the service provider's target customer.

In the business services context, portals have emerged to enable specialist service providers to be brought together to fulfil a complex service solution requiring many elements. Usually these portals are operated by service aggregators leading complex service provision projects over multiple geographies. Each complex solution will be different, requiring the aggregator to find the specialists able to complete the value chain needed. Typically, these portals operate an open bidding format, inviting bids based on capabilities, credentials, skill profiles, functional and technical attributes, availability, depth and coverage as well as price. For smaller, more specialized service providers, these portals can be a valuable route to market, offering a low-cost way of accessing the large-scale complex projects run by bigger service aggregators. However, as a channel, it may take time to establish momentum and may involve the service provider in a series of unsuccessful bids at arm's-length, all of which soak up valuable expert resource. Once on the radar of the service aggregator, it becomes more likely that opportunities will flow as account managers become aware of the capabilities (ideally receiving positive feedback from other accounts), and invite the service provider to bid for other relevant service opportunities. Depending upon the bandwidth of the service provider, it will need to be highly selective as to which aggregators it actively engages with.

Long sales cycles

In more complex services, such as business process outsourcing, the sales cycle for the service provider can be quite lengthy; the more complex the service, the longer it is. For customers considering outsourcing one or more of their business processes, this can be a strategic decision involving multiple internal functions and needing the attention of senior management, potentially up to the CEO. Most of the complexity is involved not in selecting the service provider, but in defining and scoping the processes to be outsourced. This is technically challenging, with variables including selecting where the internal and outsourced boundaries will lie, which business lines and customer segments, which geographies and which peripheral but related activities should be in or out of the scope. To add to the challenge, the process of outsourcing involves internal people, managers and other existing suppliers, all of which could be resistant to the change. Balancing the data gathering needed to scope the outsourcing invitation to tender with maintaining secrecy over what may or may not be a substantial change for affected employees is tricky. The most difficult area is often the interfaces between what is outsourced and what remains in-house. During this period, the customer needs to establish the feasibility of outsourcing through validating the capabilities of an array of possible service providers. These contenders will be desperate to help shape the invitation to tender, offering free support for the scoping and definition work, and of course an opportunity to shape it in a way that plays to their strengths. During these phases of exploration, operating-as-usual continues with business performance potentially shaping the urgency or scope of the business process to be outsourced, or suddenly bumping the project down the executive team's list of business priorities.

One additional challenge for service providers caused by lengthy sales cycles is the need to establish deep and far-reaching relationships with a potential customer. This is driven by two factors: complex service provision involves multiple business units and functions; and over a lengthy sales cycle, key personnel will change, through promotions, transfers or departures. A service provider with only one internal champion at a customer is vulnerable to all these risks, as well as internal politics, which are a huge factor when processes and functions are at risk of being outsourced.

Service providers need resilience to cope with the potential length and variability of the sales cycle, with individual opportunities constantly moving forward and back on the calendar, as well as the prospect of landing a new account moving up and down in terms of probability. Even providers of less-sophisticated services can be confronted with lengthy and variable sales cycles, an economic factor that conflicts with the fixed cost structures typical of service providers, as discussed in Chapters 14 and 15.

Critical competencies

Territory management

It is a challenge for any business, whatever the sector, to deliver a predictable, reliable, consistent service experience that fulfils the brand promise. This challenge is exacerbated if the market is geographically large, the customer base is dispersed or their requirements are complex. Add to this the possibility that many service providers may need to work through third parties, or over third-party networks to market, sell or deliver their service. Territory management is about ensuring the channels are both able *and willing* to sell and deliver the service to the market, consistent with the brand promise and values. A territory in this context can be an entire geographic region, such as North America, a cluster of related markets, such as German-speaking Europe, a single country or smaller areas.

Two primary business functions tend to require sophisticated territory management capabilities in the service sector: sales and service delivery. Territory management is also needed by the after-sale service function of any sector that sells products and solutions of any type, be they capital assets, consumer products, or online services. In each case, the supplier needs to be able to offer its customers in the territory a responsive experience, fulfilled by competent resources, motivated to meet customer expectations, in compliance with the brand's requirements that enhance the brand's reputation.

Let's look at a high-touch example of a service related to a tangible product: the provision of post-sale repairs and service for large home appliances – the type you can't bring back to the shop, like fridges, freezers, washing machines, dish-washers and so on. Ideally, of course, this service shouldn't be needed: the products shouldn't fail. However, every manufacturer knows that some customers are going to experience a product that either fails or doesn't work as it should. Motors or bearings seize, seals leak, electronic or electrical components burn out. To protect their brand reputation, manufacturers need to provide their customers with a service that can get their appliance back up and running as it should. Clearly, if every manufacturer established its own service force in the field to cover the households in every market in which its products are sold, it would be cost-prohibitive. The usual approach is to appoint a third party, or a network of third parties, that have the skills to service the products of multiple brands (a bearing is a bearing, whether it be in an Electrolux appliance or a Miele one). Even within a single country or region, this could entail appointing many service agents to ensure that they can despatch a repair engineer out to a home or office within a reasonable time. This is where customer insight is essential. At first sight, you might think you need coverage to reach any customer within 24 or 48 hours. However, it has been shown that customers in most cases (possibly freezers excepted) do not need this degree of immediacy. What they need is predictability and convenience: an agent who can commit to a given window of, say, two hours, for a visit in the late evening, even if that window is more than 72 hours after the initial contact. A critical component of territory management is understanding customer needs and expectations well enough to give you the right service provider selection criteria.

Once the number of agents required has been established, the supplier needs to ensure that each agent is capable of diagnosis and repair, carries the frequently-needed spares and has access to a technical support line for baffling diagnoses or tricky repairs. Each agent needs to be familiar with the recommended steps for diagnosis and repair and the most likely failings so as to minimize call-out time and repair costs (whether borne as the supplier's warranty cost, or charged to the customer). Additionally, the service agent's presentation, customer handling skills, call handling and paperwork should represent the brand's values positively. Typically, a supplier would adopt an accreditation model to assure itself of the technical and other capabilities required of its third-party service network. In such a model, the supplier establishes an accreditation scheme for service engineers that evolves as new models or technologies are released. A curriculum of training and exams is built and maintained, enabling engineers to prove mastery of whatever skills and content are required. This can be extended to customer service agents, salespeople and any other key roles fulfilled by the third-party agents. Often the whole curriculum is delivered online. Setting all this up can be expensive and is an up-front cost. However, it enables clear criteria for agent approval, expressed in terms of how many of each accredited role is required, together with any infrastructure or back office systems. It also supports ongoing quality control with agents needing to keep up to date with their accreditations. One more subtle advantage is that the supplier can be confident there is adequate field support even though accredited engineers may move from one agent to another, or even set up on their own.

Having built a capable service network, the manufacturer needs to ensure the network is motivated to excel in its function. This can involve motivating both the agents and the people who work within the agents. Recognition is as important as revenue, so in many networks you will see annual conferences with plenty of exposure to the senior management of the manufacturer, complete with a multitude of awards (agent of the year for all types of desired performance attributes, engineer of the year, etc). Future product road maps are shared, best practices exchanged and commitment to the network is expressed and shown. Achievements are shared, brand values are emphasized and gratitude for accomplishments are expressed and reiterated. The goal is to encourage all members of the network to feel they are part of a successful mission, appreciated for what they do and motivated to improve.

Just as important is that the manufacturer listens to its agents' feedback on frustrations, issues, concerns over compensation structures, adequacy of training, policing of the quality of the network and any other undercurrents that could distract from the quality of service provision. Being seen to be listening is as important as developing fair and effective responses. Good territory managers should know their agents well enough to distinguish the genuine issues that need to be addressed from the normal background level of grumbling. Good territory management involves proactive attention to the network's profitability, cost drivers, ease of doing business together and the factors engendering brand loyalty. The posture and tone of communication by the manufacturer (and its senior managers and territory team) can be disproportionately enhancing or damaging to the network's general feeling of brand engagement and motivation.

Pipeline management

Given that one of the challenges of the service sector is a potentially long sales cycle, visibility of the likely revenue stream is a critical success factor. In Chapter 15 we explained how to measure the pipeline and the importance of predicting in which time period (week, month, quarter) the revenue is likely to be recognized. For service providers generating annuity-type income, such as subscriptions and licence fees, predictions are possibly easier to manage. However, all service providers, whether their income is typically that of an annuity profile or a more lumpy one, need to ensure that they are actively managing that profile for two reasons. The first is that with a high fixed cost base typical of a service provider, any unexpected revenue shortfall will expose the business to a loss in that period. The second reason is that the resources needed to deliver the service have to be flexed to meet demand. The shorter the forewarning of a peak or trough in demand, the harder it is to flex resources. Unfulfilled demand is lost revenue (and dissatisfied customers); having excess resources for the level of demand is inefficient and loss-making. The combination of these two factors means that even a few short periods of operating at a loss can lead to a dismal annual performance.

The techniques used by service providers to manage their pipeline include:

- *Qualification.* It is tempting when presented with a large opportunity to commit resources to pursue it. The best service providers employ a robust qualification process of every opportunity before committing resources. They evaluate the customer's need, interest, budget and credibility as early as possible. This is especially true in B2B, where qualification of the opportunity and the buyer ensures the investment in long sales cycles pays off.

- *Clear step-of-sales process.* A disciplined sale process with clearly defined steps or phases, and gates before progressing to the next step, helps bring rigour and discipline to the pipeline management process. This builds on the benefits of a robust qualification process, which is step one. Failure to be able to complete a step should influence the assessment of success probability and the commensurate level of resources allocated to securing the sale.

- *Deal registration.* Where sales opportunities are generated by players within extended third-party networks, there is a risk that the same opportunity is being pursued by two or more players. Equally, there is a risk that sales support is being demanded by these players to land the same sale, cannibalizing resources and fostering unnecessary price pressure from internal competition. The answer is to require all opportunities to be registered, as soon as certain criteria establishing the veracity of the opportunity can be fulfilled. Once registered by one player, no other player in the network can pursue that opportunity (or if it does, it will not receive any sales or pricing support).

- *Frequent review cycle.* Experienced service providers run frequent, regular pipeline reviews, usually weekly, with whichever sales channels are in action. This enables patterns to be established and optimism to be managed. For example, any high-prospect opportunity showing no progress through the step of sales process for more than a couple of weeks, should be ascribed a lower probability and longer sales cycle than one that has progressed. This regular 'combing' of the pipeline imposes a discipline on the mindset of the sales channels themselves, improving their sales predictions and pipeline predictability.

- *Active renewal management.* Good service providers exercise disciplined renewal processes, with regular communication with customers, constant reports and reminders of the benefits of the service to the customer, prior to renewal. For customers considering early termination of services or seeking not to renew, there are pre-planned steps to save the relationship, a stepped set of incentives (including price) that are calculated by reference to the cost of the alternative – new customer acquisition. Reporting of customer churn (replacing lost customers) and lost-revenue-avoidance ensures management is focused on increasing the 'stickiness' of the service proposition. Many service providers operate a specialist team in the 'customer saving department'.

- *Service packaging and pricing.* Perhaps not an obvious contributor to pipeline management, but the design and packaging of a service proposition plays a big part in lowering barriers to sale and raising the renewal and up-sell performance of a service provider. Particularly for low-touch services, it is vital to enable easy self-management (helping customers to up-sell themselves), including breaking service increments into small upgradeable steps.

Consultative selling and relationship management

Consultative selling and relationship management are core competences for high-touch services. In helping customers navigate complexity and make what can be life-changing decisions, the service provider needs to be able to engender confidence and trust in the minds of customers during the sale process. This is best achieved through an interactive process, exploring the needs and objectives of the customers, helping them to articulate them in terms they can recognize and agree to. Asking open-ended questions, making valid constructive suggestions, testing the feasibility and relative attractiveness of options will help customers commit to buy, and to buy from the service provider that is best at this process. Customers who are uncertain simply will not buy from a provider or channel they do not trust (even though the service provider itself may be a respected brand). If the channel in front of the customer is independent, that independence will place the channel on the customer's side and help sustain a long-term relationship as a trusted adviser. The service provider will need to accept that there is a limit to its sphere of influence as the price to be paid for being able to access the independent channel's customers. In many of these cases, brokers or advisers are obliged, legally or ethically, to put their clients' interests ('best advice') above their own, and above those of the service provider. A direct sales force, working for one service provider, can also employ the consultative selling and relationship management process, though they will face a higher bar to gaining trust as an adviser.

Given the cost and time involved in consultative selling, many service providers employ the RAD model (Retain, Acquire, Develop), to allocate resources efficiently. In Figure 23.1 the model is set out for a typical

Figure 23.1   Where to prioritize

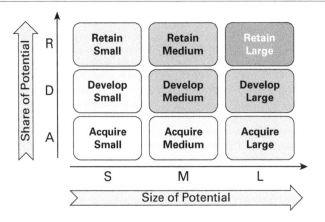

Figure 23.2   Strategies to prioritize

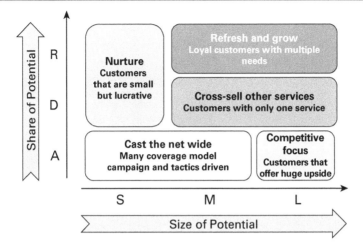

B2B context. The two axes represent the existing state of the relationship in hard financial terms: the current share of potential account value available and the potential scale of the opportunity.

Where the current share of potential is zero to low, the customer is effectively still being acquired; where it is above around 10 per cent but less than 40 per cent, the customer needs to be developed; and where it is above 40 per cent, the customer needs to be retained. Each of these three segments involves different strategies and tactics, with differing levels of cost and resource consumption. However, the decision needs to be calibrated in terms of the scale of the opportunity, which brings the other axis into play.

For different service providers at different stages of development, the deployment of resource across the nine-box matrix will vary. In Figure 23.2 we show one possible approach. In effect the service provider needs to weigh the cost of acquisition, development and retention against the lifetime value of each customer segment, and design its strategy and tactics accordingly.

The culture of sales teams will tend to be very different depending upon whether their mission is to acquire customers, develop them or retain them. These are often characterized as hunting (acquisition) and farming (retention and development). Hunters are required to bring in business, identifying the targets and risking frequent rejection before being able to get a foot in a door, maintaining a confident assertiveness without over-stepping the mark. They need to be able to gain customer trust quickly and accept small initial sales – the beachhead. Farmers, on the other hand, need to plan and execute long-term strategies to build from the foothold gained by the hunters and

'move off the beach and onto the main ground'. The handover of a relationship from the hunter to the farmer needs to be smooth and seamless
from the customer's perspective. They need to see the farmer as 'their person
on the inside' of the service provider, navigating the organization to secure
the service proposition they want. The service provider will see the farmer
as its person inside the customer, uncovering opportunities for deeper and
broader account penetration. The calibre and skillset required of both
hunters and farmers will be driven by the scale of the opportunity of each
customer. In large B2B services, worth hundreds of millions of dollars a year,
the farmers, or account managers, will be the calibre and seniority of a business unit CEO, for effectively they are commanding resources and managing
complexity that are commensurate with that role.

Price waterfall management

Very large service providers, such as utilities, telecoms or cable companies,
deal with millions of customers. They fight for market share with a small
number of equally large competitors, making for price-led competition that
in turn drives the need for extremely efficient operations. One of the tools
developed by such operators is price waterfall management – analysing the
costs incurred in selling to and servicing each customer segment. We show a
simple example in Figure 23.3.

Each step on the waterfall represents one cost element. By visualizing the
data, analysts can target the bigger steps for cost reduction, and by comparing
the waterfalls of different customer segments, they can identify why the costs of
one segment differ from another and seek to identify the underlying reasons. We
know of one utility company that has broken down its costs into around 130
steps. From this they have found that if a customer has its account serviced at a
different address (eg for billings) than the address being supplied, this additional
cost can virtually wipe out the margin earned from that customer. Conversely,
given the cost of the traditional meter-reading element of the waterfall it is clear
why utilities welcome the advent of the smart meter, which can track and report
consumption without the need for a physical visit to the supply address.

It is very powerful for the service provider to be able to measure the cost
of customer behaviour and to find ways to influence that behaviour to drive
cost out of its business, or to charge the customer for the convenience benefits associated with that cost (eg free deliveries only on orders worth $100
or more, $5 per order if under). Service providers have recognized that the
cost of customer service can be reduced through porting customers to online
self-maintenance, and can price the incentive needed to move customers
from mailed paper billings to online paperless billings. A one-off incentive

Figure 23.3 Price waterfall analysis

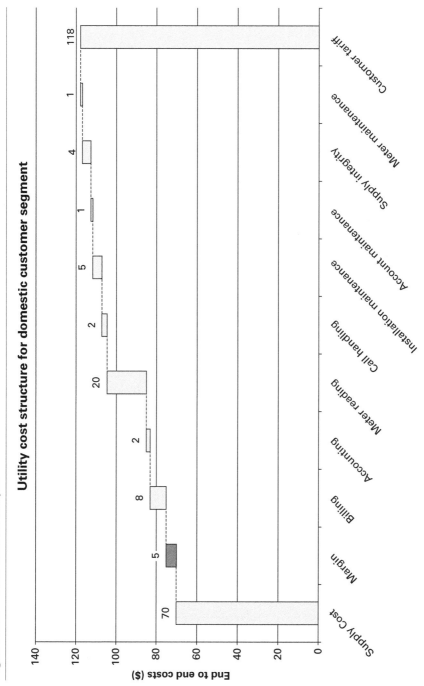

Utility cost structure for domestic customer segment

to encourage a customer to change behaviour to drive a multi-year saving for the supplier could be priced at, say, the first year's saving. Alternatively, the supplier may be able to 'nudge' customer behaviour by pointing out the environmental and convenience benefits of adopting the change, which could be much cheaper to execute.

If a service provider can understand a customer's cost drivers when in the sales process, it will be able to price its proposition more effectively. This ties back to the need for rigorous qualification, with an emphasis on identifying and filtering out customers whose behaviour is likely to drive cost into the business, and reduce the margins possible. These cost drivers can be quite subtle, like meeting public sector requirements in terms of providing evidence on an annual basis that the supplier fulfils various public policy requirements related to ethical employment and non-discriminatory practices, whereas a private sector customer may simply require an affirmation statement.

Lifetime customer value management

Service providers make their revenue over the period of a service relationship, putting great emphasis on the lifetime value of a customer. Although this is equally important to product-based businesses servicing repeat customers, for the service sector the lifetime value approach comes into strategic, tactical and operational decisions. As we have seen, the initial cost of customer acquisition can be justified only if the margins earned over time justify it. However, it would be short-sighted indeed if the cost of customer acquisition had to be justified by the first engagement with a customer, unless the service provider has a single service offer and low probability of renewal. Better to pull together a model bringing in the cost of customer acquisition, cost of customer retention and cost to serve measured against lifetime revenues and gross margins (discounted for the time value of money). Some rules of thumb have emerged, including the need for lifetime value to be greater than three times the cost of customer acquisition, and ideally it should take less than a year to recover the cost of customer acquisition. Applying the RAD model discussed above will help prioritize which customers should be targeted for cross-selling (both additional service lines and into other business units or geographies) and up-selling (premium versions of services), to grow their lifetime value.

One of the factors that destroys customer lifetime value is customer churn, which is the proportion of the customer base lost in a year, and needing to be replaced simply to stand still in revenue terms. In the early days of mobile telephony, customers were offered ridiculously attractive deals to sign up as the small number of service providers went all out for 'land grab'. However, their service delivery often failed to meet their promises, so once the term of the deal was up, customers shopped around for anyone other than their existing provider. History is repeating itself with the broadband, music streaming and media service providers such as Spotify, Apple Music, Sky, Netflix and Amazon Prime. A high level of churn means that the costs of expensive customer acquisition strategies (free music or video for three months or longer, free hubs and devices) may not be recovered. Customers quickly learn that they should not automatically renew their service contract at full rates, but threaten to leave so as to secure offers that were designed to attract new customers, not retain existing ones. Service providers with high churn are effectively being forced to pay twice (or more) to acquire one customer.

Key metrics

Set out below is an overview of the key metrics used in the service sector, many of which have been referred to above, together with their commonly-used acronyms.

Customer-centric measures

- Average Revenue Per User (ARPU): indicates consumption volume; guide to penetration; guide to segment attractiveness.
- Lifetime Value (LTV): indicates customer profitability and long-term segment value; guide to sales focus.
- Customer Acquisition Cost (CAC): marketing and sales cost per customer or segment.
- Lifetime Value/Customer Acquisition Cost (LTV/CAC): indicates long-term profitability; should be >3; should take <12 months to recover customer acquisition cost.
- Cost to Serve (CTS): service delivery cost per customer or segment; guide to customer or segment profitability; can be analysed using price waterfall to identify major cost elements and how they respond to changing customer behaviour.

- Share of Wallet or Account Penetration: proportion of the customer's relevant expenditure that has been captured by the service provider.
- Customer Churn: number of lost customers per annum/total customer base; indicates sustainability of business, drives total CAC; should be <15 per cent.

Service line-centric measures

- Discounted Cash Flows (DCF): total expected future revenues discounted by the cost of capital; indicates consumption volume at present value.
- Return on Investment (ROI): profits from service line divided by initial cost of investment; indicates long-term profitability of service line; guide to investment decisions.
- Payback (PB): time taken for discounted profit contribution to cover initial costs of investment; should be <12 months.
- Break-even volume (BEV): volume of sales units required for profit contribution to exceed cost of investment.

Insights from managing hotels, restaurants, catering and travel distribution

24

Introduction

The hotels, restaurants, catering (HoReCa) and travel sector is really a subset of the services sector, but the recent upheaval in distribution justifies special attention as it has been at the forefront of the new gig and sharing economies. The emergence of platforms such as Uber, Lyft, Airbnb, onefinestay, Trivago, Booking.com, Expedia, Bookatable and many others has been central to these developments, and the trend is emerging in many other sectors, such as freelancing (TaskRabbit, Care.com and Upwork), peer-to-peer lending (Lending Club, Zopa, Funding Circle) and Crowdfunding (Kickstarter, Seedrs, Indiegogo).

It is not surprising that the hotel and travel bookings sector experienced this platform-based distribution disruption before many others. Its traditional channels of travel agents were inefficient, expensive and provided a barrier to entry for new entrants on the supply side. Consumers were faced with a limited choice of a few well-known brands, putting power in the hands of the supplier, which exploited it through opaque propositions and inflexible practices, such as paying up-front weeks in advance, surcharges in the event of exchange-rate movements and fuel price rises. Somehow positive changes in these factors never found their way back to the consumer's pocket. The sector had seen major consolidation as leading hotel brands recognized the power of scale and travel agents responded, with major players such as Carlson Wagonlit emerging to serve the business sector.

From the suppliers' perspective, distribution was not only expensive, averaging around 18 per cent of their revenue, it was inflexible with standard commission rates to the booking and travel agencies applying across the board. Fixed, high-cost distribution costs could not continue unchallenged and the new low-cost airlines avoided third-party distribution channels altogether, setting up their own call centres, which were rapidly largely superseded by websites. Simple booking processes and extraordinarily low prices created a whole new market for low-cost flights, which created a similar expectation for low-cost accommodation, transfers and other services. Under the old distribution system, the consumer was the least well served participant – a warning signal to other sectors. With rising discretionary spending power, the opportunity for a disruptive move was too good to ignore and with the arrival of Lastminute.com, online travel agents (OTAs) had arrived.

Specialist challenges and how the sector tackles them

Continuing high-cost distribution

The new OTAs have grown rapidly, both in numbers and scale, through aggressive marketing campaigns, powerful PR and brilliantly easy to use consumer-oriented web platforms. With their ability to channel substantial consumer demand and purchasing power, the OTAs gained huge leverage over the travel service providers, whether global hotel chains, independent local bed and breakfast houses or anyone in between. The OTAs saw no reason to offer any discount from the standard 18 per cent commission, and in some cases increased it. In addition, the OTAs insisted on being given access to the lowest rack rates available, or the hotel risked being blanked on the OTA platform. For the small independent hotel or bed and breakfast, the ability to tap into global demand is well worth the 18 per cent or higher commission rates they must pay to be listed on the OTA's platform. How else could a picturesque boutique hotel in the Loire valley be able to simultaneously reach English families, American Francophiles, French weekenders, Asians doing the 'grand tour' and everyone else browsing for holiday inspiration? Previously patchy booking patterns could be converted into full occupancy or change seasonal patterns into year-round demand.

Hotels of every size rely on occupancy to drive profitability, and the larger and more expensive the hotel, the more critical it is to drive occupancy up from break-even levels of around 70 per cent to as close to 100 per cent as possible. Their core channels such as corporate accounts, group business, wholesalers and other discounters were simply too unresponsive to bridge this gap: if used too early, the hotel simply traded out room rates for occupancy but made no additional revenue; used too late and they could not fill rooms. Hotels quickly found that the OTAs could top up the occupancy base built up through its traditional channels. What started off as a useful tactical tool for hotels to brim their occupancy rates became a threat as the OTAs made room rates and availability highly transparent. Customers learnt to leave their room bookings until very late, confident that they would be able to find a room and take advantage of better rates than they could find either going direct to the hotel or committing early through traditional channels. Very quickly hotels found that upwards of 40 per cent of their room bookings were coming through OTAs, destroying their revenue per available room (RevPAR). Even worse, the guests brought in by OTAs were unlikely to use the hotel's services and restaurants, turning their platform-searching skills to finding local options for internet service, breakfast, dinner and late night options. The hotel sector needed to respond.

Ironically, the large chain hotels found they already had the best form of defence in place – the loyalty programme: it had simply been ignored or allowed to atrophy. Large numbers of customers have been enrolled, but the number of active members is astonishingly low at around 15 per cent. The best customer is a loyal one, but that loyalty needs to be recognized, repaid and treated as a genuine, two-way relationship. Customers have been well trained by the airlines to expect stepped tiers of loyalty with increasing benefits of genuine value, tailored to the frequent traveller's needs, acknowledging that the individual traveller is the one influencing choice and should be rewarded. (Increasingly rewards are also available to the organization employing the traveller and incurring the cost.) Today's typical hotel loyalty scheme is vastly improved, committing to make its best rates available only to its loyalty scheme members, providing free Wi-Fi, room upgrades, late check-outs, attractive redemption schemes and guaranteed availability. The key point is that these benefits are available *only* if the room is booked through the hotel's own direct channel. Even high-tier members receive only limited benefits if they book through an OTA. The Hilton's marketing campaign, 'Stop clicking around' explicitly targeted the OTA-oriented guest and made it clear that booking direct would save the guest the hassle of shopping around, bolstered by the commitment that room rates will always be cheaper if booked direct.

With a saving to the hotel of the OTA commission, it can afford to be reasonably generous, so even first-time stayers can sign up and start to receive benefits immediately. All the major chains have significantly revamped their loyalty programmes, with some overt plays such as room rate options that will reward the traveller with higher points for a higher price, encouraging business guests to make their employer pay for their perks. More enlightened schemes now allow frequent travellers to 'take a year off' for parental leave or similar lifestyle decisions and retain their tier in the scheme. Many are now moving away from the transactional model to a genuine lifetime value model, recognizing that a lifetime's loyalty should be rewarded with 'gold for life' awards.

Websites have become much more user-friendly, actively helping loyal guests to make the most of their points and reinstating call centres to offer concierge-style support for their most loyal members. The effect of this response by the hotels has been to reduce the OTA channel proportion back down to below 25 per cent. It is unlikely to ever fall much below 15 per cent on average, as this channel is so successful at grabbing market share, making it too important to ignore. This is a fascinating battle between supplier and channel, leveraging scale, innovation, customer insight and big data. The winner should be the customer, who now has fantastic visibility of supply and pricing, the option to book ahead or at the last minute and a virtually infinite variation between price and proposition.

Finite shelf-life products

Hotel room nights, table sittings, airline seats and cruise-line cabins all share one feature in common with fresh food – a finite shelf-life. In fact, the HoReCa and travel sectors' products have an even more finite life than fresh food. Last night's empty hotel room or a vacant seat on a departed flight has absolutely no value. Combining this with the very high fixed-cost structure of these sectors means that the distribution system needs to be optimized to ensure that there is minimum unused capacity at the time of each night, dinner, flight or sailing. To address this challenge the sector has built up a variety of distribution channels to ensure the capacity is sold in a mix that optimizes revenue (see revenue management below), reduces the risk of unsold capacity and ensures good visibility of the sales pipeline. Each channel delivers a different customer mix, average room rate, average total revenue (including revenue from room service, laundry, food and beverages, etc), and differing levels of forward visibility of revenue. The wholesale channel takes volumes to sell on through travel agencies, excursions and similar forward-booking customers over the whole year; 'groups' block out large volumes of rooms for peak periods, corporate account channels provide large volumes of good rate business year-round, though with fairly short-term visibility, and so on.

These core channels usually deliver around 70 per cent of a hotel's bookings. As the date of an unsold room approaches, the hotel will start to market capacity over the more tactical channels such as the OTAs. Not all OTAs are the same. Some will bring in high-yield customers planning months in advance, others will promote immediate availability, so offering lower-yield customers (unless it is a peak season or there is an event on). For airlines, there are low-visibility channels available to 'dump' unsold capacity in ways that do not risk cannibalizing their normal revenue models. These can include student travel and other restricted access agencies, where demand can be stimulated by supply at high discounts. These are the equivalent to the 'manager's offers' to be found in the back aisle of a grocery store of produce that is at or very close to its sell-by date.

Critical competencies

Revenue management

For most of the HoReCa and travel sectors, revenue management lies somewhere between science and a dark art and has become one of the most important functions in the business. With increasingly powerful analytics engines, big data and, more recently, artificial intelligence, the science dimension has taken big steps forward. It is well-known that two passengers seated side-by-side on a flight are very unlikely to have paid the same price for their seat. Variables include which channel they booked through, whether the flight is a simple return trip or part of a more complex itinerary, when the flight was booked, the restrictions accepted (non-changeable, non-refundable or fully flexible). Of these, the most significant will be the channel through which demand is accessed. Revenue managers look beyond revenue to yield, which factors in the total revenue from a customer as well as the cost of acquiring the booking. They will set up commissioning deals that reward all channels for bringing them high-yield business, and set up variations with specific channels that reward early visibility and last minute sales (to enable ultra-high occupancy rates). The revenue manager needs to allocate capacity to each channel and, as the date of 'expiry' moves nearer, start to actively reallocate that capacity to balance volumes needed and yield. Unsold capacity will be taken back from some channels and redistributed to channels better placed to sell that capacity, possibly at a lower yield. This is a game that needs to be played both tactically for short-term optimization and strategically for long-term optimization. This means that those channels that deliver substantial volumes of mid- to high-yield business cannot be denied capacity simply to capture a short-term opportunity, such as when a major event or festival is on for a few days. In these instances, some capacity needs to be kept available for those strategic channels (including, of course, its own high-tier loyalty scheme members, who have been promised guaranteed availability). Loyalty to channels is vital and good revenue managers know that it is a price worth paying to be able to provide capacity to its strategic channels, even when it could have sold that capacity at much higher yields for those peak days.

Key metrics

Set out below is an overview of the key metrics used in the HoReCa and travel sectors, many of which have been referred to above:

- *Customer yield.* Total revenue less the cost of customer acquisition – usually commissions paid to the channel.

- *Average room rates.* The rate paid by customers on average over the year. Usually compared to local market rates.

- *Occupancy.* The number of sold rooms as a proportion of the total available rooms.

- *RevPAR.* Revenue per available room; a function of average room rates and occupancy (so higher rates can compensate for lower occupancy, and vice-versa).

Insights from managing intellectual property distribution

25

Introduction

Intellectual property (IP) is a vast arena, encompassing many of the world's newer industries. It includes copyright IP, patented inventions and trademarks or brands. Many industry sectors are built on IP, including publishing, music, films, information technology, pharmaceuticals, consumer electronics, robotics, material sciences and the arts. Copyright IP includes:

- books, such as this one, and related rights, such as film rights (unlikely in the case of this book) and options;
- music and films and the related publishing rights, exhibition rights, public performance rights and merchandising rights;
- live performances, accessed through ticketing, broadcasts and recordings;
- images, the rights to which often form a large part of the compensation of sport and media stars;
- software, access to and the use of which is controlled by licences (ie not by the outright sale of the code);
- brands, which represent tightly controlled and managed IP, with sponsors paying dearly for the right to have exclusive presentation of their brand to the exclusion of other brands.

Patented inventions (including design patents) are used widely to protect inventions in the pharmaceutical sector as well as technology-related sectors of all types. Any inventions stemming from the world of research and development, including new drug discoveries, new materials (like graphene), new technologies, new applications of technologies and new designs rely on the registering of patents to protect the rights of inventors to exploit their inventions.

Trademarks are the registered name or identifying symbols of a product that can be used only by the product's owner. A brand is the representation and communication of the inherent values promised, and delivered, to a customer. All of them have required substantial investment to develop and substantiate and many have taken years to build. They can generate for the owner substantial competitive advantage in the form of a price premium, demand preference, sustained loyalty and higher life-time customer value. For this chapter, we are going to focus on distributable IP, which is largely based on copyright and inventions.

In a world that is moving from products to services, IP is one of the most critical components, as evidenced by the number of legal battles over IP rights, covering every aspect from who owns the rights, who has bought the rights, what the rights include (and exclude) through to the length of time that the rights exist and the new media by which rights can be exploited, all of which come down to the exact terms of the contracts involved.

IP even includes information about you, your browsing, your posts and your online behaviour, all of which represent intellectual property for Google, Facebook, Instagram and any platform providing some form of content. Newspapers have seen their industry transformed as readers have moved online, forcing publishers to decide whether to put their precious content behind a paywall or use it to drive online advertising. Piracy has devastated the income streams of musicians, artists, film-makers and photographers, changing the dynamics of these industries. Musicians used to go on the road to promote their albums. Now they allow their albums to be streamed for trivial sums to promote their live performances.

The distribution of IP, or more accurately *the rights* to IP, is moving faster than the laws that define and protect it can be updated. The ability to digitize almost any form of IP has led to an explosion of opportunity and generated huge flows of revenue that were unimaginable even 20 years ago. Today the cost of buying the rights to broadcast live sport runs to billions of dollars. The NBA announced in 2014 that it had struck a nine-year, $24 billion media-rights deal with ESPN and Turner Sports. In 2016, the English Premier League sold its TV broadcasting rights in packages of live football games costing upwards of £5 billion. With these amounts at stake, those involved in managing IP distribution have had to learn many lessons in segmenting different types of rights, packaging rights, market penetration, negotiation, controlling access, protecting rights from abuse and piracy while enabling massive market access, and all the time finding new ways to monetize IP assets. The battle between rights owners and the platforms that distribute these rights has swung to and fro, providing many insights and lessons to be drawn from the strategies and tactics both sides have employed.

Specialist challenges and how the sector tackles them

Contracts and licences

Intellectual property is, by definition, intangible. It remains the property of the author (which can be corporate as well as a 'natural person') where it is protected by copyright law, or the inventor, where it is protected by patent law. The rights to use or exploit IP are created and distributed through contracts or licences. These give great control over what, where, how, when and for how long. Contracts impose obligations as well as confer rights on the part of the user. These obligations usually limit how the user can use the IP, and pass along obligations to protect the IP should the rights include the ability to resell, or sub-publish the IP. Some examples can help to illustrate how this works:

- Many books are sold with words such as 'this publication may only be reproduced, stored or transmitted, in any form or by any means, with the prior permission in writing of the publishers'.

- Software licences under copyright law (ie not 'open-source') grant the use of one or more copies of software under an end-user agreement, but retain ownership of those copies. The licence typically contains provisions that allocate liability and responsibility between the parties entering into the licence agreement. In enterprise and commercial software transactions these terms often include limitations of liability, warranties and warranty disclaimers, and provide indemnity if the software infringes the IP property rights of others.

- Music licensing ensures that the owners of copyrights on musical works are compensated for certain uses of their work. A purchaser has limited rights to use the work without a separate agreement. These uses can be quite varied, for example the right to listen to music privately does not allow the user to play the music in a public space, broadcast or perform that music. A separate licence would be needed for these, defining the period of usage, the number of performances and the fees or royalty payments required. Many people listening to the radio at work may not realize that their employer is inadvertently breaching copyright if it has not bought PPL and PRS licences (these bodies administer the rights held in musical works or compositions).

- Image licensing in the form of art or photographs will follow similar principles to books. However, the pulling power of sport and music stars has created a whole world of marketing, brand endorsement and advertising based on their 'images'. A star's image can include his or her name, nicknames, likeness, image, photograph, signature, autograph, initials, statements, endorsement, physical details, voice and other personal characteristics. All these properties can generate royalties or payments for the stars or their agencies through specific licensing deals.

- Patented technology is accessed under licence, such as the embedding of Dolby Labs sound engineering into sound systems of all types, from home speakers to cars to full surround systems in cinemas. Throughout the technology sector you will find almost every IT vendor licenses the use of specific technologies from many other vendors, who hold the relevant patents, to offer their own products. In many cases these players are deadly rivals in the end-user market, but collaborate closely on the licensing of technologies. Hewlett-Packard's LaserJet printers dwarfed the sales of Canon's own laser printers, but every one of HP's LaserJets used Canon's laser printing technology under licence. Not all these relationships are amicable, especially where one party believes another has infringed its patents, such as Apple and Samsung, or breached agreements relating to standards-essential patents licensed on a fair non-restrictive basis, as Microsoft claimed when asked for royalties by Motorola.

- Your own browsing behaviour on web browsers, search engines, platforms, apps, etc is often possible only after you have clicked on a screen dialogue that says something like 'By clicking Allow, you allow this app to use your information in accordance with their terms of service and privacy policies' or, 'By continuing, I agree that I am at least 13 years old and have read and agree to the terms of service and privacy policy'. Most users simply click without hesitation, but if you do follow the link to the terms of service, you will be confronted with thousands of words of legalese, which in effect make you agree to grant all sorts of rights to the platform or app, etc without payment.

Contracts and licences enable IP owners to control and direct virtually every conceivable aspect of the use, distribution and revenue generation of their IP. Perhaps the greatest example of this is the way that Apple, Disney and others have directed their profits into low tax regimes by locating their IP in offshore bases and charging royalties and other fees against the revenues generated in higher tax regimes. Disneyland Paris has been profitable in only four or five years since it opened in 1992 because it pays Disney's parent company substantial royalties (6 per cent of revenue) for the use of its know-how, characters, images, music, etc plus a management fee. Apple, Google, Starbucks and Amazon have found themselves under the spotlight for generating billions of euros or dollars of sales in many countries, yet reporting either very small profits or even losses in those countries. Governments are constantly moving to close these 'loopholes', but inevitably find they are playing catch-up.

The key insight to draw here is the significance and power of the contract or licence. Because the income-generating rights are defined and controlled by contract, IP owners can shape exactly how they want to distribute these rights to third parties to gain maximum advantage. See the boxed text on how Elton John segmented his IP rights, first by type, and then by geography, to create nine discrete income streams. This enabled Elton and his management to control how and when his income flowed to him individually, and to ensure costs were properly matched to income for control purposes. With an income in 2017 estimated at $60 million, it is worth paying the price of some complexity to gain this level of control.

How Elton John used Big Pig and Frank N Stein

Elton John has enjoyed a phenomenal career since his debut album, *Empty Sky*, in 1969, selling over 300 million records as well as winning five Grammy Awards, an Oscar, a Golden Globe and a Tony. His achievements include musical theatre (*Billy Elliot, Aida*) and films (*Lion King*). His *Candle in the Wind* 1997 is the best-selling single in both the UK and US charts.

Working with his then manager, John Reid, Elton segmented his formidable stream of intellectual property into three types: composing (writing the words and lyrics), recording (albums and singles) and performing (live concerts and other live media performances). Each of these types then were further segmented by three territories, broadly The Americas, Europe and Asia. Nine companies were set up to manage these rights, each handling one set of rights in one territory. Being a creative type, Elton gave these companies names such as Big Pig Music Ltd, Frank N Stein Ltd, as well as the better-known ones of Rocket Records and Rocket Music. Big Pig, for example, handled the composing rights for Europe, whereas Rocket Records handled the recording rights. Frank N Stein Productions Ltd and Happenstance Ltd handled the tours and live performances in different territories.

The distribution of music rights is complex, with extensive use made of sub-publishing deals to ensure maximum geographic coverage and leverage of established local music promotion and distribution companies to bring music to fans in each market. Elton partnered with different writers and performers at different times, as well as writing and performing as a solo artist. The segmentation of his IP rights enabled clearer income streams and sharper focus on whether expected royalties were flowing back to the artists.

Downloading and streaming has transformed the music industry, with income from sales of vinyl records, cassette tapes, CDs all collapsing in turn, and illegal downloads further damaging revenues. As with many artists, live performances are now the main source of revenue for Elton and he has an extensive concert programme of tours interspersed with long runs at Las Vegas. Even here, there are different income streams, such as merchandising revenues, appearance fees and recordings of live performances for broadcast, all subject to different contracts.

Elton learnt the hard way about the significance of contracts. His first forays into the music world were after signing a contract with Dick James Music, effectively signing away the rights to his music for his early years. Once established as an artist, Elton sought to recover the rights to his back catalogue, and in June 1985, the British music magazine *NME* reported that Elton was suing Dick James over the rights to his earlier material.

Complex routes to markets

Intellectual property is often subject to complex routes to market, as contracts and licences are struck with any suitable organization capable of exploiting the IP for commercial gain. In the case of patented technologies, there can be a huge range of applications, and each one could need a specific contract selling access rights for specific purposes or applications, territories and patents. Often these contracts can be on a non-exclusive basis, such as the use of Dolby's technologies, which have become such an established brand that no music or speaker system, cinema or broadcaster could afford not to embed them (Dolby 3.1, 5.1, 7.1, etc). Sometimes, however, exclusivity is key to ensuring the technology is actively marketed to the highest potential markets. For a while Hewlett-Packard licensed Beats Audio technology on an exclusive basis to add a cool dimension to its consumer laptops. This was scuppered in 2015 when Apple bought Beats, forcing HP to look around for an alternative: it subsequently signed a new deal with Bang and Olufsen.

In the case of content IP (books, music, images, films, etc), each successive tier in the distribution cascade from IP creator to regional distributor to area distributor to local distributor is relied upon to be able to secure excellent market access through local market knowledge of the best distributors or publishers for each target segment in the territories under their remit. Perhaps the best illustration of how this can work is to follow the distribution of a single movie. The normal approach since around 1980 is termed a 'Standard Release' routine, using release windows. This starts with the film opening in cinemas and movie theatres. For huge block-busters, such as a new James Bond or Harry Potter film, this can be on the same date globally. For others, it can be sequenced around the world. This 'theatrical window' normally lasts around eight weeks, before moving to the next window, usually DVD/Blu-ray and VOD (video on demand), followed by the Pay TV window and finally the free-to-air TV window, up to two years after initial release for a reasonably successful film. The film distribution industry has developed 'channel cascade' templates from experience to determine how long a film should stay in each window, to maximize revenue yield. Around 95 per cent of cinema ticket sales occur in the first six weeks after release, but should a film's revenues disappoint or fall off earlier, the theatre window, or any window, can be curtailed, moving it faster down this channel cascade, or even combining windows to enable the marketing effort to be deployed across multiple channels for cost-effectiveness reasons. The emergence of new platforms such as Netflix and Amazon Prime has created new distribution cascades with release to Netflix occurring immediately after the theatrical window (for a premium price) for some movies instead of being in the VOD window. The 'Simultaneous Release' model collapses the channel cascade and puts the film out across all the major channels at the same time to leverage the release marketing effort across consumers of all channels (giving consumers their preferred choice of channel). Some films are released 'straight-to-video' (the term is still used even though the video technology itself has lapsed), meaning that it bypasses the theatrical window, or 'Straight to Pay TV'. This is often used for derivative products of a successful film franchise, to harvest useful marginal revenue yield at minimal production cost.

It is worth considering the management challenges of a dynamic channel cascade faced by the film distribution industry. Next time you visit the cinema look around you. There will be hundreds of different pieces of marketing collateral, ranging from the large billboard posters, to smaller posters inside, card standing figures, images on tickets, drinks cups, premiums, merchandising items, monthly magazines and listings leaflets. There will be trailers lasting up to a minute, 45 seconds, 30 seconds or 15 seconds. Outside the cinema context, there will be clips for TV ads, talk show clips, and radio ads using clips from the soundtrack, co-branding promotions (eg with Subway or McDonald's), huge billboard posters, bus stop posters, sides of buses, wraps of taxis – the list is virtually endless. And it's all in the local language, and most must be translated so that they work in all the languages of the territories in which the film is released. The images, artwork and clips exist in digital form as digital properties. For the window-based channel cascade, each digital property needs to be given a matching set of dates for when it can be pre-released to the different, relevant, channels for production, when it can be displayed, and when it should be retired. All these dates will be synchronized with the planned windows but, as we have seen, the success or failure of the film will determine if these windows are shortened or, occasionally, lengthened. Then overlay the possibility that the film receives an Oscar nomination or wins an award, prompting a whole new window dynamic, which though it is highly contingent, can be planned for (in hope!). Each of the distribution channels can be affected if their window of opportunity is disrupted, so the film distributor needs to balance short-term tactical actions, to maximize revenue for a specific film, with longer-term channel satisfaction to ensure market access for films that form the bulk of their output (or for those films less assured to be bankable).

Royalty reporting

The nature of IP demands that contracts and licences are struck with trustworthy counterparties. A high level of trust is involved in reporting royalties as the distributor effectively self-invoices itself for the royalties to be paid upstream. Each successive tier in the distribution cascade, from IP creator via regional distributor, area distributor and local distributor to the end-user is relied upon to accurately record the sale of licences, books, rights, etc and remit the proceeds on a defined timetable.

There may be complexity involved in the pricing and royalty rates, requiring investment by each part of the chain to be able to manage these variables (eg for volume, format, end user segment, etc) and to report the right revenues and royalties up the chain. The reporting is usually done periodically, in some cases (like books) every six months, in others more frequently. This means that, for example, the sale of a copy of this book in Costa Rica in January 2018 would be reported up at the end of the half year to the sub-publisher for Central America, which would fall into its second half year's revenues, to be reported up to the Latin American sub-publisher in the first half of 2019. This is turn would flow up to the initial publisher in the second half of 2019 and, finally, to the authors in the first half of 2020, to be paid around September 2020, some two and half years after that book was sold! Not all sectors take so long to cascade revenues upwards, and the sale of digital licences can be reported virtually simultaneously right back up the cascade to the creator.

It is usual in any licence or contract to provide the right of a royalty audit. This means that the IP owner, or initial publisher or distributor has the right to inspect the books and records of the self-reporting entity. This should be done periodically as a matter of best practice, to ensure the correct pricing, royalty rates and other technical requirements are met (such as free copies being issued only to qualifying recipients). Given even a fairly straightforward royalty report can have hundreds of line items, the potential for error is high. An early 'catch' will prevent accumulation of royalty corrections that can become unrecoverable if left undetected for too long. Obviously, fraudulent under-reporting can be a risk as well, which can be picked up with smart analysis, comparisons to similar markets or equivalent IP/titles and other techniques.

Business model differences

IP rights, licensing revenue streams or royalty streams in most cases create income streams without the need for inventory in working capital. For example, a distributor licensing corporate purchases of Microsoft Office is handling a digital transaction, activating licences on behalf of thousands of final-tier partners for millions of end-users. There is no inventory of physical products; only a few consumers still buy shrink-wrapped boxes from retailers. This means that the GMROII metric (Gross margin return on inventory investment) is infinite (there is no denominator) and the GMROWC metric (Gross margin return on working capital) reflects the net balance of receivables and payables in the denominator, so even very thin gross margins can deliver exceptionally good GMROWCs compared to any physical product.

One key difference between copyright IP and patent IP is the lifecycle. Copyright lasts for the life of the author plus 70 years for literary works, 70 years from recording or performance for sound recordings, and 70 years from the last to die of the director, screenwriter, producer or soundtrack composer. Broadcasts last 50 years from date of broadcast. Contrast that with the life of a patent, which is a mere 20 years from date of patent application. Design patents last only 14 years from the date the design patent is granted. This limited exploitation period places much greater urgency on patent IP owners to monetize their IP and maximize market access as rapidly as possible.

In the case of medical patents, it can take eight years or more for a pharmaceutical company to get a drug approved by the US Food and Drug Administration after invention. However, depending upon the drug and its application, the period of exclusivity protection, post-NDA approval, can be limited to anything from seven years to as little as three years for new clinical investigation. Exclusivity is designed to balance new drug innovation and greater public access to drugs. Once patent and exclusivity protections lapse, the drug can be marketed as a generic, which in practice means many new brand names pop up for what is the same drug. For example, penicillin, the pioneering antibiotic, is known in its various forms as Amoxil, Augmentin, Bactocill, Cloxapen, Nallpen, Piracil, Permapen, Pfizerpen, Ticar, Trimox, Unasyn, Wymox and many others.

This need to maximize revenues from a drug that may have taken years of expensive research and testing to bring to market lies behind the aggressive marketing and promotion of drugs both to patients and to prescribers. Increasingly, patients are researching their conditions online and coming to their physicians and doctors with strong views as to the treatments they would like prescribed. This 'pull' marketing approach is closely coupled with 'push' marketing aimed at the physicians and doctors themselves, the prescribing committees, best practice bodies and funding bodies involved in the approval of branded drugs for treatment regimes. This model has some similarities to the technology sector in its core dynamic, although in technology it is generally product obsolescence rather than patent expiry that frames the short window of exploitation opportunity, with the core IP continuing to earn its keep over several product lifecycles.

As we have seen, in the media context there is little time to capture the initial release revenues, so there is a great attraction in reaching the market through mass-market channels such as Amazon Prime, Apple TV, Netflix, iTunes, Spotify and others. This has led to a power tussle between the IP holder and the main platforms. Each of the major platforms offers the potential to instantly reach millions of consumers, but their proposition of a low fixed-price subscription with a free introductory period demands ruthless negotiation over rates paid for the content. Not many artists have the leverage of Taylor Swift, who famously withheld her back catalogue from

Spotify and pulled her *1989* album off Apple Music because it expected her to accept zero income for music streamed during its free period. It's a tough call for IP movie or music creators to trade-off very low royalty rates for the opportunity of global visibility and market access to millions of users. These provisioning platforms are constantly innovating ways of presenting media. Curated playlists and inbuilt 'radio' options introduce new audiences to an artist. These play a stream of music algorithmically selected to be similar to that of an artist a listener already likes. Artists can build a following through streaming media that can be monetized through concerts and downloads but, with a few exceptions, they won't get rich on the proceeds of streaming.

Critical competencies

Licensing skills and infrastructure

As you have seen, the distribution of IP rights is governed by contracts and licences. This puts enormous emphasis on the ability of the IP owner (or manager) to construct contracts and licensees that put into effect the distribution intent in a safe, secure and legally watertight framework. With global distribution opportunities comes the need to be able to manage contracts and licences on a global scale, taking account of the different legislative environments and countries in which the rights are to be exploited. This is a commercial legal capability that does not come cheap, whether established in-house or outsourced to attorneys and specialists. The best lawyers are both expert in this specialist aspect of the law and highly commercial. This means that they can balance the risks and rewards of the terms they help to negotiate, based upon years of experience as to where the real commercial risks and opportunities lie. An inexperienced lawyer may seek to impose unrealistic constraints and obligations that frustrate the deal and offer protection against highly unlikely risks or eventualities.

The most important aspect of the IP legal exploitation team's capability is the management of what can be thousands of contracts or licences covering the spectrum of IP types, specific rights, territories, terms and conditions. This is more than the administration of a comprehensive database. There is the risk of rights overlap or gaps. Overlap creates channel conflict at best and can put IP owners into litigation at worst, through breach of their own contracts or licences (for example by inadvertently granting the same rights to two channels). Gaps mean missed exploitation opportunities, ie lost revenue. Both overlaps and gaps can be very expensive in terms of real and opportunity cost as well as the time and expense of putting things right retrospectively. As with any distribution channel, rights exploitation is a power battle between the demand for and unique value of the IP and the distribution power of the different channels or platforms. That balance will determine whose terms and conditions will be imposed on the others.

The infrastructure required to distribute IP can be enormous. One of the best examples of this is software. This is a huge sector (estimated by Gartner to be $3.5 trillion in 2017), which is evolving rapidly and one that showcases the need for every element in the value chain to deliver value or risk extinction. Software comes in many forms, from machine code, through layers of middleware, up to the application layers that underpin business processes, enable networking or protect security and on to the personal productivity tools like spreadsheets, e-mail, word processing, etc that live on every personal computer. Consumer software such as games is a sub-sector that dwarfs the movie industry in size. Software can be accessed in various ways, including licences (perpetual or annual), or through subscription or consumption models.

Licence access can be enabled through activation keys that are delivered via an electronic key delivery system. The licensing rules can be very complex (and change frequently), so the distribution tier has built configurators to manage the rule sets to meet the needs of different customers. Subscription access is like licensing, but consumption access has exploded the volume of transactions involved because consumption is billed monthly by individual user. Managing this requires an infrastructure able to track consumption (metering), manage billing cycles and compute referral fees for each individual user. Distributors have invested hundreds of millions of dollars in developing and operating the infrastructure required.

The final tier, serving the end-user, plays a key role for the customer, enabling integration of software applications, managing consumption and providing training and support. From the vendor's perspective, software sold through the consumption models is like gym membership: if it's not used, it lapses. So, the final tier's role is to actively manage consumption and drive it up, through educating the user as how to realize the benefits. This is an expensive activity, so the final tier look to the distribution tier to provide tools to enable them to fulfil their role at minimal costs. These tools provide the opportunity for distributors to differentiate themselves to their final-tier customers, and demonstrate their value back upstream to the vendors relying on user activation to drive market penetration. One key role a sophisticated distributor can play here is to orchestrate the 'pull' and 'push' marketing, 'pull' being the end-user demand stimulation activity, and 'push' being the trade marketing aimed at the channel.

It would be wrong to conclude that this is simply a huge transaction–based infrastructure. Had this been the case, software distribution might have been taken over by the telecoms sector, which already had the necessary infrastructure in place. However, those software vendors that tried to leverage telcos to meet the demand for consumption sales have made little traction with market penetration. The telcos did not have the customer relationships or credibility in the IT space to be able to sell cloud-based applications (or even personal productivity suites such as Microsoft's Office 365). It's only if a product has become completely commoditized (such as most apps), that a transaction platform is sufficient for software IP distribution.

Balancing protection with market access and exploitation

Inventors and authors have two primary objectives: to monetize their inventions or content to the greatest possible extent as quickly as possible, and to protect their inventions and content from unauthorized exploitation or copying. It can take years to perfect an invention or to produce creative content, during which time no income is generated. In the case of technology or research-based inventions, the productive life may be short as newer, better inventions emerge, often long before the 20-year patent protection expires. Once patented, the race is on to put the invention into the market as rapidly as possible and into as many applications, territories and end-user segments as possible. Speed to market can be the best protection against competitors replicating the invention, albeit with sufficient alteration to avoid breaching the patents. This means teeing up exploitation and market access contracts in parallel with the patenting process. Established players, such as 'Big Pharma' and blue-chip technology players can leverage long-standing distribution systems and networks to take a flow of new inventions to market. For the biotech start-up, this is daunting, and the challenge has led to a stream of acquisitions of 'inventor companies' by established players. In fact, finding and buying inventors at the right stage of the proving process has become a core competence of Big Pharma and the technology sector. As well as investing in their own R&D, these companies can fill product pipelines by acquiring the inventions of a start-up at the point that it is clear the technology works, or earlier if the indications are positive and the competition is sniffing around. It's a fine line between waiting to ensure the invention works and can demonstrate it has a commercial application, and not losing out to a competitor willing to take a bigger bet earlier in the lifecycle. In 2015, pharma deals reached $59.3 billion, helping make the industry look like a pyramid where there are many companies developing new molecules at the bottom and a few companies commercializing drug products at the top. Big Pharma built its commercialization capabilities during the era of blockbuster drugs, learning how to navigate the drug promotion regulations, how to manage rights exploitation and protection, how to market to the complex network of buyers and prescribers, and how to manage the reimbursement processes of public and private care provision. Given that getting a novel drug to market costs an average of $2.5 billion, start-up biotech companies cannot hope to match these capabilities, though they can be nimbler at the research and early clinical development stages.

The same phenomena of M&A complementing R&D can be seen in the technology space with start-up companies being acquired by the sector giants to fill gaps in their core technologies and offerings. In the first quarter of 2017, HPE bought SimpliVity for $650 million, to boost its hyper-converged portfolio, and Nimble Storage for $1 billion to expand its storage capabilities; Intel acquired Mobileye, a specialist in autonomous car technologies for $15.3 billion; Cisco bought AppDynamics for $3.7 billion to acquire its software for monitoring application performance; and Apple bought Workflow, an iPad and iPhone automation tool. These examples give just a snapshot of the activity in this sector and while these may appear to be large sums, in the context of the acquirer and the exploitation opportunities they are not.

Authors usually do not have quite the same speed to market pressure as inventors, though they share the same desire to monetize their content. Some content is time-critical though, such as sport events, the video and audio broadcasting and narrowcasting of which is subject to a similar channel cascade as films, though for very much shorter timescales. The channels capable of showing live content will be restricted as to the audiences they can broadcast to, protecting other rights acquirers. For example, if as a UK subscriber to Sky Sports or BT Sport you expect to watch a live English Premier League football match on your iPad, you will find that you can currently only do this in the UK. If in another country you would need to be a subscriber to the local rights holder network to gain access (although this is expected to change in early 2018 for subscribers to paid content travelling within the European Union). Later on the day of the match or the following day, other channels will be allowed to show the whole match, and yet further channels will be able to show a restricted highlights package on the same day. Catch-up channels will be able to hold the match for a short period, delayed by a matter of hours or days; other channels will provide access to short snippets showing the goals scored.

It is a core competence to balance this structured market access across numerous channels and territories to maximize the monetization, while not frustrating the consumers you are trying to reach. Different products (a football match, a cricket match lasting five days, a boxing match, a tennis tournament, etc) all have different characteristics in terms of time-criticality, potential audience size, price elasticity and acceptable packaging (subscription, pay-per-view, bundled packages, etc). The more complex the structure of rights deals, the greater is the risk of channel conflict or cannibalization.

Digital content is potentially highly vulnerable to being distributed to non-paying viewers or listeners, which is a major threat to copyright exploitation and distribution channel management. Early controls to prevent this were quite crude: zoned DVDs and players attempted to limit distribution to one of six geographic territories (and three other zones including an 'all' zone). With the arrival of downloads came Digital Rights Management (DRM) technologies, which are access controls embedded in the media and provisioning platforms such as Apples iTunes. The primary objective was to stop copyright infringement by preventing unauthorized copying and distribution. This is a controversial area, with concerns over limiting legitimate rights for a purchaser such as the ability to create a back-up. The emergence of low-cost streaming services such as Spotify, Apple Music, Napster, Deezer and many others has mitigated the risk of copyright infringement, but has displaced music download sales, with much lower streaming fees for artists.

Digital watermarks are a familiar device for image copyright owners to make their products visible and searchable without losing control over the use of the image itself. Most photographers use this device to provide a low-resolution image 'spoiled' by a visible watermark, for customers to search and select the images they wish to buy as a clean high-resolution image file. What the customer may not know is that there may be an invisible watermark on their purchased image that would enable source tracking should they choose to infringe the copyright and copy or distribute the image without the owner's permission. This technique can also be applied to audio, video, text or any other digital product. These hidden digital watermarks are only perceptible under certain conditions, such as after using an algorithm. This passive technique enables distribution without causing any frustrations or unnecessary restrictions on the part of the legitimate user of copyrighted IP, while enabling detection and tracing of infringements, should they be suspected.

Piracy prevention

Piracy is a real threat to IP owners as it goes beyond the casual infringement of copyright or patent protection and deliberately seeks to steal a legitimate income stream from the IP owner. Examples of piracy include counterfeit goods (often of high-value branded goods, infringing trademarks), distribution of illegal copies (for every authorized copy of computer software in use, there is estimated to be at least one pirate copy), and the theft of trade secrets, which can include designs for products or software source code, manufacturing techniques, etc.

The prevention of IP piracy or theft is based on two key defences: denying access to the IP in the first place and removing the opportunity for pirates or thieves to exploit the IP, should they succeed in obtaining it. (Prevention of unauthorized IP access was covered to a degree under balancing protection with market access, above.) Protecting the IP depends upon the form in which it exists. Software source code, for example, is protected under layers of access controls. Films face other challenges, as pirated copies often hit the internet at or even before the official release dates. These copies, ranging from bootleg copies recorded inside a cinema to the DVD 'screeners' sent in advance to film critics and other industry insiders, can show up on major torrent sites or platforms for illegal downloading. Here, tightly controlled distribution and invisible watermarking are the major controls used. However, it is not unusual for thousands of individual people and media outlets to receive a watermarked DVD of a major blockbuster (especially if it is an Oscar contender).

Often, the best protection against exploitation of unauthorized IP is to drop the price of authorized IP access in high-risk areas and remove the incentive. Markets like China are notorious: the culture simply does not recognize individual rights in the way western cultures do. Microsoft and other software developers have been forced to adopt this strategy in several markets to protect their income streams and establish a base of authorized users. For larger commercial customers wanting to run legitimate software the challenge is one of compliance, ensuring that every user is authorized to use the software on their laptops or access it from the cloud. One of the benefits to the software sector of migrating users to cloud-based software is the greater control it offers to prevent unauthorized access. However, consumers, micro businesses and small to medium-sized businesses are more concerned with cost than compliance, so major competitors have combined in several markets to promote education about the risks of using bootleg products and the threat of being caught.

Closely related but different is grey-marketing or parallel marketing. This is where a product is legally supplied into markets by unauthorized distributors, in conflict with the vendors' channel strategy. In many jurisdictions, vendors cannot legally prevent access to supply by distributors outside of the authorized network. This situation occurs only where there is an arbitrage opportunity in the market, encouraging grey marketers to exploit the situation, which is almost always caused by price differences or availability issues. For example, on availability, should a hot product be launched in North America before Europe or Asia, and there is pent-up demand, unauthorized distributors will buy in bulk in North America and freight the product into these markets ahead of the official release day. The same issue of availability can occur at other points in a product's lifecycle, not just at launch.

An example of price differences can occur when the volume breaks on large deals are available in one market but not another. For instance, a distributor purchasing in a large European market like Germany can obtain a widget at €10 for very large volumes, which it will push it into Austria and Switzerland where the maximum volume breaks only allow the lowest purchase price to be €11. The distributor may or may not need to rely on the aggregation of demand across the entire German-speaking market to reach the highest volume break prices. Authorized distributors in these other markets will cry foul to the vendor as they will be undercut by the grey-market supplier(s). This will happen more with commodity type products where there are no local requirements (such as voltage rates, language-specifics, national type approvals, etc), and the volumes involved justify the effort of shipping and marketing.

Solutions available to the vendor looking to prevent grey-marketing to protect the integrity of their authorized channels are a mix of black arts and science. Some products, no matter how strong the demand, will simply not show up in unauthorized channels or even authorized channels at out-of-market prices, indicating that the supplier has mastered these techniques. Black arts include the use of implicit threats to authorized retailers and distributors that, should they be found to indulge in grey-marketing, future product allocations could be difficult, issue resolution and reimbursements may take rather a long time, participation in programmes will be curtailed, access to new release products will be rather limited and so on. For the unauthorized distributor, which may be authorized in its home market, these threats will be particularly potent as they will be putting its core business at risk for the sake of some marginal quick wins.

Vendors confronted by grey-marketing activities can find that it really disrupts their channel strategy, damaging their core partners and harming the vendor's ability to access market segments that grey marketers wouldn't bother with. Solutions range from needing to remove the arbitrage opportunity on price, by making the same terms available in each market (not just the largest ones) to making products market-specific, which can harm economies of scale. Both can be expensive. Alternatives include adding the element of traceability to a product or its packaging, such as serial numbers, batch codes or even RFID chips (machine readable chips costing less than a penny), to be able to identify the source of the grey-marketing supply and cut it off or at least curtail it. More black arts may be needed to keep channels and channel players in line, using a mix of carrot ('You will be prioritized next time or for marketing funds', etc) and stick ('We can't guarantee you will receive your normal allocation of the next hot new product').

Allowing the situation to drift not only damages authorized channels and players that have invested in the vendor's brand, but makes it harder to convince the channel of the vendor's channel-positive posture, undermining long-term channel development. Fast, firm, fair and visible robust action is required. It usually only takes one or two high-profile actions to bring the rest of the grey-marketing villains into line while reinforcing the vendor's status as pro-channel.

Insights from managing franchised distribution

26

Think of some of the world's biggest brands and you'll be including a fair number of franchise systems in your list. Examples include the obvious quick service restaurants such as Subway or McDonald's, automotive services such as Jiffy Lube, hotel operators such as Howard Johnson or Hilton Garden Inn and retailers such as 7-Eleven, Body Shop or Benetton. However, franchising has flourished in many other sectors such as financial services (H & R Block), cleaning and maintenance (Jani-King, Molly Maid), health and fitness (Snap Fitness), car repairs (Chips Away), retirement homes (Senior Helpers and The Senior's Choice), the technology sector (e-Backups) and printing.

In this chapter, we look at why franchising has become such a popular and successful route to market, how it works, and some of its special features as a sales and marketing channel. In the online content that supports this book, you will also find guidance on how to sell to a franchised system to assess whether it is a feasible channel for a vendor. We also look at how to engage with franchised systems if they are a potential customer or route to market for your products or services, and how to manage a relationship with them on a long-term basis. To understand whether and how to get the best out of franchising, we first need to get to grips with what a franchise is and what's special about franchised systems. For vendors looking to work with a franchised system to reach target segments, or even to set up their own franchise, we will cover the significant challenges in achieving market access, as well as the obvious benefits of leveraging 'other people's money' (OPM) to fund growth and outlet expansion as well as their self-motivation and effort.

What is a franchise?

A franchise is a right granted to an individual or group to market a company's goods or services within a certain territory or location. The franchisor grants the right and the franchisee acquires the right under a detailed contract set out by the franchisor, under which the franchisee agrees to follow quite strict rules and guidelines set out by the franchisor, which are usually related to ensuring the brand is not compromised by wayward franchisees or poor operators. In return for a franchise sale fee, the franchisor provides an operating manual, extensive training, operational guidance, brand awareness and plenty of support in the early days to help get the franchisee up and running. The franchisor earns an ongoing franchise royalty fee (set as a percentage of sales), as well as the up-front, one-off franchise fee. The franchisee gets into business operating a proven concept and business model under a well-known brand with an established supply chain and can draw on the best practice experience of hundreds or thousands of other operators (ie existing franchisees).

Note that as well as paying the up-front fee, franchisees have to invest their own money into securing the necessary leasehold premises, paying for shop conversion and fit-out (or even a new build stand-alone site) and buying specialized equipment or vehicles, and sufficient start-up and working capital to see them through the early months and into profitability. These investment costs can range from under $25,000 for a cleaning franchise up to over $1.5 million for a stand-alone fast food location, and more if it has a drive-through. Usually franchisees find that it is much easier to raise start-up and working capital when they tell their bank they are setting up a franchised rather than an independent business. This source of external investment not only saves the franchisor from the need to raise finance to fund expansion, it also brings with it the powerful force of entrepreneurial motivation. The quality of the franchisees' return on investment is in their own hands – the better they run their own business, the greater and faster the returns generated. These investors don't pile the pressure onto the franchisor to make a good return on their investment, they pile it onto themselves. Of course, this pressure is converted into expectations of the franchisor in terms of brand building and protection, new product innovations, demand generation, etc, and unhappy franchisees can be harder to satisfy than unhappy shareholders. In effect, the franchisor is in the business of selling a proven business model to entrepreneurs – but to those with perhaps only a moderate appetite for risk.

The attractiveness of the franchise concept to franchisees is mirrored in terms of what it offers to a vendor as a route to market. A vendor with a proven business model and looking to expand can harness the capital and entrepreneurial spirit of franchisees to effectively outsource its business development. Leveraging OPM, a franchise system enables a vendor to expand quickly without needing to raise additional capital itself. Nor does it need to set up an expensive management structure with many hundreds of employees to recruit, train, lead, motivate and manage before the sales build up. The alignment of motivational forces in a franchise system removes the need for much of this, plus of course it is the franchisees that are hiring and training additional people at their expense and risk.

There are some costs and risks for the franchisor that stem from the outsourcing aspect of this model. The franchisor must ensure that its brand is protected from lousy operators (or worse, dishonest ones who pass themselves off as part of the brand) so all franchisors operate some form of compliance checking process, with regular, if not frequent, visits to check that the brand and marketing materials are up to date and correctly deployed. Even more important, these visits look at the customer experience being delivered by the franchisee to ensure it meets the brand promise and adheres to the procedures as set out in the operating manual and other mandatory updates. The franchisor shares in the responsibility for driving up same-store sales, by providing strategic direction, planning and oversight of the marketing activity and driving the flow of new products and offerings to keep customers coming back. If franchisees are unhappy about the brand's effect on their sales and profits, they will not buy additional franchises themselves and will dissuade new entrants from joining the system. Growth will go into reverse and, once that happens, it is extremely difficult to turn things around.

Perhaps the most challenging part of being a franchisor is generating and processing applications from would-be franchisees where the assessment process is not really focused on the relevance of skills and experience, as it would be for recruits, but on business acumen and entrepreneurial drive balanced with a willingness to conform to the brand – not easy bedfellows. For some franchise systems, such as McDonald's, the assessment process is very demanding, with rigorous investigation of background, experience, aptitude, financial means, management skills and so on. For others, the process is designed to make the franchise accessible to a far wider pool of possible entrepreneurs and to keep the flow of new blood coming into the system.

The franchise system model

In most well-established franchise systems there are a number of recognizable elements with specific roles that together deliver the business model. In this section we will explain how the typical franchise system works and describe the role fulfilled by each of these elements. Figure 26.1 shows the typical structure of the major players in a well-established franchise system.

Some of the players may be set up at the start of the franchising business model but often they are established some way down the road as the growing pressures and demands of the system require that they be established. Let's take each player in turn and review their role before discussing the inter-dynamics at the end.

Franchisor

The franchisor is the central figure in the system, owning the rights to the concept and the brand as well as commanding the ability to define the terms under which franchisees can access these rights – in effect defining the business model available to be bought into. All the other players in the system exist only with the permission of the franchisor and their roles are usually tightly defined under relationship agreements or trust deeds. It is up to the franchisor to decide the size of the territories to be franchised and the

Figure 26.1   Structure of major players in a well-established franchise system

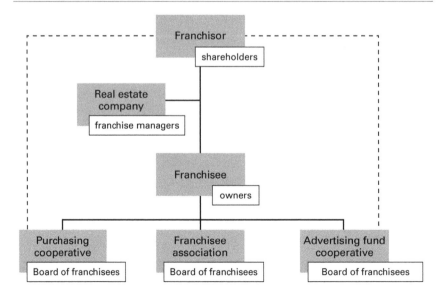

detailed terms and operating conditions franchisees must accept, including the royalty rate (usually between 4 and 8 per cent) – a key decision as the royalty rate is rarely if ever changed once set.

Franchisors have a key role to train and equip their franchisees to be able to set up and operate the concept. In many cases this involves an initial multi-week-long training programme in all the aspects of the technical side of the operation and the business skills to manage the franchise commercially, including marketing, sales, staff recruitment and management, basic accounting and business analysis as well as legal and security guidance (many franchises are cash businesses). The franchisor also has to exert strong management control over the operations and performance of franchisees to keep the wheel of success turning (see Figure 26.2).

It is extremely risky to allow or tolerate badly run franchise operations to continue, in terms of either the standards of customer service or the level of profitability. The franchisor is jeopardizing its brand as well as sending a signal to other franchisees that it's acceptable to let standards slip. Good franchisors will work with weak performers to help them clean up their operations, turn the business round and move back into profitability. At some point though, should these efforts fail to produce a response from the franchisee, the franchisor will step in and remove the franchisee from the system.

Figure 26.2 Franchise system wheel of success

Franchisee

By signing a standard agreement, franchisees join the system and agree to operate the franchisor's concept according to the operations manual and to promote its brand in the local territory. The franchisee may or may not have some latitude to localize or customize the brand, as the franchisor determines. For fast food operators, there is a tension between maintaining brand consistency and responding to local preferences or religious requirements.

Franchisees can expect to be given the tools, training and initial support to make a start in their territory; after that it's up to them to make a success of it, with the franchisor's support in the background. The franchisees' role is to build up the customer base through local marketing and by providing excellent customer service. Depending on the type of business, customer leads may flow from the franchisor as a result of its brand advertising or web presence and be steered to franchisees based on postal address or store locators online. However, this will almost never drive enough revenue, so franchisees will need to be active in local marketing to attract customers who have the proximity to become loyal and frequent customers.

Advertising fund cooperative

In most systems, franchisees pay a revenue-based fee (usually between 2.5 and 5 per cent) in addition to the franchise royalty into an advertising fund to pay for brand advertising and any marketing that covers market areas bigger than that of the individual franchisees' territories. This is how regional and national radio and TV campaigns, event sponsorships and PR activities are funded. There are tremendous economies and efficiencies of scale that can be achieved by the pooling of franchisee resources and it is the role of the advertising fund to realize them.

The advertising fund is usually a franchisee-owned cooperative established by the franchisor through a trust deed or relationship agreement that defines its charter (ie the boundaries of its role) and governance (including when and how boards are to be set up, transparency of accounting and the responsibilities and accountabilities of all involved). Because the funds come from the franchisees, the advertising fund is typically governed by a national board and a series of regional and local boards. Professional marketing people are employed by the trust to make the marketing decisions as to how best to deploy the funds and to oversee the media creation and media buying, etc.

Purchasing cooperative

A similar structure to the advertising fund cooperative is often set up to handle the purchasing and supply chain aspects of the system as a purchasing cooperative. As with the advertising fund, a professional team is put it place to be accountable to a structure of boards comprising franchisees. Note that some systems, such as Snap-on Tools, prefer to be the exclusive supplier of the core products, especially where they have a unique technology or formula. For systems where the franchisees buy from approved third-party suppliers, the purchasing cooperative is essentially a giant buying group, acting on behalf of all the franchisees in the system (or those who opt in).

Real estate company

In many systems, the franchisor prefers to retain the responsibility for signing the leases on the franchisee's locations. It passes on the lease rental costs and other lessee obligations to the franchisee, but it is the franchisor's name – or rather its real estate company's name – that goes on the lease document. This is primarily to ensure that the franchisor can retain control over the location should it find that it needs to replace the franchisee for reasons of poor performance or non-compliance.

Franchisee associations

In most systems, there are one or more franchisee associations to represent the franchisees' interests. These associations will be granted (or demand) a voice at the strategic and management decision-making levels of the system, or be consulted on forthcoming plans and trials. In some systems, the franchisee association is regarded as a valuable asset for improving the business and providing an essential communication channel; in others it is regarded the way a union would be in a highly unionized industry, somewhat warily and possibly as a block to progress.

Specialist challenges and how the sector tackles them

Any vendor contemplating setting up a franchised system to reach its markets should be aware of the unique aspects of franchising that raise not only barriers to entry but also *barriers to exit*. Each country has specific legislation governing the ways in which franchise systems operate, but there are some general principles that apply almost universally and have important implications for distribution strategy.

Exclusive territories

At the heart of a franchise agreement is the right to market in a defined territory without competition from other franchisees. In practice, these territories can be defined in terms of a specific location, which is why you will see popular brands on opposite corners of a busy road junction or within the same mall. However, this exclusivity is a factor that open distribution systems do not allow, and brings with it the ability to control the location and density of locations that the vendor seeks to achieve its distribution goals. This territory exclusivity also means that most franchise systems do not sit easily in a multi-channel strategy, as the franchisor cannot allow other channels to encroach on a franchisee's exclusive territory. The nearest to a multi-channel strategy you will usually see is the existence of company-owned stores alongside franchised stores (the rationale for such a strategy is discussed later).

Recruiting franchisees

Franchisors cannot make claims about the potential profitability of a franchise opportunity in any of their franchisee recruitment marketing (which makes sense given the number of unknowns involved in making a profit, including the applicant's own abilities). Therefore, to enable an aspiring franchisee to assess the merits or otherwise of a franchising opportunity the franchisor is obliged to make full disclosure of all the pertinent facts (which are defined in each country's legislation). This set of disclosures is pretty exhaustive and must be backed up by evidence – just like a share offer prospectus. As an example, the disclosure document requirements in the United States are set by the Federal Trade Commission; they are shown in Table 26.1.

You can see that this is a pretty onerous obligation and all the information must be kept up to date. Ironically, few franchisees will wade through all this detail (and even fewer will understand it), so in practice most will ask to talk to other existing franchisees about their business. Given the legal exposure, the franchisor needs to make sure its franchise sales team are fully aware of the legal constraints under which they operate and do not make illegal claims. For a new brand selling its first franchises, this can feel like operating with one hand tied behind the back. Most franchisee applicants

Table 26.1 Franchise Disclosure Document as regulated by the US Federal Trade Commission

- The franchisor and any predecessors
- Litigation history
- Bankruptcy (ie, any franchisees who may have filed)
- Listing of the initial franchise fee and other initial payments
- Other fees and expenses
- Statement of franchisee's Initial Investment
- Obligations of franchisee to purchase or lease from designated sources
- Obligations of franchisee to purchase or lease in accordance with specifications or from authorized suppliers
- Financing arrangements
- Obligations of the franchisor; other supervision, assistance or services
- Exclusive/designated area of territory
- Trademarks, service marks, trade names, logotypes and commercial symbols
- Patents and copyrights
- Obligations of the franchisee to participate in the actual operation of the franchise business
- Restrictions on goods and services offered by franchisee
- Renewal, termination, repurchase, modification and assignment of the franchise agreement and related information
- Arrangements with public figures
- Actual, average, projected or forecasted franchise sales, profits or earnings
- Information regarding franchises of the franchisor
- Financial statements
- Contracts
- Acknowledgment of receipt by respective franchisee

are usually looking to choose between alternative franchise business options so they will become familiar with the limits on what the franchisors can say about their respective opportunities.

Contracts and disclosures

In many channels, contracts with channel partners either do not really apply (as in the retail channel) or are used only as a last resort to force a change in behaviour of the channel partner or to lever them out. However, in franchise systems, the entire relationship is governed by contract and the details matter. Obviously the rate of royalty paid from franchisee to franchisor is critical, but so are the rights and obligations of each party. Knowing how to use the contract, how to draft the terms and when to apply 'tight' or 'loose' contractual controls is a strategic competence and can take years to develop in the context of the franchisor's own business.

Exiting the franchise channel

Once set up, it is extremely difficult to exit from a franchise channel as a franchisor. There are only two ways to do this – agree a compensation payment with each franchisee, which can run into one or more years' revenue (not profits); or buy up the franchisees and operate them as a company-owned channel or close them. Both options can be extremely expensive, so many businesses have avoided entering the franchise channel for fear of the cost of exit, should the strategy not deliver the required results, or a change in channel strategy be needed.

Growth and store development

'System' is a good word to describe the way a franchised business works. When the elements work together effectively, tremendous results can be achieved. McDonald's, Subway, Starbucks and many others have built up global businesses in one generation or less. Although each system has its own unique strategy, there are a number of common concepts that have underpinned their rapid development.

Once the brand concept has been established and proven, growth is vitally dependent on finding and securing the right sites in which it can flourish. McDonald's is recognized as among the best at this in any sector (franchised or not). Starbucks is a master at securing mall and other primary high-traffic locations. Location is only part of the success factor – matching the franchisee to the location is the other. There are two types of franchisee: the single-unit-owner (SUO) and multi-unit-owner (MUO). It is perhaps simplistic but helpful to think of SUOs as people (or families) and MUOs as businesses.

Consider the possibility of a site in a new mall – you might need to commit to the lease 18 months before the site is even built and the mall could take three years to fill all its sites and build up the level of footfall for the site to break-even. You would not want to put an SUO into that site, or even a small MUO, as it would have to carry the costs of running at a loss for three years before the profits start to come in and as a result could fail, putting site retention in jeopardy. The same logic applies to airport and hospital locations or roadside service stations.

Larger franchise systems run into the issue of store density, where many stores are opened within a short distance of each other. Appearances can be deceptive, however, as it is traffic flow that really determines the degree to which opening a new store impacts the sales of existing stores. For example, you will often find Starbucks outlets near each of the main entrances or hubs in a large shopping mall – there are four outlets in one mall in Singapore. Starbucks knows that the people who enter and leave through one entrance will generally not pass by the other ones, and not taking the other sites would leave the way clear for a competitor. Eventually, however, as the franchise system 'fills in the white space', adding more and more stores to the map, new stores will cannibalize the existing ones' sales.

Concept and new product development

To drive growth (and reverse falling sales), franchisors need to keep the concept fresh and relevant and to introduce new products and offerings. While this may appear an obvious strategy, it is far more challenging to introduce new offerings in a franchise system than a normal distribution system for the following reasons:

- Any new concept extension or offering may increase operating costs or equipment costs for franchisees – something that may drive marginal franchisees into losses or bigger losses. McDonald's McCafe cost over $100,000 in fit-out and equipment costs alone.

- Advertising and promotion of new offerings requires significant marketing spend and special advertising – which will be at the expense of supporting the core offering, and may not be backed by the advertising fund boards.

- New concepts and offerings need trials to ensure they work and to establish the new operating procedures to be communicated across the system – franchisees need to be recruited to do this and help win support, but this raises issues of who pays for these costs and whether compensation would be paid if the trials prove to lose money.

- All the elements need to be in sync to make a success: the advertising fund, the purchasing cooperative, the franchisees and the franchisor. Achieving this takes time, consultation and persuasion.

- Rolling upgrades (such as décor) can cause problems because it takes time to recoup the costs of the upgrade and some stores will look smart and more appealing while those in marginal locations may wish to delay additional expenditure but suffer from a comparative disadvantage.

Critical attributes and competencies

A quick look at the range of sectors in which franchised systems operate might suggest that you can franchise any form of business. While this might be possible, there are some types of business that lend themselves to franchise systems as an effective distribution model. There are a number of critical attributes and competencies that render a business franchise-ready, discussed below.

Consistency of offering is critical to the brand

There are many businesses, usually service-oriented, where a consistent offering or customer experience is a key aspect of the brand. Almost everyone who goes into a McDonald's wants to find the Big Mac, fries and milkshake on the menu and for the meal to taste the same as the first one they experienced. They expect to receive the same fast, friendly service wherever they go, with the toilets spotlessly clean in every site. A similar expectation of a predictable standard of room is true of Hilton or the printing facilities and shipping services expected to be found at every FedEx. This is important because business units with standardized offerings, processes, equipment and facilities are fundamental to a franchised system. They lend themselves to controllable replication with clear documentation, standards, structured training, and tight metrics. The brand itself benefits from consistency of experience across multiple outlets as well as the ability to deliver on the promise made in marketing communications.

Proven concept

To scale up a business through franchising, it is vital to have a strong sustainable demand for the concept and core offerings. The early phases of most well-known franchise brands represent the period when the core concept is being fine-tuned and usually reduced to the core elements. Unnecessary products, services or features that add cost but are rarely purchased are eliminated and a solid understanding of what customers want and are prepared to pay for is established. Usually the concept needs to be simple – both to communicate to the customer and to increase its replicability.

Proven business model

No franchise system is going to grow if the existing franchisees are struggling to make money, so there must be a sound business model that can cope with normal business cycles and local market variations. There are three key dimensions to the definition of a successful business model:

1 Profitable in terms of net profit after all operating costs, royalties and financing costs (including the notional cost of franchisees' own labour). This usually implies that a strong gross margin and/or low overheads are required to ensure fluctuations do not push the business below break-even.

2 Positive cash flow from operations. Many franchised businesses are 'cash' businesses with little or no need to provide customer credit. This means that business growth does not consume cash or need working capital financing.

3 Quick payback of the original investment made by the franchisee, including the cost of buying the franchise, equipping and fitting out the location and the working capital needed – ideally within two years. Many franchises can be bought and established for under $200,000 and some for even less, which suggests an annual operating profit of $100,000. However, more substantial business units, such as a McDonald's stand-alone store with drive through, which costs upwards of $1 million, may take longer to build up the revenues necessary to achieve payback.

Territory and operational management

Territory and operational management covers the whole range of activities in which the system engages to build the business and deliver a consistently excellent customer experience across all the locations. As a system of distribution, the franchisor and each franchisee rely on their fellow franchisees to maintain operational standards and fulfil the brand promise. To achieve consistency over several thousand outlets each owned and managed by an independent entrepreneur is a huge challenge, which is usually surprisingly well achieved. Most people would cite McDonald's as an exemplar of clean, bright, attractive restaurants where you will be greeted with a smile and served promptly and accurately. On reflection, most would also admit this would be pretty true of any of the quick service restaurant chains. Even the hotel chain franchises, which suffer from variable property standards (older properties sometimes just cannot match newer ones) will ensure that the staff, from front desk to janitor, make customers feel welcome and appreciated. How do the franchise systems achieve this? They use a number of techniques in combination:

- *Define and communicate standards for all operations*: the way to perform just about every aspect of a franchise system's operational activities is defined in the operations manual and communicated through training courses, websites, road shows, convention workshops and newsletters. Best practices are captured and disseminated alongside regular updates and reminders on a cyclical basis. Good franchisors have made a virtue out of necessity, with their operations documentation a model of clarity and presentation – often visual, with few words – in a highly structured, easy-to-follow format. This has become essential as many franchisees experience high levels of staff turnover and employ many young staff, sometimes with poor attention spans and limited experience of disciplined environments.

- *Motivation and recognition schemes*: go to any franchise event or meeting and there will inevitably be a host of awards, roll calls of honour and other ways of recognizing performance and achievement at the grassroots level. Franchisees are encouraged and expected to do the same with their own staff, providing recognition for service (stars on a name badge), customer service and performance with awards, badges, bonuses and nomination to regional and national awards.

- *Compliance monitoring*: standards will not be maintained unless they are monitored across the franchise system. Compliance visits to observe whether standards are being followed are carried out on some kind of frequency, ranging from half-yearly to monthly. These are undertaken by consultants/inspectors who are experts in the standards and best practices and work from a checklist. Different scoring philosophies apply with some franchise systems adopting a checkbox, in-or-out-of-compliance approach, and others more of a consultative advisory approach, with only serious breaches registering an out-of-compliance rating. Franchises marked out of compliance are given a fixed period to rectify issues and then re-marked. Typically, compliance is a factor in deciding which franchisees are eligible to be offered an additional franchise, as the system does not want to encourage franchisees that cannot run a clean operation.

- *Customer feedback*: the best guide to how well the system is delivering customer experience is to ask customers, although it is hard to gather more than the extreme views (good and bad). To overcome the reluctance of customers to bother telling you what sort of experience they had, franchise systems are increasingly turning to technology and incentives. Customers are being encouraged to go to a website and answer a few short questions about their experience, enter a code on the printed till receipt and in return download a voucher for a reward (a cookie, drink, etc). An alternative approach is to pay mystery shoppers to conduct clandestine visits and record the details of their experience.

- *Turn-around teams*: where a franchisee is in real trouble (or heading that way), some form of turn-around team is sent in to advise and support the franchisee. By providing a safety net of this sort, it sends a positive signal that the franchisor wants its franchisees to succeed and is not just a policeman. Ultimately, if the franchisee doesn't engage with the turn-around team or fails to follow through on an agreed turn-around action plan, the franchise will be removed and the franchisee exited from the system. Some systems operate a bottom 10 per cent focus, effectively putting all franchisees in this class into special measures.

The franchisee's role encompasses more than just serving the customer – it includes building up the local customer base and marketing to the local area. Traditional techniques such as directory listings, newspaper advertising, sampling, leafleting, bag-stuffers, table-top cards and point of sale and window displays all help communicate to current and prospective customers. Smartphones can identify the customer's location, enabling tools to be developed that can send communications to customers within easy access of a franchise location. Apps such as Voucher Cloud, Around Me and TripAdvisor can all steer customers to active marketing participants. With the increasing fragmentation of media, local radio and even local or specialized TV channels can now be relevant to a franchisee's store in terms of marketing options.

Each franchisee will be supported by local, regional and national marketing under the stewardship of advertising fund boards and will be sent materials to use in their locations to support the wider campaigns (tie-ins to World Cups, Olympics, national rollouts of new products or price points, etc). While it may be optional for them to adopt these materials and price points, usually it is in all the franchisees' interests to align with the marketing and offer a consistent array of products at consistent price points.

All franchise systems are brands – making and delivering a promise to customers. Their financial and incentive model enables them to grow quickly, with franchised businesses representing the most effectively distributed brands in the world in terms of numbers of branded distribution points and the market reach and coverage that represents. They act cohesively and consistently despite the apparent potential to behave like the many thousands of independent operators that the franchisees really are. Part of the reason for this is that decisions are made within effective governance structures, allowing every part of the system to concentrate on what it was designed to do and to trust the other parts of the system to fulfil their roles. In many ways franchised systems were early adopters of the disaggregated models that are now emerging in all sectors of business and enterprise. As such, they can offer many lessons for other distributions systems, even if franchising is not a feasible distribution model for your business.

> For readers interested in learning how to engage with franchised systems, there is a bonus online chapter available at www.koganpage.com/SMC3

Key metrics

We start by looking at how the franchise outlet's performance is measured – the measures the franchisee uses at single- and multi-unit level. The second set of measures are used by the franchisor to manage the overall franchise system.

Franchise outlet-level measures

Revenue, sales or turnover

This is typically measured and reported on a weekly basis for each outlet and is called Average Unit Volume or AUV (the 'unit' is the franchised unit or outlet, not the unit of sale). Despite the reference to volume, AUVs are reported in the local currency or franchise system's 'home' currency, which for a United States-based system would be US$. AUVs are used as the basis for calculating royalties so there is a lot of focus on a franchisee's AUV performance and any franchise holder looking to acquire an additional franchise needs to deliver strong AUVs and strong growth in AUVs.

Revenue and activity are also measured in units, somewhat confusingly, where units are a standard measure of the business. In QSRs (Quick Service Restaurants) the unit is a hamburger or sandwich. In some businesses, there is a 'stat unit' that equates all activity in terms of the standard unit, such as cases for groceries or cups for a coffee shop. Items that don't fit the unit are converted to unit-equivalents, for example a dessert in McDonald's could be a half unit. Units are helpful when calculating other measures such as productivity (see below) and to eliminate the effects of price changes or inflation in tracking activity levels. For example, a growth in AUVs without a growth in units would indicate that all the growth has come from price changes. Units are more useful measures when making comparisons between stores in different regions or countries, as they eliminate any foreign exchange aspects and local purchasing power differentials.

The third measure of top line activity attempts to get at the level of traffic passing through the franchised outlet and can be called customer count, transaction count, or a business-specific equivalent. The link between customer count and AUVs is a key measure used to interpret the top-line performance of a franchised outlet – the Average Cheque (or Check for North Americans). This is the equivalent of Average Basket for a retailer and shows the typical spend of a customer in a single transaction. If a QSR franchisee can get every customer to buy a 'side' and a drink with every unit, then its Average Cheque will be higher than the franchisee that can only get a few customers to do so.

Operational measures

One area that franchisees of many systems have in common is the scheduling and productivity of their staff. Many franchise outlets are open for long hours with variable levels of activity; for example, the peak periods of breakfast, lunch and dinner hours for a quick service restaurant with quiet periods in between. Many of the staff in these outlets are part-time, so the franchisee may employ as many as 30 people to cover the hours of 10 full-time equivalents. This requires constant juggling of schedules to ensure there is enough cover in place for the busy times (and preparation) without incurring excessive costs.

Customer feedback

New technologies are now enabling the direct measurement of customer satisfaction at the outlet level. In addition, many systems employ some form of mystery shopping to assess the quality of the customer experience delivered by each franchise outlet, with the results fed back to the franchisee. Mystery shopping is carried out by an agency that employs trained observers to go into stores and make a purchase. Each visit is scored against criteria set by the franchisor and aims to cover each aspect of the customer experience.

Franchise system-level measures

Financial and operational measures

The measures used by the franchisor to manage the system financially and operationally are focused on three main objectives:

1 Understanding how well the system as a whole is performing and identifying the reasons behind good and bad trends.

2 Understanding which parts of the system are performing well or poorly.

3 Identifying best practices or initiatives that could be rolled out to lift performance across the entire system.

One of the principal tools used by franchisors is the rolling up of all the measures used at the franchise outlet level to provide system-wide averages and league tables. With hundreds or thousands of almost identical business units, grouped in a multitude of different tables, it is possible to spot trends quickly, identify meaningful correlations and see the outlets or franchisees that are clearly doing something special (or the opposite).

There is one additional measure that the franchise system uses that the franchisees themselves do not, and that is the degree of compliance. Each franchisee can expect a compliance visit on some degree of frequency (usually quarterly or monthly). In contrast to the mystery shopper, the compliance visit is carried out with the full knowledge of the franchisee and usually by a field support person or field consultant (titles vary) who is known to them. The compliance visit focuses on all the operational aspects of running the franchise, including ensuring all the latest edicts and updates have been implemented and that the official front- and back-of-house processes are being followed.

Development and growth

A core focus of the system is growth (remember franchising is all about growing without the franchisor needing to inject its own capital). Development measures include:

- *Store count*: the number of stores or outlets in the system. Can be sub-totalled in many ways, such as by type (stand-alone, drive-through) or ownership (franchised, company-owned).

- *Stores added*: the gross or net number of stores added to the system (opened) in a period, usually a year. Different systems adopt different rules as to how to treat a store move (or relocation) and other unusual events. Gross stores added is the number of stores opened in the period; net stores added is the gross number less the number that have closed in the same period.

- *Store density*: the number of stores per million of population. For example, if the franchisor has 25,000 stores in the United States with a population of 307 million (according to the *CIA World Fact Book* in 2010), this gives a store density of 1 per 12,280 people. It is an excellent measure of market penetration and coverage.

There are numerous strategies for franchisors to drive system growth in terms of whether to build in clusters or allow new stores to open wherever the franchise applications occur. However, the measures above are retrospective, reflecting the results of the work done to build the system. They don't give any indication as to how well the pump-priming activities to continue the growth of the system are performing – the equivalent of monitoring lead generation in a more traditional business model. Franchise systems will use some or all of measures around the:

- *franchise sales process* – number of enquiries, leads in negotiation and sold, with relevant conversion rates;
- *location sourcing and building* – number of locations in lease negotiation, various build and fit-out stages, through to store opening;
- *estate maintenance* – numbers of outlets in relocations, refurbishments, transfers (between franchisees), etc.

All of these measures tell the franchisor whether it is doing enough to achieve its growth targets and where there are any bottlenecks or choke points that will impede its progress.

Core proposition

The final set of measures includes ones that are familiar to most businesses, but they play a special role in franchise systems, ensuring that their core proposition remains attractive and competitive. These are the measures that show how attractive a business proposition the franchise is to a potential franchisee:

- *Franchise cost*: the total cost to a franchisee of taking on a franchise. This is usually made up of three elements: franchise fee paid to buy the franchise; store build/fitting costs, to secure the lease, build or convert the space to meet the franchisors' requirements and install all the necessary equipment; and working capital required to fund the trading cycle.
- *Payback*: how long it takes for the money invested in setting up a new franchise to be repaid through profit. From the franchisor's perspective, a shorter payback increases not only the attractiveness of its franchise proposition, but also accelerates the time required for a single unit owner to be ready to add another unit and become a multi-unit owner.

- *Return on investment*: shows how attractive the franchise proposition is as a capital investment. It is the average annual profit divided by the investment expressed as a percentage. The figures ignore the 'sweat equity' or time and commitment of the franchise owner in its calculation of the investment.

Key ratios

Ratio	Calculation	Interpretation	Ratio increase means...
Achieved margin %	$\dfrac{\text{Actual price received} - \text{Supplier cost}}{\text{Actual price received}} \times 100$	Used to compare to buying margin % by retailers	Good performance
Average project size	$\dfrac{\text{Total (project) sales}}{\text{Number of projects}}$	Effectiveness measure – as size drives utilization	Good performance
Average store size	$\dfrac{\text{Actual sales space}}{\text{Average number of stores}}$	Indicator of a retailer's core proposition	Large changes mean shift in core proposition
Buying margin %	$\dfrac{\text{Expected retail price} - \text{Supplier cost}}{\text{Expected retail price}} \times 100$	Used as benchmark for achieved margin %	Good performance
Contribution margin %	$\dfrac{\text{Sales} - \text{Cost of sales} - \text{Variable costs}}{\text{Sales}} \times 100$	Profitability measure – shows true return on sales	Good performance
Contribution margin return on inventory investment (CMROII)	$\dfrac{\text{Contribution profit}}{\text{Inventory}} = \dfrac{\text{Contribution profit}}{\text{Sales}} \times \dfrac{\text{Sales}}{\text{Inventory}}$ 'Earn' × 'Turn'	Productivity measure – shows true return on capital tied up in inventory	Good performance
Contribution margin return on working capital (CMROWC)	$\dfrac{\text{Contribution profit}}{\text{Working capital}} = \dfrac{\text{Contribution profit}}{\text{Sales}} \times \dfrac{\text{Sales}}{\text{Working capital}}$	Productivity measure – shows true return on working capital	Good performance

Metric	Formula	Description	Performance
Days payable outstanding (DPO)	$\dfrac{\text{Accounts payable}}{\text{Cost of sales}} \times 365 \text{ days}$	Shows time taken to pay suppliers	Bad performance
Days sales outstanding (DSO)	$\dfrac{\text{Accounts receivable}}{\text{Sales}} \times 365 \text{ days}$	Shows time taken to collect payment from customers	Good performance (up to a limit, beyond that can be bad)
Gross margin %	$\dfrac{\text{Sales} - \text{Cost of sales}}{\text{Sales}} \times 100$	Basic profitability measure – indicates value added	Good performance
Gross margin return on inventory investment (GMROII)	$\dfrac{\text{Gross profit}}{\text{Inventory}} = \dfrac{\text{Gross profit}}{\text{Sales}} \times \dfrac{\text{Sales}}{\text{Inventory}}$ 'Earn' $\times$ 'Turn'	Productivity measure – shows basic return on capital tied up in inventory	Good performance
Gross Margin Return on Working Capital (GMROWC)	$\dfrac{\text{Gross profit}}{\text{Working capital}} = \dfrac{\text{Gross profit}}{\text{Sales}} \times \dfrac{\text{Sales}}{\text{Working capital}}$ Working capital = Inventory + Accounts receivable – Accounts payable	Productivity measure – shows basic return on working capital	Good performance
Inventory days (DIO)	$\dfrac{\text{Inventory}}{\text{Cost of sales}} \times 365 \text{ days}$	Shows time taken to sell inventory	Bad performance
Inventory turn	$\dfrac{365 \text{ days}}{\text{Inventory days}}$	Shows speed at which inventory is turning over	Good performance

(continued)

Ratio	Calculation	Interpretation	Ratio increase means...
Mark-up %	$\dfrac{\text{Sales} - \text{Cost of sales}}{\text{Cost of sales}} \times 100$	Shows amount of profit added to cost of product	Good performance
Net margin %	$\dfrac{\text{Sales} - \text{Cost of sales} - \text{Overhead costs} - \text{Interest}}{\text{sales}} \times 100$	Profitability of business activity for a period	Good performance
Operating margin %	$\dfrac{\text{Sales} - \text{Cost of sales} - \text{Overhead costs} - \text{Interest}}{\text{sales}} \times 100$	Profitability of trading operations for a period	Good performance
Potential growth capacity %	Net margin after tax % × Working capital turn	Rate of sales growth that can be financed internally	Good performance
Profit per square foot	$\dfrac{\text{Gross profit or DPP}}{\text{Average sales space (square feet)}}$	Profitability of sales space in a retailer	Good performance
Recoverability	$\dfrac{\text{Final contract price paid by customer}}{\text{Total resources used} \times \text{Standard prices}}$	Proportion of billable work that customers will pay for	Good performance
Return on capital employed (ROCE)	$\dfrac{\text{Net profit before tax}}{\text{Total assets} - \text{Non-interest-bearing liabilities}}$	Productivity of capital employed in the business	Good performance

Metric	Formula	Description	Rating
Return on invested capital (ROIC)	$= \dfrac{\text{Operating profit after tax}}{\text{Invested capital}}$ $\dfrac{\text{Operating profit after tax}}{\text{Total assets} - \text{Excess cash} - \text{Non-interest-bearing current liabilities}}$	Productivity of capital employed in the trading operations of the business (or allocated to the relevant part of the business)	Good performance
Return on net assets (RONA)	$\dfrac{\text{Operating profit}}{\text{Cash} + \text{Working capital} + \text{Fixed assets}}$	Productivity of assets employed in the business	Good performance
Sales per square foot	$\dfrac{\text{Sales}}{\text{Average sales space (square feet)}}$	Productivity of sales space in a retailer	Good performance
Sales per store	$\dfrac{\text{Sales}}{\text{Average number of stores}}$	Productivity of stores in a retailer	Good performance
Sales pipeline	$\dfrac{\text{Booked sales plus probability of expected sales}}{\text{Average monthly targeted sales}}$	Size of order book and expected sales	Good performance
Utilization	$\dfrac{\text{Billable time}}{\text{Standard time}} \times 100$	Productivity of people in a service business	Good performance (up to a limit, beyond that can be bad)
Value creation (VC)	Operating profit after tax − (Invested capital × WACC)	Profits generated in excess of cost of capital employed	Good performance
Working capital turn	$\dfrac{365 \text{ days}}{\text{Working capital days}}$	Shows speed at which working capital is turning over	Good performance

GLOSSARY OF TECHNICAL TERMS

accounting principles The principles governing the preparation of financial statements.

accounts payable (US term) Persons or business to whom amounts are due for goods or services purchased on credit (also known as 'trade payables'). Also includes other amounts payable within 12 months from the date of the balance sheet. (UK term is creditors.)

accounts receivable (US term) Amounts owing to the company. Accounts receivable are amounts owed from customers. (UK term is debtors.)

accumulated depreciation The cumulative amount of depreciation written off a fixed asset at a balance sheet date.

achieved margin The actual gross margin achieved on selling products. It is then compared to the buying margin.

acid test – quick ratio Liquid assets divided by current liabilities. 'Liquid assets' are normally represented by cash plus debtors; but long-term debtors (if any) would be excluded. If inventories were reckoned to be 'liquid' (for example, in a retailing chain with a very rapid rate of stock turnover) then they too might, exceptionally, be included.

advertising fund A franchisee-owned cooperative established within a franchise system to plan and deliver advertising and marketing on behalf of the franchisees. By pooling their resources, franchisees can secure economies of scale and scope for the money they pay to the advertising fund.

advocate channel A channel that influences the awareness and preferences of the end customer, by acting as a specifier (such as an architect) or as a paid adviser (such as a technical consultant or independent financial adviser). Although this is not a channel that a supplier can sell its products through, it is a critical channel to include in a channel strategy as a 'sell-with' channel.

aggregator A channel player that leverages information from multiple online sites or large volumes to gain a role in the supply chain. Its proposition to customers is ease of use (one-stop shopping) or price advantages (through accessing higher levels of discounts or other economies of scale), or both.

amortization The reduction in value of a liability over a period due to regular repayments.

annuity model *see* **consumption model**

ARPU *see* **average revenue per user**

asset turnover Measure of the utilization of the assets of the business, ie how many dollars of sales each dollar invested in assets produces.

AUV (Average Unit Volumes)   The headline measure for the sales or revenues of a franchised outlet per week.

average basket   *see* **average cheque**

average cheque; average check (also average ticket; average basket)   The average sales value of a single transaction. A useful measure to track over time to assess whether customers are increasing their spend each visit to the store or website.

average revenue per user (ARPU)   A measure of customer productivity, used in sectors working with the consumption model. Helps to assess attractiveness of customers and customer segments, and used to justify an appropriate level of customer acquisition cost.

average ticket   *see* **average cheque**

B2B   *see* **business to business**

B2C   *see* **business to consumer**

balance sheet   Statement of the assets, liabilities and shareholders funds of a company at a particular date. International accounting standards require that share capital, reserves, provisions, liabilities, fixed assets, current assets and other assets must be separately identified.

basis point   A basis point is one-hundredth of 1 per cent or 0.01 per cent.

BEV   *see* **break-even**

book value   The monetary amount of an asset as stated in its balance sheet. It usually represents acquisition cost less accumulated depreciation. In the case of land (or land with buildings on it), marketable securities or foreign currencies book value can be market value.

borrowing ratio (gearing ratio)   Ratio of debt to equity. Normally expressed as percentage. 100 per cent and over is high. Most public companies aim for 50 per cent or less.

break-even   The volume of activity or sales in units at which the contribution profit earned on those sales is exactly equal to the fixed costs in the business. At this volume the business makes neither a profit nor a loss.

business to business (B2B)   A generic term for describing the sales of products of services to business customers.

business to consumer (B2C)   A generic term for describing the sales of products of services to consumers as the end-customers. Can be applied to final-tier partners, as in retailers serving the B2C space.

buying margin   The gross margin expected when making a purchasing commitment. In some sectors, such as clothes retailing, this can be many months before the products arrive in the stores ready to be sold.

CAC   *see* **customer acquisition cost**

capacity utilization   The proportion of a service provider's billable capacity (measured in time terms such as hours or days) that is absorbed by billable activity on customer projects. High capacity utilization means that the service provider is very busy and is good for the business.

capital commitments   The amount of contracts for capital expenditure not provided for and the expenditure authorized by the directors but not contracted for that must be disclosed in the accounts.

capital employed   Capital employed is long-term capital. It consists of equity capital (ordinary share capital and reserves) plus long-term liabilities. Looked at from the asset side, capital employed equals net assets (= fixed assets plus working capital = total assets less current liabilities).

cash budget/cash flow   A plan of future cash receipts and payments based on specified assumptions concerning sales growth, credit terms, etc.

cash-to-cash cycle   The time taken for the cash paid out to suppliers for products to be returned to the business having been invested in inventory and receivables from credit customers, measured in days.

channel   A route to market for a supplier. Sometimes used loosely ('the channel') to describe only the indirect channel or trade channel, but when applied correctly refers to any specific route to market, which can include the direct channels such as sales force, catalogue, direct mail and the web.

channel value proposition   The relationship offering of a supplier to its trade channel partners. Perceived by the channel as the strategic and commercial value of a relationship with a particular supplier. It is built up from the comprehensive array of terms and conditions in the contract supported by the sales and marketing programmes, inter-business process investments, relationship support, strategic alignment and many other aspects of the relationship.

comps sales   *see* **same store sales**

connect rate   The proportion of customers who purchase a second item to accompany the main item. For example, the number who buy an extended warranty with the purchase of a household appliance, or the proportion who buy a drink to accompany their burger or sandwich.

consumption model   A business model based on customers consuming products or services over time, rather than purchasing them outright. Also known as an annuity model, which refers to the long-term sustainable revenue stream generated from this consumption.

contribution   Contribution profit (or margin) is the gross profit less other variable costs incurred.

co-op funds   Marketing funds allocated as a fixed percentage of sales by a supplier to be spent by a channel player on driving increased sales through that player.

corporate reseller   A final-tier player that specializes in selling into corporate customers, usually in the realm of information technology, business equipment, etc.

cost of goods sold or cost of sales   The price paid for getting goods and services to the point and condition where they are ready for sale.

cost structure   The profile of the overhead costs incurred by a business. Can also be used in reference to the balance between fixed and variable costs.

cost to sell   The costs incurred in *generating* a sale through a channel. Typically these costs are buried in traditional management accounting analyses and need to be extracted or estimated using an activity-based costing approach.

cost to serve   The costs incurred in *fulfilling* a sale through a channel, and can include all the costs over the lifecycle of the product, including warranty, service and support as well as the relationship management costs. Typically these costs are buried in traditional management accounting analyses and need to be extracted or estimated using an activity-based-costing approach.

credit period   The amount of time that it takes a person who has made a purchase on credit to pay.

creditors (UK term)   Persons or business to whom amounts are due for goods or services purchased on credit (= 'trade' creditors). Also includes other amounts owing within 12 months from the date of the balance sheet. (US term is accounts payable.)

cross-sell   The sales technique of adding sales of other product lines to the core product when engaged with a customer. An example is the adding of accessories and consumables to the core purchase.

current assets   Those assets which are either already cash or can reasonably be expected to become cash within one year from the date of the balance sheet. Examples: accounts receivable, inventories.

current liabilities   Liabilities which are expected to be paid within one year from the date of the balance sheet (eg trade creditors, proposed dividend, current taxation).

current ratio   Ratio of current assets to current liabilities.

current taxation   Tax payable within one year from the date of the balance sheet.

customer acquisition cost (CAC)   The cost of acquiring a customer. Usually includes all relevant marketing and sales costs incurred in generating leads through to customer sign-up. Often compared to lifetime value to ensure that the cost is not uneconomic.

customer churn   The number of customers lost per annum divided by total customer base expressed as a percentage. It indicates sustainability of business, as the higher the churn, the harder the service provider must work simply to maintain revenues.

customer count   The number of customers visiting a store or website in a specified period.

days inventory outstanding (DIO)   A measure of how long the business holds its inventory between purchase and sale, expressed in days. Used to show how quickly the inventory is turning.

days payable outstanding (DPO)   A measure of how long the business is taking to pay its suppliers' credit invoices, expressed in days.

days sales outstanding (DSO)   A measure of how long customers are taking to pay their credit invoices, expressed in days.

DCF   *see* **discounted cash flows**

debtors (UK term)   Amounts owing to the company. Trade debtors are amounts owed from customers. (US term is accounts receivable.)

depreciation   Expense recording the using up of fixed assets through operations. Accountants usually measure it by allocating the historical (acquisition) cost less scrap value of the asset on a straight-line or reducing-balance basis. Amount of depreciation must be disclosed in the profit and loss account. The accumulated (provision for) depreciation is deducted from the cost in the balance sheet to give the net book value.

    Depreciation (of fixed assets) is the process of allocating part of the cost of fixed assets as expense to a particular accounting period. Accumulated depreciation is the total amount so provided to date for assets still held by the company; it must be shown separately in the balance sheet or in the notes to the accounts.

    Net book value (NBV) is the difference between the cost of a fixed asset (or, in some cases the amount of its valuation) and the accumulated depreciation in respect of that asset. It does not represent market value.

    Residual value is the amount for which a fixed asset can be sold at the end of its useful life. The expected residual value is taken into account in calculating depreciation during the asset's life by writing off a constant percentage of the asset's original cost.

    The reducing-balance method writes off a constant percentage of the declining net book value of a fixed asset shown at the start of each accounting period. The percentage rate used is higher than for the straight-line method.

    Accelerated depreciation is any depreciation method which charges higher amounts in the early years of an asset's life than in the later years. Reducing balance is one such method.

DIO   *see* **days inventory outstanding**

direct channel   A route to market that involves the supplier in dealing directly with its customers and not going to market through intermediaries. Examples of direct channels are any type of sales force which calls on customers, catalogues, direct mail and the web.

disclosure document   The legal documentation that a franchisor is required to publish about its business together with the rights and obligations of the franchisor and franchisee and any other material information required by the franchisee before he or she decides to purchase a franchise.

discounted cash flows (DCF)   The total expected future revenues discounted by the cost of capital, to reflect the time value of money, ie later cash flows are valued lower than current ones.

distributor   A business that buys from suppliers and sells to other types of channel player (usually in the final tier) who in turn sell on to end customers. It does not sell directly to end customers.

DPO   *see* **days payable outstanding**

DSO   *see* **days sales outstanding**

dunning   The process of collecting payment from a debtor or account receivable.

earnings per share (EPS) Net profits after tax divided by the number of ordinary shares. This measure is often used to compare the overall performance of a business to the previous year.

EBITDA (Earnings before interest, tax, depreciation and ammortization) Represents the free cash flow generated from operations.

EDM (Electronic Direct Mail) Describes an email sent direct to a customer or potential customer.

end cap The display located at the end of an aisle in a retail store. Typically these locations attract an above-average level of passing customer traffic or footfall and stand out from the normal shelves, so are regarded as a premium location.

equity share capital Any issued share capital which has unlimited rights to participate in either the distribution of dividends or capital.

everything as a service (XaaS) The collective term for 'X as a service', 'anything as a service' or 'everything as a service'. The acronym refers to an increasing number of services that are delivered over the internet or through the cloud.

final tier The generic name given to channel players that sell to end customers. Refers to their location in a channel or distribution model as the final tier before reaching the customer.

financial statements Statements showing the financial position (balance sheet), profit for a period (income statement) and the sources and uses of funds for a period (funds flow statement).

fixed assets Assets held for use in the business rather than for re-sale. In general the movement for the year should be shown in the accounts.

footfall The number of customers entering a store or passing through a particular section of the store.

franchise A right granted to an individual or group to market a company's goods or services within a certain territory or market.

franchise system The group of players or entities that work together under agreements with the franchisor to operate the franchised business. It usually comprises the franchisor, franchisees, advertising fund and its boards, purchasing cooperative and its boards and one or more franchisee associations.

franchisee A holder of a franchise; a person who is granted a franchise.

franchisor The owner of the brand and business model who licenses the rights to their use.

gearing The ratio of net borrowings to capital employed. A measure of how much of the money in the business is owed; also known as leverage.

GMROII Gross margin return on inventory investment (GMROII) can be calculated by multiplying gross margin (earn) by the sales to inventory ratio (turn). A measure of the productivity of different products in inventory.

GMROWC Gross margin return on working capital (GMROWC) is calculated by dividing gross profit by working capital. A measure of how efficiently working capital is being used.

Gold-tier dealer or partner A dealer or partner that is in the top tier of a Gold/Silver/Bronze three-tier partnership model. A Gold-tier dealer or partner may be in the top tier through the volume of sales it makes or through meeting the top accreditation requirements.

goodwill   The excess of the price paid for a business acquired over the fair value of its identifiable assets acquired less liabilities assumed.

gross margin   Gross profit divided by sales expressed as a percentage.

gross profit   The difference between sales and cost of sales or cost of goods sold. Also known as the trading margin.

historical cost   The usual basis of valuation in published financial statements. Favoured because it is more objective and more easily verifiable by an auditor. Its use can be attacked on conceptual grounds, especially in times of inflation. In practice historical cost is usually replaced by market valuations for land, marketable securities and financial assets denoted in foreign currencies.

holding company   Company which controls another company, called its subsidiary. The balance sheet of the holding company must show separately its investment in subsidiaries (including basis of valuation) and amounts owing to and owed by subsidiaries. Holding companies are required to publish consolidated accounts which combine the financial statements of all the companies in the group.

IaaS   *see* infrastructure as a service

IFA   *see* independent financial intermediary

income statement (US term)   A financial statement summarizing the results of a business's trading activities for a period. (UK term is profit and loss account.)

independent financial adviser (IFA)   A major route to market for financial services providers. IFAs provide financial advice to consumers as to how to meet their personal long-term financial goals using pension and investment products.

indirect channel   Any route to market that involves a supplier selling through intermediaries such as distributors or final-tier trade players.

infrastructure as a service (IaaS)   The provision of essential corporate services through virtualized internet-enabled computing, or cloud computing. Enables users to pay for infrastructure as they use it (and scale it up when required), instead of making the up-front investment in their own infrastructure.

intangible assets   Goodwill, patents and trademarks, intellectual property of any sort, brands, etc. There are strict rules governing how intangible assets should be valued.

intellectual property   The collective term for ideas, inventions and creative works of the mind. It includes patents for inventions, trademarks, industrial designs, software, images, recordings, performances and many other categories.

inventory (US term)   Raw materials, work-in-progress and finished goods, usually valued at the lower of cost or market value. (UK term is stock.)

inventory days   Measures the average number of days inventory is held before it is sold.

inventory turn   Measure of working capital management, which represents how many times the inventory has been sold and replaced in a given period.

IP   *see* intellectual property

liabilities   Amounts owing by a company.

lifetime value (LTV)   A measure of the value of a customer of customer segment over its expected lifecycle. Usually calculated in net present-value terms. Indicates customer profitability and long-term segment value.

liquidity   The ease with which current assets and current liabilities can be transformed into cash.

listing fees   Fees demanded by retailers from suppliers for including the suppliers' products in their stores, ie to include them in their list of products.

LTV   *see* **lifetime value**

marketing funds   The money allocated by a supplier to be spent by a channel player according to rules defined by the supplier to ensure the marketing drives sales for the supplier through the channel player. Can be allocated on a discretionary basis or in direct proportion to sales, in which case they are often termed co-op marketing funds.

mass merchant   A type of retailer that offers a very broad array of categories in its stores, catalogues or online. Leading retail mass merchants include discount store and department store operators, and some of the larger grocery chains have some stores that include such large non-food sections that they could also be considered to be mass merchants.

minority interest   That part of a subsidiary company's shareholders' funds that is not held by the holding company. Usually shown as a separate item on the liabilities side of a consolidated balance sheet.

multi-unit owner   A franchisee who owns more than one franchised outlet in a franchise system.

net assets   Total assets less total liabilities.

net current assets   Current assets less current liabilities.

net margin (before or after tax)   Net profit divided by sales expressed as a percentage. Can be applied to net profit before tax or after tax.

net present value   Net present value is the present value of future cash flows discounted back using an interest rate which is normally the company's cost of capital.

net profit (before or after tax)   Net profit is the operating profit less interest. Can be expressed as before tax or after tax.

net worth   Assets less liabilities in the proprietorship section of a balance sheet, usually referred to as shareholders' funds or share capital and reserves.

omni-channel   A type of consumer sales or retailing that orchestrates multiple sales motions (store, online, catalogue) as well as communications and fulfilment channels to provide a complete customer experience.

online travel agents   Travel agents offering a platform or portal for booking travel online.

operating profit   The profit made after deducting overheads from the gross profit, but before deducting interest.

OTA   *see* **online travel agents**

overheads   The selling, general and administrative costs incurred by a business that are not included in cost of sales (or cost of goods sold).

overtrading   Running the business at a level of sales above that which can be supported by the capital available within the business.

parent company   *see* **holding company**

Pareto's Law   An empirical observation sometimes known as the '80:20' principle. It applies in many ways, but the simplest is where 20 per cent of products deliver 80 per cent of the sales, or 20 per cent of customers account for 80 per cent of sales.

payable days   Measures the average number of days it takes to pay for purchases on credit.

payback, payback period   The time taken for an investment to recoup the initial outlay.

pipeline management   *see* **sales pipeline**

planograming/planogram   Planograming is the process of working out the layout and display of product categories, product lines and individual SKUs in a retail store to maximize sales or profitability. The result is a planogram, which is a map of where categories are sited in the store and where each product sits on the shelf.

platform or **platform provider**   A business model that facilitates exchange between providers and customers. The internet has enabled platform providers to take a powerful role in areas such as taxi services (eg Uber), travel and accommodation (eg Expedia, Airbnb) and many others. The term 'platform' can be used more generically to describe a business based on a high fixed cost infrastructure such as railways or hotels.

potential growth capacity   Measures the amount by which the company can grow using its existing financial resources.

professional services firm   Any type of business selling professional services such as lawyers, accountants, consultants, etc, either to private individuals or to companies.

provision   An estimate of the loss in the value of an asset which is charged against the profits. Examples include provisions for future warranty costs, bad debts and inventory obsolescence. Can also refer to providing for a known liability of which the amount cannot be determined with accuracy such as the outcome of outstanding litigation or claims against the business.

purchasing cooperative   A franchisee-owned cooperative established within a franchise system to handle purchasing and supply chain management on behalf of the franchisees.

qualification   The process of validating a potential customer's business value, including assessing their ability to buy, the seriousness of their intent, their likely cost of acquisition and cost-to-serve, and judging the probability of their choosing the supplier. Good qualification processes ensure scarce sales skills are directed to high quality opportunities.

ranging   Deciding on the range of products to offer in a retail store, including the assortment of how many models and sizes to offer in each category and in what depth.

receivable days   *see* days sales outstanding

receivables   *see* accounts receivable

recoverability   The proportion of billable activity (valued at sales prices) that can be billed to a customer by a service provider.

reseller   A trade channel player that buys and resells products to end customers. A term used mainly by suppliers as it describes the role the player fulfils for them.

reserve   A specific application of retained earnings which prevents them from being available for distribution to shareholders. An example is capital redemption reserve, which is created when retained earnings have been used to buy back shares, and is needed to prevent the capital of the business being reduced. The term reserve is often used inappropriately as a vague term or even a substitute for the meaning applied to provision or even surpluses of cash.

retained profits   Profits which are retained and not paid out as dividends. Also called accumulated profits when shown in the balance sheet and represents the retained profits since the business was started.

return on capital employed (ROCE)   Net profit before tax (EBIT) divided by shareholders funds expressed as a percentage.

return on invested capital (ROIC)   Operating earnings after tax divided by invested capital (total assets less excess cash minus non-interest-bearing liabilities). This is often used to assess the value creation capabilities of a firm in an intuitive way. It is a measure of the operating business performance, with the treasury aspects (ie excess cash) stripped out.

return on investment   The profits from an investment or project less the initial cost of investment divided by the initial cost of investment. Used as a guide to investment decisions, the higher the return, the better the project's expected or actual outcome.

return on net assets (RONA) (before or after tax)   Net profit (before or after tax) divided by net assets employed expressed as a percentage. A measure of how well the company is utilizing its assets to produce a return on shareholder investment.

return on shareholders' funds (ROSF)   Profit after tax divided by equity shareholders' funds expressed as a percentage.

revenues (US term)   The value of all goods and services sold in a period. (UK term is sales.)

RevPAR   Revenue per available room, a metric used in the hotel sector for tracking earning performance. It is a function of occupancy and average room rate achieved.

ROI   *see* return on investment

SaaS   *see* software as a service

sales (UK term)   The value of all goods and services sold in a period. (US term is revenues.)

sales cycle   The time it takes on average for a lead to be converted into a confirmed order.

sales pipeline   The measure of revenue visibility equal to the average number of months sales booked as orders (or orders plus expected value of outstanding bids). Can also be used in a more generic way to refer to a business's view of the number of enquiries or leads, prospects, bids or proposals and unfulfilled orders outstanding that gives it some ability to predict its future levels of sales or revenues.

same store sales   These are sales of stores that have been opened for one year or more. Because it takes time for a new store to ramp up to full productivity, analysts will often turn to this measure to filter out the effect of distortions caused by a rapid store expansion programme. Sometimes referred to as 'comps' sales.

seasonality   The sensitivity of a business to uneven sales over the year. A seasonal business is one that is highly uneven such as one selling sun-tan lotions in the UK. Seasons can be artificial, not just related to nature's seasons, for example Back to School and the end of the public sector financial year, which often involves a rush to spend unused budgets to ensure they are not cut in future years.

sell-with channel   *see* **advocate channel**

share capital   The ownership of a share gives the shareholder a proportionate ownership of the company. The share capital is stated in the balance sheet at its par (nominal) value.

share of wallet or account penetration   The proportion of the customer's relevant expenditure that has been captured by the retailer, supplier or service provider.

shareholder   Member of a company through ownership of shares in the company. Shareholders are the capital backers of a business, either by investing directly or by buying the shares second-hand. Private companies' shares are usually traded directly between individuals; public companies' shares can be traded through the stock markets.

shareholders' funds   The proprietorship section of a company balance sheet. Includes the share capital, any share premium and the retained earnings.

short-term loan   A loan with an original maturity of less than 12 months.

SKU   An acronym for stock-keeping unit. Each different size and weight and packaging of a product is a unique SKU, so the 250 g box, the 450 g box and the 450 g box with a special promotion are each individual SKUs.

software as a service (SaaS)   The provision of the functionality of a software product as a web-enabled service. Office 365 is an example of SaaS, where users can log into their browser and operate their spreadsheets, word processing and presentations as if they were using an installed version of Office.

SPIFF   A special reward given by manufacturers or service sources to a dealer's sales team for encouraging the sale of their own products, usually run as a very short-term programme, such as a 'SPIFF day'. (SPIFF is possibly an acronym for sales promotion incentive for funds.)

stock (UK term)   Raw materials, work-in-progress and finished goods, usually valued at the lower of cost or market value. (US term is inventory.)

store density The number of stores or outlets in a retail chain or franchise system divided by the number of people in the population. Used as a measure of market penetration or saturation, low numbers such as one store per 12,000 people are called high densities.

straight-line depreciation Cost less estimated scrap value of an asset divided by its estimated economic life.

subsidiary Company that is owned by another company (either entirely or substantially, defined by technical rules).

SUO (Single Unit Owner) A franchisee who owns a single store.

territory management The business function of running a geographic area to meet business objectives, usually sales and operating service standards.

trade channel A route to market that comprises intermediaries that sell to the end customer (*see also* indirect channel). Sometimes loosely called 'the trade'.

trading margin *see* **gross margin**

unsecured loan or borrowings Money borrowed by a company without the giving of security.

up-sell The sales and marketing technique of encouraging a customer to buy a better, more expensive or higher-margin product when considering a purchase. Many suppliers offer a range comprising of 'good, better, best' products to encourage the customer to trade up. Some also offer a basic model that is so stripped down that its only real feature is a low price to generate customer interest on which up-selling techniques can be engaged.

utilization The key measure of productivity used in service providers. It can be applied to the entire service part of the business, individual divisions or teams and even each individual billable member of staff. High utilization means that a high proportion of the time of billable staff is going into productive, revenue-generating work. Excessively high utilization over time will lead to burnout and quality issues.

value creation (destruction) Operating profits generated in excess of the cost of capital. If profits exceed cost of capital, management has created value and if the reverse is true, management has destroyed value.

value proposition An analysis and quantified review of the benefits, costs and value that an organization can deliver to customers or partners. It represents the complete business case for doing business together.

vendor Term for supplier often used by distributors and channel players.

waterfall (analysis) A tool used to break out the components of cost or margin for a customer, segment or product. By analysing the components and identifying their drivers, a business can prioritize strategies for reducing costs and increasing margins.

weighted average cost of capital (WACC) The average cost of capital, representing the expected cost of all of a company's sources of capital. Each source of capital, such as equities, bonds and other debt, is weighted in the calculation according to its prominence in the company's capital structure.

wholesaler   *see* **distributor**

work-in-progress   Partly completed manufactured goods.

working capital   Inventory plus accounts receivable less accounts payable. This represents the capital required by a business to fund its trading cycle. As the business grows it will need more working capital, unless it can improve the working capital cycle.

working capital cycle   Measures the average number of days working capital is tied up in the business. The lower the figure, the more efficiently working capital is being recycled.

working capital requirement   Measures the amount of working capital required in a company given its level of sales and how quickly its working capital is recycled.

working capital turn   Measures how many times the company generates its working capital during a period. The higher the turn, the better the generation capacity.

XaaS   *see* **everything as a service**

yield   Another term for return. Usually refers to the annual return generated by an asset or investment.

INDEX

Note: The index is filed in alphabetical, word-by-word order. Within main headings, numbers, acronyms and 'Mc' are filed as spelt out. Page locators in *italics* denote information contained within a Figure or Table.

accelerated depreciation 344
Accenture 201, 273
account managers (management) 22–23, 88, 92, 125–26, 199, 206, 211–13, 278, 284–86
  see also project accounting; project management
account penetration 290, 350, 386
accounts payable 54, 74, *102*, 186, 340
accounts receivable 43, 54, 78–79, 80, *102*, 113, *155*, 187, 340
accreditation 116, 142, 200, 203, 281
accumulated depreciation 340
achieved margins 269, *336*, 340
acquisition sales teams 285
  see also mergers and acquisitions (M&As)
activity-based-costing (ABC costing) 69
ADP 273
advance payments (up-front payments) 186–87, 188
advertising 107, 242, *247*, *266*, *270*, 273, 300, 325, 329
advertising fund cooperative *318*, 320, 340
advocate channel (advocacy) *10*, *137*, 138–40, *145*, 146–48, *177*, 216–17, 263, 340
after-sales policy 261
  see also post-sales (second-level technical) support; returns
aggregators *15*, 17–18, 24–26, 29, 30, 276–77, 278, 340
agricultural machinery 225
Airbnb 4, 36, 37, 291
Airbus 225, 228, 232
airline (aviation) industry 16, 21, 169–71, 180, 225–26, 228, 232, 277, 293, 295
Alain Afflelou 258
Alibaba 18, 246
alliances 205, 265
Alstom 230
Amazon 18, 31, 241, 246, 250, 257, 262, 263, 301
Amazon Prime 28, 262, 289, 303, 306
amortization 50, 113, 127, 178, 180, 229, 340

analysis
  business model *22*
  data analysis 236, 262–63
  price waterfall 286–88, 351
  sensitivity 197
annuity model *see* consumption model
Apple 263, 300, 301, 303, 310
Apple iTunes 250, 251, 306, 311
Apple Music 28, 289, 307
Apple Stores 29–30, 257, 268
apps 29–30, 249, 329
ASOS 246
ASSA ABLOY Group 236
assets 205, *207*, 211, 232
  current 54, *102*, *152*, *155*, 343
  fixed 51, 54, 55, 57, 94, *101–03*, 104, *124*, *163*, 345
  intangible 223, 242, 275, 299, 346
  net 54, *102*, 347
  net current 54, *102*, *152*, *155*, 347
  see also return on net assets (RONA)
attach rates 180
Auchan 256
automation 24, 47, 49, 113, 118, 225, 310
automotive industry 42, 79, *134*, 138–39, 144–45, 315
  see also car rentals; car servicing; Toyota
average cheque (basket/ticket) metric 179, 267, 331, 341
average cost of processing orders 70
average order sizes 70
average order value 267
average project size *163*, 169, *191*, *336*
average revenue per user 289, 341
average room rate 294, 296
average store size 268, *336*
average transaction value *266*, 267
average unit age 239, 240
average unit volume 330–31, 341
aviation (airline) industry 16, 31, 169–71, 180, 225–26, 228, 232, 277, 293, 295
awareness-building *10*, 47, 49, 119, 120, 202, 246, *260*, *264*

balance sheets 50, 51, 54–55, 90, 100, 102, 211, 341
banking sector 181, 192, 222, 276
BAT 44
Beats Audio 303
benchmarking 70, 84, 92–93, 184, 214–15
BestBuy 263
BEV (break-even) 71–72, 110, 121, 170, 172–73, 181–82, 290, 292, 341
Big Pharma sector 139, 309–10
Big Pig Music Ltd 302
billable time 158, 165, 166–68, 173–74, 191, 196
black box discounts 141–42
blended margins 62–66, 128, 267
Boeing 225, 226, 228
bonuses 142, 173
books 28, 297, 299, 303, 304
boundary roles 212
bow-tie model 125–26
brand 202, 209, 297, 298, 320, 326
    see also co-branding
brand promise 7, 11, 14, 279, 317, 327
break-even (BEV) 71–72, 110, 121, 170, 172–73, 181–82, 290, 292, 341
briefings 216–17
broadline distributors 41, 45, 46, 56, 78, 207–08
brokers 13, 17, 24, 134, 147, 249, 274, 284
B2B (business-to-business) 27, 32, 35–36, 139, 215, 341
    services sector 273, 275, 282, 284–85, 286
B2C (business-to-consumer) 27–28, 32, 215, 273–74, 277, 341
buffer stocks 112–13, 114
building sector 96, 134, 136–37, 226
    see also construction sector
bulk breaking (breaking bulk) 42, 43, 48, 129, 256
burnout 112, 167
business case formulation 126–29
business cycle fluctuations 227–28
business mix strategy 193
business models 5, 6–7, 20–23, 52–72, 149–56, 327
business planning 203, 209
buying margins 269, 336, 341

C-suite 231
call centres 183, 273, 275, 276, 292, 294
Candle in the Wind (John) 301
Canon 300
capacity utilization 151, 164–65, 178–79, 341

Capita 273
capital employed 71, 184, 196, 342
    see also return on capital employed (ROCE)
capital goods sector 222, 225–40
    see also automotive industry; building sector; construction sector
car rentals 27–28, 169–70, 171
car servicing 144–45
Carrefour 247, 256, 261
cash and carry wholesalers 17, 41
cash floats 81, 188
cash flow 19, 27, 51, 67–68, 156, 186–87, 188–89, 234, 327, 342
    discounted 290, 344
cash-to-cash cycle 73, 183–85, 187, 342
catalogues 241, 244, 245–46
category killers 247
category 1 sales pipeline 159–61
category 3 sales pipeline 159, 161
category 2 sales pipeline 159, 161
catering sector see hotels, restaurants and catering (HoReCa) sector
Caterpillar 201, 225, 234, 235, 236
change management 12, 112
channel conflict 19, 31–32, 120, 121, 255, 276, 307, 311
channel enablement 238–39
channel value proposition 12, 21–23, 120, 198–17, 342
channels 229–30, 342
    see also advocate channel (advocacy); aggregators; channel conflict; channel enablement; channel value proposition; conferences; direct channels; final-tier channels; first-tier channels; franchises; gig economy; indirect channels; multi-channels (omni-channels); multiple-tiered channels; one-tier channels; online retail channels; online travel agents (OTAs); original equipment manufacturers (OEM); retailers; smartphones; two-tier channels
Charles Schwab 16, 96
chemicals sector 79, 96
China 17, 230, 312
Chipotle 31
Cisco 4, 135, 142, 310
click and collect 255, 256, 261, 262
click-throughs 179, 277
cloud solutions 24, 25–26, 27, 29–30, 135, 170, 229, 312
CMROII 86–89, 336
CMROWC 89–93, 336

co-branding 205, *207*, 304
co-op funds *48*, 342
Coca-Cola (Coke) 14, 21
commission *see* sales commission
communication 171, 249, 281–82, 328
comparable store sales *see* same store sales
Comparethemarket.com 18, 31, 276
comparison websites 18, 31, 33, 249–50,
  276–78
compensation models 32, 141–48, 252, *253*
compensation payments, franchise exit 324
  see also rebates
competencies 25, 81, 138–39, 231–39,
  259–65, 276, 279–89, 295–96,
  307–14, 326–30
competitor analysis 22, 206
compliance (monitoring) 142, 312, 317,
  321, 328, 332
concept 326–27
concept extensions 325–26
conferences 46, *48*, 147, 216, 217, 223, 281
conflict, channel 19, 31–32, 120, 121, *255*,
  276, 307, 311
connect rate 87, 125, 129, 252, 342
consignment stock *42*, 44, *48*
consistency 30–31, 178, 261, 320, 326, 327
consolidation services *42*, 43, 208, 210
construction sector *134*, 222, 225
  see also building sector
consultants (consultancies) 138, 146,
  216–17, 328
consultative selling 231, 258, 284–86
consumer ecosystem 35–36, 263–65
consumer goods sector 221, 222, 241–72
consumers 34–35, 254–58, 263–65
  see also customers
consumption billing 265
consumption model 27, 188–89, 229, 232,
  258, 308–09, 342
content IP 303
  see also books; films; images; music
contention rates 181
contract-based value delivery 151
contracts 151, 157–59, 170, 184, 188, 203,
  299–308, 323–24
  see also final contract price paid by
  customer
contribution margin return on inventory
  investment 86–89, *336*
contribution margin return on working
  capital 89–93, *336*
contribution margins 66–70, 86–93,
  110–11, 127, *336*, 342
convenience 28–29, 171, 242, 244, *255*,
  256, *260*

conversion rates *266, 267*
Coolblue 246
copyright exploitation 311
copyright IP 297, 305–06
  see also books; brand; films (film
  distribution); images; live
  performances; music; software
core competencies 25, 81, 138–39, 232,
  262, 276, 284, 309, 311
core offerings, distributors 41–45, 47–50
corporate resellers *134*, 342
cost of sales (cost of goods sold) *54*, 60, 75,
  151, *152, 155*, 172, 342
cost structure 50, 69–70, 72, 107, 150, 156,
  169, 252, 294, 342
cost to sell 20, 127, 128, 343
cost to serve 68–69, 104–06, 200, 288,
  289, 343
costs 11, 13–14, 15, 43, 68, 69
  capital goods 228
  direct *152, 155*
  direct product 271
  fixed 18–19, 51, 69–70, 109–11, 172,
    282, 294
  franchise 324, 333
  HoReCa sector 292–94
  indirect *152, 155*
  operating 188, 239
  retail sector 243
  variable 51, 109
  see also activity-based-costing (ABC
    costing); cost of sales (cost of goods
    sold); cost structure; cost to sell; cost
    to serve; customer acquisition cost;
    full costing; overheads; overtime
Couchsurfing.com 37
counterfeit goods 235, 237–38, 312
credit management function 25, 49, 51, 113
credit period (terms) *42*, 43, 57, 75, 79–81,
  187, 343
  see also prompt payment discounts
creditor days *see* days payable outstanding
  (DPO)
creditors 343
cross-selling 63, 70, 88, 200, 214, 245, 272,
  275, 288, 343
current assets *54, 102, 152, 155*, 343
current liabilities *54*, 101–03, *124, 163*,
  191, 343
customer acquisition cost 30, 31, 156, 178,
  180, 181, 288–89, 343
customer churn 28, 288–89, 290, 343
customer count 331, 343
customer days *see* days sales outstanding
  (DSO)

customer experience (journey) *10*, *153*,
    242–43, 259–60, 263–64
customer lifetime modelling 181
customer lifetime value 181, 268, 288–89,
    294, 347
customer loyalty *10*, 11, 266, 267–68, 296
    loyalty schemes 4, 68, 170–71, 179,
        223, *247–48*, 259, 293–94
customers 11, 28, 42, 50, *153*, 170–71,
    179, 289–90, 329, 331
    new 202, 209
    see also consumers; contribution
        margins; customer acquisition cost;
        customer churn; customer experience
        (journey); customer lifetime value;
        customer loyalty; footfall

data analysis 236, 262–63
data mining 262, 263
days inventory outstanding (DIO/inventory
    days) 75–76, 81, 83, 185–87, *337*,
    343, 346
days payable outstanding (DPO) 74–75,
    81, 82, 100, *337*, 343
days sales outstanding (DSO/debtor
    days) 78–80, 81, 82–83, 100, 187,
    337, 343
deal registration 283
delayed investment strategy 110–11
Deliveroo 36, 37
delivery logistics 28–29, 43, 245–46
    see also click and collect; Deliveroo
Dell 4, 14–16
demand generation 26, 47, *48*, 49, 199,
    266, 316
demonstration centres (demonstrations) 32,
    147, 252
depreciation 178, 196, 340, 344
design patents 298, 306
diamond model 125–26
Dick James Music 302
differentiation 14, 22, 32, 118, 122, 125,
    141, 149, 176–77, 308–09
Digital Rights Management 311
digital watermarks 311, 312
DIO (inventory days) 75–76, 82, 83,
    185–87, *337*, 343, 346
direct channels 15–16, 293, 344
    see also catalogues; sales forces (teams);
        websites
direct costs *152*, *155*
direct product costs 271
direct product profitability 271–72
disclosure documents 322, 323–24, 344
discounted cash flows 290, 344

discounts 49, 56, 60, 64, 66, 69, 75, 76–77,
    141–42
    see also rebates
diseconomies of scale 114
disintermediation 24–26
Disneyland Paris 301
disposal services *233*, *260*, 263, *264*
distribution models *see* aggregators; direct
        channels; distribution strategy;
        distributors; envelope-level
        distribution; final-tier channels; high-
        touch distribution; indirect channels;
        low-touch distribution; multiple-
        tiered channels; narrow bandwidth
        distribution; one-tier channels;
        original equipment manufacturers
        (OEM); 'over-distribution'; platform-
        based service business model; release
        models, film distribution; two-tier
        channels
distribution strategy 9–15, 24–26, 28, 34,
    36, 38, *50*, 50–51, 121–30
distributors 18, 41–130, 207–11, 344
    IT 4, 17, 25–26
    specialist 16, 19, 133, 201, *247*
    third-party 292
Dixons 244
Dolby 300, 302–03
domestic trade services 176–77
downtime 179
DPO (days payable outstanding) 74–75,
    81, 82, 100, *337*, 343
DSO (days sales outstanding/debtor
    days) 78–80, 81, 82–83, 100, 187,
    337, 343
dunning 82, 344

earn and turn 82, 84–86, 89, 127
earnings per share 51, 345
eBay 246
economic value added *see* value creation
    (VC)
economies of scale 109–14
ecosystem thinking 35–36, 263–65
Edrington Group 122
80:20 rule (Pareto's Law) 49, 56, 78,
    348
electronics sector 41, 96, 297
emerging markets 17
engagement process 13, 120–24
English Premier League 298–99
envelope-level distribution 256, 262
equipment metrics 239–40
estate maintenance 268, 321, 333
Europe 44, 75, 235, 273, 279, 313

see also France; Germany; Greece;
 Turkey; UK
EVA *see* value creation (VC)
evaluation *10*
everything as a service (XaaS) 273, 345
exclusive territories 322
exclusivity 116–17, 128, 147, 199, 302–03,
 306, 322
extended supply chains 229–30
extension of vendor role 136–37, *140*,
 145, *207*

fashion sector 80, 245, 256
fast moving consumer goods (FMCG)
 brands 221, 222
Federal Trade Commission (US) 322–23
FedEx 47, 326
fee for function model 142–45
feedback 50, 206, 250, 259, 281, 329, 331
films (film distribution) 142–44, 297,
 303–04, 312
final contract price paid by customer 175
final-tier channels 7, *15*, 19, 25, 41,
 133–217, 345
finance agreements 228, 232, 234
finance-driven costs 68, *69*
financial services sector *96*, 138, 147–48,
 274, 276
 see also banking sector; insurance sector
financial statements 54, 345
 see also balance sheets; income
 statements; profit and loss accounts
first call status distributors 208
first-level technical support (pre-sales
 support) *42*, 43, 46, 66, 67,
 141, 203
first moment of truth 265
first-tier channels *15*, 17, 18–19, 26,
 41, 136
Five Ps 4
fixed assets 51, *54*, 55, *57*, 94, *101–03*,
 104, *124*, *163*, 345
fixed costs 18–19, 51, 69–70, 109–11, 172,
 282, 294
fixed-price contracts 158–59
fixed-term service, support and maintenance
 contracts 158–59, 188
floorplan financing schemes 234
FMCG brands 221, 222
Fnac Darty 256, 257
Food and Drug Administration (US) 306
food wagons 37
footfall 18, 265–67, 272, 324, 345
Forrester and Gartner 217
France 122, 230, 256, 263

franchise system 224, 315, 317, 318–21,
 322, 324, 325–34, 345
franchisee associations *318*, 321
franchisees *318*, 320, 322–24, 345
franchises 224, 315–34, 345
franchisors 316, 317, 318–19, 322–23, 345
Frank N Stein Ltd 302
freelancing 36, 291
fulfilment distributors *45*, 47
full costing 173
full profit portfolio 236–38
funding 71, 73, 204, *207*, *208*, 244, 250, 252
 see also advertising fund cooperative;
 marketing funds; peer-to-peer
 lending; purchasing cooperative;
 shareholder funds

gearing 345
 see also leverage
General Electric (GE) 228, 236
Germany 79, *91*, 142, 244, 273, 279, 313
gig economy 4, 36–38
global distribution channels 234–35
gold-tier partners 199–200, 345–46
Google 29–30, 254, 263, 298, 301
Google Adwords 29, 277
Google Analytics 265
Google Translate 33
GPS location 236, 249
Greece 79, *91*, 92
grey-marketing 223, 313–14
gross margins (GMs) 59–61, 64–65,
 126–28, 172–74, 176–82, 214,
 337, 346
 gross margin return on inventory
 investment (GMROII) 84–86, 89,
 129, 305, *337*, 345
 gross margin return on working capital
 (GMROWC) 89, 129, 305, *337*, 345
gross profit 54, 55, 60–63, 72, 84–85, *152*,
 155, *173–74*, 177, 346
growth management 107–14, 129, 196–97,
 201–03, 209
 see also potential growth capacity

Happenstance Ltd 302
healthcare sector *96*, 216–17, 222, 226,
 274–75, 276
Hewlett-Packard (HP/HPE) 4, 28, 135,
 148, 205, 235, 300, 303, 310
high-tech sector 70, 142, 230
 see also Apple; Apple iTunes; Apple
 Music; Apple Stores; Cisco; Dell;
 Hewlett-Packard (HP/HPE); IBM;
 Intel; Microsoft

high-touch distribution 274–75,
    280–82
Hilton Hotel Group 293, 315, 326
holidays, utilization calculation 166
Hollister Co 242
hotels, restaurants and catering (HoReCa)
    sector 4, 169–71, 188, 223,
    291–96, 328
    see also Airbnb
Huawei 230

IaaS 27, 29, 30, 273, 346
IBM 135, 216, 230
images 297, 300
incentives 23, 48, 49, 56, 69, 75–77, 88,
    170–71, 213, 286, 288
    see also bonuses; rewards; SPIFFS
income statements 54, 55, 346
    see also profit and loss accounts
Independent Financial Advisers
    (IFAs) 274, 276
independent retailers 247
indirect channels 9, 24–25, 346
    see also distributors; final-tier channels;
    Independent Financial Advisers
    (IFAs); resellers; retailers; third-party
    distributors; TV
indirect costs 152, 155
information technology (IT) 96, 134,
    135–36, 138, 139–40, 142, 221, 226,
    229, 300
    see also apps; information technology
    (IT) distributors; information
    technology (IT) systems; software;
    Software as a Service (SaaS);
    streaming; Wi-Fi
information technology (IT) distributors 4,
    17, 25–26, 41, 63
information technology (IT) systems 56,
    89, 111, 113, 179, 183
infrastructure as a service (IaaS) 27, 29, 30,
    273, 346
installed base 237, 239
insurance sector 180, 276, 277
intangible assets 223, 242, 275, 299, 346
integrators 32, 35, 36, 137–40, 207, 216
Intel 14, 18, 230, 310
intellectual property 223, 235, 297–314,
    346
internal organization 12, 23
internet 181, 215, 236, 245, 312
Internet Service Providers (ISPs) 170,
    258–59
inventory 19, 47, 49, 52–53, 68–69, 75–78,
    79, 114, 262, 346

    see also contribution margin on
    inventory investment; days inventory
    outstanding (DIO/ inventory days);
    gross margin return on inventory
    investment (GMROII); inventory
    turn; stock
inventory turn 84–86, 111, 113, 337, 346
investments 57–58, 110–11, 327, 333
    see also return on invested capital
    (ROIC); return on investment
IT see information technology (IT)
iTunes 250, 251, 306, 311

James Hardie 35–36
John, Elton 301–02
Just Eat 36

knowledge value chain 138, 139
Komatsu 225, 236

lead generation 204, 207, 208, 333
legal requirements 32, 165, 274, 284, 298,
    307, 319, 322
leverage 50–51, 211
liabilities 104, 152, 155, 347
    current 54, 101–03, 124, 163,
    191, 343
    long-term 54, 94, 102, 109
licensing
    intellectual property 223, 299–308
    software 6, 27, 188–89, 275, 297, 299,
    308–09, 312
    technology 26, 300, 302–03
licensing skills 307–08
lifetime value see customer lifetime value
like-for-like sales see same store sales
liquid assets 240
liquidity 43, 83, 347
listening skills 281
listing fees 34, 243, 347
live performances 28, 297, 301, 302
location 37, 147, 229–30
    franchises 321, 322, 324–25, 333
    inventory 114
    retail 53, 242–43, 247
logistics 42, 43, 68, 69, 208–09
    returns 34, 66, 67, 256, 262
    reverse 127, 245, 262
long-term contracts 158, 184
long-term liabilities 54, 94, 102, 109
loser products (losers) 87, 88–89, 271
low ball, pricing 64–65
low-tech sectors 142
low-touch distribution 275–76, 283
loyalty 10, 266, 267–68, 296

loyalty schemes 4, 68, 170–71, 179, 223,
247–48, 259, 293–94
see also Preferred Partner Programmes

M&As (mergers and acquisitions) 117,
230, 310
McDonald's 304, 317, 324, 325, 326, 327
management 104, 154
see also C-suite; strategic account
managers (SAMs)
manufacturing sector 225, 227, 228, 230,
273
margin mix 62–66, 203, 210, 266, 267
margins 56, 203, 210
see also achieved margins; blended
margins; buying margins;
contribution margins; gross margins
(GM); margin mix; net margins;
operating margins
mark-ups 60, 338
market 13, 28, 76, 79, 202, 209
market access 11, 12, 13–14, 24–38,
309–11
market information (research) 48, 49,
198–99, 213
market penetration 202, 224, 299, 308,
309, 333, 351
market share leaders 126–28, 213–14
marketing 42, 45, 46, 49, 68, 69, 204, 205,
210, 211
grey 223, 313–14
pull 306, 308–09
push 306, 309
marketing funds 48, 129, 152, 155, 199,
203–04, 244, 250, 252, 347
marketplaces 246, 248, 257
see also Amazon
mass merchants 247, 347
measures see metrics
MediaMarkt/Saturn 244
medical patents 306
mergers and acquisitions (M&As) 117,
230, 310
metrics 6–7, 239–40, 265–72, 289–90, 296,
330–34
average cheque (basket/ticket) 179, 267,
341
average cost of processing orders 70
average order size 70
average project size 163, 169, 191, 336
average revenue per user 341
average room rate 294
average store size 336
average unit volume 341
CMROII 86–89, 336

CMROWC 89–93, 336
DIO/inventory days 75–76, 81, 83,
185–87, 337, 343, 346
DPO 74–75, 81, 82, 100, 337, 343
DSO 78–80, 81, 82–83, 100, 187, 337,
343
footfall 18, 324, 325
GMROII 84–86, 89, 129, 305, 337, 345
GMROWC 89, 129, 305, 337, 345
NOPAT 97, 100, 190, 192
potential growth capacity 108–09, 338,
348
profit per square foot 338
repeat customer rate 266, 267
revenue 289, 293, 296, 330–31, 341,
349
ROCE 94–96, 127, 151, 152, 338, 349
ROIC 97–98, 100, 151, 152, 339, 349
RONA 94–95, 339, 349
sales 317, 339, 350
WACC 97–98, 100, 351
see also benchmarking
metro locations 230
Microsoft 4, 15, 135–36, 205, 216, 300,
312
Microsoft Office 365 27, 305, 309
microtransactions 29–30
middle-class market 28
millennials 27–28, 34
mining sector 225, 227–28, 229, 230, 232,
233, 235
Mitie 273
mobile phones 181, 258
see also smartphones
Mobileye 310
'moments of truth' (Procter &
Gamble) 254, 265
MoneySuperMarket.com 18
motivation (motivational events) 147, 281,
282, 315, 316, 317, 328
Motorola 300
multi-channels (omni-channels) 19, 30–32,
246–53, 261, 265–68, 347
multi-unit-owner franchises 324–25, 347
multiple shipments 44
multiple-tiered channels 15, 17, 24–25, 29
music 28, 243, 251, 274, 289
IP 297, 298, 299–300, 301–02, 307,
311
mystery shoppers 329, 331

narrow bandwidth distribution 78, 81
national retailers 247
NBA 298
negative inventory 186

net assets *54, 102*, 347
    see also return on net assets (RONA)
net current assets *54, 102, 152, 155*, 347
net margins 70–72, *270, 338*, 347
net operating profit after tax (NOPAT) 97,
    100, 190, 192
net profit *55*, 347
net worth 276, 347
Netflix 28, 289, 303, 306
new entrants 128–29, 214–16
newspaper industry 298, 329

occupancy rate 296
OEM *15*, 18
office supplies sector 78, 96
oil lubricants 20
omni-channels (multi-channels) 19, 30–32,
    246–53, 261, 265–68, 347
one-tier channels *15*, 16, 18–19
Onefinestay.com 37
online retail channels 15, 34, 244–53,
    256–57, 261, 275
    see also Amazon; eBay
online travel agents (OTAs) 4, 292–96, 347
operating cost per hour 239
operating costs 188, 239
operating margins 70–72, *338*
operating profit after tax (NOPAT) 97,
    100, 190, 192
operational management 327–30
operational metrics 239, 331, 332
opportunities identification *22*
optional services *42*, 44
order consolidation *42, 43*, 208, 210
    see also average cost of processing
        orders; average order size; average
        order value
organization, internal *12*, 23
original equipment manufacturer
    (OEM) *15*, 18
'other people's money' (OPM) 315, 317
    see also funding
outsourcing 25, 44, 45, 48, 49–51, 56–57,
    136–37, 278–79
'over-distribution' 118
over-stocking 19, 23
overheads 56–57, 72, *152*, 168, 174, 178,
    204, 210–11, 347
overtime 166, 167
overtrading 57, 58, 348
ownership, capital goods 228–29, 239

parallel marketing *see* grey-marketing
Pareto's Law (80:20 rule) 49, 56, 78, 348
partnerships 119–29, 201

see also account managers
    (management); gold-tier partners
parts *see* spare parts (spares)
passing it to the street 141
patents 223, 298, 302–03, 305–06, 309
payback 290, 327, 333, 348
payment terms 30, 185–88, 245, 246,
    276
    see also advance payments (up-front
        payments); compensation payments;
        discounts; incentives
peer-review sites 250
peer-to-peer communication 249
peer-to-peer lending 291
penalties 69, 170
people-based service business model
    151–69, 172–82, 183–87, 190–95
performance ranking 142
pharmaceuticals sector 96, 138, 139,
    216–17, 297, 298, 306, 309–10
pipeline management *see* sales pipeline
piracy prevention 298, 312–14
planning
    business 203, 209
    utilization 164, 165–69
planograms *143*, 243, 348
platform-based service business model *15*,
    18, 25–26, 155–56, 169–71, 178–82,
    188–89, 195–96, 348
plumbing services 176–77
political environment 230
pop-up stores 36, 37, 243
portfolio management 86–89, 125
portfolio pricing 63
positioning 21–23, 87, *125*, 202, *207*, 209,
    246–48, 263
post-sales (second-level technical)
    support *42, 43, 45*, 48, 49, 137, 263,
    280–82
potential growth capacity 108–09,
    338, 348
pre-sales support (first-level technical
    support) *42, 43*, 46, 66, 67,
    141, 203
Preferred Partner Programmes 141
price leaders 140, *247*
price waterfall management (analysis)
    286–88, 351
pricing 44, 87, *125*, 175, 246, 246–48,
    251–52, 283
    low ball 64–65
    portfolio 63
    see also price leaders; price waterfall
        management
printing sector 259, *260*

prioritization strategies 284–85
product completer role 137, *140*, *145*, *207*
product information *42*, 43, 49
product managers 46, 56, 61, 63, 85–86
product resale 149–50
product/service mix 149–50
productivity 84–93, 166, 204–07, 211, 214, 272, 331
products *42*, 43, 49, 87–89, 123, *124*, 125, 149–50, 196–97, 325–26
    see also product completer role; product managers
profit (profitability) 55–58, 64, 109–12, 192–93, 210–11, 236–38, 266, 267, 269–72, 327
    final-tier distributors 203–04
    gross *54*, 55, 60–63, 72, 84–85, *152*, *155*, *173–74*, *177*, 346
    net 347
profit and loss accounts 53, 67, 70, 100, *102*, 107, 346
    see also income statements
profit per square foot 272, *338*
project accounting 184
project management *42*, 44, 194
    see also account managers (management); project accounting; project size
project size *163*, 168–69, *191*, *192*, 194, *336*
promotions 14, 179, *247*, 254, 259, 261, *270*, 304, 325
    see also SPIFFS
prompt payment discounts 60, 75, 76–77
pull marketing 306, 308–09
purchasing cooperative *318*, 321, 348
push marketing 306, 309

qualification 282, 288, 348

RAD model 284–85, 288
ranging *143*, 243, 246, 348
real estate companies *318*, 321
rebates 46, 49, 141, 142–43, 200, 252, *253*
receivables *see* accounts receivable
recognition awards 281, 328
recoverability 174–76, 238, *338*, 349
refresh cycle metric 239
regional retailers *247*
Reid, John 301
release models, film distribution 303–04
renewal management 180–81, 283
rental equipment metrics 240
repair ratios 240
repair services *134*, 263

repeat business 194–95
repeat visits 266, 267
replacement services 28, *134*, 226–27, 236, *260*, 263
resellers *134*, 135–36, *140*, 206, 229, 349
reserves 109, 349
residual value 228, 240, 344
resource alignment 205, 211
restaurants 224
    see also hotels, restaurant and catering (HoReCa) sector
retail grouping solutions 243
retailers 16, 53, 215, 222, 241–72
    see also online retail channels
retention and development sales forces 285–86
return on brand investment *see* CMROWC
return on capital employed (ROCE) 94–96, 127, 151, *152*, *338*, 349
return on invested capital (ROIC) 97–98, 100, 151, *152*, *339*, 349
return on investment 7, 290, 316, 334, 349
return on net assets (RONA) 94–95, *339*, 349
returns logistics 34, 66, 67, 256, 262
revenue 157–59, 238, 349
revenue metrics 289, 293, 296, 330–31, 341, 349
revenue per room available (RevPar) 293, 296, 349
revenue pull-through 202, *207*
reverse bow-tie model 125–26
reverse logistics 127, 245, 262
review cycle 283
review sites 31, 250
rewards 170–71, 276
    see also bonuses; incentives; SPIFFS
RFID chips 314
rights gaps 307–08
rights overlaps 307–08
ROCE (return on capital employed) 94–96, 127, 151, *152*, *338*, 349
Rocket Records 302
ROI (return on investment) 7, 290, 316, 334, 349
ROIC (return on invested capital) 97–98, 100, 151, *152*, *339*, 349
rolling upgrades 326
Rolls Royce 228, 236
RONA (return on net assets) 94–95, *339*, 349
Royalties 300–01, 302, 304–05, 307, 316, 319, 320, 324, 330
rules of engagement 201

SaaS 27, 29, 30, 273, 350
sales (sales management) 60, 63–64, 68,
       69, 152, 157–71, 239, 240, 282, 349
    see also cost of sales (cost of goods
       sold); discounts; sales commission;
       sales cycles; sales forces (teams);
       sales metrics; sales pipeline
sales commission 4, 60, 67, 109, 147–48,
       236, 250, 276, 292, 295
sales cycles 196, 278–79, 282, 283
sales forces (teams) 16, 63, 66, 162, 199,
       200, 201, 284, 285–86, 322
sales metrics 268–69, 272, 317, 333,
       339, 350
sales per square foot (sales space
       productivity) 268–69, 272, 339
sales per store 268, 339
sales pipeline 159–63, 191, 193, 195, 196,
       282–83, 294, 339, 350
same store sales 269, 317, 350
Samsung 300
scheduling 153, 331
Scoring Points 259
seasonality 77–78, 80, 170, 193, 350
second moment of truth 265
second-level technical (post-sales) support 42,
       43, 45, 48, 49, 137, 263, 280–82
security systems market 35–36
segmentation
    final-tier distributors 199–200
    IP 301, 302
selling skills 231, 258, 284–86
sell-with channels 146–47, 216–17, 350
    see also advocate channel (advocacy)
sensitivity analysis 197
service (services) 4, 26–29, 149–56,
       222–23, 238, 240, 273–90
    domestic trade 176–77
    people-based business model 151–69,
       172–82, 183–87, 190–95
    platform-based business model 15, 18,
       25–26, 155–56, 169–71, 178–82,
       188–89, 195–96, 348
    repair 134, 263
    replacement 134, 226–27, 236,
       260, 263
    sales commission 147–48, 276
    see also service leaders; service level
       agreements (SLAs); service providers;
       service, support and maintenance
       contracts
service leaders 247
service level agreements (SLAs) 170, 229
service providers 137, 138–39, 140, 145,
       153, 154–56, 207

service, support and maintenance
       contracts 158–59, 188
share of wallet 290, 350
shareholder funds 54, 57, 72, 102, 108
shareholders 95, 97, 192, 318, 350
shopping cart abandonment rate 267
showrooming 255, 258, 267
showrooms 263
Siemens 225, 230
simultaneous release distribution
       model 303
single-unit owner franchises 324–25, 351
skills development 19, 180, 193, 231, 258,
       281, 284–86, 307–08
    specialist 154, 156, 176–77, 178
    see also training
SKUs 42, 49, 60, 63, 86, 87, 113, 114,
       129, 350
SLAs (service level agreements) 170, 229
sleeper products (sleepers) 87, 271
small contracts 157, 158
smaller vendors 128–29, 214–16
smartphones 33, 244, 246, 249, 267, 329
Smith, Delia 79
Snap-on Tools 321
social media 4, 31, 34, 249–51, 263
software 6, 27, 32, 188–89, 243, 275, 297,
       299, 308–09, 312
Software as a Service (SaaS) 27, 29, 30,
       273, 350
software source code 312
sole traders 248
solution integrators 137–38, 140, 145, 207
Sonos 258
spare parts (spares) 42, 77, 134, 226, 228,
       234, 236, 240, 280
    counterfeit 235, 237–38
specialist distributors 16, 19, 78, 116, 133,
       201, 211, 247
specialist skills 154, 156, 176–77, 178
specialized logistics services 208–09
speed to market 309, 310
SPIFFS 48, 48, 350
sport, and IP 298–99
Spotify 28, 289, 306, 307, 311
staff, scheduling 153, 331
standard prices 175
standard release routine 303
standard time 166
standardization 204, 210, 213, 326
Starbucks 301, 324, 325
stat units 330–31
stock 43, 79, 350
    buffer 112–13, 114
    consignment 42, 44, 48

see also inventory; over-stocking; stock-keeping units (SKUs); stock-outs
stock-keeping units (SKUs) 42, 49, 60, 63, 86, 87, 113, 114, 129, 350
stock-outs 55, 77, 113
store count 332
store density 333, 351
store openings 268
store productivity 268
stores 242–44, 246, 252, 256, 258, 261, 262, 268, 332–33, 351
stores added 332
straight to Pay TV release 303
straight-to-video release 303
strategic account managers (SAMs) 212–13
strategy
business mix 193
distribution 9–15, 24–26, 28, 34, 36, 38, 50–51, 121–30
prioritization 284–85
streaming 28, 289, 302, 307, 311
subcontractors 45, 136, 164, 165, 175–76, 184, 185
subscription access 308
Subway 304, 315, 324
supermarkets 122, 243, 256
supplier days *see* days payable outstanding (DPO)
suppliers 45–51, 74–75, 243–44
supply chains 226–27, 229–30, 261–62
supply fulfilment 48, 49
see also bulk breaking (breaking bulk); consignment stock; logistics; supply chains
surveys 206
sustainability 94–106
Swift, Taylor 306–07

Taittinger 122
target inventory levels 77
tax management 71
technical briefings 216–17
technical help 147, 204, 210, 215–16
post-sales 42, 43, 45, 48, 49, 137, 263, 280–82
pre-sales 42, 43, 66, 67, 141, 203
technology 24–25, 202, 300, 302–03, 310
see also apps; automation; cloud solutions; Digital Rights Management; electronics sector; high-tech sector; information technology (IT); internet; internet service providers (ISPs); low-tech sectors; mobile phones; RFID chips; TV

telecommunications sector 70, *134*, 224
telemetry 227, 236
territory management 279–82, 327–30, 351
Tesco 247, 259, 262
third-party collection points 262
third-party distributors 51, 292
see also indirect channels; outsourcing
tiered value proposition 235
time dimension of capacity 151
timesheets 158, 166, 184
total resources used 175
Toyota 263
traceability 314
tracking 29, 236, 237, 239, 246, 249, 262, 311, 331
trade channels 351
see also indirect channels
trade discounts 141–42
trade-in capability 234, 240
trade secrets, theft 312
trademarks 48, 223, 297, 298, 323
trading margin *see* gross profit
traffic builder products (traffic builders) 87, 271
training 147, 204, 211, 238–39, 275, 281
transaction-driven costs 68, 69
transaction processing 68, 69, 179
transport equipment 225, 229
travel sector 18, 37, 38, 96, 171, 188, 223, 291–96
treasury function 71
trials 321, 325
TripAdvisor 31, 250, 329
TurboTax 29
Turkey 79
turn-around teams 329
TV 298–99, 303, 304, 306, 320, 329
two-tier channels *15*, 16–17
two-way communication 249

Uber 4, 36, 37, 291
UK 79
ultimate moment of truth 254, 265
unboxing videos 263
Unilever 17
unique strength identification 21, 22
Uniroyal 123
United Airlines 31
United States (US) 21, 230, 273
Federal Trade Commission 322–23
Food and Drug Administration 306
unrecovered customer abuse 240
unused resources (unallocated resources) 173–74

up-front payments (advance
    payments) 186–87, 188
up-selling 70, 288, 351
uptime 178, 222, 226–27, 234, 239
used equipment metrics 240
user enablement 238–39
utilization 164–71, 178–79, 339, 341, 351
utilization planning (people utilization
    planning) 165–69

vacation utilization calculation 166
value *see* customer lifetime value
value-add 59–61
    see also contract-based value delivery
value added distributors 45, 46
value creation (VC) 98–106, 163, 190–95,
    339, 351
value creation tree 99–101, 103, 163,
    190–95
value proposition 7, 12, 20–23, 232, 235,
    247, 351
    channel 120, 198–217, 342
variable costs 51, 109
vendors 128–29, 200–07, 208, 211–13,
    214– 17, 252–53, 264,
    308–09, 351
Verizon 31
videobroadcasting 310–11
videos 263
volume 178, 214
volume sensitivity 150, 169–70

warehouse in the dark operations 113
warehousing 16, 47, 55, 56, 69, 74, 78,
    109, 112, 113

waterfall management (analysis) 286–88,
    351
watermarks 311, 312
websites 57, 179, 245, 292, 294, 329
    comparison 18, 31, 33, 249–50,
    276–78
    see also review sites
weighted average cost of capital
    (WACC) 97–98, 100, 351
wholesalers 13, 17, 18, 41, 43
Wi-Fi 249, 293
winner products (winners) 87, 271
work-in-progress 183, 184, 185, 352
Workflow 310
working capital 55–58, 73–83, 92,
    108, 112–14, 183–89, 333, 339,
    352
    see also contribution margin return on
    working capital (CMROWC); gross
    margin return on working capital
    (GMROWC)
working capital cycle 58, 73–74, 80–83,
    352
working capital requirements 108, 333,
    352
working capital turn 80, 92, 108, 339,
    352

XaaS 273, 345
Xcite 257

yield 223, 295–96, 303, 352

zero moment of truth 254, 265
zero-sum game 213

CPSIA information can be obtained
at www.ICGtesting.com
Printed in the USA
JSHW011013120922
30395JS00007B/72

9 780749 482145